LINCOLN CHRISTIAN COLLEGE AND SEMINARY

W9-CBU-319

Storytelling in Religious Education

Storytelling in Religious Education

Susan M. Shaw

Religious Education Press
Birmingham, Alabama

Copyright © 1999 by Religious Education Press
All rights reserved

No part of this publication may be reproduced, stored in a retrieval system, or transmitted, in any form or by any means, electronic, photocopying, recording, or otherwise, without the prior permission of the publisher.

The paper in this book meets the guidelines for permanence and durability of the Committee on Production Guidelines of the Council for Library Resources.

Library of Congress Cataloguing-in-Publication Data

Shaw, Susan M. *Susan Maxine), 1960–
   Storytelling in religious education / Susan M. Shaw.
     p.   cm.
   Includes bibliographical references and indexes.
   ISBN 0-89135-111-6
   1. Storytelling in Christian education. I. Title.
   BV1534.3.S43 1999
   268'.67—dc21   99-13512
                                         CIP

Religious Education Press
5316 Meadow Brook Road
Birmingham, Alabama 35242-3315
10 9 8 7 6 5 4 3 2

Religious Education Press publishes books exclusively in religious education and in areas closely related to religious education. It is committed to enhancing and professionalizing religious education through the publication of serious, significant, and scholarly works.

PUBLISHER TO THE PROFESSION

In memory of
Jim Moss
who taught me to appreciate literature and
Jim Colquitt
who taught me to love it

97580

CONTENTS

PART III: DEVELOPMENT AND STORYTELLING

PREFACE

Early in life I developed a great love for literature. During my doctoral work at The Southern Baptist Theological Seminary in Louisville, Kentucky, I decided to write a dissertation suggesting a role for literary fiction in the church's religious education curriculum. Several years later, while I was teaching religion at California Baptist College in Riverside, I spent a semester as a visiting scholar at The School of Theology at Claremont, where I met Mary Elizabeth Moore. I told her about my dissertation, and she suggested I contact James Michael Lee at Religious Education Press to see if he might be interested in developing a book from my dissertation. Although Lee felt that fiction alone was too narrow a topic for a Religious Education Press book, he explained that he had been looking for someone to write a book on storytelling in religious education, and he asked if I would be interested. Given my love for stories, I responded enthusiastically in the affirmative.

My journey with this book has taken a few interesting twists and turns, including my own career change from teaching religion to teaching women studies at the university level. In the middle of the process of writing the book, I returned to school to earn a graduate degree in women studies. The perspective I acquired had a role in shaping this book as I sought to integrate my concerns regarding gender, race, and class with storytelling and religious education.

This book rests on solid grounding in social scientific research, but it is intended to be a very practical tool for religious educators who desire to use storytelling in religious instruction. I use the general term "storytelling" here and throughout the book to include of all the ways in which people employ narrative—drama, visual art, literary fiction, music, and ritual, as well as oral storytelling.

Narrative is a very basic way by which people experience, understand, and act in the world. As a seemingly universal human characteristic, narrative ability offers religious educators a profound means through which to facilitate the desired goals of religious instruction. Stories can touch, challenge, and change learners on cognitive, affective, and behavioral levels as they are used effectively within religious instruction. The goal of this book is to provide religious educators with both a foundation in storytelling and concrete tools that will allow them to add storytelling to their repertoire of religious instruction teaching techniques.

The first part of the book provides theoretical and social scientific underpinnings for storytelling in religious instruction. Part 1 explores historical, theological, psychological, and educational perspectives on storytelling with special attention to implications for religious instruction. Because stories are such an integral part of human experience and identity, storytelling in religious instruction can engage learners in cognitive, affective, and behavioral modes of learning that can lead to powerful, life-changing learning outcomes. Chapter 1 offers specific and practical suggestions about how to find, choose, prepare, and tell stories in religious instruction. Special attention is given to the effective practice of storytelling in a religious instruction setting. Chapter 2 explores some of the history of storytelling, particularly as it relates to education. From ancient oral storytelling to contemporary forms of oral and written narrative, storytelling's history reflects its character as an effective instructional tool. Chapter 3 takes a close look at the nature of story primarily through the perspective of literary authors and critics, most of whom are or were people of faith. This chapter suggests that faith and narrative are closely related, that stories help people re-create, reexperience, and understand their life experiences in such a way that particular stories become the mythic frameworks or metanarratives out of which people live. Chapter 4 analyzes the relationship of stories to theology, especially in terms of stories' usefulness to the theological enterprise. Theology begins in reflection on religious experiences that are first expressed in narrative form. Although theology provides abstract categories and classifications for these experiences, theological concepts are essentially related to the stories out of which they arise. Chapter 5 examines the narrative nature of human lives or the "storied psyche," noting the particular roles narrative may have to play in the development of learners' faith identity. This chapter contends that through stories, people create cohesion from their random experiences and build identity, meaning, and community. Chapter 6 analyzes the usefulness of storytelling in achieving a number of educational goals in a variety of domains. This chapter also offers examples of structured experiences that use storytelling as a central teaching technique.

Part 2 of the book examines numerous types of stories appropriate for use in religious education. From myths and parables to children's stories and folktales to biblical stories, literary stories, and life narratives, stories express and evoke ideas, emotions, attitudes, values, and behaviors. Out of its own unique characteristics, each type of story offers religious educators a particular possibility for creating teaching/learning situations that can achieve the goals of religious instruction. Each chapter in part 2 examines the characteristics of various types of stories and suggests ways of using them in religious instruction.

Part 3 focuses on connections between storytelling and human development. Narrative experience changes as people develop, just as needs and abilities develop throughout life. These chapters examine some of the major issues and tasks of the developmental periods of childhood, adolescence, and adulthood and suggest how stories can appropriately connect with learners' life needs to create optimal learning situations.

A common thread throughout the book is its emphasis on storytelling as a tool to facilitate religious living. Although stories are without a doubt a wonderful form of entertainment, their close connection with the human psyche gives them a much more significant role in human life than entertainment alone. Stories invite learners into a realm of possibility in which they may learn new ways of being faithful people in the world. I hope that this book will encourage and equip religious educators to utilize storytelling in exciting and effective ways in a variety of religious education contexts in order to help learners become more faithful, loving, justice-seeking people.

Many centuries ago, a rich sultan in Baghdad gave a banquet in honor of the birth of his son. All the nobility who partook of the feast brought costly gifts, except a young sage who came empty-handed. He explained to the sultan, "Today the young prince will receive many precious gifts, jewels and rare coins. My gift is different. From the time he is old enough to listen until manhood, I will come to the palace every day and tell him stories of our Arabian heroes. When he becomes our ruler he will be just and honest."

The young sage kept his word. When the prince was at last made sultan, he became famous for his wisdom and honor. To this day, an inscription on a scroll in Baghdad reads, "It was because of the seed sown by the tales."[1]

I did not make my journey to completion of this book alone. Without the assistance and support of a number of people, this project would have been impossible. First and foremost, I would like to thank James Michael Lee for his keen editorial eye and his constant encouragement. I am undoubtedly a better scholar because of his persistent demand for excellence in scholarship and in writing.

Next, I must thank the many students who assisted me with library research: Renee Baker, Cathy Collinsworth, Jennifer Hostettler, Tami Hotard, and Terri Trosper. I am especially indebted to Terri, who spent a great deal of her summer assisting me with the final details of the manuscript. I must also thank John Hendrix, William Rogers, Daniel Aleshire, Doris Borchert, Robert Proctor, and Findley Edge, who laid a foundation in religious education for me. Sandy Maurer provided invaluable assistance in keyboarding the first draft of the manuscript while I was making the transition from writing longhand to writing at a computer keyboard. While I was teaching there, George Fox University provided a summer faculty grant that assisted me with research; the librarians at George Fox did an amazing job of making needed books and articles accessible. Lisa Lawson has been extremely helpful in providing clerical assistance. I am especially indebted to Oregon State University director of Women Studies Janet Lee, who has given me unfailing support and encouragement. I also want to thank Ainsworth United Church of Christ in Portland, Oregon, my church family, which loves, supports, and nurtures me. And finally, I am grateful to Tisa Lewis, Julie Smith, Linda Givens, and Karen Massey, whose life stories are inextricably woven into mine.

Susan M. Shaw

---

[1]William J. Bausch, *Storytelling: Imagination and Faith* (Mystic, Conn.: Twenty-Third, 1984), p. 50.

PART I

FOUNDATIONS OF STORYTELLING IN RELIGIOUS EDUCATION

1

On Telling Stories

A rabbi, whose grandfather had been a disciple of the Baal Shem, was asked to tell a story. "A story," he said, "must be told in such a way that it constitutes help in itself." And he told: "My grandfather was lame. Once they asked him to tell a story about his teacher. And he related how the holy Baal Shem used to hop and dance while he prayed. My grandfather rose as he spoke, and he was so swept away by his story that he himself began to hop and dance to show how the master had done. From that hour on he was cured of his lameness. That's the way to tell a story."[1]
—Martin Buber

I grew up to the cadence of story. My mother read to me at night until I was able to read for myself. My Sunday school teachers told me stories of brave queens and wise kings and wicked priests and foolish disciples. Every year my church staged a Christmas pageant in the city auditorium and reenacted the ancient story of a poor, young, pregnant woman, her husband, and the birth of the baby who brought hope to us all. As soon as I was old enough, I had a library card, and I read Beverly Cleary, then C. S. Lewis, then William Faulkner and Flannery O'Connor and Alice Walker. In my imagination, I was the hero of my daydreams, in which I rescued people trapped in burning buildings and sank the winning shot at the buzzer and wrote the Great

---

[1]Martin Buber, *Tales of the Hasidim: Early Masters* (New York: Schocken, 1961), pp. v–vi.

3

American Novel. I recognized myself in the stories I heard, and I constructed myself with the stories I told myself about who I was.

Once, as a college teacher, I was given the unenviable task of making announcements before a mandatory chapel service. As I walked to the podium, students were still noisily entering chapel—late, as students so often are. Other students who were already seated were talking and rustling papers. I stepped to the microphone and began my feeble attempt to get their attention and work my way through announcements about yearbooks, club meetings, and basketball games. After a few minutes, and with the feeling that no one in the building had heard a word I'd said, I launched into my introduction of the day's program. As it happened, the topic for the day was story. And so, with only the transition of a deep breath and a sigh on my part, I moved from "will be tonight at 7:00 in the gym" to "once upon a time . . . ," and the entire room fell silent. With that one phrase, the students were spellbound because they knew it was time for a story. And I came to realize the profound and universal appeal of story.

Narration seems to be a universal human activity.[2] People think, dream, enact, and tell stories. In so doing, they engage in a process of self-creation and meaning making that is an important condition of learning.[3] Learners first engage a subject narratively, since experience is constructed through the narration that embeds it with meaning.[4] In

---

[2]Barbara Hardy, "Narrative as a Primary Act of Mind," in *The Cool Web*, ed. M. Meek, A. Warlow, and G. Barton (London: Bodley Head, 1977), p. 13; Robert Coles, *The Call of Stories: Teaching and the Moral Imagination* (Boston: Houghton Mifflin, 1989), p. 30; David Lodge, "Narration with Words" in *Images and Understanding*, ed. H. Barlow, C. Blakemore, and M. Weston-Smith (Cambridge: Cambridge University Press, 1990), p. 141.

[3]Hunter McEwan and Kieran Egan, introduction to *Narrative in Teaching, Learning, and Research*, ed. Hunter McEwan and Kieran Egan (New York: Teachers College Press, 1995), p. xi; Jefferson Singer, "Seeing One's Self: Locating Narrative Memory in a Framework of Personality," *Journal of Personality* 63 (September 1995): 429–457.

[4]Peter L. Berger and Thomas Luckman, *The Social Construction of Reality* (New York: Doubleday, 1966). Derek Edwards suggests that discourse provides "not just a way of seeing, but a way of constructing seeing." Derek Edwards, "Categories are for Talking: On the Cognitive and Discursive Bases of Categorization," *Theory and Psychology* 1 (November 1990) p. 523. Likewise, Mary McClintock Fulkerson notes that reality is textualized, that is, the signifying processes themselves constitute the objects perceived. *Changing the Subject: Women's Discourses and Feminist Theology* (Minneapolis: Fortress, 1995), p. 8.

other words, narrative gives shape to experience and turns the raw data of experience into meaning.[5] Therefore, narrative represents a primary or privileged form of discourse[6] and a significant way of knowing.[7] Narrative also offers possibilities of legitimating notions of reality or destabilizing them.

The primacy of narrative in discourse and in learning suggests that narrative should be considered and used as a significant component of religious instruction. If the goal of religious instruction is religious living,[8] narrative offers one important way for religious educators to facilitate integration of religious experiences, religious ideals, and religious living. Learners experience their lives narratively, and in many respects they live out their lives in accordance with the self-narratives they have constructed.[9] These self-narratives are shaped within the metanarratives, or larger stories, of the dominant culture and within interactions with other people.[10] Religious instruction provides both a metanarrative and community context within which learners may hear, examine, create, and live stories that facilitate the goals of religious instruction.

Because narrative is such a primary human activity, stories are powerful. Stories that are communicated well invite learners into a transformative realm in which old ways of living may be opened up to new possibilities. The universality of human ability to tell stories, however, does not imply that stories are automatically and universally well communicated. Professional storytellers often spend months refining a story before they are ready to perform it. Achieving the goals

---

[5]Roy F. Baumeister and Leonard S. Newman, "How Stories Make Sense of Personal Experiences: Motives that Shape Autobiographical Narratives," *Personality and Social Psychology Bulletin* 20 (December 1994): 676–690.

[6]McEwan and Egan, introduction to *Narrative in Teaching Learning and Research*, p. x.

[7]Recognition of narrative as a way of knowing has been an essential part of recent feminist theory and research. See, for example, Mary Belenky et al., *Women's Ways of Knowing: The Development of Self, Voice, and Mind* (New York: Basic, 1986).

[8]James Michael Lee, *The Flow of Religious Instruction* (Birmingham, Ala.: Religious Education Press, 1973), pp. 11–12.

[9]Jerome Bruner, *Actual Minds: Possible Worlds* (Cambridge: Harvard University Press, 1986); and Jerome Bruner, *Acts of Meaning* (Cambridge: Harvard University Press, 1990).

[10]Janet Lee, "Women Re-Authoring Their Lives Through Feminist Narrative Therapy," *Women and Therapy* 20 (November 1997): 2.

of religious instruction through storytelling will not occur if religious educators do not carefully construct and refine the stories they communicate. For this reason, knowing how to communicate stories is imperative as a starting point for religious educators when using stories with learners.

CHOOSING A STORY

Religious educators should begin preparing to communicate a story by selecting a story that is appropriate for the teaching/learning session. The appropriateness of a story is determined by three important and interrelated factors: learners/audience, religious instructional objectives, and setting.

Learners/Audience

Learning begins with learners.[11] Likewise, defining a religious instructional objective and choosing an appropriate story begin with the needs and abilities of learners. Although religious instructional objectives are in dialogue with theology, they are not determined by theology but rather by the interests, needs, goals, desires, and learning styles of the learners.[12] The goal of religious instruction is not primarily theological understanding but religious living. Religious living is facilitated when religious educators arrange the elements of religious instruction so that the learner's experiences live on productively in subsequent experiences.[13]

This religious instruction paradigm suggests that religious educators' knowledge of learners is paramount. In addition to knowing the theoretical foundations of learning and human development, religious educators should know the actual learners themselves. This is especially important in selecting stories because learners are drawn to stories that resonate with their experiences. The closer the identification, the more powerful the narrative experience.[14]

---

[11]John Dewey, *Experience and Education* (New York: Collier, 1938); Carl Rogers, *Freedom to Learn for the 80s* (Columbus, Ohio.: Merrill, 1983).

[12]James Michael Lee, "The Authentic Source of Religious Instruction," in *Religious Education and Theology*, ed. Norma H. Thompson (Birmingham, Ala.: Religious Education Press, 1982), pp. 100–197.

[13]Dewey, *Experience and Education*, pp. 27–28.

[14]Charles A. Smith, *From Wonder to Wisdom: Using Stories to Help Children Grow* (New York: Plume, 1989), p. 16.

For example, I once taught a religion course at a conservative Christian college that required students to work through some very difficult issues of faith. As part of the course, I asked the students to read Ferrol Sams's *The Whisper of the River*, a novel that tells the story of a conservative young Christian boy who has gone to a Christian college and has had his faith challenged. This novel provided my students with the opportunity to form a very close identification with the protagonist and his college experiences. In so doing, the story operated to validate the feelings and experiences of the students.

Learners may, however, identify with a story's protagonist even when that character is quite different from the learners and when the protagonist's situation is different from theirs. In this instance, identification may occur because the story shares an emotion experienced by learners or because the story deals with relationships that are important to learners. Since stories invite learners to see the world through the eyes of the protagonist, or, in other words, to become the protagonist, these stories allow learners to enter into the Other through the powerful connections and commonalities that humans share. Part of the power of the story of the Good Samaritan is that Jesus's listeners had the option to identify either with the man in the ditch or with the Samaritan and briefly to experience the world of the Other. In this way, story functions to destabilize presuppositions and prejudices while at the same time suggesting alternative constructions of self and others.

In choosing stories for religious instruction, religious educators should ask themselves which stories are most likely to engage learners. Which stories resonate with learners' experiences? Which evoke appropriate emotional experiences? Which are developmentally appropriate? Which stories are learners ready to hear? Which stories invite learners to enter into the Other? And, finally, which of these stories would be likely to bring about the desired learning outcome?

Religious Instructional Objectives

The general goal of religious instruction—religious living—in itself is too broad to be pedagogically useful to religious educators in planning teaching/learning sessions. For this reason, it is necessary for religious educators to define specific objectives in order to provide direction in structuring learning experiences which will lead toward achieving the objective.[15] Objectives may fall into cognitive,[16] affective,[17] or lifestyle domains.[18] For example, a lifestyle religious instructional objective in the category of exposure might be a demonstrated awareness of the physical, emotional, social, and spiritual needs of people living with HIV/AIDS by listing and defining these needs. This objective could be achieved, for example, by telling and discussing a story of an HIV positive person in which these needs are evident. Many books, such as Mary Fisher's *My Name Is Mary*,[19] chronicle the daily struggles of people living with this disease. Another procedural possibility could be showing a video such as *Philadelphia* that documents the life of a person who has HIV/AIDS and discussing the needs evidenced in the story.

Once the objective is defined, religious educators may then begin to design appropriate learning experiences to bring about the desired learning outcome. The religious educator should choose a story only when this narrative procedure has been demonstrated to be an effective procedure in achieving the desired learning objective. Stories can be an important teaching tool to facilitate a host of religious instructional objectives in the cognitive, affective, and lifestyle domains (as I shall discuss later). Depending on the objective, narrative experiences can be shaped to introduce information, encourage analysis, engage emotions, invite participation, and model behavioral change.

As religious educators begin to construct learning experiences using narrative (stories), the learning objectives and educational research will suggest both the stories to be communicated and the best methods to communicate the stories. Story options range from fairy tales to biblical stories to biographies to personal experiences. Part 2 examines in detail the many types of stories available to religious educators. Options for communicating stories include storytelling performance, role play, drama, mime, music, dance, drawing, painting, sculpting, video (watching and creating), audiotape, reading, and

---

[15]Lee, *Shape of Religious Instruction*, p. 231.

[16]Benjamin S. Bloom and David Krathwohl, *Taxonomy of Educational Objectives: Handbook I: Cognitive Domain* (New York: McKay, 1956).

[17]Benjamin S. Bloom, David R. Krathwohl, Bertram B. Massia, and Bertram B. Masia, *Taxonomy of Educational Objectives: Handbook II: Affective Domain* (New York: McKay, 1964).

[18]James Michael Lee, *The Content of Religious Instruction* (Birmingham, Ala.: Religious Education Press, 1985), pp. 608–735.

[19]Mary Fisher, *My Name Is Mary* (New York: Simon and Schuster, 1995).

writing. Examples of narrative experiences will be woven throughout this book.

Environment

The physical and emotional environment of religious instruction plays an important role in setting the context for a narrative experience. When and where a story is related has a profound effect on the ways in which learners experience the story. Research in proxemics—the interaction of an individual with personal, social, and environmental space—indicates that space exerts influence on a person's behavior and social interaction.[20] Where a building is located, how a room is arranged, and how physically close people are to one another all have a decided impact on a learning experience.

Generally, storytelling in religious instruction should be an intimate activity. Both religious educators and learners should be mutually engaged in the storytelling experience. On the whole, having learners seated at desks in rows while religious educators tell stories from the front of the room is not the most appropriate arrangement of space for achieving the desired outcomes of religious instruction. A semicircle or a circle suggests a more open and egalitarian environment in which learners are encouraged to be active contributors to the process of constructing knowledge.[21] During storytelling, religious educators may think of the classroom (or living room) as their performance arena. Space should be used in this case as part of the story. Religious educators may move around the room as they tell stories, or they may stand on a desk or even sit in the circle, depending on which is most appropriate to the story and to the desired outcomes. By moving closer to learners, religious educators may make use of proximity to convey acceptance, familiarity, and belonging,[22] important environmental characteristics for religious instruction.

---

[20]For a detailed discussion of proxemics in religious instruction, see James Michael Lee, *Content of Religious Instruction*, pp. 442–444.

[21]Patrick W. Miller, *Nonverbal Communication*, 3rd ed. (Washington, D.C.: National Education Association, 1988), pp. 112–114; Sam Neill and Chris Caswell, *Body Language for Competent Teachers* (New York: Routledge, 1993), pp. 26–31. For more on the construction of knowledge, see Belenky et al., *Women's Ways of Knowing*; Michael Polanyi, *Personal Knowledge* (Chicago: University of Chicago Press, 1958).

[22]Edward T. Hall, *The Hidden Dimension* (Garden City, N.Y.: Doubleday, 1969), p. 113–129.

Closely related to the arrangment of physical space is the creation of psychological/emotional space. The arrangement of physical elements, including religious educators' own nonverbal communication, plays an important role in creating psychological space. Additionally, the attitudes and values conveyed by religious educators also contribute to the kind of atmosphere in which religious instruction takes place.[23] When stories are used in religious instruction, the learning space should be open, welcoming, and participatory so that it fosters an interpretive community of discourse.[24] Within this context, community members learn and help negotiate the values, beliefs, language, and lifestyle of the community. Discourse is a central metaphor for understanding the nature of learning space because the nature of knowledge is dialogic and constructive.

Constructivist thought recognizes the relative positions of the knower and the known.[25] It also emphasizes the fluidity and inessential nature of the self, language, and truth.[26] From a constructivist position, knowledge is seen as a creation, a construct, which comes into being in terms of those who are engaged in the knowing. Consequently, constructivists ask not only "who" "what," "why," and "how" of the subject matter, but they also ask who is asking the questions, why the question is being asked at all, and how the answers are achieved.[27] Constructivists understand knowledge as contextualized; in other words, all knowledge exists in a context, and as contexts shift so does knowledge.

The standpoint or social location of each learner will offer opportunities for varying perspectives out of which to construct knowledge. Each individual comes to the learning environment with a limited perspective based on life experiences and social location. As many perspectives are shared in the learning situation, learners create possibilities for wider visions and multiple angles on knowledge. Consequently, the more diverse the voices that are included in the

---

[23]Richard L. Swanson, "Toward the Ethical Motivation of Learning," *Education* 116 (Fall 1995): 43–50.

[24]For more on interpretive communities, see Stanley Fish, *Is There a Text in This Class? The Authority of Interpretive Communities* (Cambridge: Harvard University Press, 1980).

[25]Belenky et al., *Women's Ways of Knowing*, pp. 137–141.

[26]26See, for example, the work of such deconstructionists as Jacques Lacan, Jacques Derrida, Hélenè Cixous, Luce Irigaray, and Julia Kristeva.

[27]Belenky et al., *Women's Ways of Knowing*, p. 139.

learning experience, the greater the possibility for more inclusive, interconnected learning.[28]

A constructivist position is important for religious instruction because it helps religious educators recognize the relativity of any piece of knowledge while at the same time valuing that piece of knowledge within its social and historical context. Practically, this position suggests that no one religious educator or learner possesses ultimate truth. But it also suggests that each person's experiences and perspectives are valuable resources in the instructional process of constructing knowledge. Often, approaches that tend toward absolutism have silenced the voices of learners who are not part of a dominant culture and have made their experiences invisible and invalid. Constructivism, in contrast, demands that all voices and all experiences become part of the discourse, and, in fact, tends to highlight the voices which have generally been excluded from full participation in the creation of knowledge.[29] In religious instruction, in particular, constructivism is important because it is a practical affirmation and implementation of an underlying belief in the value of all people. A constructivist approach in religious instruction creates an environment in which the multiple ways in which learners experience God are valued and are intentionally incorporated in the construction of communal knowledge.

In religious instruction, the learning space provides an arena for multiple voices to forge shared knowledge which is then individually appropriated by members of the learning community. Individuals also develop ownership of specific zones of the common knowledge in which they choose to specialize and contribute to the common knowledge from these areas.[30]

---

[28]Frances A. Maher and Mary Kay Thompson Tetreault, *The Feminist Classroom: An Inside Look at How Professors and Students are Transforming Higher Education for a Diverse Society* (New York: Basic, 1994), pp. 191–200.

[29]Nancy C. M. Harstock, "The Feminist Standpoint: Developing the Ground for a Specifically Feminist Historical Materialism," *Feminism and Methodology*, ed. Sandra Harding (Bloomington: Indiana University Press, 1987), pp.159–160.

[30]Ann L. Brown and Joseph C. Campione, "Psychological Theory and the Design of Innovative Learning Environments: On Procedures, Principles, and Systems" in *Innovations in Learning: New Environments for Education*, ed. Leona Schauble and Robert Glaser (Mahwah, N.J.: Erlbaum, 1996), p. 319.

Key to developing this kind of learning space are respect for diversity and shared authority. As early as the 1960's Carl Rogers argued that respect for the learner was a key element for creating an optimal climate for learning.[31] Creating respect for diversity in learners begins as religious educators consciously acknowledge how their own standpoints affect their constructions of knowledge. This is particularly significant for storytelling because positional knowing operates by exploring relationships between individual narratives and larger interpretive frameworks.[32] For example, if a religious educator is a white male, he brings a certain perspective and particular privileges to the learning setting based on his experience of maleness and whiteness. If he assumes that this perspective is normative, then he will render invisible the experiences of those who are Other, and he will squelch any opportunity for real diversity and authentic dialogue.[33] If, however, he acknowledges his position and its relative privilege, he may then allow for the legitimacy of different experiences, positions, and perspectives. As these diverse narratives are then woven together in religious instruction (the larger interpretive framework), multiple voices are valued, and a common knowledge may be created that more accurately reflects the complexity of the community. And, the more voices involved, the more multidimensional the knowledge.[34]

Closely connected to respect for diversity is shared authority. An optimal learning space will allow learners the authority of their own knowledge and experience.[35] In traditional schooling paradigms, authority has resided almost wholly in the teacher who is seen as the expert. Shared authority challenges the traditional schooling paradigm by acknowledging that learners already bring a great deal of knowledge and expertise to the learning experience. Shared authority also acknowledges narrative authority.[36] Narrative authority is the

[31]Carl Rogers, *Freedom to Learn* (Columbus, Ohio.: Merrill, 1969), pp. 221–237.

[32]Maher and Tetreault, *The Feminist Classroom*, p. 210.

[33]bell hooks, *Teaching to Transgress: Education as the Practice of Freedom* (New York: Routledge, 1994), pp. 35–44.

[34]Maher and Tetreault, *Feminist Classroom*, p. 18.

[35]For more on shared authority in the classroom, see Celia Oyler, *Making Room for Students: Sharing Teacher Authority in Room 104* (New York: Teachers College Press, 1996).

[36]Maher and Tetreault, *Feminist Classroom*, pp. 150–155.

authority given the voice of each learner's story. When interpretive authority, the authority to name and interpret one's experiences, is located in each voice, many different perspectives emerge and interact, providing insights from a wide variety of positions. As a result, respect for diversity and acknowledgment of narrative authority play important roles in creating an open and respectful learning space that can help facilitate desired learning outcomes of religious instruction through storytelling.

Timing

The timing of relating a story is also a significant factor in creating the most appropriate instructional atmosphere for achieving desired learning outcomes through narrative experience. In Navaho tradition, for example, certain stories can only be told in winter because these stories are deemed to be so powerful they can upset the weather.[37] Generally, in Africa, stories are not to be told during the day, especially during planting or hoeing season.[38] Stories should be communicated at pedagogically appropriate moments to maximize their religious instructional potential. In some instances, stories may be used at the beginning of a teaching/learning session to draw learners into the session; at other times stories may be told spontaneously in response to a teachable moment created by a learner's question; at yet other times a story may be the central focus of the teaching/learning session and may be accorded a significant portion of time (as in the showing of a movie or acting out of a play); and sometimes a story may be used at the end of a session to bring closure. In Hebrew tradition, when children asked the meaning of the law, this teachable moment became the opening for a story, and so they heard the story of how the LORD brought the people of Israel out of Egypt (Deut. 6). Many Hebrew stories became associated with particular festivals and were recited each year during their observance.[39] In each of these instances, stories were told at the most appropriate time in order to achieve a desired religious outcome. Religious educators should, then, keep the importance of timing in mind as they plan teaching/learning sessions.

---

[37]Suzanne Martin, "Stories in Season," *Storytelling* 4 (Fall 1992): 22.

[38]Anne Pellowski, *The World of Storytelling* (New York: Bowker, 1977), p. 103.

[39]James King West, *Introduction to the Old Testament*, 2d ed. (New York: Macmillan, 1981), p. 462.

FINDING STORIES

Many religious educators may be hesitant to use storytelling because they do not think they have effective stories to communicate. Yet a wealth of storytelling resources is readily available (See the Appendix for a brief list of story resources). The Bible, children's literature, collections of myths, legends, and folktales, biographies, novels, short stories, and movies all provide potential stories for religious instruction. Oral traditions of family, church, and community often provide rich reservoirs of narrative material that can be shaped into effective stories. And most readily available, personal experiences can be mined for stories appropriate to learning goals.

The key to finding stories is alertness. Religious educators should constantly watch for stories that may be useful in religious instruction. Reading reviews of new releases of novels, biographies, children's stories, plays, and motion pictures may provide numerous leads toward effective stories. Listening for stories in conversations and on the news may prove helpful. Oral histories provide rich material for stories and can provide insight into the histories and traditions of a community.[40] Stories permeate every community and culture, whether in oral, written, visual, or enacted form. Finding appropriate stories for religious instruction involves giving specific attention to these stories as potential resources for teaching/learning.

Furthermore, by paying attention to the stories all around them, religious educators may also become more aware of the conventions of storytelling (which are discussed in chapter 3) which will allow more effective facilitation of the creation of original stories. This capacity may be helpful in two ways. First, as religious educators become more aware of how effective stories are constructed and communicated, they may be more able and more confident in creating their own stories to use in religious instruction. Second, they may, in turn, be more effective in helping learners fashion stories.

ANALYZING STORIES

Religious educators should begin preparation for using a story in religious instruction by first ascertaining whether or not the story will

---

[40]Suzanne Martin, "Hearing Other People's Voices," *Storytelling* 5 (Winter 1993): 13–16.

facilitate achievement of desired learning outcomes and then analyzing the story in order to have a complete understanding of it. Analysis also offers helpful clues about adaptation and about appropriate uses of dialogue, movement, and props. The more religious educators understand a story and are aware of the story's dynamics, the more effective they will be in communicating it.

Storyteller Doug Lipman suggests beginning by "finding the *Most Important Thing*" about the story.[41] The "Most Important Thing" is the key idea the religious educator wants to convey. One story may have many "Most Important Things," depending on goals, tellers, listeners, and context. Each "Most Important Thing" may be equally valid, but each leads to a different way of adapting and communicating a story. For religious educators, identifying the "Most Important Thing" should, of course, be closely tied to the desired learning outcome. Religious educators should begin by defining the instructional objective and then selecting a story whose "Most Important Thing" will help facilitate the achievement of the objective.

Next, religious educators should examine the characters in the story. Storyteller Nancy Kavanaugh argues that character development is one of the most important parts of story preparation.[42] She offers five helpful suggestions for analyzing and developing believable story characters: (1) describe the character's qualities; (2) describe the character's appearance; (3) describe the habitat of the character; (4) describe the relationship of the character to other characters in the story; and (5) describe the character's movements.[43] Other important qualities to examine include the character's background, emotions, and motives. The more complex and rich the characterization, the more believable the character.

Awareness of the organization of the story, or its plot, is another significant aspect of story preparation. A story plot typically revolves around a protagonist or group of protagonists who face a dilemma, a struggle, or an imbalance. Whatever brings about the conflict is the inciting incident. It is the inciting incident that then gives rise to the story's action. Following the inciting incident, the action of the story rises toward a turning point and climax, as the struggle is won or lost, the dilemma solved or not. After the climax comes the denouement (or

---

[41]"Finding the Most Important Thing," *Storytelling* 6 (May 1994): 16–18.
[42]"5 Tips for Making Characters Real," *Yarnspinner* 16 (December 1992): 3.
[43]Ibid.

the return to balance) and the conclusion of the story. Identifying the high points of the story offers religious educators clues about pace, voice, and movement.

Finally, a careful examination of the story's atmosphere is an essential part of analysis. Generally, a story has one predominant mood. It may be suspenseful or sad or silly. Just as the "Most Important Thing" may vary from teller to teller or from context to context, the mood of a story may vary as well. The story of Abraham's negotiations with God over the fate of Sodom may be told as a tale of suspense. Will God destroy the city or will Abraham convince God otherwise? Or it may be told as a humorous tale. Abraham's audacity to bargain with God and to lecture God about doing the right thing is full of humorous possibility. The story may also be told as a tale of tragedy. To what state has Sodom fallen that so few righteous people can be found in it? All of these possibilities are implicit in the text. Ascertaining which mood to create depends on the desired effect of the story toward the learning objective.

ADAPTING STORIES

Because each communication of a story (with the exception of audio/video tapes) is a unique experience, adaptation of the story inevitably occurs. Each recounting of a story is a process of authoring; each story is being constructed in and through the telling. Therefore, no two tellings of a story are exactly the same.[44] Word choice, intonations, or movements may change. Different groups of learners may require different forms of a story. For example, simpler words may need to be used to tell a story to preschoolers than to adults. Groups performing improvisations on story lines will always create variations in the tale. At other times, religious educators may wish to adapt stories created by other storytellers to make the tales more effective in facilitating the desired outcomes of religious instruction.

In the case of stories created by other storytellers, some guidelines apply. Generally, the essence of the story should be retained. Thus the fundamental elements of the story should be retained (plot, major characters, atmosphere). Although stories from oral tradition are easily and ethically adaptable, written stories present certain dilemmas. Many written stories are copyrighted. Permission to tell these stories

---

[44]Maguire, *Creative Storytelling*, p. 109.

in professional public performance may need to be obtained, although this will not usually be the case for stories used in religious instruction.[45] When using a written story, religious educators should take great care to keep the core of the story intact.

Beyond these general guidelines, religious educators may adapt stories in many ways. The point of view of the narrator, for example, may be changed so that the story is told from first person perspective rather than third. The historical setting may be changed so that a story is moved, for example, from the biblical period into the contemporary world. Details may be changed to suit learners better. In Portland, Oregon, characters may wear flannel shirts and hiking boots, while in Cape Cod they may wear button-down oxford shirts and deck shoes. Dialects may be used, both for the general narration and/or for the voices of characters. The story may be lengthened or shortened as necessary. Props, music, and dance may be added. The medium used to communicate the story may itself be changed. The story may be told, sung, drawn, watched, or acted out. All of these adaptations should serve to further the learners' connection with the story in order to facilitate desired outcomes.

PREPARING LEARNERS FOR A STORY

For an effective narrative experience, religious educators should prepare learners for the story. Among the Jicarilla Apache, children were given kernels of corn to chew during storytelling. Because corn was perceived as sacred as a symbol of life and stories were considered holy, the Jicarilla Apache believed that eating the corn would help the children remember the stories and their importance.[46]

In a contemporary religious instruction setting, learners may be given a listening assignment when a story is to be told: Listen for an idea that is new to you; listen for something that makes you uncomfortable; listen for what motivates a character. Listening assignments also work well when a story is communicated through drama or video. These assignments should be made with the desired learning outcome in mind.

Another preparatory device that invites direct participation is story enactment. When learners are to enact a story, religious educators

---

[45]Roger Rose, "Getting Permission," *Storytelling* 6 (September 1994): 14–15.
[46]Pellowski, *The World of Storytelling*, p. 110.

should provide sufficient guidance for learners to be able to carry out the task. For example, when I taught an overview of the history of the intertestamental period at a college in Oregon, I asked students to act out significant moments of the Maccabean revolt, scenes from the Maccabean dynasty, and scenes from the life of Herod the Great. I gave each student a role to play, a name tag for the character, props, and a synopsis of the plot. Students then had to organize themselves, plan the action, and act out the story for the rest of the class. Students found this activity particularly helpful because of the number of names repeated during this period.

Learners may also be instructed to participate in storytelling by giving responses throughout the story. Among the Nez Perce, listeners were expected to exclaim, "E!" (yes) after every few sentences.[47] During the Jewish festival of Purim, when the story of Esther was told, the people stamped their feet and made noise with special noisemakers every time the name of Haman was mentioned.[48] This device is useful in both formal and informal contexts. Learners may be given a refrain to repeat or may be asked to make noises or movements at appropriate times in the story. In this way, learners become active parts of the telling of a story.

HOW TO TELL A STORY

Stories are communicated in many ways. Long before the advent of writing or audio/video recording technology, stories were told orally. Stories were handed down as entertainment and instruction from one generation to the next. Everyday people did (and still do) tell stories to relive, to understand, and to share their experiences. The primacy of oral storytelling as a means of entertainment and instruction continues in the present. Consequently, oral storytelling provides religious educators with a familiar and readily available method for using stories in religious instruction.

Although storytelling is often used in religious instruction, insufficient preparation may diminish its effectiveness in achieving the desired learning outcome. Once an appropriate story is selected and oral storytelling is chosen as the desired communication technique,

---

[47]Ibid.

[48]Barry L. Bandstra, *Reading the Old Testament: An Introduction to the Hebrew Bible* (Belmont, Calif.: Wadsworth, 1995), p. 462.

religious educators should perfect the telling of the story before they share the story with learners.

Several years ago, I attended my first storytelling concert at the National Conference on Storytelling in San Antonio. Professional storytellers from the Southwest wove a spell of wonder as they told of *Senor Tigre* and *El Conejo*, of clever and beautiful Italian women, and of Coyote, the Trickster. From the moment the first storyteller stepped into her story, the audience was captivated by the magic of storytelling.[49]

This experience offered a sharp contrast to the halting or wooden repetitions often offered as stories in religious instruction. The storytellers of the National Conference on Storytelling were not relating the facts of an event; they were creating an experience. And this is the task of religious educators who would be storytellers.[50] Telling a story well is offering a gift to God and to others. Holocaust survivor and Nobel Peace laureate Elie Wiesel suggests that "God made man because He loves stories."[51]

Telling a story well requires hard work, discipline, and practice. Few people tell stories well spontaneously, and too often stories told in religious instruction lose their effectiveness because they are not told well. The following suggestions offer some guidelines for religious educators to use in preparing and performing storytelling.

Remembering Stories

I often serve as a guest preacher for churches in my area, and I always preach (almost word-for-word) from a manuscript. Through the years, I have had a recurring dream where I get up to preach and my manuscript is missing or I have forgotten I was preaching and have not prepared a sermon. I think in some way this dream captures a fear that I, and probably most speakers, have—going blank, forgetting what I am supposed to say. Memory is an important capacity for a storyteller, and the fear of forgetting the story may hinder or even prevent some religious educators from telling stories. But in the storytelling

---

[49]Suzanne Martin, "Altered States," *Storytelling* 5 (Summer 1993): 20–23.

[50]See Timothy Arthur Lines' discussion of the religious educator as storyteller in *Functional Images of the Religious Educator* (Birmingham, Ala.: Religious Education Press, 1992), pp. 226– 267.

[51]Elie Wiesel, *The Gates of the Forest*, trans. Frances Frenaye (New York: Schocken, 1966).

experience, each story is a creation, an experience in which a story-teller creates the story anew in the telling. The storyteller is a person in relationship with an audience, and in telling a story the storyteller does not so much perform a script as create an experience of mood, characters, and events.[52] Thus the storyteller does not memorize stories but remembers them.[53]

Metamemory is the knowledge people have about the strengths, weaknesses, and workings of their own memory.[54] It involves three related skills—awareness, diagnosis, and monitoring.[55] Awareness of the need to remember is a key prerequisite to effective memory.[56] Knowing that they need to remember affects how learners approach what needs to be remembered. Being aware that they need to remember stories, religious educators read and listen to stories with requisite attention to the defining aspects of the narrative. Simple awareness of the need to remember should heighten religious educators' effectiveness in remembering stories.

Beyond awareness of the need to remember, religious educators also need to understand what is necessary for remembering. Diagnosis is composed of two related skills: assessing task difficulty and determining retrieval demands.[57] Assessing task difficulty involves understanding differences in the difficulty of various memory tasks. For example, the amount of information to be remembered, the familiarity of information, the speed at which information is given, and how information is organized all affect the level of difficulty of remembering.[58] Diagnosing retrieval demands involves determining what kinds of encoding are necessary in order to retrieve memories successfully. For example, a learner listens to a story differently depending on

---

[52]Jack Maguire, *Creative Storytelling: Choosing, Inventing, and Sharing Tales for Children* (New York: McGraw-Hill, 1985), p. 100.

[53]Norma J. Livo and Sandra A. Rietz, *Storytelling: Process and Practice* (Littleton, Colo.: Libraries Unlimited, 1986), p. 101; Marsh Cassady, *Storytelling Step by Step* (San Jose, Calif.: Resource, 1990), p. 102.

[54]A. L. Brown et al., "Learning, Remembering, and Understanding," in *Handbook of Child Psychology. vol. 3: Cognitive Development.* ed. J. H. Flavell and E. M. Markman (New York: Wiley, 1983), pp. 263–340.

[55]Robert V. Kail Jr., *The Development of Memory in Children*, 2d ed. (New York: Freeman, 1984).

[56]John A. Glover, Royce R. Ronning, and Roger H. Bruning, *Cognitive Psychology for Teachers* (New York: Macmillan, 1990), p. 103.

[57]Ibid., pp. 103–105.

[58]Ibid., p. 104.

whether she is expected to recognize elements of the story or to retell the story.[59] Consequently, a religious educator can affect and enhance the ways learners listen to a story by providing learners with a listening assignment during the telling of the story. In other words, the religious educator provides an encoding clue before the story is told, and this clue should help learners remember and retrieve significant aspects of the story.

Finally, monitoring is the assessment of how well the narrative material is being committed to memory. Monitoring lets religious educators know how much of a story is adequately learned, how much is mastered, and how much needs more work. For example, if a learning objective in religious instruction involves the memorization of a Bible story, a religious educator may monitor learners' progress by having them tell the story. The monitoring process is significant because it allows religious educators to know when to shift attention from parts of the story that have been learned to parts that still require work.[60]

Although metamemory allows religious educators to be aware of the ways in which their memory works in learning stories, knowledge of encoding and retrieval processes is also helpful. Encoding has to do with the ways material is stored in the memory. Effective encoding depends on levels of processing and organization of knowledge. Learners remember material better if they deal with its meaning rather than its superficial elements.[61] Furthermore, memory is enhanced when learners make decisions during encoding[62] and when learners encode the same information in different but related ways.[63] A clear organizational structure in the material also facilitates memory of the

---

[59]Ibid., pp. 104–105.

[60]Ibid., pp. 105–106.

[61]Fergus I. M. Craik and R. S. Lockhart, "Levels of Processing: A Framework for Memory Research," *Journal of Verbal Learning and Verbal Behavior* 11 (December 1972): 671–684.

[62]Larry L. Jacoby, Fergus I. M Craik, and Ian Begg, "Effects of Decision Difficulty on Recognition and Recall," *Journal of Verbal Learning and Verbal Behavior* 18 (October 1979): 585–600.

[63]Fergus I.M. Craik and E. Tulving, "Depth of Processing and the Retention of Words in Episodic Memory," *Journal of Experimental Psychology: General* 104 (September 1975): 268–294. See also J. R. Anderson and L. M. Reder, "An Elaborative Processing Explanation of Depth Processing" in *Levels of Processing in Human Memory*, ed. L. S. Cermak and F. I. M. Craik (Hillsdale, N.J.: Erlbaum, 1979), pp. 385–404; and Neff Walker, "Direct Retrieval from Elaborated Memory Traces," *Memory and Cognition* 14 (July 1986): 321–328.

material.[64] For example, when the elements of a plot are linked by causality, a clear organizational structure is formed, and learners are better able to remember the story as they move through the narrative from one event of the plot to the next.

Certain encoding procedures seem to be especially well suited to facilitating story memory. One of the most important of these is rehearsal, which involves repetition of the material to be remembered. There are two different types of rehearsal: maintenance rehearsal and elaborative rehearsal.

Maintenance rehearsal refers to the process of repeating information over and over to keep it actively in short-term memory.[65] This sort of rehearsal, such as repeating a phone number until it is written down or dialed, is highly efficient for a short time but less helpful for complex information to be remembered for a long time.

Elaborative rehearsal, however, provides much more effective encoding for complex information.[66] Elaborative rehearsal involves relating the information to be learned to other information.[67] In terms of storytelling, for example, once the basic plotline is learned, elaborative rehearsal may include connecting the story to a previously learned genre of story or relating additional information to be told in the narrative to the plot line so that the information is associated with the plot as the story moves along. For example, in the apocryphal story of Daniel and Bel, a group of Babylonian priests and their families are using a secret entrance to the temple of Bel in order to sneak in and consume food and drink offerings left there for the idol. Daniel exposes these people to the king by scattering ashes on the floor of the temple after the priests have set out the offering and left the temple. The next morning the king and Daniel enter the temple. The food is gone, and the king is convinced Bel has eaten it until Daniel points out the footprints in the ashes.

---

[64]Glover, Ronning, and Bruning, *Cognitive Psychology for Teachers*, p. 111.

[65]Roberta L. Klatzky, *Human Memory: Structures and Processes*, 2d ed. (San Francisco: Freeman, 1984).

[66]Michele L. Simpson et al., "Elaborative Verbal Rehearsals and College Students' Cognitive Performance," *Journal of Educational Psychology* 86 (June 1994): 267–278.

[67]Fergus I. M. Craik and R. S. Lockhart, "CHARM Is not Enough: Comments on Eich's Model of Cued Recall," *Psychological Review* 93 (July 1986): 360–364.

The story of Daniel and Bel is quite similar to a story form familiar to most religious educators and learners—the detective story. Connecting the elements of the Daniel and Bel story to that form as it is rehearsed can help religious educators encode the story as a detective story. Elaborative rehearsal can also help link details of the story to the plot. Dialogue, descriptions, and elaboration can all be connected to the plot line as the story is rehearsed.

Another helpful procedure for encoding story is imagery. Dual coding—encoding through both words and image—enhances memory by linking verbal and nonverbal information.[68] By creating images of the story, religious educators can strengthen the encoding of the story in their memories. As religious educators rehearse the story, they should picture the story in their minds, noting sights, sounds, smells, tastes, and textures.[69] In this way, the words of the story are stored in the memory along with rich sensory images of the narrative.

Mnemonics provide a helpful memory strategy by pairing new information with well-learned information. Most people have probably used some form or another of mnemonics while studying for a test (creating a sentence using the first letter of a list of words to be memorized, for example). Storyteller Jack Maguire suggests a mnemonic device called loci as an excellent procedure for learning stories.[70]

Loci dates back to the times of the ancient Greeks. As the story goes, the poet Simonides was attending a great banquet. He was called outside, and just then, an earthquake struck. The roof of the banquet hall collapsed, mangling all those inside so badly that even their loved ones could not identify the bodies. But Simonides was able to identify each person by remembering where each person had sat at the banquet table. Hence, the method of loci involves the use of location to help people remember information.

---

[68]Alan Paivio, *Imagery and Verbal Processes* (New York: Holt, Rinehart and Winston, 1971); Alan Paivio, "Dual Coding and Episodic Memory: Subjective and Objective Sources of Memory Trace Components" in *Human Memory and Cognitive Capabilities: Mechanisms and Performances*, ed. F. Klix and H. Hafgendorf (Amsterdam: North-Holland, 1986), pp. 225–236; Alan Paivio, Virginai A. Diehl, and Carol Bergfeld Mills, "The Effects of Interaction with the Device Described by Procedural Test on Recall, True/False, and Task Performance," *Memory and Cognition* 23 (November 1995): 675–688.

[69]Milbre Burch, "Finding and Learning Stories," *Storytelling* 6 (May 1994): 15.

[70]Maquire, *Creative Storytelling*, pp. 104–105. See also Glover, Ronning, and Brunning, *Cognitive Psychology for Teachers*, pp. 120–121.

Remembering stories through loci begins with visualizing each of the main chronological components of the story as a separate visual image. Next, religious educators will attach the first of these chronological components to a specific place in a familiar room. Then they will continue around the room, connecting each chronological component to a memorable place in the room. Later, as religious educators tell the story they can recall the events by taking a mental walk around the room and visualizing each component. This technique can also work by visualizing a familiar road or the rooms in a familiar house.

Encoding the information to be remembered, however, is only half of the memory process. The information must also be retrieved. Retrieval is not simply a matter of calling up information that has been encoded. Rather, empirical research suggests that retrieval is actually a matter of reconstruction.[71] Instead of remembering and recalling every detail of an event, people store key elements and then, in bringing them up, combine these elements with general knowledge to reconstruct the experience.[72] This process explains the propensity toward memory errors. Since only the gist of the event is often encoded, reconstruction relies on connecting events from probable information from one's general knowledge. The likelihood of proper reconstruction of an event, however, increases when cues present at encoding are also available at retrieval.[73] Thus, if a religious educator encodes a story using the method of loci, retrieval and reconstruction of the story will be strengthened if the religious educator uses the image of the room to recall the story.

Religious educators may also use their voices, movement, and props as cues for story encoding and retrieval. The voice is a storyteller's performance instrument. Inflection, tone, enunciation, rhythm, and pace are all important parts of effective performance and can also act as effective memory cues. As religious educators develop stories

---

[71]Jean M. Mandler, *Stories, Scripts, and Scenes: Aspects of Schema Theory* (Hillsdale, N.J.: Erlbaum, 1984); Randy J. Spiro, "Constructive Processes in Prose Comprehension and Recall" in *Theoretical Issues in Reading Comprehension*, ed. Randy J. Spiro, B. C. Bruce, and W. F. Brewer (Hillsdale, N. J.: Erlbaum, 1980).

[72]Fredric C. Bartlett, *Remembering a Study in Experimental Psychology* (Cambridge: Cambridge University Press, 1932); Ulric Neisser, *Cognitive Psychology* (New York: Appleton-Century- Crofts, 1967).

[73]Endal Tulving and Sonia Osler, "Effectiveness of Retrieval Cues in Memory for Words," *Journal of Experimental Psychology* 77 (August 1968): 593–601.

for telling, they should be aware of how they use their voices to tell the story.[74]

Research indicates that vocal intonation is probably the most understood and valid mode of nonverbal communication.[75] Vocal intonation includes such components as rhythm, pitch, loudness, rate, inflection, enunciation, and intensity. If vocal cues contradict verbal messages, vocal cues will dominate.[76] Vocal intonation can convey emotion and meaning, as well as personal and physical characteristics such as dialect region, race, and education. Among the Clackamas Chinook, storytellers never used words to convey the feelings of characters in their stories but rather relied on voice and gesture to express emotions.[77]

Body movement, or kinesics, likewise convey information and emotion.[78] In fact, gestures are often comprehended more quickly than speech.[79] In the story of Zorba the Greek, when two characters who speak different languages meet, they decide to communicate by gestures: "He was to speak first. As soon as I couldn't follow him, I was to shout: 'Stop!' Then he'd get up and dance. D'you get me boss? He danced what he wanted to tell me. And I did the same. Anything we couldn't say with our mouths we said with our feet, our hands, our belly or with wild cries: Hi! Hi! Hopla! Ho-heigh!"[80]

Storytellers generally use three types of gestures: descriptive, directive, and emphatic.[81] Descriptive gestures are used, for example, to demonstrate height or size. Directive gestures point attention in a specific direction, and emphatic gestures highlight or emphasize, as in

---

[74]Livo and Reitz, p. 111; Cassady, p. 109. On paralanguage in religious instruction, see also Lee, *Content of Religious Instruction*, pp. 400–404.

[75] R. J. Haamersma and R. Mark, "Importance and Use of Nonverbal Communication," *Texas Personnel and Guidance Journal* 5 (Spring 1977): 7–16; B. Eckman, "Making Valid Nonverbal Judgments," *English Journal* 66 (November 1977): 72–74.

[76]A. Mehrabian, "Communication without Words," *Psychology Today* 2 (September 1968): 53– 55.

[77]Pellowski, *World of Storytelling*, p. 110.

[78]L. I. Gurley-Dilger, "Body Signals," *Science Teacher* 53 (September 1986): 63–64; Judith L. Hanna, *To Dance Is Human: A Theory of Nonverbal Communication* (Chicago: University of Chicago Press, 1987). See also Lee, *Content of Religious Instruction*, pp. 423–441.

[79]Miller, *Nonverbal Communication*, p. 17.

[80]Nikos Kazantzakis, *Zorba the Greek*, trans. Carl Wildman (New York: Simon and Schuster, 1952), p. 73.

[81]Cassady, *Storytelling Step by Step*, p. 140.

pounding on a table or shaking a fist. Gesture can enhance character development, and it can signal plot movement from one scene or character to the next.

Props may also serve as means for developing a story and helping religious educators remember stories. Folklorist Lyle Dickey theorizes that native Hawaiians devised string figures and chants as memory aids to help keep alive the people's oral traditions.[82] Storyteller Cherie Karo Schwartz suggests that artifacts may also bring learners closer to the experiences of the story by providing them with touchpoints.[83] For example, the *shekarisi* of the Congo region often hold a representation of one of the favorite symbols of the heroes of the epics they recount.[84] Religious educators can effectively use picture books, dolls, natural objects, string or paper games, or any of a number of other items as props. Certainly in Christian tradition, most congregants benefit from the presence of bread and wine (or, in certain conservative groups, grape juice) in the reenactment of the Lord's Supper. These props explicitly call Christians to remember the story of Jesus' passion.

All of these suggestions offer religious educators viable ways of remembering stories. Ultimately, each religious educator will have to try out various methods and see which work best. Finally, practice, practice, and more practice will make religious educators adept storytellers.

Beginning Stories

The beginning of a good story is an invitation. Storytellers invite the audience to listen, to enter into the story world. When telling stories, religious educators should not rush into the story but should first set the tone by the way the story is begun. Religious educators may use a formulaic phrase such as "Once upon a time . . ." or "there once was a . . ." Learners will recognize these phrases as a signal that a story is about to follow. Religious educators may also use opening rituals such as lighting a candle or dimming the lights to alert learners that a story is beginning. Some storytellers have used a call-and-

---

[82]Pellowski, *The World of Storytelling*, p. 147.

[83]"Using Objects in Storytelling and Teaching," *Storytelling* 6 (November 1994): 161–168.

[84]Pellowski, *World of Storytelling*, pp. 148–149.

response device to invite listeners into a story. In Mohawk tradition, for example, the storyteller calls out, "Ho?" and interested listeners respond, "Hey!"[85]

In one way or another, as determined by the goals of religious instruction, the beginning of a storytelling experience should engage learners' interest. Religious educators may develop their own ways of inviting learners along, and beginnings may need to be adapted for various audiences. The goal is to get learners involved in the story immediately so they will accompany the storyteller on the journey.

Telling Stories

Effective presentation of stories is essential for an optimal experience on the part of learners. Nervous energy in the religious educator will probably precede storytelling, but it can be channeled into excitement in performance. Religious educators for whom storytelling is a new procedure may even develop stage fright, which can exhibit itself in trembling, fidgeting, or talking too fast. To avoid excessive nervousness, religious educators should learn to relax before a storytelling experience. Storytellers Priscilla Howe and John Benedetto offer the following physical and mental warm-ups for storytellers:

1. Warm up the voice by singing a simple song or by vocalizing up and down a scale.
2. Stretch the mouth; stick out the tongue; make faces.
3. Stand in a relaxed position. Breathe deeply. Hold the breath for a moment. Then release slowly. Pause. Then repeat this procedure several times.
4. Roll the head gently to the right and then to the left.
5. Roll the shoulders forward and then backward.
6. Drop the jaw. Open the mouth wide. Move the jaw from side to side.
7. Stretch the body as much as possible.[86]

Storyteller Ellin Greene contends storytellers should exercise the speech organs just as athletes exercise their muscles. Such exercises may include sticking out the tongue and moving it from side to side of the mouth, trying to touch the nose and then the chin with the tongue, rotating the tongue clockwise and then counterclockwise, repeating

---

[85]Maguire, *Creative Storytelling*, p. 159.
[86]"Physical and Mental Warm-ups for Tellers," *Yarnspinner* 17 (March 1993): 5.

tongue twisters, rounding and stretching the lips, and moving and rotating the jaw.[87]

During the story, regular breathing helps religious educators remain relaxed. It also helps maintain the tempo of the story. As Howe and Benedetto point out, a common mistake people make during storytelling is talking until they are almost breathless and then taking shallow breaths.[88]

Experienced storytellers appear relaxed in front of an audience. Their interactions with the audience seem personal and spontaneous. Religious educators can learn such confidence and ease by watching and imitating professional storytellers and by rehearsing stories until they are comfortable with them. Practicing storytelling in front of a mirror and then in front of a small group of friends can also increase confidence. As storyteller Marsh Cassady suggests, knowing a story well is the most important component for a successful telling of it.[89]

Ending Stories

A good ending to a story is as important as a strong beginning. The story journey should be brought to a closure that directly leads to the religious instruction objective. Religious educators should neither drag out a story nor simply come to a halt. Formulaic endings provide a smooth transition from the story world to the world of the learners. I once heard one storyteller modify a typical formula and conclude her fairy tale with "and they lived, as may we all, happily ever after." A formulaic ending conveys completion to learners; they recognize that the story is over. Religious educators may also use a concluding ritual to signal the end of the story. If, for example, a candle were lit at the beginning of the story, it could be extinguished at the end. The ending serves as a bridge between the storytelling experience and what is to follow. The ending and the activities to follow, of course, will be determined by the goals of religious instruction.

---

[87]Ellin Greene, *Storytelling: Art and Technique*, 3d ed. (New Providence, N.J.: Reed Reference, 1996), pp. 70–72.

[88]Ibid.

[89]Cassady, *Storytelling Step by Step*, p. 137.

FACILITATING STORYTELLING

Although religious educators can and should bring stories to religious instruction, they should also help learners become storytellers.[90] People learn much about themselves as they tell their stories. Each person also has stories from which other learners can benefit. Furthermore, the very act of learners sharing stories tends to facilitate community among the participants in the learning group.

Religious educators may draw learners into storytelling by first demonstrating the art for them. Such direct modeling allows learners to discover the essentials of effective storytelling. Religious educators may also show video clips or play audio tapes of storytelling to provide other examples of effective storytelling. A demonstration may be followed by a discussion about the process of storytelling in order to allow learners to analyze components of stories and to identify techniques of storytelling.

One effective way to begin the facilitation of storytelling is to ask learners to share their own personal experiences. Since these experiences are already in learners' memories, the basic elements of story are already present. Character, plot, motivation, conflict, and setting are already formed in learners' minds and are thus readily accessible for a shared narrative. Religious educators may suggest that learners keep a journal of significant events as a resource for personal stories. Personal stories can provide religious educators with a significant tool for assisting learners in examining their own lived religious experience and developing strategies for lived faith in light of the personal myths learners articulate.

Personal storytelling can lead naturally into the telling of family stories.[91] Family stories, like personal stories, already reside in learners' memories. But because family stories were heard rather than experienced directly, they call for more development and preparation by learners. Religious educators may assign learners to collect stories from their own family members and then incorporate them into stories

---

[90]Two particularly helpful resources on facilitating storytelling are: Leland B. Jacobs, "Successful Storytelling," *Early Years* 15 (December 1984): 764; and Norma J. Livo, "Storytelling," *Media and Methods* 19–20 (September 1983): 24–26.

[91]Rives Collins and Pamela J. Cooper, *The Power of Story: Teaching through Storytelling*, 2d ed. (Scottsdale, Ariz.: Gorsuch Scarisbrick, 1997), pp. 23–33.

for sharing in a religious instruction setting. Family stories can be important in religious instruction as one means of providing a larger context for learners' personal myths. Family stories may serve as the metanarrative for learners' own narratives of their faith journey.

Learners may also want to learn to tell traditional stories, such as myths, folktales, fairytales, and biblical stories, many of which originated in oral traditions. These are the stories that embody and create people's experience of the world.[92] In the religious instruction context, these stories can help learners explore their own experiences through interaction with common human experiences embodied in these stories, or they can help learners experience worldviews different from their own and perhaps contribute to learners' growing inclusivity of other people and other ideas. These stories may also allow learners to explore the narratives that have helped keep oppressive ideas and systems in place and to suggest new, more just narratives for creating the world.[93]

Learners can search collections of traditional tales and can compare variant forms in order to discover the story they want to tell. Because such stories first existed in oral tradition, they usually follow a typical construction which makes them easy to remember and to tell. Often learners may already know the basics of the story and may need simply to learn how to tell the story.

Finally, learners may wish to move into creating their own stories. Religious educators may wish to try out original stories with a group first.[94] A group can create its own stories, for example, by having the religious educator begin a story. After a set amount of time, say, thirty seconds, the next person picks up the story and continues it, and so on. Or religious educators may foster the telling of original stories by providing some trigger to help learners get started.[95] Pictures, incomplete sentences, and objects can be used to stimulate learners' imaginations.

---

[92]Alida Gersie and Nancy King, *Storymaking in Education and Therapy* (London: Jessica Kingsley, 1990).

[93]Pam Gilbert, "'And They Lived Happily Ever After': Cultural Storylines and the Construction of Gender," in *The Need for Story: Cultural Diversity in Classroom and Community*, ed. Anne Haas Dyson and Celia Genishi (Urbana, Ill.: National Council of Teachers of English, 1994), pp. 124–142.

[94]Norma J. Livo and Sandra A. Rietz, *Storytelling Activities* (Littleton, Colo.: Libraries Unlimited, 1987), p. 51.

[95]Thomas N. Turner and Tommy Oaks, "Stories on the Spot: Introducing Students to Impromptu Storytelling," *Childhood Education* 73 (Spring 1997) pp. 154–157.

Learners' stories can be shared in a group both informally and formally. A story may emerge informally as an anecdote as the conversation triggers a relevant memory. Other times, depending on the goals of the learning session, religious educators may wish to have a time dedicated to learners' formal telling of a prepared story to the group. During these times, learners should be encouraged to be attentive to and supportive of the storyteller. In addition to oral storytelling, learners may also enact their stories, or they may wish to create a videotape, or they may draw their stories. Depending on the goals of religious instruction and the nature of the story, many forms of storytelling may be appropriate for communicating stories.

Following a story, time should be set aside for discussion and feedback. Feedback helps storytellers improve their stories and their skills, and time for debriefing is essential to allow learners to explore the implications of stories for lived faith. Although the stories themselves may create powerful experiences, reflection may intensify those initial reactions and further contribute toward achieving the goals of religious instruction. Helpful discussion of a narrative experience may focus on such questions as: How did you feel as you heard the story? What new things did the story suggest to you? Did the story challenge you in any way? Have you had experiences similar to those in the story? What happened in your experiences? What does the story suggest to you about faith? What did you learn from the story? What are situations in your life where you might apply what you learned from the story?

As learners become conscious and intentional storytellers, they will experience faith in a variety of ways. On one level, stories can introduce learners to new information and can help them reflect critically on their own experiences. But on a more significant level, stories can be life-changing encounters with Mystery and Awe. This potential of narrative is what makes it such an important tool for religious instruction. Narrative can be a powerful means of facilitating lived Christian faith.

OTHER TECHNIQUES FOR
COMMUNICATING STORIES

In addition to oral storytelling, stories can be communicated effectively through a number of other modes. Depending on the goals of a learning session, some stories will best be communicated through methods that are most effective in the cognitive domain (reading or writing a story); others in the affective domain (watching a motion picture); and yet others in the lifestyle domain (enacting the Christian story through lived experience). Some of these methods will be interwoven throughout the rest of the book as examples for effective narrative experiences in religious instruction.

Enacting a story, using movement, creating art, singing and playing music are all methods of storytelling that involve learners physically in a story. These forms of storytelling make learning direct, utilizing the body and the senses to enhance the learning experience. Watching demonstrations, watching movies, listening to music, or viewing art are storytelling methods that call on learners to use their imaginations, even more than the previous, more direct methods. Through these techniques, learners indirectly share experiences by identifying with characters (instead of becoming the characters as in dramatized stories). Writing stories, reading stories aloud, and reading literature are primarily verbal modes of storytelling and operate at the highest level of abstraction in terms of instructional technique. Thus the words chosen to convey the story must be used with precision, creating in the imagination vivid pictures of the characters and events of the story. Selected properly for a particular learning session, any one of these techniques may be effective for achieving the goals of that session.

Stories are an important resource in the repertoire of religious educators because, as I explain in chapter 6, stories can help achieve goals of religious instruction in cognitive, affective, and lifestyle domains. Stories seem to be inherent forms of human experiencing and learning. Thoreau suggests that many people have dated the beginning of an era in their lives from the reading of a book, and C. S. Lewis and Frederick Buechner both point to stories as essential elements in their own personal faith journey.[96] Stories connect us to ourselves, our community, the human family, and to God. The following story comes from Hasidic tradition: Once, long ago, when one of the great rabbis saw misfortune threatening Israel, he would go to a certain place in the forest where he would light a fire and say a special prayer. A miracle would then happen, and disaster would be averted. Years later

---

[96]C. S. Lewis, *Surprised by Joy: The Shape of My Early Life* (New York: Harcourt, Brace, and Jovanovich, 1955); Frederick Buechner, *The Sacred Journey* (New York: Harper and Row, 1982).

when other misfortunes threatened Israel, the rabbi's disciple went to God to intercede. He returned to the same place in the forest and said, "Master of the Universe, I am not able to light the fire, but I can still say the prayer." Again, a miracle would happen. Many years later, yet another rabbi went to intercede for Israel. He would go to the place in the forest and say, "Master of the Universe, I cannot light the fire, and I do not know the prayer, but I do know the place, and it must be sufficient." And it was. The miracle happened. Finally, many, many years later, misfortune threatened again. Another rabbi sat in his armchair in his study and with his head in his hands prayed, "Master of the Universe, I cannot light the fire, and I do not know the prayer. I cannot even find the place in the forest. But I can tell the story, and it must be sufficient." And it was.[97]

---

[97]Elie Wiesel, *The Gates of the Forest*, trans. Frances Frenaye (London: Heinemann, 1966).

2

A Brief History of Storytelling

Some things know their own story and the stories of other things,
too; some know only their own. Whoever knows all the stories
has wisdom, no doubt.[1]

—Mario Vargas Llosa

Mario Vargas Llosa's *The Storyteller* relates the experience of a
young Peruvian man captivated by a photograph he sees in an exhibit
in a Florence museum. The photo is of a group of primitive Amazon-
ian Indians sitting in a circle, spellbound, all eyes focused on the one
in the center of the circle—*el hablador*, the storyteller. The
habladores traveled from settlement to settlement carrying current
news and tales of the past. Part priest, part medicine man, they were
the memory of the community who "using the simplest, most time-
hallowed of expedients, the telling of stories, were the living sap that
circulated and made the Machiguengas into a society, a people of interconnected and interdependent beings."[2]

Storytelling is an ancient art found across all races, ethnicities, cultures, and nationalities. Originating as an oral event, storytelling eventually grew to encompass oral and written narratives, as well as visual
narratives such as drama and the visual arts. Although retaining some
common characteristics, oral and written stories have developed

---

[1]Mario Vargas Llosa, *The Storyteller*, trans. Helen Lane (New York: Penguin,
1989), p. 131.
[2]Ibid., p. 93.

34

distinct processes and laws of composition.[3] In current discussion, the term storytelling most often connotes the oral act of composing narrative.[4] Storyteller Marsh Cassidy defines storytelling as "an oral art form that provides a means of preserving and transmitting ideas, images, motives, and emotions that are universal."[5] Anne Pellowski offers this definition: "The entire context of a moment when oral narration of stories in verse and/or prose is performed or led by one person before a live audience; the narration may be spoken, chanted, or sung, with or without musical, pictorial, and/or other accompaniment, and may be learned from oral, printed, or mechanically recorded sources; one of its purposes must be that of entertainment or delight and it must have at least a small element of spontaneity in the performance."[6]

The distinguishing characteristic of oral stories over against written narrative is the method of composition; it is a distinction of form rather than content. Each oral performance is a separate act of creation that exists only in the moment of the telling. The oral storyteller does not compose or memorize a fixed text but creates a story with each performance. Whereas elements of the story, such as plot, character conception, events, or motifs, may be transmitted, the story itself is not. The story cannot be separated from the performance.

Oral narrative is also marked by its traditional story grammar. Oral storytelling is often formulaic, following patterns traditioned by the culture of the teller. The story event itself then is the product of the interaction of tradition and individual talent, traditional plots and motifs being reshaped by originality and individual expression.

A third significant distinction between oral and written narrative is the place of the narrator. Usually, in oral narrative no ironic distance exists between the narrator and the storyteller. The narrator is authoritative, reliable, omniscient, and objective, whereas in written narrative

---

[3]For a more in-depth discussion of the relationship between oral and written narrative, see: Robert Scholes and Robert Kellogg, "The Narrative Tradition" and "The Oral Heritage of Written Narrative," in *The Nature of Narrative* (London.: Oxford University Press, 1966), pp. 3–56.

[4]Throughout this book, the term "storytelling" will, on the whole, be used in its broadest sense to encompass oral, visual, and written forms of narrative. When specific forms are addressed, they are noted in the text.

[5]Marsh Cassidy, *Storytelling Step by Step* (San Jose, Calif.: Resource, 1990), p. 5.

[6]Anne Pellowski, *The World of Storytelling*, rev. ed. (New York: Wilson, 1990), p. 18.

the narrator is self-conscious, a creation of the author. While traditional oral narrative consists rhetorically of a teller, the teller's story, and an implied audience, written narrative consists rhetorically of the imitation or representation of a teller, the teller's story, and an implied audience.[7]

Despite these differences in form, oral and written narratives share a number of common elements that are essential to any story: characters, setting, conflict, plot, and meaning. Characters are the personalities involved in the narrative action and may be characterized in mythic or mimetic terms. A mythic character is traditional, archetypal, whereas a mimetic character is ordinary, everyday. Setting is the physical background or element of place in a story. Conflict is the external struggle of the characters against the environment or one another or the inner struggle of the characters within themselves. Plot is the dynamic, sequential element or the structure of action, and meaning is the function of the relationship between the world created by the storyteller, the "real world," and the world reconstructed by the listener or reader. Understanding a narrative implies the construction of a satisfactory relationship or set of relationships between the worlds.[8]

At the core of storytelling, whether oral, visual, or written, there lies a common human need to give expression to experience, to construct meaning of the events of life. The ability to tell stories is one of the defining characteristics of human beings. The apprehension of story grammar, consisting of these common elements, seems to be universal across ages, races, cultures, and time. Human identity itself is narratively constructed as people live out narratives and understand their lives in terms of the narratives they live out.[9] Walker Percy even labels humanity *homo symbolificus*, symbol monger.[10]

In the act of storytelling, humans create experience, meaning, identity, and community. The telling of stories seems necessary for humans to explain and understand experience. In telling, hearing, seeing, and

[7]Scholes and Kellogg, *Nature of Narrative*, p. 53.

[8]For more detailed definitions of narrative elements, see: Scholes and Kellogg, *Nature of Narrative*, and Cleanth Brooks and Robert Penn Warren, *Understanding Fiction* (New York: Appleton-Century-Crofts, 1943).

[9]Stephen Sykes, "The Grammar of Narrative and Making Sense of Life," *Anglican Theological Review* 67 (April 1985): 123.

[10]Walker Percy, *The Message in the Bottle* (New York: Farrar, Straus, and Giroux, 1975), p. 17.

reading stories, people experience aspects of common human existence, out of which they come to create meaning of their own experiences.

As such an integral part of human identity, story probably emerged almost simultaneously with language itself. Pellowski has identified seven theories of the origins of storytelling:

1. Storytelling grew out of playful, self-entertainment needs of humans.
2. It satisfied the need to explain the surrounding physical world.
3. It came about because of an intrinsic religious need in humans to honor or propitiate the supernatural force(s) believed to be present in the world.
4. It evolved from the human need to communicate experience to other humans.
5. It fulfilled an aesthetic need for beauty, regularity, and form through expressive language and music and body movement.
6. It stemmed from the desire to record the actions or qualities of one's ancestors or leaders, in the hope that this would give them a kind of immortality.
7. It encoded and reserved the norms of social interaction that a given society lived by.[11]

Many examples of stories or story fragments exist in texts from a number of ancient cultures: Babylonian, Canaanite, Hittite, Sumerian, Egyptian, Chinese. A number of stories have ancient roots and are found in some form in widely divergent cultures. These stories have been told and retold, passed from one part of the world to another, and recast in the language and culture of each teller. Many stories across cultures embody similar themes of common human experience, such as parent-child relationships, initiation into adulthood, and encounters with Mystery.

The oldest written description of a storytelling event is found in the Egyptian Westcar Papyrus, dated 2000–1300 B.C.E. In it, the sons of Cheops, the great pyramid builder, entertain their father by telling him tales.[12] The Golenischeff Papyrus, from approximately the same period, describes a conversation between a sailor and a nobleman who

---

[11]Pellowski, *World of Storytelling*, pp. 10–11.

[12]"Tales of the Magicians," in *Egyptian Literature*, trans. and ed. Epiphonius Wilson (London: Colonia, 1901), pp. 159–169.

has returned from an unsuccessful venture and is afraid to report to the ruling powers. The sailor tells his stories of adventure to the nobleman as examples of how such misfortunes can happen to anyone.[13] The earliest known heroic epic is the Sumerian story of Gilgamesh, which was taken over by the Babylonians when Sumerian civilization collapsed in 2000 B.C.E.[14] Reflections of this epic are found in the Greek epics of Homer and the flood story of the Hebrew Scriptures.[15]

The oldest written version of a story is "The Tale of Two Brothers," found in an Egyptian papyrus dating from around 1250 B.C.E.[16] In this story, a younger brother rejects the advances of his sister-in-law. Afraid the younger brother will publicly denounce her, she tells her husband that the younger brother tried to seduce her. The angry older brother tries to kill the younger brother, who escapes wounded into the wilderness and eventually dies there. At this point the gods intervene and reveal the truth to the older brother who is able to find his younger brother's body and resuscitate it. This type of cautionary tale also appears in ancient Chinese, Sumerian, and Sanskrit texts, and the biblical account of Joseph and Potiphar's wife may derive from the Egyptian tale.

The Hebrew Bible contains many forms of folktales that were collected by the Israelites and later incorporated into their sacred writings. The text itself, however, relates very few instances of storytelling events. In Judges 9:7, Jotham uses a story to convince the people of Shechem of their misdeed in anointing Abimelech king, and in 2 Samuel 12:1–7, Nathan the prophet uses a story to convict David of his sin with Bathsheba.

Once the written texts of the Hebrew Scriptures were fixed, emphasis shifted away from the more dynamic retelling and reinterpreting of biblical stories characteristic of oral tradition, although Jewish people who lived in oral cultures seemed more free in their storytelling,

---

[13]Ibid., pp.173–176.

[14]Ellin Greene, *Storytelling Art and Technique*, 3d ed. (New Providence, N.J.: Bowker, 1996), p. 2.

[15]Ibid.

[16]Jack Maguire, *Creative Storytelling: Choosing, Inventing, and Sharing Tales for Children* (New York: McGraw-Hill, 1985), p. 32. For the text of the story, see Adolf Erman, *The Literature of the Ancient Egyptians: Poems, Narratives, and Manuals of Instruction, from the 3rd and 2d Millenium B.C.*, trans. Aylward M. Blackman (New York: Arno, 1977), pp. 150–161.

adapting biblical material as well as tales and legends of heroic and common people.[17] Even so, Jewish scholars and leaders continued to use storytelling to a great degree as a means of both conveying and interpreting Jewish faith.[18] Interestingly, hundreds of years later storytelling became an integral part of Hasidic ritual and teaching, particularly as the Hasidim used stories as a way to introduce children to the life of the community.[19]

Other ancient religious traditions made great use of storytelling. Sanskrit scriptures make numerous references to the practice of storytelling.[20] The Tripitaka, part of the Buddhist scriptures, contains a number of dialogues, lives of saints and sages, fables, and other types of tales.[21] And while Taoism and Confucianism do not have the same wealth of story material, their proponents too use story to propagate belief.[22]

Many ancient peoples used stories as an educational tool. Both Plato and Aristotle include storytelling in their educational paradigms and comment on the importance of choosing appropriate tales for children. In *The Republic* (c. 400 B.C.E.), Plato writes,

---

[17]Birger Gerhardsson, *Memory and Manuscript: Oral Tradition and Written Transmission in Rabbinic Judaism and Early Christianity*, trans. Eric J. Sharpe (Lund: CWK Gleerup; Copenhagen: Enjar Munksgaard, 1961).

[18]For more information on Judiasm and Jewish storytelling, see: Louis Ginzberg, *The Legends of the Jews*, trans. Henrietta Szold (Philadelphia: Jewish Publication Society of America, 1909); Ephraim E. Urbach, *The Sages: Their Concepts and Beliefs*, trans. Israel Abrahams (Jerusalem: Magnes, 1975); George Foot Moore, *Judaism in the First Centuries of the Christian Era* (Cambridge: Harvard University Press, 1962); Michael Fishbane, *Biblical Interpretation in Ancient Israel* (Oxford: Clarendon, 1985).

[19]Martin Buber, *The Legend of the Baal-Shem* (New York: Schocken, 1955); Jerome R. Mintz, *Legends of the Hasidim: An Introduction to Hasidic Cultural and Oral Tradition in the New World* (Chicago: University of Chicago Press, 1968); Louis I. Newman, *The Hasidic Anthology: Tales and Teachings of the Hasidim* (New York: Bloch, 1944).

[20]*Kaushitaki Brahmana Upanishad*, pt. 3, *The Sacred Books of the East*, vol. 19, ed. F. Max Müller (Oxford: Clarendon, 1879–1910); and *Grihya-Sûtras*, *The Sacred Books of the East*, vol. 30, ed. F. Max Müller (Oxford: Clarendon, 1879–1910).

[21]In the Buddhist work *The Questions of King Milinda* (300–400 C.E.) a sage reassures the king that the recitation of stories is positive. *Sacred Books of the East*, vol. 36, pp. 92–96.

[22]See the writings of Chuang-Tze (c. 100 B.C.E.).

We begin by telling children stories which, though not wholly destitute
of truth, are in the main fictitious; and these stories are told them when
they are not of an age to learn gymnastics. . . . Let the censors receive
any talk of fiction which is good, and reject the bad; and we will desire
mothers and nurses to tell their children the authorized ones only. Let
them fashion the mind with such tales, even more fondly than they
mould the body with their hands.[23]

The stories Plato wishes to have censored are ones that he accuses
of telling lies, which he defines as making erroneous representations
of the nature of gods and heroes. Rather, he wants children to hear
tales that are models of virtuous thoughts. In his *Politics*, Aristotle
agrees that the Directors of Education should be careful what stories
the children hear because these stories will prepare the children for
adult life and should therefore be representations of the occupations
they will pursue.[24] The educational value of storytelling was also expressed in the *Panchatantra* (c. 400 C.E.), a work compiled for the education of the royal children of India:

Whoever learns the work by heart,
Or through the storyteller's art
Becomes acquainted;
His life by sad defeat—although
The king of heaven be his foe—
Is never tainted.[25]

Among the Xhosa and Zulu people of Africa, storytelling was considered training in listening and telling, and children were expected to
listen to and learn the stories they heard from their elders.[26]
Several references to storytelling as entertainment appear in Greek
and Roman literature. Both Euripides and Aristophanes mention storytelling in their plays. In *Heracles* (c. 423 B.C.E.). Euripides has Am-
phitryon advise his daughter-in-law Megara to spend the time waiting
for her husband's return by consoling her children with stories.[27] In

---

[23]Plato, *The Republic* (trans. Benjamin Jowett) 2.377.
[24]Aristotle, *Politics* (trans. Benjamin Jowett) 7.1336.
[25]Introduction to the *Panchatantra* (trans. Arthur Ryder)
[26]Greene, *Storytelling Art and Technique*, p. 3.
[27]Euripides, *Heracles* (trans. Philip Vellacott) 66–98.

Aristophanes' *Lysistrata* (c. 411 B.C.E.), the chorus of old men tell a reversal of the story of Atalanta.[28] In *The Wasps* (c. 422 B.C.E.), Bdelycleon instructs Philocleon on how to behave in polite society by telling stories.[29]

Roman literature, likewise, makes reference to storytelling. Horace describes this scene in one of his satires:

> O evenings, and suppers fit for gods! with which I and my friends regale ourselves in the presence of my household gods. . . conversation arises, not concerning other people's villas and household, nor whether Lepos dances well or not; but we debate on what is more to our purpose, and what it is pernicious not to know—whether men are made happier by riches or by virtue; or what leads us into intimacies, interest or moral rectitude; and what is the nature of good, and what its perfection. Meanwhile, my neighbor Cervius prates away old stories relative to the subject.[30]

Cervius then goes on to tell the story of the country mouse and the city mouse as a response to a discussion on wealth.

In his *Metamorphoses*, (c. 7 C.E.) Ovid depicts a storytelling situation that later became common throughout Europe—women spinning and telling tales to make the time pass more quickly:

> Alonly Mineus daughters ben of wilfulnesse, with working
> Quite out of time to breake the feast, are in their houses lurking:
> And there doe fall to spinning yarns, or weaving in the frame,
> And kepe their maidens to their worke. Of which one pleasant dame
> As she with nimble hand did draw hir slender—veede and fine,
> Said: Whyle that others idelly doe serve one God of wine,
> Let us that serve a better Sainct Minerva, finde some talke
> To ease our labor while our handes about our profite walke
> And for to make the time seeme shorte, let eche of us recite,
> (As every bodies turne shall come) some talke that may delight.[31]

---

[28]Aristophanes, *Lysistrata* (trans. Jack Lindsay) 66–98.
[29]Aristophanes, *The Wasps* (trans. Moses Hadas) 1170–1262.
[30]Horace, *Satires* (trans. Arthur Golding) 2.6.
[31]Ovid, *Metamorphoses* (trans. Arthur Golding) 4.1.41–50.

Like the Greeks, the Romans continued to use storytelling as an educational as well as entertainment form. In his *Institutio Oratoria*, Quintillian writes, "Let boys learn, then to relate orally the fables of Aesop, which follow next after the nurse's stories, in plain language, not rising at all above mediocrity, and afterward to express the same simplicity in writing."[32] And in his first- century C.E. *Geography*, the Roman historian Strabo writes:

> Man is eager to learn and his fondness for tales is a prelude to this quality. It is fondness for tales, then, that induces children to give their attention to narratives and more and more to take part in them. The reason for this is that myth is a new language to them—a language that tells them, not of things as they are, but of a different set of things. And what is new is pleasing, and so is what one did not know before, and it is just this that makes men eager to learn. But if you add to this the marvelous and the portentous, you thereby increase the pleasure, and pleasure acts as a charm to incite the learning. At the beginning we must needs make use of such bait for children.[33]

Ancient Greek and Roman cultures also marked the beginning of the development of a tradition of written narrative, which may not have been seen as a positive movement by all. In *Phaedrus*, Plato relates the story of the Egyptian god Theuth who discovered the use of letters. Theuth took his discovery to the god Thamus so that the Egyptians would be allowed to benefit from it. "This . . . will make the Egyptians wiser and give them better memories," Theuth explained. "It is a specific for both the memory and for the wit." Thamus replied,

> This discovery of yours will create forgetfulness in the learners' souls, because they will not use their memories; they will trust to the external written characters and not remember of themselves. The specific which you have discovered is not an aid to memory, but to reminiscence, and you give your disciples not truth, but only the semblance of truth; they will be hearers of many things and will have learned nothing; they will appear to be omniscient and will generally know nothing; they will be tiresome company, having the show of wisdom without the reality.[34]

---

[32]Quintillian, *Institutio Oratoria* (trans. James J. Murphy) 1.9.2.
[33]Strabo, *Geography* (trans. Horace Leonard Jones) 1.2.8.
[34]Plato, *Phaedrus* (trans. Benjamin Jowett) 275.

The movement of epic from oral to written tradition marked the beginning of modern narrative. In Western literature, Homer was both the culmination of the art of oral storytelling and the beginning of written.[35] Homer's epics were not the creations of a single author's mind but the redaction of a tradition of oral composition preceding Homer for centuries. The homeric epics do not distinguish between myth and history, but as Greek culture began to make this distinction it gave rise to two narrative forms that are the primary Greek contribution to the development of Western written narrative. The separation of narrative into fact and fiction gave birth to the genres of history and romance, and these two streams were not united again in written narrative until the emergence of the novel.

The storytelling of the early Christian church followed a similar path from oral to written narrative with the assistance of redactors. Many of the teachings of Jesus were preserved in parable form, and most of the gospel stories themselves circulated as oral units for a number of years before their inclusion in the New Testament text.

Using oral sources, written sources such as Q (German *Quelle* "source"), and their own literary ingenuity, the synoptic writers preserved and created stories with a particularly evangelistic intent based on their understandings and theological reflection about the life of Jesus. The variations among similar stories in the synoptics (the resurrection accounts, for example) point to the fluidity of the oral tradition, which allowed for the development of differing accounts. And, given the probability of at least two of the writers' awareness of the work of the third, these variations tend to imply the writers' own acceptance of the process of oral tradition. The writers did not feel compelled to harmonize differing accounts but were willing to include them in the text as they were appropriate to the writer's theme and structure.[36]

---

[35]Scholes and Kellogg, *Nature of Narrative*, p. 57.

[36]For more information on the construction of the New Testament text, see John S. Kloppenborg, *The Formation of Q: Trajectories in Ancient Wisdom Collections* (Philadelphia: Fortress, 1987); Rudolf Bultmann, *The History of the Synoptic Tradition*, trans. John Marsh (Oxford:Blackwell, 1972); David L. Barr, *New Testament Story*, 2d ed. (Belmont, Calif.: Wadsworth, 1995); Edwin D. Freed, *The New Testament: A Critical Introduction*, 2d ed. (Belmont, Calif.: Wadsworth, 1991); Edgar V. McKnight, *What Is Form Criticism?* (Philadelphia: Fortress, 1969).

Outside of the gospel narratives themselves, the early church also found other types of stories to be useful. Early in church history, stories of saints and exempla were transmitted and often used in sermons as illustrations.[37] An exemplum is a fable or anecdote to which a moral has been appended. The earliest known examples in Christian preaching date back to the homilies of St. Gregory the First (c. 600 C.E.). In his *Ecclesiastical History of the English Nation*, the Venerable Bede records the gift of story given to a brother in the monastery of the Abbess Hilda (c. 680 C.E.). In a dream, Caedmon was told to sing the beginning of created beings, and he began to create spontaneously verses recounting the story of creation. Upon waking, he shared his gift with the abbess, who then had him teach the entire sacred history, which Caedmon converted into verse. Bede writes:

> He sang the creation of the world, the origin of man, and all the history of Genesis: and made many verses on the departure of the children of Israel out of Egypt, and their entering into the land of promise, with many other histories from holy writ; the incarnation, passion, resurrection of our Lord, and his ascension into heaven; the coming of the Holy Ghost, and the preaching of the apostles; also the terror of future judgment, the horror of the pains of hell, and the delights of heaven.[38]

The church also found storytelling through drama to be useful, although the church's attitude toward the stage had not always been positive. Drama had its origins in religion. Shamans would act out an event to ensure its happening. The masks used in these religious rituals also had educational value. Greek drama originated in the sixth century B.C.E. with Thespis and developed through the work of Aeschylus, Aristotle, and Aristophanes, in particular. The Romans recognized the entertainment value of drama and developed its spectacle side. When the church took control of Rome, drama was banned because of its association with spectacle. The high drama of the Middle Ages, then, evolved out of the Mass. The earliest church plays were reenactments of the passion, death, and resurrection of Christ. Later

---

[37]For example, see Thomas Frederick Crane, *The Exempla or Illustrative Stories from the "Sermones Vulgares" of Jacques de Vitry* (London: D. Nutt for the Folk-lore Society, 1890).

[38]The Venerable Bede, *Ecclesiastical History of the English Nation* (London: J. M. Dent, 1916), p. 207.

morality plays developed, which were allegorical renditions of people's spiritual journey in this world.

As the Roman Empire spread throughout Europe and Asia, it carried with it tales acquired from a number of different cultures. After the empire's fall, tales were disseminated primarily by gypsies who migrated from the East to Europe. They were soon followed by Christians participating in the Crusades or making pilgrimages, who carried tales back and forth across the continents.

In the fourteenth century, Geoffrey Chaucer wrote of a pilgrimage within England to the religious shrine of Canterbury, which became an occasion for storytelling. The host of the inn at which the pilgrims lodged the night before they began the trip suggested they tell stories along the way to shorten the trip:

> This is the poynt, to speken short and pleyn
> That ech of yow, to shorte with your weye,
> In this viage, shal telle tales tweye,
> To Caunterbury-ward, I mene it so,
> And hom-ward he shal tellen otehre two,
> Of aventures that whylom han bifalle,
> And which of yow that bereth him best of alle,
> That is to seyn, that telleth in this cas
> Tales of best sentence and most solas,
> Shal have a soper at our aller cost
> Here in this place, sitting by this post,
> Whan that we come agayn from Caunterbury.[39]

This pilgrimage then became the frame for the telling of the famous *Canterbury Tales*.[40]

The first professional storytellers were bards or singer-storytellers. Bards either sang of the great deeds of past leaders or recited genealogies and sang about historic events.[41] Bardic storytellers are described in Homer's *Odyssey*. According to custom the bard accompanied

---

[39]Geoffery Chaucer, *The Canterbury Tales* (Oxford: Oxford University Press, 1978), pp. 20–21.

[40]Katharine S. Gittes, *Framing the Canterbury Tales: Chaucer and the Medieval Frame Narrative Tradition* (New York: Greenwood, 1991); Leonard Michael Koff, *Chaucer and the Art of Storytelling* (Berkeley, Calif.: University of California Press, 1988).

[41]Greene, *Storytelling Art and Technique*, p. 3.

himself on a lyre held in both hands. After about two hundred years, the bards exchanged lyres for a staff, which freed one of the storyteller's hands. This allowed the storyteller to gesture and to use the staff as a prop, leading to a more dramatic style of storytelling. Bards were known throughout the Roman Empire as well as in Asia, Africa, the South Pacific, and the Americas.[42]

While the crusaders were moving across Europe and Asia, two distinct schools of storytelling were evolving from native Celtic tradition: the Cymric school of bards in Wales and the Gaelic school of ollamhs in Ireland.[43] These schools gave the art both a formal structure of skill training and performance guidelines and an ability to create stories spontaneously through imagination. Both schools were divided into ranks, and high-ranking storytellers were held in great regard by their societies. In the Cymric school, the "chief of song" was granted a free holding of land by the king, and, in the Gaelic school, a high-ranking ollamh was allowed to wear five colors, only one fewer than royalty.

England's conquest of Wales and Ireland brought about the end of these schools of storytellers. They took to the road, becoming itinerant bards and minstrels throughout Europe and the Near East. As their context shifted from courts to public squares, their tales shifted from stories of royalty and significant historical events to stories of common people, animals, and popular superstitions. In Europe and the Middle East, French troubadours, Muslim *rawis*, and Russian *skomorokhi* all wandered throughout their countries weaving stories and entertaining the public.[44]

The invention of the printing press in the fifteenth century had an inestimable impact on the nature of storytelling. Before Gutenberg's invention, books were costly and rare. Few people were literate, and fewer still could afford to buy more than one or two books in a

---

[42]Ibid., p. 4.

[43]For more on Welsh and Irish bards, see James C. Morrice, *A Manual of Welsh Literature* (Bangor, North Wales: Jarvis and Foster, 1909); George Sigerson, *Bards of the Gael and Gall* (New York: Lemma, 1974).

[44]For more information on troubadours, see Abbe Charles De La Rue, *Essais historiques sur les bardes, les jongleurs et les trouveres normands et anglo-normands*, 3 vols. (Caen, 1854); and Anthony Bonner, *Songs of the Troubadours* (New York: Shocken, 1972). To read more about *Skomorokhi*, see Russell Aguta, *Russian Minstrels: A History of the Skomorokhi* (Philadelphia: University of Pennsylvania Press, 1978).

lifetime. With the advent of the printing press, reading material became readily available to a mass audience. More and more people learned to read, and many storytellers became authors. The number of professional storytellers declined as storytelling became a common domestic activity. The greatest threat to storytelling, however, came with the notion that the printed version of a story was the "correct" one. With this attitude came an inhibition to spinning tales that existed in some form in print.

This era also saw the rise of the literary tale—a story written specifically to be read—and an emphasis on narrative art. Although new stories were produced in literary form, ancient tales were also given new constructions. Francois Rabelais, for example, combined old French tales of the giant Gargantua with his own stories of Gargantua's son Pantagruel in *Gargantua and Pantagruel*.[45]

Pope Gregory I had defended narrative painting in the sixth century when Serenus, Bishop of Marseilles, had ordered all the religious images to be removed from churches so that the people would focus on the words of the clergy and the texts. In response, Gregory argued that pictures allowed illiterate people to understand the stories they could not read. In the fifteenth century, the Renaissance theorist Alberti and the Dominican theorist Michele da Carcano both promoted narrative art as a means of instructing those who could not read.[46] Later, pictures were used to clarify the meaning of words for readers. The first children's picture book, *Orbis Pictus* (c. 1657), used pictures to define the meanings of the accompanying words.[47]

The European colonization of the Americas gave birth to a plethora of stories. The adventures of explorers gave rise to incredible tales of the wonders of the New World. As multitudes of immigrants poured into this land, they brought with them their stories, which blended into the folktales of what was to become the United States.

Of course, long before white settlers reached the Americas, native traditions had been rich with their own folklore. Native North American narrative has a number of shared types of stories. One group of

---

[45]Francois Rabelais, *Gargantua and Pantagruel*, trans. Jacques LeClercq (New York: Heritage, 1942).

[46]Anabel Thomas, *Illustrated Dictionary of Narrative Painting* (London: John Murray, 1994), pp. ix–x.

[47]Perry Nodelman, *Words about Pictures: The Narrative Art of Children's Picture Books* (Athens: University of Georgia Press, 1988), pp. 3–4.

these is the mythological stories that account for the way the world received its present shape and include stories of the origin of the earth and humanity, the theft of fire, the flood, the development of languages, and the establishment of human institutions.[48] Another type of traditional Native American tale is that of the trickster. The trickster combines both human and animal traits and is at once creator, culture hero, spoiler, and buffoon.[49] Hero stories also abound in Native American tales. In most of these stories, the hero is an extraordinary mortal who is subjected to various ordeals, much like the protagonists of the Greek hero cycles. A variation of this tale is the story of the unpromising hero who achieves unexpected success. Often, the hero's quest is quite similar to the Greek story of Orpheus and Eurydice, in which the hero journeys to the land of the dead to bring back a loved one. Another set of stories centers on girls who marry animal husbands and on their resultant offspring. For Native Americans, stories give order to the universe, embodying their mythic ideas in tales of the primeval world, the trickster, and the hero. Although details of these stories shift from Native culture to Native culture, the common thread of giving expression to experience remains at the core of storytelling.

Like Native American tradition, African folklore is filled with common types of stories.[50] Some stories deal with a high god, a supreme being who seems to be neither a personified nature power nor a glorified ancestral ghost.[51] Often the numerous stories that attempt to account for the origin of death are somehow linked with a high god. Other religious stories are centered on nature powers, ancestral ghosts, and haunting demons. Animal stories that originated with the development of totemism are populated most prominently by the hare, the tortoise, the spider, the antelope, the jackal, the chameleon, the elephant, the lion, and the hyena. Transformations of humans into animals or animals into humans is also a common occurrence in African stories. Many African tales were transported to Europe as travelers crossed the

---

[48]Susan Feldman, introduction to *The Storytelling Stone: Traditional Native American Myths and Tales* (New York: Dell, 1965), p. 31.

[49]Ibid., p. 17.

[50]See, for example, Richard M. Orson, *African Folklore* (Bloomington: Indiana University Press, 1972).

[51]Alice Werner, " African Mythology," in *The Mythology of All Races*, vol. 7, ed. John Arnott MacCulloch (New York: Cooper Square, 1964), p. 116.

continent; others came to America with slaves.[52] One particular cycle of African slave tales became the B'rer Rabbit stories eventually collected by Joel Chandler Harris.[53]

By the late eighteenth century, oral storytelling as entertainment for educated and literate adults had practically died out in Europe. Educated Europeans had come to prefer the more polished literary tales. The appearance of the Grimm Brothers' *Kinder und Haüsmärchen* (1812– 1815) renewed interest in oral tradition among the educated. This collection of stories, with its notes and comments, created an acceptance of storytelling as an academic discipline and brought the art to the forefront of study and discussion. "Collecting" tales became fashionable among society's elite, though the stories were written down in such a refined style that much of the oral flavor of the original tales was lost.

These collections, however, became the basis for the children's story hour as American public libraries began to expand their work with children. Storytelling in the public library actually became the reading aloud of written texts rather than spontaneous oral composition of a story. By the late 1920s, this type of institutionalized storytelling had also spread to municipal recreation departments. As similar institutions were established in other countries, the storytelling component was carried along.

Storytelling in the nineteenth and twentieth century church is most closely connected with the Sunday School movement. Pellowski associates the rise of storytelling in Protestant churches in the United States particularly with the number and influence of black and white preachers from the South, especially among Methodist and Baptist

---

[52]Margaret N. Coughlan, *Folklore from Africa to the United States: An Annotated Bibliography* (Washington, D.C.: Library of Congress, 1976).

[53]Although Harris's works helped preserve this particular group of African tales, his presentation of the tales through African American storytellers reinforced and perpetuated stereotypes of Black Americans in the slave system of the antebellum South. For a critique of Harris's depictions of African Americans, see Darwin T. Turner, "Daddy Joel Harris and His Old-Time Darkies," in *Critical Essays on Joel Chandler Harris*, ed. R. Bruce Bickley, Jr. (Boston: Hall, 1981), pp. 113–129. The B'rer Rabbit stories are found in Harris's Uncle Remus works, for example: *Uncle Remus: His Songs and Sayings* (New York: Appleton, 1880); *Nights with Uncle Remus: Myths and Legends of the Old Plantation* (Boston: Osgood, 1883); *Uncle Remus and His Friends: Old Plantation Stories, Songs, and Ballads with Sketches of Negro Character* (Boston: Houghton, Mifflin, 1892).

congregations, who gradually developed a more dramatic style than had been common in the Puritan-influenced areas of the United States.[54] Late nineteenth century Sunday schools, which populated almost every town in the United States usually had a small collection of storybooks with biblical themes. In the early twentieth century, a number of books on storytelling in religious education were published, such as Edward Porter St. John's *Stories and Story-telling in Moral and Religious Education* (1910) and Margaret W. Eggleston's *The Use of the Story in Religious Education* (1920). From 1900 to 1940, religious education held storytelling in high regard. Stories were considered the best way of expressing religious truth and the procedure most appropriate to the ways children learn. The types of stories told were primarily from oral folk traditions across cultures and across the world. From 1940 to 1970 a shift occurred in the thinking of religious educators about storytelling. Storytelling became suspect, and the types of stories told shifted to literary tales written for didactic and moralistic purposes. Beginning in the 1970s, renewed interest in storytelling arose among religious educators. Again, storytelling became a significant procedure for religious education, and the types of stories told began to encompass both oral and written tales.[55] Although the focus of storytelling in religious education has remained on children, recent developments have begun to recognize the effectiveness of storytelling in adult religious education as well. Of particular interest in the arena of the academic study of religion is the development and exploration of narrative theology that has occurred in recent years.[56]

Storytelling remains a vital tradition. Organizations committed to oral storytelling, such as the National Storytelling Association, provide information and education about the tradition and offer a network for persons interested in the art. The literary tale remains as well an integral part of modern culture. Recent years have seen a revival of interest in and study of story among educators and psychologists as well as theologians. Perhaps in the midst of a cyber world, humanity is

---

[54]Pellowski, *World of Storytelling*, p. 61.

[55]Michael Edward Williams, "Passing Over: A Model for the Use of Storytelling with Adults in Religious Education Based Upon the Hermeneutic Approach of John S. Dunne" (Ph.D. diss., Northwestern University, 1983), p. 146.

[56]An overview of narrative theology is presented in chapter 4.

again discovering the necessity of the mythological for their existence as human beings.

Tasurinchi, the Machiguenga, never tired of listening to the hablador. Often he made him repeat the same stories: "That way, once you've gone, I can tell myself all over again what you're telling me now." Once as the hablador told his stories, Tasurinchi's daughter fell asleep. Her father woke her with one shake, saying: "'Listen, child! Don't waste these stories.'"[57]

---

[57]Llosa, *Storyteller*, p. 61.

3

The Nature of Story

*Are you the one who tell stories? the stranger asked. The man
took five gold coins from his pocket and placed them in her hand.
Then sell me a past because mine is filled with blood and lamen-
tation, and I cannot use it in my way through life. . . . She began
to speak. All that afternoon and all that night she spun her tale,
inventing a worthy past for the warrior, putting into the task all
her vast experience and the passion the stranger had evoked. She
spoke for a very long time, because she wanted to offer him the
novel of his life, and she had to invent it all. . . . She sighed,
closed her eyes, and when she felt her spirit as empty as that of a
newborn child, she understood that in her desire to please him
she had given him her own memory. . . . She had delved deeply
into her own story and now could not take back her words; but
neither did she want to take them back, and she surrendered herself to the pleasure of blending with him into a single story.*[1]

—Isabel Allende

STORY AS EXPERIENCE

I love movies. In fact, I will sit through just about any movie. I greatly
enjoy sinking into a chair in a darkened theater and being swept away
into other places, other lives, other worlds. When *Star Wars* was rere-
leased in 1997, I remembered seeing it in a theater as an adolescent,

---

[1]Isabel Allende *Eva Luna* (New York: Knopf, 1988), pp. 249–250.

and I realized that the folks in their twenties and teens now had only seen it on videotape. They had never had the opportunity to watch Luke Skywalker, Princess Leia, and Han Solo battle the forces of Darth Vader and the evil Empire on the big screen. At last, however, they had the opportunity to see one of the most exciting, innovative movies of all time in the otherworldly place of the movie theater.

What was it about *Star Wars* that so captured Americans' collective imagination? What is the secret behind our love affair with movies in general? I think primarily we are drawn to movies because they are a form of storytelling. They appeal to our desire for narrative, and, most of all, they tell our stories. *Star Wars* may have posited other galaxies and alien life forms, but the story it told was a story of common human experiences—alienation, danger, betrayal, courage, good and evil. *Star Wars* is a powerful story because when we see it, we write ourselves into it. We recognize our struggles in the struggles of Luke, Han, and the Princess, and for a couple of hours we become those characters, fighting the forces of evil and triumphing over the Empire.

Stories are acts of experience, expression, and recognition.[2] Narrative begins in experience. People experience their lives narratively and live out narratives they construct. Experience is the raw material of story. From experience, storytellers construct narratives—they imbue events with meaning. The resultant story then becomes a cognitive, affective, and behavioral experience for those who hear it as they recognize themselves in the story. In other words, storytellers render their experience in the story, and, if the story is true to human experience, learners find themselves participating in the story as well.

Walker Percy suggests that the function of story is to tell learners something they already know experientially but do not consciously know that they know. This, he says, gives learners a sensation of recogniton.[3] Dorothy Sayers explains that the storyteller says, "Look! Recognize your experience in my own."[4]

Priest and storyteller William J. Bausch has found thirteen characteristics of stories in his experiences:

---

[2]Dorothy Sayers, *The Whimsical Christian* (New York: Macmillan, 1969), p. 86.

[3]Walker Percy, *Conversations with Walker Percy*, ed. Lewis A. Lawson and Victor A. Kramer (Jackson: University of Mississippi Press, 1985), p. 9.

[4]Sayers, *Whimsical Christian*, p. 89.

1. Stories provoke curiosity and compel repetition.
2. Stories unite people in a holistic way to nature, the common stuff of existence.
3. Stories are a bridge to one's culture, one's roots.
4. Stories bind people to all of humankind, to the universal human family.
5. Stories help people to remember.
6. Stories use a special language.
7. Stories restore the original power of the word.
8. Stories provide escape.
9. Stories evoke right-brain imagination, tenderness, and therefore wholeness.
10. Stories promote healing.
11. Every story is each person's story.
12. Stories provide a basis for hope and morality.
13. Stories are the basis for ministry.[5]

Powerful stories are true to common human experiences, such as relationships, conflicts, or emotions. Because of these common experiences, learners are able to identify with stories whose specifics may be far removed from their actual experiences. So, for example, *Star Wars* resonates with earth-bound humans because it deals with those common experiences, such as losing one's family, searching for one's identity, struggling to do good.

Identification with a story allows learners to experience the specifics of the story vicariously. This experience creates space for learners to learn from the story's experience as if they had actually participated in it—which they have, imaginatively, through the story. Stories, therefore, are an experiential learning process, involving cognitive, affective, and behavioral modes of learning, so that learners participate in stories, reflect on them, understand them, create meaning of them, and act on them. In so doing, learners reorder their own experiences—cognitive, affective, and behavioral—into meaningful patterns and responses.

---

[5]William J. Bausch, *Storytelling: Imagination and Faith* (Mystic, Conn.: Twenty-Third, 1984), pp. 30–62.

STORY AND MEANING

A story, then, is much more than an interesting plot. Although a story begins in character and action, it also consists of meaning that is created in the action of the story itself and not in a moralistic addendum to the story. Rather, in a story, the plot is related to and integrated with character development, out of which grows meaning.

Flannery O'Connor suggests that characters are shown through action, and action is controlled through characters. This results in meaning that derives from the whole presented experience.[6] Thus characters and action interact within a story to create meaning, which is the story itself. In other words, character, action, and meaning are inseparably bound up together in a story.

This means a story cannot be reduced to one thematic statement about its meaning. On the contrary, the story itself is the meaning. O'Connor insists that a story says something which cannot be said any other way. Every word in the story is necessary to say what the meaning is. One tells a story because a statement would be inadequate.[7] C. S. Lewis concurs. In "On Stories," he claims that story does what theory cannot by creating images of what reality may well be like at its core. He further argues that the images in stories ultimately do grow out of what humans perceive as the real world. He describes landscapes that make him expect to see a giant raising its head over the next ridge. Nature, he writes, "has that in her which compels us to invent giants: and only giants will do."[8] He adds in "On Three Ways of Writing for Children," sometimes stories may just say best what is to be said.[9]

Cleanth Brooks and Robert Penn Warren also maintain that the meaning of a story is the story itself. The story itself, they explain, states the theme so precisely that for an exact statement of it, one must turn to the whole body of the story itself.[10] O'Connor adds, "A story

---

[6]Flannery O'Connor, *Mystery and Manners* (New York: Farrar Straus, and Giroux, 1969), p. 90.

[7]Ibid., p. 96.

[8]7C. S. Lewis, "On Stories," in *Of Other Worlds: Essays and Stories*, ed. Walter Hooper (New York: Harcourt, Brace, and Jovanovich, 1966), p. 8.

[9]Ibid., p. 23.

[10]Cleanth Brooks and Robert Penn Warren, *Understanding Fiction*, 2d ed. (New York: Appleton-Century-Crofts, 1943), p. 287.

really isn't any good unless it successfully resists paraphrase, unless it hangs on and expands in the mind."[11] A story, then, does not contain the answer but is the answer.[12]

Understanding story as meaning prevents the twofold danger of either dismissing stories as mere entertainment or overemphasizing the didactic elements in stories, thus misconstruing the storyteller's intentions and violating the integrity of the stories. In particular, those stories appropriate for religious instruction are not simply a means of improvement or entertainment but are a revelation of the often unsuspected and unexplored depths of humanity.[13] A story implies meaning beyond its particular characters and events, which can be extended to apply to other characters and events.[14] What is learned in story is not so much information or knowledge in the usual sense but is far closer to wisdom, understanding, or lived truth.[15] Story, then, is a unique medium that both creates and explains experience. The meaning of a story is to be found in experiencing it.

Stories embody truths and invite learners to participate in lived truths through their experiences of stories. Stories render human experiences in narrative form, imbue those experiences with meaning, and invite learners to participate in the recreation of those experiences in the narrative experience. Stories, then, explain humans to themselves, not by describing truths about the external world but by creating and recreating experiential truths of human lives.

FAITH AND STORY

As a construct, faith is a confluence of numerous subjective elements—theology, psychology, sociology, art, so much so that no one perspective can encompass its totality. Rather, different valid constructs of faith arise from these different perspectives and are

---

[11]O'Connor, *Mystery and Manners*, p. 108.

[12]Brian Wicker, *Story-Shaped World: Fiction and Metaphysics: Some Variations on a Theme* (Notre Dame, Ind.: University of Notre Dame Press, 1975), p. 43.

[13]Owen Barfield, "The Concept of Revelation," *Journal of the American Academy of Religion* 47 (June 1979): 297.

[14]Brooks and Warren, pp. 298–299.

[15]Sallie McFague, *Literature and the Christian Life* (New Haven: Yale University Press, 1966), p. 107.

complementary interpretations of the reality of faith.[16] Thus, faith is a psychological process of selecting, organizing, and interpreting experiences.[17] Faith is also a product of socially organized practices of faith communities.[18] Furthermore, faith is a lifestyle, encompassing cognition, emotion, and behavior.[19] It is a complex practice of acting, trusting, and believing. Faith is both a gift and a discipline; it is both a source of action and a consequence of action.[20] Faith is the intertwining of people's ways of being in the world and their constructions of ultimate meaning.

Natural or nonreligious faith is a common human experience. From a psychological perspective, James Fowler suggests that faith is a way of finding intellectual coherence in and giving meaning to experiences.[21] Faith is that which gives persons' lives ultimate meaning. Furthermore, Fowler contends, faith forms a way of cognitively seeing everyday life in relation to the "ultimate environment."[22] He suggests humankind is *homo poeta*—humans live by meaning. By this, he means that faith grasps the ultimate conditions of existence and unifies them into a comprehensive image which guides how people shape their responses and initiatives.[23] As such, faith is a process, not a substance. The image Fowler suggests is an inner representation that unites information and feeling. Fowler argues that these images are prior to and deeper than concepts. He adds that when persons think, they call up images and then, in a process that involves both forming and expressing, they narrate what their images "know." The narration may take the form of story, poetry, symbol, proposition, or concept.

---

[16]James Michael Lee, "Growth in Faith through Religious Instruction," *Handbook of Faith*, ed. James Michael Lee (Birmingham, Ala.: Religious Education Press, 1990), p. 287.

[17]Ibid., p. 276.

[18]Ibid., p. 278.

[19]James Michael Lee suggests that through the centuries, many theologians and theological groups have asserted that faith is inclusive of all three domains, but most have also asserted the dominance of one of these domains. For more, see ibid., pp. 280–286.

[20]V. Bailey Gillespie, *The Experience of Faith* (Birmingham, Ala.: Religious Education Press, 1988), p. 26.

[21]James W. Fowler, *Stages of Faith* (San Francisco: Harper and Row, 1981), p. 4.

[22]Ibid., p. 24.

[23]Ibid., p. 25.

Thus, inner images become articulated, shared images. These images represent what a person holds to be true or ultimate conditions of existence.[24]

Although faith certainly contains the cognitive component Fowler emphasizes, faith is much more than cognition. Faith is a lived reality, a lifestyle.[25] Theologians John Cobb and David Ray Griffin suggest that faith is fundamentally a mode of existence.[26] Theologian John Macquarrie contends that faith is an existential attitude that includes acceptance and commitment and that religious faith looks to the wider being in the context of which individuals have their own being.[27] New Testament scholar Rudolf Bultmann defines faith as adherence to the gospel message. It is, he writes, an act of obedience.[28]

Liberation theologians, in particular, emphasize faith as lifestyle. Walter Rauschenbusch suggests, "Faith is an energetic act of the will, affirming our fellowship with God and man, declaring our solidarity with the Kingdom of God, and repudiating selfish isolation."[29] For Rauschenbush, faith means seeing God at work in the world and sharing in that work in order to bring about a just social order. Similarly, feminist theologian Judith Plaskow argues that the biblical prophets understand faith as social justice. She contends that the intention of Hebrew prophetic and legal religion is to connect faith with the concrete world. In Judaism, she argues, faith is the expression of one's relationship with God in the whole of life.[30]

Religious faith is intimately related to experiences of God.[31] And although occasionally these experiences may be special or acute, the difference is one of degree. For persons of faith, God permeates and is present in all experiences, including the mundane. The lens of faith is

---

[24]Ibid., p. 26.

[25]Gillespie, *Experience of Faith*, p. 56.

[26]John B. Cobb Jr., and David Ray Griffin, *Process Theology: An Introductory Exposition* (Philadelphia: Westminster, 1976), p. 31.

[27]John Macquarrie, *Principles of Christian Theology*, 2d ed. (New York: Scribner's, 1977), p. 80.

[28]Karl Rudolf Bultmann, *Primitive Christianity in its Contemporary Setting*, trans. Reginald H. Fuller (Philadelphia: Fortress, 1956), p. 202.

[29]Walter Rauschenbush, *A Theology for the Social Gospel* (Nashville: Abingdon, 1981), p. 102.

[30]Judith Plaskow, *Standing Again at Sinai: Judaism from a Feminist Perspective* (San Francisco: HarperSanFrancisco, 1970), pp. 216–217.

[31]Gillespie, *Experience of Faith*, pp. 30–45.

what allows people to see God in all of life. As Bailey Gillespie suggests, faith may well consist of the very act of living itself.[32]

Out of their experiences of God, people act in the world to bring about the community of God. Experience is followed by commitment and action. Dietrich Bonhoeffer contends that the response of a disciple is an act of obedience. He suggests that faith is the condition for obedience and obedience is the condition for faith.[33]

In 1939 American friends helped Bonhoeffer escape Germany, where he opposed Nazism and German aggression. When he arrived in England from the United States, his friends there realized that he was determined not to desert the politically oppressed people of Germany. He wrote in a letter to Reinhold Niebuhr, "I shall have no right to participate in the reconstruction of Christian life in Germany after the war if I do not share the trials of this time with my people . . . . Christians in Germany will face the terrible alternative of either willing the defeat of their nation in order that Christian civilization may survive, or willing the victory of their nation and therby [sic] destroying our civilization. I know which of these alternatives I must choose; but I cannot make this choice in security."[34] Bonhoeffer returned to Germany to work with the Confessional Church and the political underground movement. He was arrested by the Gestapo in 1943 and held in Gestapo prisons until 1945, when he was taken to the Buchenwald concentration camp. In the prisons and concentration camps, he ministered to his fellow prisoners. Eventually, he was moved to the Flossenberg concentration camp and was executed by a special order of Gestapo chief Heinrich Himmler only days before liberation by the allies.

For Bonhoeffer, faith expresses itself in total commitment to the demand of the gospel. It is a way of being in the world that engages people in action to bring about God's community. Faith, then, is inextricably tied up with lifestyle. People are people of faith not because of what they profess to believe but because of how they choose to live.

---

[32]Ibid., p. 39.

[33]Dietrich Bonhoeffer, *The Cost of Discipleship*, rev. ed. (New York: Collier, 1959), pp. 61–69.

[34]Quoted in G. Liebholz, "Memoir," in *Cost of Discipleship*, p. 16.

Faith and Stories

Closely tied to faith are stories. People experience their lives narratively. They tell stories to recreate, reexperience, and understand these experiences. Their stories reflect the meanings they have made of their experiences and become the mythic frameworks or metanarratives out of which they live.[35]

Stories are primarily concerned with human existence. The human condition is always under scrutiny in stories. Walker Percy suggests that stories offer an alternative mode of exploration of human existence. He says science, for example, can bring persons to a certain point and then no further. Science cannot answer the question of what humans are or what they ought to do. Therefore, for him, stories are the best way to deal with human behavior. He claims, "When it comes to the ultimate mysteries of the human mind, the psychiatrist must yield to the artist, to the writer."[36]

Stories touch threads of commonality in human existence as they create and illuminate human experience. Joseph Conrad claims that stories awaken a feeling of "unavoidable solidarity" that binds people to one another and to the natural world.[37] Although each story relates a particular experience of particular characters, the events and attitudes are common.

Stories deal in precisely the common experiences and attitudes that characterize human existence. While unique in their own right, story characters are also in some sense Everyman and Everywoman as well. Through varied situations and characters, stories explore experiences, feelings, and responses that are common to humans. Thus, strong identification with characters or situations in stories occurs. Through this dynamic comes potential for expanded experiences of human existence. Through stories, learners enter into the lives, situations, and feelings of others and learn both about common human existence as well as their own lives.

O'Connor contends that if storytellers are fulfilling their artistic task, they will suggest images of reality as it can be glimpsed in some

---

[35]John Shea, *Stories of God: An Unauthorized Biography* (Chicago: Thomas More, 1978), p. 52.

[36]Percy, *Conversations with Walker Percy*, p. 94.

[37]Joseph Conrad, preface to *The Nigger of the Narcissus* (New York: Doubleday, 1914), p. xiv.

aspect of the human situation.[38] In this glimpse of reality, learners experience some aspect of human existence; they come to a deeper experiential understanding of what it means to be human. Percy suggests the function of the storyteller is to help people know themselves.[39] Stories, then, are revelatory. Stories transcend the particular personal circumstances of an individual's experience, which may in themselves prevent the individual from plumbing the learning potential of those experiences. In stories, however, learners come to know themselves as they reexperience parts of their own lives in the experiences of stories, and they come to feel with and respond to all of humanity as they enter into the commonality of stories.

Stories, therefore, may be epiphanies. Henry David Thoreau, for example, exclaims, "How many a man has dated a new era in his life from the reading of a book."[40] Stories tell truths about humanity, and the experiencing of these truths may be a moment of awakening for learners. Throughout his autobiographical *Surprised by Joy*, C. S. Lewis relates how what he terms "joy" was mediated to him through such stories as *Squirrel Nutkin* and *Phantastes, a Faerie Romance*. In fact, Lewis traces his conversion process through his reading of such writers as Sir Philip Spencer, John Milton, Samuel Johnson, and G. K. Chesterton.[41] Stories, then, mediate a kind of knowledge that is experiential. The truths of stories are made, not by logical persuasion, but by experiential engagement. Stories do not convince by argument; they surprise by identification.[42]

This engaging characteristic of story then offers great potential for learning in religious education. Stories may create broadening and humanizing experiences whereby learners may more fully engage in authentic human existence. On a cognitive level, stories may raise critical issues and disrupt preconceived patterns of thinking. In so doing, stories may facilitate critical reflection and hence moral and ethical development. One significant factor in cognitive forms of

---

[38]O'Connor, *Mystery and Manners*, p. 158.

[39]Percy, *Conversations with Walker Percy*, p. 98.

[40]Henry David Thoreau, *Walden, The American Tradition in Literature*, ed. Sculley Bradley et al., 4th ed. (New York: Grosset and Dunlap, 1974), 1: 1291.

[41]C. S. Lewis, *Surprised by Joy: The Shape of My Early Life* (New York: Harcourt, Brace and Jovanovich, 1955).

[42]See also Frederick Buechner, *The Sacred Journey* (San Francisco: Harper and Row, 1982).

development is disruption of implicitly held assumptions.[43] Cognitive development occurs as ideas or assumptions come into conflict, making simplistic answers no longer viable. John Shea calls this the experience of disenchantment and suggests that it is the beginning of mature religious consciousness.[44] As human cognitive development reaches higher stages, persons are able to recognize the relativity of ideas and hold paradoxical and contradictory ideas in tension. Stories help people learn to think about meaning, values, and truths by holding these elements in a healthy tension that challenges unquestioned preconceptions. By experiencing the lives of others, learners may be better equipped to engage in processes of critical reflection.[45]

Learners who are able to see commonality in disparate characters and situations may come to accept differences as not only tolerable but also positive. They may come to understand self and others in more complex and variegated ways. They may learn to behave toward all people in just ways. The experiences of stories are rarely simple, univocal expressions. They are paradoxical, ambiguous. Learners who are able to accept and to appreciate the creative tensions of stories may also come to accept and to appreciate people who are different.

Stories also offer a rich potential for affective development. Humans are full of paradox and ambiguity. By allowing room for the variety of human experiences, stories create room for openness to the richness of diversity. By re-creating human experiences, stories may carry learners into new experiences and perspectives, allowing learners to feel for a while what it is to walk in another's shoes. Stories may create empathy—an emotional identification of the self with a character—which creates the feeling of participation in the character's experiences. Thus, although learners do not directly participate in the events related in stories, they often feel as if they have participated in them. In feeling as if they have lived through certain situations,

---

[43]See, for example, the description of stage 3 synthetic-conventional faith in Fowler's *Stages of Faith*, pp. 151–173.

[44]Shea, *Stories of God*, p. 33.

[45]For more information on critical inquiry and faith, see Richard E. Creel, *Religion and Doubt: Toward a Faith of Your Own*, 2d ed. (Englewood Cliffs, N.J.: Prentice-Hall, 1991); Daniel Taylor, *The Myth of Certainty: The Reflective Christian and the Risk of Commitment* (Waco, Tex.: Jarrell, 1986); Douglas Alan Walrath, *Counterpoints: The Dynamics of Believing* (New York: Pilgrim, 1991).

learners experience what it is to be Other; they broaden their emotional range. In this way, stories may create humanizing experiences. As learners enter into the experiences of others, they may experience a greater breadth and depth of human existence, and as learners experience various aspects of human existence, they themselves may move toward becoming more fully human.

To be fully human is to participate authentically in the life of the world; it is to be one with others, with God, and with the natural world. As a medium of liberation, stories can free learners from the provincialism, prejudice, and narrow-mindedness that prevent unity. Stories may awaken learners to the richness of authentic human existence. Stories may challenge untested assumptions and disrupt simplistic views with richer, more diverse views that encompass the paradox and ambiguity which characterize human existence. Stories may invite learners into the Other in a way that brings about a transformation of behavior, affect, understanding, and belief.

Stories as Sacrament

Perhaps stories' greatest potential for religious education lies in the incarnational and sacramental nature of stories. O'Connor suggests that whatever truths a storyteller sees must be embodied in the concrete and the human. She points out that Christ did not redeem humanity by a direct intellectual act but became incarnate in human form and now speaks through the mediation of a visible church.[46] Stories may incarnate human experiences of wonder and may draw learners into encounters with the sacred. Religious educator John Westerhoff suggests, "The arts incarnate our experience of mystery, wonder and awe and thereby aid us to encounter the holy or sacred."[47] Nathan Scott claims stories may invite learners to enter the world of I and Thou. He explains that the language of the artist is not the language of communication but of communion.[48]

Of particular interest to religious educators are stories in which the sacred, the holy, may be encountered. These stories lead people to

---

[46]O'Connor, *Mystery and Manners*, p. 176.

[47]John H. Westerhoff III, "What Has Zion to Do with Bohemia?" *Religious Education* 76 (Winter 1981): 5.

[48]Nathan Scott, *The Broken Center: A Definition of the Crisis of Values in Modern Literature* (New York: National Council of the Protestant Episcopal Church, 1959), p. 5.

participation in the greater Whole, the encompassing Mystery, the Divine. For different people, different stories may effect this encounter. I can recall several stories that engaged me, personally, in an encounter with God. The first time I read C. S. Lewis's *The Lion, the Witch, and the Wardrobe*, I fell in love with the mighty, gentle lion, Aslan, and felt anew the wonder of the love of Christ. The first time I read T. S. Eliot's *The Cocktail Party*, I heard again my call to ministry. Later, when I read that play aloud with a group of students at California Baptist College, I was renewed in my convictions about the call and shape of ministry. When I heard a Holocaust survivor speak at Oregon State University of forgiving her Nazi tormentors, I again experienced the power of forgiveness. Biblical stories of Jesus, Graham Greene's *The Power and the Glory*, J. D. Salinger's *Franny and Zooey*, Gail Godwin's *Father Melancholy's Daughter*, Herman Hesse's *Journey to the East*, Alice Walker's *The Color Purple*, Reynolds Price's *Tongues of Angels*—all of these stories have invited me into the presence of the Holy.

Sacred stories are stories that embody some human experience so true, so authentic for learners that they usher those learners into the presence of Mystery. In penetrating the concrete world of human existence, stories create images of human reality. Learners' encounter with these images in stories may provide moments of epiphany. In these moments, learners are invited into the awe and mystery of the depths of human existence. Such encounters open the way for learners to come to new commitments, behaviors, feelings, and understandings and thus move toward a fuller humanity that stories invite them to try out. In this way, stories offer possibilities for transformation.

Walker Percy offers an example of a commuter on a train. There is a great deal of difference, he contends, between an alienated commuter riding a train and the same commuter reading a book about an alienated commuter riding a train. Percy argues the nonreading commuter "exists in true alienation, which is unspeakable," whereas the reading commuter "rejoices in the speakability of his alienation and in the new triple alliance of himself, the alienated character, and the author." For the reading commuter, the reading of the book is an experience of feeling, "Yes! That is how it is!" Percy calls this experience an "aesthetic reversal."[49] The alienated man on the train reads a book

---

[49]Walker Percy, *The Message in the Bottle* (New York: Farrar, Straus and Giroux, 1975), p. 83.

about an alienated man on a train and so is no longer alienated. Thus, Percy says, literature of alienation is actually the triumphant reversal of alienation through its representation. It is "an aesthetic victory of comradliness, a recognition of plight in common."[50] In the experience of reading, the commuter immerses himself in the plight of one like himself and thus transcends his particular situation in experiencing and recognizing the larger picture of the human situation. This experience, then, mediates joy in his fuller experience of self as a human being.

In stories, learners experience their own experiences embodied. Such identification with stories opens the way for encounters with the Mystery incarnated in stories. Through their embodiment of common human experiences, stories draw people deeper into the awe and wonder of life's depths. In those feelings of the mystery and wonder of human life, religious experiences can occur. As stories engage the experiential dimensions of learners, they can act as catalysts for encounters with the Divine. By plumbing human depths, stories can recreate experiences of the sacred which permeate human existence.

Thus, stories may open the way for hitherto neglected avenues of encounter with God. The experience of stories allows a particular distance and freedom. Stories do not directly attack or confront learners or reiterate tired and outworn arguments. Rather, stories create experiences that invite learners in. Homiletics professor Fred Craddock calls this experience "overhearing."[51] Old themes couched in new forms arrest attention and invite learners to explore again realities with which they assume familiarity. Craddock contends that the language of theology, for example, has been overused to the point of bankruptcy. He sees the task of stories as to enable learners to "walk down the corridors of their own minds, seeing anew old images hanging there . . . to pronounce the old vocabulary so that someone hears a new cadence in it."[52]

Likewise, C. S. Lewis asks, "Why did one find it so hard to feel as one was told one ought to feel about God or about the sufferings of Christ?" He answers, "I thought the chief reason was that one was told one ought to." He explains that the obligation itself can freeze the very feelings it intends to elicit. Yet in stories, stripped of their

---

[50]Ibid., p. 93.
[51]Fred B. Craddock, *Overhearing the Gospel* (Nashville: Abingdon, 1978), p. 104.
[52]Ibid., p. 38.

"stained-glass and Sunday School associations," those images appear in their real potency.[53] For example, the first time learners hear the story of Clarence Jordan, founder of Koinonia Farms and translator of *The Cotton Patch Gospels*, they learn from a distance about injustice and racism in the 1940s and 50s in the South. Eventually, learners may move closer to the story and begin to feel anger and dismay. Finally, apart from Jordan's story, learners may develop and bear a new consciousness of racial injustice and a new commitment to work to bring about racial justice. Thus, what begins as overhearing ends as hearing.[54] The distance between learners and the story is closed, and the learners begin to hear a word being addressed to them. Narrative is seductive, Percy says. "'Once upon a time something happened.' That's almost an irresistible act of communication, transaction."[55]

Stories and Learners

I do not remember the first time I heard the story of Jesus. It was always there, in the stories that my preschool Sunday school teachers told me, in the bedtime stories my mother read me, in the missionary stories I learned in Girls in Action (GAs) on Wednesday nights, in the lives of those Christian women who surrounded me and nurtured me from the crib. For me, Jesus was as real and present as my little friends Pam or Marney or my Sunday school teacher Mrs. Jett.

When I was six, a traveling evangelist came to our church. He told another story, a story of an angry God who punished sinners and sent the unrepentant to hell. This God seemed nothing like the gentle Jesus who until that time had filled my imagination. Quickly, the gentle Jesus was replaced by images of eternally burning fires, devouring worms, and the screams of the damned. Unwilling to risk the fires of hell, I walked the aisle of my church to the strains of "Just As I Am" to accept Jesus as my Lord and Savior.

For many years, I carried with me this image of an angry and judgmental God ready to smite me at any moment if I dare disobey. Gentle Jesus was a constant companion, but lurking not too far away was the ever watchful, critical Father. When I was in seminary, Baptist

---

[53]C. S. Lewis, "Sometimes Fairy Stories May Say Best What's to Be Said," in *Of Other Worlds: Essays and Stories,* ed. Walter Hooper (New York: Harcourt, Brace and Jovanovich, 1966), p. 37.

[54]Craddock, *Overhearing the Gospel,* p. 112.

[55]Percy, *Conversations with Walker Percy,* pp. 242–243.

minister and storytelling comedian Grady Nutt was killed in an air-
plane crash. "What kind of God would do this?" I wondered. "Has
God nothing better to do than crash small planes into the ground?" At
that moment, the faith I had could no longer carry me. The old stories
did not work anymore. And about that time, I read Frederick Buechner's *The Sacred Journey*. And I overheard the good news. And I read
Annie Dillard's *Pilgrim at Tinker Creek*, and I again experienced the
grace of the God I had known in those days "once below a time," to
borrow Buechner's phrase, before the traveling evangelist had cast me
out of Eden and barred the entryway. I read Flannery O'Connor's *Wise
Blood* again and Graham Greene's *Brighton Rock* and began to weave
for myself a new story of God, one that embraced me in unconditional
love and empowered me to practice love in the world.

Stories are powerful and can work powerfully and redemptively in
the lives of learners. Stories have the potential to mediate encounters
with the Divine, and they have potential to scar the imagination and
limit the scope of one's possibilities. For religious educators, this
means that the choosing of stories is a sacred and important task. Appropriate stories mediate encounters with God, challenge learners to
engage in authentic lives, model justice, and bring about the desired
outcomes of religious instruction.

Understanding the role of learners in story experiences is paramount in utilizing stories in religious education. Learners are not passive recipients of story information but are active creators of story
texts. Learners reconstruct the stories they read, hear, or see from their
own standpoint. This means each learner will construct a slightly different story from the experience offered by the storyteller.

Learners enter experiences of stories as whole beings. Stories affect
learners as entire human beings. Thus, the faith of learners is an extremely important part of story experiences. Learners operate out of
their faith; they behave in ways that betray what they ultimately hold
to have meaning and value. Faith is shown, then, less in professions
than in actions. T. S. Eliot suggests that the common ground between
religion and stories is behavior. He says religion imposes judgments,
ethics, and behavior toward other humans, and stories affect behaviors
toward other humans as well as patterns of self.[56]

---

[56]T.S. Elliot, "Religion and Literature," in *Religion and Modern Literature*, ed.
G. B. Tennyson and Edward E. Ericson, Jr. (Grand Rapids, Mich.: Eerdmans, 1975),
p. 24.

What happens to learners in stories is a vicarious and holistic experience of life that generates experience and self-creation. Dorothy Sayers explains that in the image of the storyteller's experience, learners reexperience some experience of their own which they had never understood, formulated, nor expressed until that moment. When learners encounter the story, then, they say, "It is though a light were turned on inside us."[57] This experience puts new experiences of self within grasp. It renders learners through an experience so that they are changed by it.

Stories, then, are learning experiences which give fresh shape and structure to experience in general.[58] Of course, the attitude of learners toward stories is a significant factor in the efficacy of the stories. Literary critic J. Hillis Miller suggests that learners approach stories, not as scientists to physical objects, but as one person to another in charity.[59] Learners should approach stories openly, willing to enter into story experiences and be transformed by them. Literary critic Vernon Ruland maintains that authentic works of art do not so much need learners to pass judgment on them as first to stand in judgment over learners.[60] In other words, artistic expressions such as stories challenge learners to be open to new experiences and to recreate themselves in light of these experiences.

When teaching a rather conservative and literalistic group of college students at a small, Christian college, I discovered the importance of creating a fertile story context for learners. I especially remember realizing the importance of helping learners understand how to approach stories when I found the students engaged in a heated debate about whether or not they could trust Zooey Glass's advice in J. D. Salinger's *Franny and Zooey* because he was not "born again." From this discussion, I realized that I needed to go back and provide the students some basic interpretive tools for approaching stories. I also remember offending another group of students when I retold some of the biblical stories in humorous ways. They thought I was laughing at the Bible.

---

[57]Sayers, *Whimsical Christian*, p. 87.

[58]McFague, *Literature and the Christian Life*, p. 103.

[59]J. Hillis Miller, "Literature and Religion," in *Religion and Modern Literature*, ed. G. B. Tennyson and Edward E. Ericson Jr. (Grand Rapids, Mich.: Eerdmans, 1975), p. 45.

[60]Vernon Ruland, *Horizons of Criticism: An Assessment of Religious-Literary Options* (Chicago: American Library Association, 1975), pp. 227–228.

Religious educators should be especially aware of where learners are in relation to stories. Often learners may need to be taught interpretive skills, such as identifying images and analyzing characters. At other times, learners may need to be encouraged to hear stories from other perspectives. For example, in studying biblical stories, I often ask learners to retell a particular story from the perspective of a minor character in the story. Often, I remind learners not to analyze the story for theological correctness but to experience the story as an expression of human existence.

Fortunately, because stories are not primarily cognitive, they can often break free of intellectual constraints and dogmatic barriers to engage learners in experiences and perspectives far different from their own. Sometimes, like C. S. Lewis, learners are caught up, even against their conscious wills, in the transformative power of stories, and, like many of Flannery O'Connor's characters, they are stalked by the searing, revealing grace of God, which can free, forgive, redeem, and transform.

Faith and the Storyteller

Storytelling is itself an act of faith. In telling a story, narrators posit meaning in the world and suggest the possibility of transformation of the self and the world. Storytellers image in narrative form what they perceive to be fundamental conditions of human existence. The storytellers' context for these conditions is informed by faith. Quoting Toynbee, who said all issues are ultimately religious, Percy contends the "religion" of storytellers becomes relevant when they are telling stories of ultimate issues. He says, "It would not have mattered a great deal if Margaret Mitchell were a Methodist or an atheist. But it does matter what Sartre's allegiance is, or Camus's or Flannery O'Connor's."[61] He goes on to explain that he himself writes in a Christian context, although he does not conceive his vocation to preach Christian faith in his novels.

On the contrary, Percy's worldview is informed by certain ideas about humanity related directly to his Christian perspective which do become central in his work. Flannery O'Connor does not attempt to evangelize in her stories, though certainly her views of grace are paramount in these stories. Likewise, James Joyce's Catholicism is always

---

[61]Percy, *Message in the Bottle*, pp. 110–111.

an integral element in his works, even in the form of overt struggle with Church dogma. Nonetheless, Joyce's intent is neither to convert people to Catholicism nor to turn them away from it. Catholicism is simply part of his worldview and is therefore central in his artistic vision. Even an atheistic worldview can inform stories appropriate for religious instruction. O'Connor suggests these unbelieving searchers do have an effect on those who believe: "We begin to examine our own religious notions, to sound them for genuineness, to purify them in the heat of our unbelieving neighbor's anguish."[62]

Thus, while storytellers' faith informs their worldviews, their intent is not to proselytize. Discussing the task of the novelist, O'Connor distinguishes proselytizing from writing authentic stories:

> We see people distorting their talents in the name of God for reasons that they think are good—to reform or to teach or to lead people to the Church . . . . None of us is able to judge such people themselves, but we must, for the sake of truth, judge the products they make. We must say whether this or that novel truthfully portrays the aspect of reality it sets out to portray. The novelist who deliberately misuses his talent for some good purpose may be committing no sin, but he is certainly committing a grave inconsistency, for he is trying to reflect God with what amounts to a practical untruth.[63]

Although the type of story O'Connor describes is meant to provide Christians an alternative to "secular" literature, the attempt is misguided. Such stories are not faithful to human experience; they are not true. Storytellers, rather, should use their craft to express the truths of human existence. O'Connor claims the storyteller's obligation is to truth, and not to the learner's taste, happiness, or morals.[64] Percy goes so far as to suggest immorality in stories is a result of falling short of trying to arrive at truth, catering to bad taste, or writing for other reasons than to express what the storyteller perceives as truth.[65]

C. S. Lewis admits that his *Chronicles of Narnia* did not grow out of an attempt to say something about Christianity to children. He did not draw up a list of Christian principles and then hammer out

---

[62]O'Connor, *Mystery and Manners*, p. 160.
[63]Ibid., p. 174.
[64]Ibid., p. 172.
[65]Percy, *Conversations with Walker Percy*, p. 191.

allegories to embody them. Instead, the *Chronicles* all began with images—a faun carrying an umbrella, a queen on a sledge, a great lion. He adds that originally there was nothing Christian about the images at all. That element, he says, pushed itself in of its own accord.[66]

Storytellers do not begin with statements of facts or bodies of knowledge to convey. Rather, they begin with their own experiences, their own visions of truth. Dorothy Sayers even claims that storytellers often do not know their own experiences until they create the stories which reveal them. She explains that a person experiences something only when she can express it: "The thing reveals itself to him in words and so becomes so fully experienced for the first time. By thus recognizing it in its expression, he makes it his own—integrates it into himself. . . It is no longer something happening to him, but something happening in him."[67] In incarnating human existence in stories, storytellers appeal not simply to cognitive capacities with fact and statement but moreso to emotions and lifestyles. Conrad suggests that storytellers speak "to our capacity of delight and wonder to the sense of mystery surrounding our lives."[68]

Storytellers, then, engage in a process of making the invisible visible, of making the unspeakable spoken, of incarnating mystery and wonder for learners to experience. In this quest for incarnation, any human experience may become significant and relevant. Conrad says, "There is not a place of splendour or a dark corner of the earth that does not deserve if only a passing glance of wonder and pity."[69] All experience is potential resource for stories. In the arranging of experience into stories, storytellers demonstrate their faith in a world which is meaningful and in the hope that human beings can transform themselves.

Stories and Community

Among the Yoruba, stories are an important part of wedding and child-naming celebrations. Stories at wakes for the dead are common in Ireland, Europe, and some parts of Africa. In India storytellers perform in the streets and marketplaces. Among the Xhosa and Zulu,

---

[66]Lewis, "Sometimes Faerie Stories May Say Best What's to Be Said," p. 36.
[67]Sayers, *Whimsical Christian*, pp. 85–86.
[68]Conrad, preface to *The Nigger of the Narcissus*, p. xii.
[69]Ibid.

stories are performed within families. An integral part of children's social life is listening to and learning narratives so they can perform them when they are parents and grandparents.[70]

Stories are, across culture, communal experiences. Percy's example of the alienated commuter reading about an alienated commuter demonstrates the communal nature of written narrative. The communal nature of oral narrative is, however, even more striking. Oral narrative involves at least two people in each other's presence, both actively engaged in paying attention to one another, each affecting the other in their shared purpose of exploring the human condition. In both written and oral narrative, story creates community and is created by community.

Just as stories and identity emerge together, stories and community emerge simultaneously. Community among persons begins as they share experiences and grows as they create stories together, building a common pool that gives identity to their relationship. As community develops day by day, it creates its stories from its experiences and is created by those stories as they become part of the community's mythology or metanarrative. As shapers of identity, stories become an important part of the basis for community and a guiding force in the development of the community's life. In communities, people share a common memory, a common pool of stories which provide the framework for the community's identity and life.[71] Within the community, individual identity is shaped by one's experience of the life of the community, including the stories which the community creates and then passes on as part of a living tradition. In turn, individuals through their new experiences and creativity, add to the community's stories and help give shape to the evolving community.[72]

---

[70]Anne Pellowski, *The World of Storytelling* (New York: Bowker, 1977), pp. 47–53.

[71]For more on the relationship of memory and community life and identity, see Russell A. Butkus, "Dangerous Memories: Toward a Pedagogy for Social Transformation," in *Religious Education as Social Transformation*, ed. Allen J. Moore (Birmingham, Ala.: Religious Education Press, 1989), pp. 201–233.

[72]For more on building communities, see Evelyn Eaton Whitehead and James D. Whitehead, *Community of Faith: Crafting Christian Communities Today* (Mystic, Conn.: Twenty-Third, 1992).

A Christian community is a community experiencing God and interacting with a tradition that includes stories of God's actions in history. Within that tradition, persons are influenced by their contact with the Christian story, and they give shape to the ongoing story as they live out their own stories. Thus, persons are given a hermeneutic by the community with which to shape and evaluate their own stories, and, at the same time, their stories critique and give shape to the community's hermeneutic. Ethicist Stanley Hauerwas suggests Christianity can partly be conceptualized as one set of coherent metaphors and stories that constitute an understanding of the world and a possible life plan.[73]

Christian community is created and sustained through its experiences and stories of God.[74] As the Christian community lives out its story, it gives birth to other stories which continue to shape the evolving identity of the community. Without its stories, communities would not exist, because their identity is held in their stories.

The Senecas tell the story of a young boy named Poyeshao who went hunting for birds for his foster mother. Along the way, he ran across a stone that offered to tell him stories in exchange for the birds he'd killed. Poyeshao gave the stone his birds, and the stone began to tell him stories of long ago. The boy returned for several days to bring the stone birds and to hear the stories. One day his foster mother, who had become suspicious because of the few birds Poyeshao brought home, sent another young boy to find out what Poyeshao did in the woods all day. The boy followed Poyeshao into the woods, and when he heard the stone begin to talk he joined Poyeshao. The boy gave the stone his birds, and again the stone began to tell stories. After several days, the foster mother hired two men to follow the boys in their daily trek into the woods. Soon they too joined the boys in hearing the stories. At nightfall, the stone told the four to bring all the people in the village to hear the stories. The next day, everyone came to hear the stone, and each brought something for the stone. Then the stone told them it would tell them the stories of long ago. "Some of you will remember every word that I say, some will remember part of the words, and some will forget them all—I think this will be the way, but each of

---

[73]Stanley Hauerwas, *Vision and Virtue: Essays in Christian Ethical Reflection* (Notre Dame, Ind.: University of Notre Dame Press, 1974), p. 75.
[74]Shea, *Stories of God*, pp. 58–59.

you must do the best you can. Hereafter, you must tell these stories to one another." Then the stone began to tell the stories.

For three days, the stone told the stories. Then it said, "I have finished! You must keep these stories as long as the world lasts; tell them to your children and grandchildren, generation after generation. One person will remember them better than another. When you go to someone to ask for one of these stories, carry something to pay for it. I know all that happened in the world before this. I have told it to you. When you visit one another, you must tell these things and keep them up always. I have finished!"

And so has it been among the Senecas ever since.[75]

Stories, Faith, and Religious Education

Faith is a way of life people learn from experiences within a faith community.[76] Learning in faith involves cognitive, affective, and behavioral dimensions of growth and development within the context of the faith community, and stories can play an important part in bringing about development in faith within religious education. Religious educators may use stories to address desired learning outcomes in each of the three learning domains. I address these domains in greater detail in chapter 6, but a brief discussion here may prove helpful.

Cognitive learning involves information storage and retrieval, reasoning, inferring, problem solving, conceptualizing, classifying, relating, symbolizing, imagining, and creating.[77] Religious educator Daniel Aleshire suggests three cognitive learning skills that are especially important for faith development: learning stories of the believing community, developing a capacity for critical reflection, and imagining new paradigms in which faith fashions new experiences and perceptions.[78] These skills allow learners to receive and reshape the narratives of the faith community, to think about beliefs and reconstruct them in light of new information or different experiences, and to

---

[75]Adapted from Susan Feldman, "The Storytelling Stone," in *The Storytelling Stone: Traditional Native American Myths and Tales* (New York: Dell, 1965), pp. 259–266.

[76]Lee, "Growing in Faith through Religious Instruction," pp. 297–298.

[77]For a detailed discussion of cognitive development, see John H. Flavell, *Cognitive Development*, 2d ed. (Englewood Cliffs, N.J.: Prentice-Hall, 1985).

[78]Daniel O. Aleshire, *Faithcare: Ministering to All God's People through the Ages of Life* (Philadelphia: Westminster, 1988), pp. 67–69.

envision new ways of acting in the world. Using narratives in religious instruction may be one way to facilitate development of these important faith skills.

Growing up Southern Baptist, I heard the story of Lottie Moon every December during Southern Baptists' foreign missions emphasis month. Lottie Moon had been a missionary to China and was instrumental in establishing the offering that grew to be the primary support for Southern Baptist foreign missions work. For us little girls in Girls in Action (GAs), Lottie Moon was a role model of a faithful Southern Baptist woman who had answered God's call. I learned the rest of the story in seminary. Apparently, Lottie Moon, who was very short, would travel around the Chinese countryside and stand up in her rickshaw to address the people. Some male missionaries were upset at what they called her "preaching," an improper behavior for women. As a result of the agitation of these male missionaries, the Foreign Mission Board passed a resolution against Lottie Moon. Lottie Moon heard about it and fired off a letter to the Foreign Mission Board demanding that they provide her with $500 for her passage home so that upon her return she could present the board with her resignation. The board never sent the money, and Lottie Moon became one of the most respected missionaries in Southern Baptist history. For me, the rest of the story addressed the last two cognitive learning skills: it offered a challenge to think critically about Southern Baptists' stance on women in ministry, and it offered a vision of the possibility of Southern Baptist women in ministry, a vision shaped by Lottie Moon's story, for thousands and thousands of little girls in Southern Baptist churches.

Affective learning in faith has to do with developing a capacity for love of God and love of others. Beliefs alone do not have the power to motivate people; passion—emotion—is necessary to compel people to behave in certain ways.[79] Aleshire suggests four ways in which religious instruction may influence and fashion emotionality: naming, expressing, disciplining, and discovering.[80] Naming helps learners to identify their emotions. The process of expressing allows learners to speak or demonstrate their emotions. Disciplining helps learners to channel their emotions into appropriate responses, and discovering

---

[79]Lee, *Content of Religious Instruction*, p. 205.
[80]Ibid., pp. 54–56.

helps learners to find and experience their emotions. Emotions are learned by experience and observation.[81] Stories provide the potential for helping learners name, express, discipline, and discover emotions.

In the eleventh century Indo-Persian story cycle, *The Thousand and One Nights*, King Shahrayar learns of the unfaithfulness of his wife and his brother's wife. Together they vow never to allow another woman to betray them. Each night the king demands his vizier to bring a virgin to share his bed with him, and the next morning he has her put to death. Finally, only the vizier's two daughters are left. The elder daughter, Scheherazade, insists on being presented to the king first, and she insists that her younger sister attend her. That night as the king and Scheherazade prepare for bed, the younger sister enters the chamber and begs Scheherazade to tell her stories. The king agrees, and Schehrazade complies. By morning she has not yet finished the first tale, and the king is so enthralled with the story that he postpones her execution until the next morning. This scenario continues for innumerable nights until at last the king feels that the storyteller can restore his happiness and trust. And so he marries Scheherazade and convinces his brother to marry her sister. The Indo-Persian culture that gave rise to *The Thousand and One Nights* believed that stories were curative. Even today in Hindu medicine fairy tales are given to people with emotional disturbances to help them heal, and in Muslim societies visitors tell sick people stories of endurance and triumph to help them heal.[82]

Behavioral learning in religious instruction involves helping people learn to behave in faithful ways. Behavior may be learned through reinforcement, modeling, and behaving.[83] Reinforcement involves rewarding desired behaviors. In faith communities, reinforcement may be as simple as a thank-you in public worship for assistance in church maintenance or an appreciative note for providing child care during a young adult church activity.[84] Modeling teaches behavior as learners

---

[81]Michael Lewis and Carolyn Saarni, "Culture and Emotions," in *The Socialization of Emotions*, ed. Michael Lewis and Carolyn Saarni (New York Plenum, 1985), p. 10.

[82]Jack Maguire, *Creative Storytelling: Choosing, Inventing, and Sharing Tales for Children* (New York: McGraw-Hill, 1985), pp. 38–39.

[83]Aleshire, *Faithcare*, pp. 61–64.

[84]Ibid.

observe others behaving.[85] Learning is even more powerful when learners identify with models or perceive themselves to be like models. Behaving as a means of learning behaviors involves engaging learners directly in behaviors to be learned. Learners may participate in an organized missions trip to work in soup kitchens in an inner city as a way of learning ministry. Again, stories also provide a means for achieving these goals. Stories can reinforce, model, and engage.

A lawyer came to Jesus asking what he had to do to inherit eternal life. Jesus asked him, "What is written in the Law?" The young man responded, "You shall love the Lord your God with all your heart and all your soul and all your strength and all your mind. And you shall love your neighbor as yourself." Jesus answered, "Quite right. Do this and you will have life." But the lawyer wanted to justify himself, and so he asked, "And who is my neighbor?" And Jesus told the story of the Good Samaritan. When he finished, he asked the lawyer, "So, who do you think was a neighbor to the man who fell among thieves?" The lawyer answered, not wanting to admit it was the Samaritan, "The one who showed him mercy." And Jesus said, "Go and do likewise."

Stories are an essential part of religious instruction. Passing on stories, developing new stories, creating spaces in which Mystery may be encountered, and helping learners live out stories—all are important tasks for religious instruction. Religious educators may facilitate faith development by creating learning experiences in which learners may engage in experiencing and practicing faith in cognitive, affective, and behavioral ways. Stories provide one mode for religious educators in structuring learning experiences to enhance faith development. Stories can pass on Christian tradition; stories can invoke powerful emotions; stories can model and invite faithful lifestyles. An important task of religious educators is providing these narrative experiences, whether in reading biblical stories aloud, enacting dramas, watching movies, or performing folktales, which will invite learners to grow in faith and live faithful lives in the world. And, like the Senecas, some will remember every story. Some will remember a part of the stories, and some will forget them all. But all must do the best they can.

---

[85]For more on observational learning, see Albert Bandura, "Social Learning through Imitation," *Nebraska Symposium on Motivation: 1962*, ed. M. R. Jones (Lincoln: University of Nebraska Press, 1962); Albert Bandura, *Social Learning Theory* (New York: General Learning Press, 1971).

4

The Value of Stories for Theology

Soon it became clear to us: you can't teach disbelief
to a child,
only wonderful stories, and we hadn't a story
nearly as good.[1]
—Stephen Dunn

Theology begins in reflection upon religious experiences that are first expressed in narrative form. It is a conscious, theoretical exploration of pretheoretical religious awareness and meaning. The discipline of theology reflects upon the religious story in which people participate and in which they experience God.[2] Out of these experiences and stories, theology may create abstract systems and classifications, but these concepts can never be completely unrelated to the narratives from which they arise. Thus theological ideas are always tied to religious stories.[3]

Stories, then, provide one of the most significant ways of talking about God available to theological discourse. One way humans can know God is by knowing God's stories. Because God is more than the scope of human senses, language, and knowledge, the most

---

[1]Stephen Dunn, "At the Smithville Methodist Church," in *Local Time* (New York: Morrow, 1986), p. 54.

[2]For more on how people "live in story," see John Dominic Crossan, *The Dark Interval: Towards a Theology of Story* (Allen, Tex.: Argus, 1975).

[3]John Navone, *Towards a Theology of Story* (n.p.: St. Paul, 1977), p. 41.

78

appropriate ways of talking about God are analogical,[4] and, as ethicist Stanley Hauerwas argues, "stories are required by those matters we can only describe analogically."[5] Thus, to talk about God is to tell God's stories.[6]

As Hauerwas points out, God is not a concept but a name.[7] In biblical thought, a name was more than an appellation; it summed up the essence of a person.[8] Telling someone a name was an act of self-disclosure. A refusal to give one's name implied an unwillingness to give all of oneself, since to have someone's full name implied a power over or a possession of that person. Thus, God's willingness to give God's name to Moses (Genesis 3:13–14) was significant for the development of God's relationship with the people of Israel.[9] In the Exodus, God made his name known to Moses and the people of Israel. *YHWH* was the same God who had led the patriarchs as *El Shaddai* but now was covenanting with the people whom God had delivered from the Egyptians. A relationship begun with Abraham was now extended to a people, and these covenant people became not only the recipients of a promise but also participants in a story.[10]

The centerpiece of this unfolding story was the Shema:

> Hear O Israel: The Lord our God is one Lord; and you shall love the Lord your God with all your heart, and with all your soul, and with all your might. And these words which I command you this day shall be upon your heart; and you shall teach them diligently to your children, and shall talk of them when you sit in your house and when you walk by the way, and when you lie down, and when you rise. And you shall bind them as a sign upon your hand, and they shall be as frontlets between your eyes. And you shall write them on the doorposts of your

---

[4]John Macquarrie, *God-Talk: An Examination of the Language and Logic of Theology* (London: SCM, 1967), p. 214.

[5]Stanley Hauerwas, "Story and Theology," *Religion in Life* 45 (Fall 1976): 346.

[6]For more on analogy, see David B. Burrell, *Analogy and Philosophical Language* (New Haven: Yale University Press, 1973); and David Tracy, *The Analogical Imagination* (New York: Crossroad, 1981).

[7]Ibid., p. 347.

[8]Roy L. Honeycutt, Jr., *Exodus*, Broadman Bible Commentary, rev. ed. (Nashville.: Broadman, 1973), 1:396.

[9]Ibid., p. 314.

[10]John Bright, *A History of Israel*, 3d ed. (Philadelphia: Westminster, 1972), p. 148.

house and on your gates. And when the Lord your God brings you into the land which he swore to your fathers, to Abraham, to Isaac, and to Jacob, to give you, with great and goodly cities, which you did not build, and houses full of all good things, which you did not fill, and cisterns hewn out which you did not hew, and vineyards and olive trees, which you did not plant, and when you eat and are full, then take heed lest you forget the Lord, who brought you out of the land of Egypt, out of the house of bondage. (Deuteronomy 6: 4–12)

The Shema stood uniquely as the focal point of Hebrew life. Its commandment of absolute love and proclamation of the singleness and unity of God had no parallel expression in the Pentateuch.[11] Here, the Israelites were again introduced to YHWH, the personal name for God, which later the Jews refused to speak for fear of profaning it. YHWH, they were told, was one. Unlike the gods of other Near Eastern religions, YHWH was exclusive. YHWH was not many, but one, not represented in diverse forms and appearances as other nature deities, but a single, unified being. And the proclamation made clear that this being alone was to be the recipient of the Israelites' love and obedience.[12]

The Israelites had come to know and understand YHWH through their experiences with God. As the deuteronomic historian recalls, YHWH had chosen Abram to be the father of the Hebrew people; YHWH had emancipated the people from slavery to the Egyptians; YHWH had provided manna in the desert; YHWH had led the people into the promised land; and YHWH had made a covenant with these people, promising them provision and protection on the condition of their obedience. This condition made the teaching of God's law paramount in Hebrew life, especially as those who had experienced the exodus first hand died and generations who had not seen God's mighty acts were born. The Shema reflected the Israelites' desire that subsequent generations know the story of YHWH's covenant with them and respond with obedience to YHWH's law. The Shema recognized the importance of teaching God's covenant story diligently to the Hebrew children. The teaching of the covenant story was taken so seriously by the Israelites that they carried out the suggestions of the Shema

---

[11]John D. W. Watts, *Deuteronomy*, Broadman Bible Commentary, (Nashville: Broadman, 1970): 2:214.

[12]James King West, *Introduction to the Old Testament*, 2d ed. (New York: Macmillan, 1981), p. 187.

literally, wearing phylacteries around their wrists and foreheads, and placing a mezuzah on their doorposts. These little boxes contained passages from the Torah. When their children would ask the meaning of the boxes, the Israelites had a teachable moment, a moment when children were open and inquiring, to tell their children the story of God's acts in their history.[13]

For Christians, the story of God's acts in human history continues in the Christ-story of the New Testament and in the stories of the Christian community across the centuries. To be Christian is to incorporate these stories as one's own and to shape one's life in interaction with them. These stories form many of the images that define the identity of the Christian community and help shape the lives of those within the community. Theologian James McClendon identifies such story images as the very substance of religion.[14] For example, the stories of Scripture give rise to dominant images—the Exodus or the Last Supper—which help give shape to the lives of those who apply them to themselves. Hence, the Exodus has become a primary image for theologies of liberation as oppressed peoples and their allies identify with the plight and liberation of the people of Israel.[15] Within these theologies, work for justice is a reenactment of this story. The stories of the Christian community, particularly the Christ-story, help show Christian people what it has meant to be Christian and help Christian people construct their own Christian identity as participants in the ongoing Christian story.

Theologian John Navone argues that stories create the very context that allows for belief. In storytelling, people create meaning of the facts of experience. Stories express people's need to understand the world as intelligible, coherent, and meaningful, and stories of God represent people's will to believe these things about the world. Narrative consciousness, Navone suggests, functions on the premise that meaning exists. Human tendency to create stories and myths, he says, indicates belief that the universe is not absurd.[16] This narrative consciousness assumes intelligibility over indifference, meaning over absurdity, and being over nonbeing. It is ontologically grounded in being

---

[13]See Claus Westermann, *A Thousand Years and a Day: Our Time in the Old Testament*, trans. Stanley Rudman (Philadelphia: Fortress, 1957), pp. 179–180.

[14]James McClendon, *Biography as Theology: How Life Stories Can Remake Today's Theology* (Nashville: Abingdon: 1974), p. 93.

[15]For example, see Cyris H. S. Moon, *A Korean Minjung Theology: An Old Testament Perspective* (Hong Kong: Plough, 1985).

[16]Navone, *Towards a Theology of Story*, p. 39.

or Being-in-Itself (God). Humans' will to believe in an intelligible world evidenced in narrative consciousness opens people up to the possibility of meaning. Since people tell stories, they assume there is intelligibility in the world, and, since people revise their stories, they apparently anticipate further intelligibility.[17] If humans did not believe in meaning, they would not tell stories. Human willingness to choose meaning over absurdity opens up space for belief. When people tell stories, they imply belief in meaning.[18]

STORIES AS THEOLOGICAL TOOLS

Central to Christian faith is a story; it is a story that begins in the covenant faith of God's people and continues in the life of one person who fully lives out faith, trusting God even to death on a cross. Because Christian faith is so intimately connected to a particular story, theology must take narrative into account as one primary expression of faith experiences and understandings.[19] Story is not the only appropriate means of theological reflection, but it is a valuable and important one. Christian theological reflection implies not only the formulation and exploration of concepts but also the implementation of Christian conviction in lived Christian faith. Narrative helps people both reflect on religious experience and live out religious truths in their own lived stories. Hauerwas explains that a "theory is meant to help you know the world without changing the world or yourself, a story is to help you deal with the world by changing it through changing yourself."[20] Such an emphasis on story does not deny the significance of the intellectual and theoretical explorations of faith, but it does offer a context in which to understand the parameters of intellectual and theoretical exploration and the relationship of theological understandings to lived faith.[21]

---

[17] Ibid., p. 40.

[18] To read more about connections between grace, meaning, and story, see: Andrew M. Greely, *Religion: A Secular Theory* (New York: Free Press, 1982), pp. 53–69.

[19] Sallie McFague, *Speaking in Parables: A Study in Metaphor and Theology* (Philadelphia: Fortress, 1975), p. 139.

[20] Hauerwas, "Story and Theology," p. 341.

[21] For uses of narrative theology in religious education, see Jerry H. Stone, "Narrative Theology and Religious Education," *Theologies of Religious Education*, ed. Randolph Crump Miller (Birmingham, Ala.: Religious Education Press, 1995), pp. 255–285.

Stories provide the grammatical setting for religious convictions.[22] Christian convictions do not exist as entities separable from the story of which they are a part. Rather, the story gives rise to the convictions, and the story context provides the setting for the exploration of the validity of any religious conviction. Christian convictions develop partly from persons' interactions with the Christian story, and Christian convictions are tested out in the lived stories of those who participate in the Christian community. Christian convictions are not ideas to be held in an intellectual vacuum but are lifestyle implications to be lived out in the world. As the normative story of Christian faith, the biblical story is not an illustration to explain a point but a way to involve persons actively in a particular style of life.

Theologian Terrence W. Tilley has offered three primary tasks of story theology: to discover the narratives that form Christian tradition, to transform (when necessary) the narratives of Christian tradition, and to proclaim the Good News.[23] As theology explores the narratives of Christian tradition, it finds that Christian faith expresses itself in a wide variety of experiences open to multiple meanings. There is no one exclusive Christian story. Rather, people participate in their own stories in interaction with the Christian story. The encounter with the Christian story always occurs at a particular historical moment in a particular culture to a person with a particular set of life experiences. The task of narrative theology, then, is to explore the experience of the Christian story, discovering the structures of people's own pasts which they impose upon the story as they live it out. In so doing, people may recognize the limitations of their own experiences of the Christian story. Thus, to affirm one's own experience with the Christian story is not to deny the legitimacy of the experiences of others. In this way, each Christian contributes to a communal Christian wisdom. Navone suggests, "What one authentic and dedicated Christian experience tells us of the Christ-story and its truth from his standpoint is not the whole of reality, but it is an important part of the whole. If he does not testify to the truth of this story, who will? The understanding of the truth of this story is not exhausted and absolutized by any one Christian's 'telling' of it."[24] The reality of the Christian story is always more

---

[22]Ibid.

[23]Terrence W. Tilley, *Story in Theology* (Wilmington, Del.: Michael Glazier, 1985), pp. 11–16.

[24]Navone, *Towards a Theology of Story*, p. 29.

than any one person's experience of it. Thus, no one person's story is normative for Christian living. Rather, because of the limitations of people's experiences of the Christian story, others' stories should be heard and valued for the unique experience and perspective of the Christian story they offer as a way to enrich others' experiences.

As culture changes, the narratives of tradition may need to change in order to remain relevant. Story theology can address this task by creating, telling, and living stories that embody the Christian story in culturally relevant ways. One important component of this task involves creating new ways of expressing the tradition in new contexts. For example, because contemporary people no longer believe in the Ptolemaic universe of Genesis 1, religious educators need to find ways to narrate the creation story in our existential context, providing a faith interpretation of scientific discoveries about the origins of the universe. Feminist theologians have been especially helpful in challenging the limitations of traditional narratives. For example, Judith Plaskow argues that Jewish women must confront their exclusion from the definitive texts of Judaism and must recreate the central Jewish categories of Torah, Israel, and God to be inclusive of women.[25] Likewise, Elisabeth Schüssler Fiorenza argues from a Christian perspective that women must reconstruct the narratives of tradition to reflect the participation of women in the Christian community from its origins.[26]

Second, religious educators also need to create and recount completely new stories. Because contemporary persons live in a time and in a culture that are vastly removed from the world of the biblical writers, religious educators need to create and tell their own faith stories which embody the truth of the Christian story in their culture. These stories may take the form of myth, parable, fiction, biography, autobiography, or folktale. The point is that these are contemporary stories that embody contemporary appropriations of the Christian story in contemporary culture.

Third, religious educators need to live out new stories by making the gospel relevant to the social and moral problems of their time. Story theology then becomes a form of lived faith whereby persons

[25]See Judith Plaskow, *Standing Again at Sinai: Judaism from a Feminist Perspective* (San Francisco: HarperSanFrancisco, 1990).

[26]See Elisabeth Schüssler Fiorenza, *In Memory of Her: A Feminist Theological Reconstruction of Christian Origins* (New York: Crossroad, 1992).

reflect on their experiences of the Christian story in their lives and in the world in order to engage more fully in incarnating the Christian story through their actions in the world.

In so doing, they fulfill the third task of story theology, which is to share Good News by telling stories and by living true and authentic stories. Story is a way of being in the world and thus retelling the Christian story. In the way Christians live, they embody and proclaim their appropriation of the gospel. Thus, orthodoxy and orthopraxis are inseparable. Faith and action coexist in a necessary relationship in persons' ways of being Christian in the world as they live out authentic and true faith stories. Hence, theology and ethics are not distinctly separate disciplines but are connected by narratives. Story theology explores these narratives, transforms them when necessary, and proclaims them through authentic Christian lives. The story at the center of Christian faith is ultimately a call to engage in a particular way of being. It is the call to experience, appropriate, and embody the Christian story in lived Christian faith, true to one's own story and vision and open to the story and vision of others.

STORY AS A PLAN FOR LIVING

Rooted in the Shema is a theology of remembering. When people look for evidence of God in their lives, they eventually turn to their memories. There, in those stories, they recall those moments of heightened awareness of the presence of God. They look back and see a pattern of God's involvement in their lives.[27] They can also turn to the memory of others who have preserved stories and patterns of experience with God, from the authors of the biblical text to the long line of participants in faith communities.[28] Personal memories, the memories of the biblical writers and the communities that preserved the oral narratives, the memories of other faithful persons, and the memory of the faith community itself all act to affirm the interconnectedness of God's story and human stories. These memories provide the context for

---

[27]For example, see Frederick Buechner, *The Sacred Journey* (San Francisco: Harper and Row, 1982) and Frederick Buechner, *Now and Then: A Memoir of Vocation* (San Francisco: HarperSanFrancisco, 1983).

[28]For example, see *Conversions: The Christian Experience*, ed. Hugh T. Kerr and John M. Mulder (Grand Rapids, Mich.: Eerdmans, 1983).

Christian living.[29] They recall the activity of God in human lives, and they call for patterns of living consonant with the Christian story.

Journey Stories

Journey stories are one of the most characteristic human stories. In journey stories, the protagonist leaves home in search of wholeness, which is ultimately found through the triumph of the spirit in the midst of experiences of adversity, failure, and mortality. The Bible itself is full of such journey stories—Abraham, Moses, Elijah, Jesus—with the Exodus and the Christ story dominating the Hebrew Scriptures and New Testament respectively. People of faith, in biblical terms, are people on a journey.

The multiplicity of journey stories the Bible presents suggests that persons come to God in different places. Each story affirms something unique about God and opens readers' eyes to some new facet of who God is. For example, the accounts of the four Gospel writers represent four perspectives of the story told by the life of Jesus; yet each affirms the truthfulness of the story his life told.[30]

The challenge these stories offers to learners today is to the authenticity and truthfulness of the stories their lives tell. As Christian people on a journey, they are called to live truthful lives that affirm the claims of the gospel. Their lives are to be a truthful enactment of the gospel story. Their commitment is to tell with the stories of their lives the story of God as they seek to bring about reconciliation, atonement, unity, and peace.

The Drama of Salvation

Faith journeys begin at the initiation of the Spirit of God. God calls persons to the journey and guides and empowers them for the journey. God comes to Abram with the command to leave his home and begin a pilgrimage; God confronts Moses in the wilderness to call him to lead the Hebrews out of Egypt; the Spirit of God descends upon believers gathered for the festival of Pentecost to empower them to carry the gospel beyond the reaches of prejudice and religious intolerance. The journey, then, is the human response to God's initiating call.

---

[29]John Shea, *Stories of God: An Unauthorized Biography* (Chicago: Thomas More, 1978), p. 59.

[30]Ibid., pp. 64–66.

The journey is a response to the claim of God on one's life. Through individual responses, the community experiences the call of God to become a pilgrim community. The journey is not made alone. To be a pilgrim is to be part of a covenant community which travels together. Hence, salvation is not personal, individual assent to a particular collection of propositions but is active participation in the ongoing life of God's pilgrim community, which understands itself in relation to the story of God told by the life story of Jesus and invites others to join its pilgrimage through its witness to the possibility of authentic existence as the people of God.

These people of God are characterized by faith, hope, and love.[31] These words describe their way of being in the world. In this context, faith is the act of putting one's trust in God; it implies belief in meaning in existence over absurdity and suggests such meaning is found ultimately in God and one's relationship to God and others. Hope is the anticipation of good. It is the vision that looks beyond one's self and one's circumstances to the activity of God in the world working to bring about good. Love is response to God's initiating love. Love requires moving outside self and participating in the oneness of the universe. It is the ultimate embodiment of atonement. Of course, these qualities are achieved only partially by most of those who journey. The pilgrimage is a quest for wholeness during which incremental transformations occur through the experiences and encounters of the journey.

The journey is also a story of homecoming. It is coming to terms with the meaning of one's life and accepting one's place in one's ultimate environment. Homecoming is accepting the demands of authentic existence and finding one's place in being with others and being with Mystery. Homecoming is a metaphor for the theological language of atonement, making persons at-one with others and with God. This at-oneness occurs through the efficacy of the Christian story as it is experienced, heard, appropriated, and lived out by the people of God.

Yet homecoming is not without cost. Those for whom atonement becomes a way of life make a difficult pilgrimage. In all journey stories, something is always left behind. Abram leaves the comfort of his homeland; Jesus leaves his place in his family; Lottie Moon leaves

---

[31]Navone, *Towards a Theology of Story*, p. 56.

family, friends, and native country to cast her lot with the poor of China; Dietrich Bonhoeffer leaves the safety of England to return to his native Germany to oppose Hitler. Yet in this renunciation of some things, the pilgrim finds freedom to live truthfully. The journey of faith demands risk and vulnerability. The image of the journey suggests conversion is not entrance to a safe harbor but rather an ongoing movement whose direction has been established.[32]

Given the necessity of risk, the faith traveler must also take into account the possibility and,' ultimately, inevitability, of death. As faith travelers seek to enact the Christian story in the world, suffering becomes a reality, from loss of property to loss of status to loss of life itself. The truthfulness of faith is made evident in its steadfastness in the face of suffering. In exploring the lives of Martin Luther King Jr. and Dag Hammarskjöld, McClendon comes to the conclusion that

> theology must hear her witnesses, discover her own truth, shape her doctrine in faithfulness to that truth. I do not mean that theological passion should replace thought; there must be clear thought even about passion and about death. I mean that in the community which includes the doctrine of at-one-ment in its storehouse of treasure, the community whose sacred images include the Suffering Servant, there can be no clear thought which does not think truly, and passionately, about that somber treasure.[33]

The journey stories of faithful pilgrims witness to the truth of the gospel. They call people of faith to live in response to the authentic, experiential possibilities disclosed in the stories of these persons whose lives have been shaped by the transforming power of the Christian story and particularly to the realization of the potential to be fully human embodied in the story lived by Jesus. In turn, the truthfulness of Christians' lives bears continuing witness to the truth of the gospel story. The stories Christians tell with their lives are evidence that the Good News is true.

Albert Schweitzer, noted theologian and accomplished musician, startled friends and acquaintances in 1905 by announcing his decision to study medicine and to become a missionary doctor in equatorial Africa. His controversial *The Quest of the Historical Jesus* upset

---

[32]Ibid., p. 63.
[33]McClendon, *Biography as Theology*, p. 107.

conservatives and liberals alike by challenging cherished views about the person and nature of Jesus. For Schweitzer, elaborate Christologies led away from the simple truths revealed in Jesus' own words and life. Rather, he saw Jesus as a person with a mission to awaken people to the community of God. As Schweitzer struggled with the implications of this idea, he decided he would make his life his argument: "I would advocate the things I believed in terms of the life I lived and what I did. Instead of vocalizing my belief in the existence of God within each of us, I would attempt to have my life and work say what I believed."[34] Schweitzer's hospital at Lambarene then became the evidence of the truthfulness of Schweitzer's life and his response to the Christian story. For Schweitzer, Christ became known only as a person responded to the invitation to "Follow me." To experience the Christian story involved enmeshing one's own life in its demands for justice and peace. Schweitzer's life told a story that continues to validate the claims of the gospel. His story suggests to us that the gospel is true.

---

[34]Quoted in Norman Cousins, *Dr. Schweitzer of Labarene* (New York: Harper, 1960), p. 191.

5

Psychological Perspectives on Storytelling

The stories people tell have a way of taking care of them. If sto-
ries come to you, care for them. And learn to give them away
where they are needed. Sometimes a person needs a story more
than food to stay alive. That is why we put these stories in each
other's memory. This is how people care for themselves.[1]

—Barry Lopez

Jungian therapist James Hillman claims stories are good for the soul.[2]
As Hillman notes, story and psyche are closely interwoven. People
create meaning, identity, and community as they hear stories, create
narratives of their life experiences, and participate in common human
stories.[3] Stories are an essential part of human wholeness and human
wellness.[4] In the *cantadora* tradition of storytelling, *La Invitada* is
"the guest" or the empty chair present at every telling. Sometimes
during a telling, the soul of an audience member will come and sit in

---

[1]Barry Lopez, *Crow and Weasel* (San Francisco: North Point, 1990), p. 48.

[2]James Hillman, "A Note on Story," *Parabola* 4 (Fall 1979): 43.

[3]Michelle Dykstra, "Story, Psyche, and Supper: A Psychological Interpretation of the Eucharist," Ph.D. diss., Fuller Theological Seminary, 1992, p. 38.

[4]Psychologist George S. Howard suggests that psychotherapy is a means of repairing stories. "Culture Tales: A Narrative Approach to Thinking, Cross-Cultural Psychology, and Psychotherapy," *The American Psychologist* 46 (March 1991): 194.

the empty chair because it has a special need the story fulfills or a brokenness the story mends.[5]

Beginning with Sigmund Freud's psychoanalytic theories, depth psychologists from a wide variety of perspectives have attempted to understand the complex relationship between story and psyche. Some have even referred to the human personality as "storied psyche" or have suggested the nature of human conduct is "storied."[6] This chapter will briefly examine a few of the major contributions of various schools of psychology toward a useful understanding of storytelling in religious education.

STORIES IN PSYCHOLOGICAL TRADITION

Three separate but related psychological perspectives on narrative can provide an important foundation for religious educators' understanding and use of stories. The theories of Sigmund Freud, Carl Jung, and Jerome Bruner offer helpful possibilities for an exploration of the storied psyche in terms of the unconscious, the collective unconscious, and cognition. Each of these theorists has made helpful contributions for religious educators' appropriation of storytelling in religious instruction, and their ideas have continued as significant components of the discourses of narrative psychology.

Sigmund Freud

Perhaps Freud's most significant contribution toward an understanding of the storied psyche was his exposition of an underlying structure—part science, part mythology—which purported to explain conscious and unconscious experience. For Freud, the power of the structure to explain and complete the story was the important thing.[7] The most important element of this structure for the purposes of storytelling in religious education is what Freud termed the "unconscious." The unconscious is distinct from the preconscious, which consists of latent ideas that make their way into consciousness as soon as they become strong. The unconscious, on the other hand, is composed of

---

[5]Clarissa Pinkola Estes, *Women Who Run with the Wolves: Myths and Stories of the Wild Woman Archetype* (New York: Ballantine, 1992), p. 464.

[6]Ibid.; and Theodore R. Sarbin, ed. *Narrative Psychology: The Storied Nature of Human Conduct* (New York: Praeger Special Studies, 1986).

[7]Alan Parry, "A Universe of Stories," *Family Process* 30 (March 1991): 37.

latent ideas that do not penetrate into consciousness, no matter how strong they become, because they meet with active resistance. Nonetheless, the product of unconscious activity may, with a certain amount of exertion, pierce into consciousness.[8]

Freud saw that dreams as the primary vehicle by which this unconscious material is brought into the conscious.[9] He contended that parallels exist between the symbols of dreams and myths.[10] The individual's story, for Freud, was simply the particularized version of the underlying myth. Myths provided categories through which the conscious mind could work with unconscious material. Thus, an individual's dream stories could be properly understood by a specialist in structure and myth, better even than by the storyteller, who was only the instrument of the structure.[11]

Freud laid the foundation for the significance of stories in psychoanalytic theory. In Freudian theory, stories were integrally related to the psyche through the unconscious structure of mythology which provided a means by which the conscious mind could begin to deal with unconscious material. Freud's disciple Carl Jung, however, would be responsible for the development of a more thorough psychological theory of the storied psyche.

Carl G. Jung

Jung began his practice of depth psychology as a disciple of Freud but eventually broke with him to create his own distinctive school of analytical psychology, which is, nonetheless, indebted to Freud. Like Freud, Jung saw the significance of stories in understanding the psyche and in achieving health. Jung, however, saw the unconscious as composed of the personal unconscious, which closely parallels Freud's notion of the unconscious, and the collective unconscious, which is of much more importance.[12] The collective unconscious is

---

[8]Sigmund Freud, "A Note on the Unconscious in Psychoanalysis," in *A General Selection from the Works of Sigmund Freud*, ed John Rickman (Garden City, N.Y.: Doubleday, 1957), pp. 49–51.

[9]ibid., p. 52.

[10]Sigmund Freud, "The Origin and Development of Psychoanalysis," *A General Selection from the Works of Sigmund Freud*, ed. John Rickman (Garden City, N. Y.: Doubleday, 1957), p. 21.

[11]Parry, "Universe of Stories," pp. 37–38.

[12]Carl G. Jung, "The Structure of the Psyche," in *The Portable Jung*, trans. R. F. C. Hull, ed. Joseph Campbell (New York: Penguin, 1971), p. 38.

the repository of all human experience going back to humanity's earliest beginnings. It contains the entire spiritual heritage of humanity's evolution, which is passed down in the brain structures of every individual.[13] The content of this inheritance is the collection of symbols and patterns that express themselves in dreams and which exert influence on the individual psyche itself. Fundamental to the development and functioning of the psyche are the archetypes, which are typical modes of apprehension or preexistent forms that shape certain psychic contents.[14] Archetypes are the archaic remnants or primordial images of the collective unconscious that appear in the individual psyche.[15] These archetypes are not specific mythological images or conscious representations but are tendencies to form such representations of the motif. These representations can then vary a great deal in detail without losing their basic pattern.[16] These archetypes or patterns are inherited from the history of the human race, not as specific representations but as instinctive trends.[17] The appearance of these archetypes in the individual psyche is then given shape in specific representations by the experiences and worldview of the individual.

Jung contended that psychological health depends on the integration of the conscious and the unconscious. "For the sake of mental stability and even physiological health, the unconscious and the conscious must be integrally connected and thus move on parallel lines. If they are split apart or 'dissociated,' psychological disturbance follows."[18] This connection occurs through dream symbols, which carry messages from the instinctive to the rational parts of the mind. The interpretation of these symbols "enriches the poverty of consciousness so that it learns to understand again the forgotten language of the instincts."[19] According to Jung, modern humanity's

---

[13]Ibid., pp. 44–45.

[14]Carl G. Jung, "Instinct and the Unconscious," in *The Portable Jung*, trans. R. F. C. Hull, ed. Joseph Campbell (New York: Penguin 1971), p. 57; and Carl G. Jung, "The Concept of the Collective Unconscious," in *The Portable Jung*, trans. R. F. C. Hull, ed. Joseph Campbell (New York: Penguin, 1971), p. 60.

[15]Carl G. Jung, "Approaching the Unconscious," in *Man and His Symbols*, ed. Carl G. Jung (New York: Dell, 1964), p. 75.

[16]Ibid., p. 58.

[17]Ibid.

[18]Ibid., p. 37.

[19]Ibid.

rational rejection of these symbols has put them at the mercy of the psychic underworld.[20] In the process of demythologizing the world, humanity has lost its spiritual values and has consequently experienced disintegration and dissociation.[21]

Jung's answer to this dissociation of instinct and rationality was an understanding of myth and symbol that allows persons to create meaning of their lives. Jung warned that loss of the numinous strips persons of their ability to make sense of their lives but that myth and symbol allow persons a sense of wider meaning to their existence beyond the mundane tasks of daily living.

Jung traced the origins of myth to the dreams and fantasies of primitive storytellers, whom he likened to those later generations have called poets or philosophers. He noted that primitive storytellers did not concern themselves with the origins of their fantasies. Yet by the time of ancient Greece, human minds were advanced enough to realize that the tales of the gods were archaic and exaggerated traditions of long-buried kings or chieftains. Since these people already viewed myth as too improbable to mean what it said, they tried to reduce it to a generally understandable form.[22]

According to Jung, a similar demythologizing has taken place in the contemporary world in relation to dream symbols. As myths were dismissed as elaborations of rational history, dream symbols are dismissed as bizarre forms in which repressed contents of the psyche appear to the conscious mind.[23] This devaluing of myth and symbol creates a split in the psyche, distancing the rational mind from the instinctive mind and distancing the individual psyche from the common history of the human race.

Remythologizing of the psyche, on the other hand, reunites conscious and unconscious, rational and instinctive. Understanding of the ancient myths provides a framework for understanding the contemporary psyche of the individual. Archetypal patterns emerge from the collective unconscious in contemporary and individual symbols in the dreams of modern human beings in ways that, when understood, help the individual confront present life tasks.[24] For example, the Wild

---

[20]Ibid., p. 84.

[21]Ibid.

[22]Ibid., p. 78.

[23]Ibid.

[24]For further discussion of myth and dream, see Joseph Campbell, "Myth and Dream," in *The Hero with a Thousand Faces* (New York: Pantheon, 1949), pp. 3–25.

Woman archetype represents the innate, instinctual self that in women is often circumscribed by the cultural roles into which women are forced. She allows women to be in touch with their own inner rhythms, to claim their own lives.[25] Likewise, the hero archetype facilitates development of the individual's ego-consciousness—awareness of strengths and weaknesses—to equip the individual to deal with the difficult tasks of life.[26] Thus, the hero symbol arises in dreams when the ego needs strengthening—that is, when the conscious mind needs assistance in some task that it cannot accomplish without drawing on the sources of strength that lie in the unconscious mind.[27]

Thus, dreams and the archetypes that emerge therein assist persons in integrating their lives and support them in the tasks they must accomplish.[28] Myths allow persons to acknowledge patterns of existence from which they can create meaning of the disjointed events of their lives. For Jung, healing the rift between conscious and unconscious is the path to meaning and to individual and societal health. The symbols of the unconscious, Jung contended, are indeed meaningful and provide a key to the human soul:

> Dreams provide the most interesting information for those who take the trouble to understand their symbols. The results, it is true, have little to do with such worldly concerns as buying and selling. But the meaning of life is not exhaustively explained by one's business, nor is the deep desire of the human heart answered by a bank account.[29]

Jungian James Hillman has observed that people who have connections with stories fare better in therapy than those to whom stories must be introduced.[30] In psychotherapy, the analyst and patient together rewrite the patient's case history into a new story that has meaning for the patient. Hillman explains that Jungian psychotherapy

---

[25]Estes, *Women Who Run with the Wolves*, pp. 8–10.

[26]Joseph L. Henderson, "Ancient Myths and Modern Man,"in *Man and His Symbols*, ed. Carl G. Jung (New York: Dell, 1964), p. 101.

[27]Ibid., p. 114.

[28]See Carl G. Jung, "Dream-Analysis in its Practical Application," in *Modern Man in Search of a Soul*, trans. W. S. Dell and Cary F. Baynes (New York: Harcourt, Brace and World, 1933), pp. 1–27.

[29]Jung, "Approaching the Unconscious," p. 93.

[30]Hillman. "Note on Story," p. 43.

brings about an awareness of the dominance of fantasy in life as persons tell themselves into one story and then another. Implicit in these personal references are common themes that emerge in myth, fairy tale, and legend. Fantasy, he explains, is the attempt of the psyche itself to remythologize consciousness. "Soul-making goes hand in hand with deliteralizing consciousness and restoring its connection to mythic and metaphorical thought patterns."[31] In fact, he adds, "Literalism is sickness."[32]

The soul finds life in story, in dream, in myth and metaphor. This story from Yiddish tradition illustrates Hillman's point about the power of dreams and metaphors. One night, Ayzik, the son of Reb Yekl, dreamed of a treasure hidden under the Warsaw bridge. Ayzik traveled to Warsaw and tried to reach the spot under the bridge but saw a soldier standing guard there. He paced back and forth on the bridge, waiting for the soldier to leave. Eventually the soldier became aware of the man pacing on the bridge. He went to Ayzik and asked what he wanted. Ayzik told him the truth. He told him that he had dreamed of a treasure under the bridge. The soldier laughed and told Ayzik to go home. "Just because I dreamed about a treasure in the oven at the home of Ayzik, the son of Reb Yekl, in Cracow doesn't mean I have to go there." Ayzik returned home, where he took apart his oven and found a great treasure that made him a very rich man.[33]

Contemporary culture needs to be re-storied, made aware of archetypes at work in human psyches and freed from the narrow confines of rationalism and literalism that destroy the soul. Humans need to learn to live in and through stories, valuing the instinctive patterns of the unconscious, which unite contemporary people to the history of the human race and help people make sense of the world they experience.

Jungian psychology suggests a significant role for storytelling in religious education.[34] As participants in the task of soul making, religious educators need to know the great myths and the archetypal patterns embodied in them. They, in turn, may then make learners aware

---

[31]Ibid., p. 93.

[32]Ibid.

[33]Beatrice Silverman Weinreich, ed., *Yiddish Folktales*, trans. Leonard Wolf (New York: Schocken, 1988), p. 23.

[34]See James Michael Lee's chapter on the significance of the unconscious content of religious instruction in *The Content of Religious Instruction* (Birmingham, Ala.: Religious Education Press, 1985), pp. 475–607.

of these archetypes at work in their own psyches. Furthermore, religious educators may use their understandings of archetype and myth to examine the archetypal patterns present in biblical stories. For many in our time, demythologizing of Scripture by higher criticism on one hand or fundamentalist literalism on the other have stripped away the mythic quality of biblical stories, reducing them to time and culture bound narratives with little historical or mythical value or to mere factual accounts, which, in fact, become impossible to reconcile or harmonize.

Jung warned that often religion itself becomes a substitute for religious experience.[35] He argued that this substitution replaces immediate experience with suitable symbols invested in a solidly organized dogma and ritual, which are maintained by authority in the Catholic Church and insistence on faith and the evangelical message in Protestant churches. The effect, he explained, is to shield people from immediate religious experience. For Jung, immediate religious experience is contextualized within larger patterns that are part of the living process of the unconscious. These larger patterns, such as repentance, sacrifice, and redemption, are not the inventions of the church but represent stories and psychical phenomena from all over the world and across the ages. For Jung, they are like dreams, reflecting the activity of the unconscious.[36]

Religious education has an important role to play in remythologizing Scripture. Exploration of the mythic quality of biblical stories can provide a framework for learners to understand the same patterns at work in their own lives. In this way, Scripture can become a dynamic component of the religious education process, connecting with both the immediate life of the learner and the rich heritage of the entire past of the human race.

Jerome Bruner and Narrative Thinking

The psychological research of cognitive psychologist Jerome Bruner shifts the focus on narrative from an emphasis on experience and affect to emphasis on cognition, with narrative as a particular mode of

---

[35]For more on Jung and religious experience, see Fredrica R. Halligan, "Jungian Theory and Religious Experience," in *Handbook of Religious Experience*, ed. Ralph W. Hood Jr. (Birmingham, Ala.: Religious Education Press, 1995), pp. 231–253.

[36]Carl G. Jung, *Psychology and Religion* (New Haven: Yale University Press, 1933), pp. 52–57.

thought. Bruner has suggested that cognition is characterized by two modes of thought, which he has labeled propositional thinking and narrative thinking.[37] Propositional thinking is logical, analytical, and abstract. Narrative thinking, in contrast, is imaginative, intuitive, and concrete. Although propositional thinking aims at the construction of theoretical interpretations and abstract paradigms, narrative thinking aims at description of concrete actions in particular times and places as paradigmatic experiences. Related to this are two thinking factors identified by J. P. Guilford.[38] According to Guilford, intellectual production is the generation of new information from known information. Convergent thinking pertains to new information determined by known information. Divergent thinking, on the other hand, pertains to new information determined minimally by known information. Whereas convergent thinking calls for the "right" answer, divergent thinking demands, in Jerome Bruner's terms, that learners go "beyond the information given."[39] As Guilford argues, educators have often emphasized convergent thinking and "right" answers at the expense of divergent thinking and creative answers.[40] In religious instruction, stories, rather than propositions, may function as modes of divergent thinking, propelling learners toward creative thought and new ways of behavior.[41]

In contrast to propositions, which are publicly available and empirically verifiable, stories focus on people and on the causes of their actions—their intentions, goals, and subjective experiences.[42] Bruner suggests that people carry within themselves their own cast of characters taking part in an internal drama. He adds that life can be described

---

[37]See Jerome Bruner, *Actual Minds, Possible Worlds* (Cambridge, Mass.: Harvard University Press, 1986).

[38]Joy P. Guilford, *The Nature of Human Intelligence* (New York: McGraw-Hill, 1967).

[39]Jerome Bruner, *Beyond the Information Given: Studies in the Psychology of Knowing*, ed. Jeremy M. Anglin (New York: Norton, 1973).

[40]Joy P. Guilford, "Creativity: Its Measurement and Development" (paper presented to educators of Sacramento County, California, January 20, 1959), p. 24, quoted in Jacob W. Getzels, "Creative Thinking, Problem-solving, and Instruction," *Theories of Learning and Instruction*, ed. Ernest R. Hilgard (Chicago: University of Chicago Press, 1964, p. 248.

[41]Lee, *Content of Religious Instruction*, pp. 176–177.

[42]Paul C. Vitz, "The Use of Stories in Moral Development: New Psychological Reasons for an Old Education Method," *American Psychologist* 45 (June 1990): 710.

as a script that is constantly being rewritten and which guides the unfolding internal drama. He says that the internal cast is a way of grouping internal demands; myths are the idealized models of these cast members.[43] Bruner has also observed that when people encounter an exception to the ordinary, they almost always explain it with a story. The story is designed to give the exceptional behavior meaning in a manner that implicates both an intentional state on the part of the protagonist and some element of the culture.[44]

Bruner cites the work of Albert Michotte, who constructed an experimental apparatus that allows an observer to view colored rectangles in motion to demonstrate that viewers perceptually experience causality and, very likely, intentionality in the movements.[45] Of particular interest to Michotte were the links between perceptual displays and the semantic content of observers' responses. For Michotte, the inference of causality in the subjects' responses provided a clue to the subjective organization of causality.[46]

Michotte's experiment suggests a narrative compatibility in psychic structure. Built into the psyche is a tendency to imbue the movements of inanimate objects with meaning, to suggest that one action caused another and that the first action occurred with intention. In other words, every person has a natural, innate tendency to tell stories.[47]

Bruner suggests four reasons why intentionality is important in narratively framed explanations of the world. First, people do believe that the course of events is not independent of human wishes, beliefs, and feelings, that their acts and points of view do change reality. Second, stories preserve "mattering," whereas convergent descriptions do not; that is, stories affirm that experiences matter, have consequences, and have significance. Third, stories maintain discourse at the level of the

---

[43]Jerome Bruner, *On Knowing: Essays for the Left Hand* (Cambridge: Belknap, 1979), pp. 28– 29.

[44]Jerome Bruner, "Culture and Human Development: A New Look," *Human Development* 33 (November-December 1990): 347.

[45]Albert Michotte, *The Perception of Causality*, trans. T. R. Miles (New York: Basic, 1963).

[46]Georges Thines, "The Experimental Phenomenology of Albert Michotte," in *Michotte's Experimental Phenomenology of Perception*, ed. Georges Thines, Alan Costall, and George Butterworth (Hillsdale, N.J.: Erlbaum, 1991), p. 16.

[47]For a related discussion on narrative epistemology as a fusion of image and language, see Kristie S. Fleckenstein, "Images, Words, and Narrative Epistemology," *College English* 58 (December 1996): 914–933.

particular and the personal; they create concrete paradigms of public experience. Finally, stories, unlike logic, are not stopped dead by contradiction. In fact, stories demand ambiguity and clashes of human experience and perception.[48]

Narrative knowing allows people to make sense out of their experiences. People's lives may even be interpreted as narratives, and those narratives can function as organizing principles for people's actions.[49] A self-narrative can be both a self-constructed story of one's life or an almost literal acting out of life in accordance with a narrative model.[50] This sort of narrative thinking has both cognitive and social ramifications. Stories influence what learners believe and can affect how they may act in the future. New stories are incorporated into the cognitive structures that represent the knowledge and experience of the storyteller or the learner. As stories are incorporated, they can alter the content and organization of a learner's world knowledge and beliefs. And, since prior knowledge is actively used in creating stories, each new story enriches the cognitive resources available for future acts of narrative thought.[51] Narrative thinking thus provides an enriched way for learners to organize their experiences—thoughts, memories, perceptions, and actions—in meaningful ways that allow them to make sense of the world.

Stories, then, have an important role to play in the cognitive domain of religious instruction. Stories can help learners store, retain, and recall information. More importantly, however, stories can help learners move beyond information to new ideas and new plans for behavior. And finally, stories can help learners make meaning of their lives by making sense of their experiences.

Daniel Aleshire was one of my seminary professors. When I started seminary, his daughter, Jenny was a preschooler. Dan often used what we called "Jenny stories" as teaching devices in a behavioral foundations of religious education course. During the section of the course

---

[48]Bruner, "Culture and Human Development," pp. 349–350.

[49]Theodore R. Sarbin, "The Narrative as a Root Metaphor for Psychology," in *Narrative Psychology: The Storied Nature of Human Conduct*, ed. Theodore R. Sarbin (New York: Praeger Special Studies, 1986), p. 9.

[50]Vitz, "Uses of Stories in Moral Development," p. 711.

[51]John A. Robinson and Linda Hawpe, "Narrative Thinking as a Heuristic Process," in *Narrative Psychology: The Storied Nature of Human Conduct*, ed. Theodore R. Sarbin (New York: Praeger Special Studies, 1986), p. 116.

on developmental psychology, he would often tell one or another Jenny story to illustrate a point of developmental theory. For example, when discussing the concrete ways in which children think, Dan told the following story. He had planned a party at his house for the students enrolled in one of his doctoral seminars. He decided to provide party favors, and so he took Jenny with him to a Christian bookstore to pick up trinkets. He was laughing as he picked out pencils engraved with Bible verses and bookmarks with pictures of Bible stories. Finally, Jenny turned to him and asked, "Daddy, why are these funny?"

More significantly, Dan would often tell stories that embodied truth in such a way that we students experienced an "aha" moment, a moment in which our perceptions or feelings or understandings shifted in important and lasting ways. Later, after Dan's son was born, he added Jonathan stories to his repertoire. One Sunday morning, as Dan's family was gathering in the car, he asked Jonathan, then two and a half years old, where they were going. "Church!" Jonathan shouted. "What do you learn at church?" Dan asked. Jonathan replied, "Jesus loves me this I know."

An Epistemology of Difference

A recent trend arising within many different schools of psychological thought provides another significant perspective on storytelling as a means of expressing, understanding and valuing difference.[52] Influenced particularly by postmodernism and feminism, various schools of psychology are paying attention to and contributing new ideas to epistemologies of difference. From a wide variety of perspectives, many current thinkers in psychology have begun to critique the foundational assumptions of psychology itself in order to create room for difference in psychological theories.

A great deal of what psychologists claim to know is based on generalizations resulting from positivist research, usually done with men.[53] Hence, for example, one branch of psychology offers stage

---

[52]For an excellent collection of essays on stories, difference, oppression, and liberation, see George C. Rosenwald and Richard L. Ochberg, eds., *Storied Lives: The Cultural Politics of Self- Understanding* (New Haven: Yale University Press, 1992).

[53]See Naomi Weisstein, "Psychology Constructs the Female, or The Fantasy Life of the Male Psychologist," *Roles Women Play: Readings Toward Women's Liberation*, ed. Michele H. Garsko (Belmont, Calif.: 1971, pp. 68–83; and Carol Gilligan, *In a Different Voice: Psychological Theory and Women's Development* (Cambridge: Harvard University Press, 1982).

theories of human development. Often such theories assume the existence of a stable, coherent self and reason as the means by which to examine human existence and discover "truth."[54] The difficulty, however, is that theoretical generalizations cannot account for the psyche or experiences of any given individual. Each individual is a construction, not only of epigenetic wiring but also, if not more so, of particular experiences experienced and interpreted within a particular culture.[55]

These differences, which are obscured in stages and categories, are made manifest in stories. Stories offer a representation of the complexities of an individual psyche within a specific cultural context. Stories complicate and destabilize fixed notions of truth by appealing to the particular rather than the universal, to the intuitive rather than the analytic, to relationship rather than isolation. Stories help learners see that knowledge and truth are constructs[56] rather than givens and that in telling stories learners are engaged in the construction of knowledge.[57] In this way, stories underline the agency of all learners as knowers in the educational process.[58]

---

[54]Jane Flax, "Postmodernism and Gender Relations in Feminist Theory," *Signs* 12 (Summer 1987): 624.

[55]Ellyn Kaschack, *Engendered Lives: A New Psychology of Women's Experience* (New York: Basic, 1992), pp. 29–30.

[56]James Michael Lee defines a construct as "a concept which has the added meaning of having been deliberately invented or consciously adopted for a particular purpose. This purpose is enhanced usefulness. The reason a construct is 'constructed' is functional, namely, to make a concept more useful. Because a construct is functional, it helps us to analyze a set of particulars more carefully, to discover hitherto unknown but fruitful relationships among various kinds of particulars, and to generate new particulars and constructs." Lee goes on to explain faith as a construct. As a construct, faith can enrich and be enriched by other constructs, such as grace, hope, redemption, and the like. "Growth in Faith through Religious Instruction," in *Handbook of Faith*, ed. James Michael Lee (Birmingham, Ala.: Religious Education Press, 199), pp. 271–272. Recognizing faith or knowledge as a construct creates openness for diversity and dialogue. Rather than accept faith or knowledge as objectively defined, universally valid and agreed upon concepts, a constructionist position allows room for the agency of the knower in what is known or the faithful in the faith that is practiced. One of the advantages of such a position is its valuing of diverse perspectives and experiences.

[57]For more on the social construction of knowledge, see Mary Field Belenky et al., *Women's Ways of Knowing: The Development of Self, Voice, and Mind* (New York: Basic, 1986).

[58]Sandra Harding, "Introduction: Is There a Feminist Method?" in *Feminism and Methodology*, ed. Sandra Harding (Bloomington: Indiana University Press, 1987), p. 3.

Stories are also powerful tools in the construction of identity. Gender, race, ethnicity, and sexual orientation are socially constituted identities, constructed partially by individuals' appropriations of stories and representations of personal experiences in story form. But whatever meanings are constructed from experiences are not outside culture, which is itself unstable, plural, and contradictory.[59] This suggests that constructed meanings, as well as cultures and identities, are not fixed and unchanging. Rather, they are more like kaleidoscopes, constantly shifting and creating new patterns. Stories, then, provide an important means for reflecting the complex, contradictory, and changing identities of human beings. Perhaps better than any other formulation, stories reflect the particularities of difference and call into question fixed notions of knowledge or truth.

This attribute of stories is particularly valuable for religious educators as they attempt to create learning situations that help learners value all people and love their neighbors as themselves. Several years ago, I took a group of conservative college students to the Metropolitan Community Church of San Francisco, a predominantly gay and lesbian congregation. Most of the twenty students who attended the service went into the church with a great deal of discomfort and with rather strong convictions about the sinfulness of most of the congregants. That evening a young, gay, African-American minister preached, telling his story as a gay Christian within the context of Paul's defenses of freedom in the Christian Testament. For the first time, many of these students were able to question the interpretations of homosexuality they had been taught all of their lives. Suddenly, their propositions did not square with their experiences of these gay Christians and their experience of this young preacher's story. His story invited them to see not just the issue but also his life from another standpoint. Most left the service that night with a new openness to gay and lesbian Christians and to all gay and lesbian people.

Religious educators should be attentive to the variety of stories used in religious instruction. The more stories, the more standpoints. The more standpoints, the truer to the complexities of human experience. Religious educators should also encourage learners to tell their

---

[59]Catherine Belsey and Jane Moore, "Introduction: The Story So Far," in *The Feminist Reader: Essays in Gender and the Politics of Literary Criticism,* ed. Catherine Belsey and Jane Moore (New York: Blackwell, 1989), p. 10.

own stories. As learners tell their stories, they may feel their standpoints valued and validated, and they will contribute to the community
wisdom created by the group. These opportunities can play an important role in helping learners construct their own voices and develop
their own identities by allowing their stories to be heard.

COMMUNITY, MEANING, AND IDENTITY

The themes of community, meaning, and identity constitute major
psychological understandings of the storied psyche. From a variety of
psychological perspectives, stories seem significant in making meaning of one's life. Stories give cohesion to the random experiences of
life and bind them together in ways that are meaningful to the individual.[60] The patterns of an individual's narrative constructions give
shape to the emerging identity of the individual in the context of the
patterns of narrative received by the individual from her community.
Reciprocally, the narratives constructed by the individual continue to
contribute to the shape of the ongoing story of the community of
which he is a part. Understanding the roles of community, meaning,
and identity in the structure and function of the psyche is an important
task for religious educators in using stories in religious instruction.

Stories and Community

All people áre born into communities whose narratives influence their
experiences, feelings, understandings, and constructions of self.[61] In
turn, people add their narratives to their community's ongoing story,
thus reshaping and redefining the community itself. On one level, people participate in archetypal patterns of human experience; at another
level, individuals' experiences and expressions of these archetypes is
influenced by the specific community of which they are a part. For example, primitive and modern societies have numerous ways of recognizing a person's emergence from childhood into adulthood. This experience of initiation both provides a meaningful transition from
childhood into adulthood and assimilates the individual into the life of

---

[60]Theodore R. Sarbin, "Steps to the Narratory Principle: An Autobiographical
Essay," *Life and Story: Autobiographies for a Narrative Psychology*, ed. D. John Lee
(Westport, Conn.: Praeger, 1994), p. 8.

[61]Howard, "Culture Tales," pp. 190–191.

the community. The form this experience takes, however, varies greatly from culture to culture.

Jung claims that each person experiences a feeling of wholeness, a complete sense of the self (the totality of the psyche). As individuals mature, their individualized ego consciousness emerges from the self.[62] Yet the emergence of the individual ego, the center of the field of consciousness,[63] comes at the cost of severe injury to the original sense of wholeness. Thus, the ego must continually return to reestablish its relation to the self in order to maintain psychic health. In other words, with the break from childhood comes injury to the parent archetype, which must be healed through the process of assimilation into the community.[64]

Initiation rituals provide examples of how the injured original parent archetype is healed as the individual is assimilated into the life of the community. The group becomes a kind of second parent to which the young are symbolically sacrificed, only to reemerge into a new life.[65] When the original parent archetype is overcome in the process of ego differentiation, the individual experiences alienation from the powers of the unconscious. Initiation rites address this problem by taking the individual back to the deepest level of the ego-self identity in which a symbolic death is experienced as the individual's identity is temporarily dissolved in the collective unconscious. From this state, the individual is ceremonially rescued by the rite of new birth. In this act, the individual ego is assimilated into the larger group.[66] This ritual of death and rebirth provides a meaningful rite of passage from one stage of life to another.

Among the Ndembu people of Zambia, the girls' puberty ritual, *Nkang'a*, occurs when a young girl begins to experience breast development. In this ritual, a young girl lies motionless at the foot of a mudyi tree for about eight hours covered with a blanket while other women dance around her. The site is known as the "dying place"

---

[62]See Carl G. Jung, "The Relations between the Ego and the Unconscious," in *The Portable Jung,* trans. R. F. C. Hull, ed. Joseph Campbell (New York: Penguin, 1971), pp. 70–138.

[63]Carl G. Jung, "Aion: Phenomenology of the Self," in *The Portable Jung,* trans. R. F. C. Hull, ed. Joseph Campbell (New York: Penguin, 1971), p. 139.

[64]Henderson, "Ancient Myths and Modern Man," p. 120.

[65]Ibid., p. 121.

[66]Ibid., p. 123.

because there she leaves childhood and enters into womanhood. She lies on her side in a position representing both birth and death; in Ndembu culture, this position is both the fetal position and the position in which corpses are buried. The girl's mother cannot be a part of the early stages of the ritual. In her stead are the village women who are taking the girl into their ranks away from the mother. Later, the girl will be received again by her mother, not as a child but as a member of the village women.[67]

Beyond the archetypal patterns that are given various expressions in diverse communities, communities amass their own collection of stories which are derived from the community's historical sense of itself. These stories emerge from the common experience of the historical community.[68] These stories serve a socializing function and have a significant impact on the lives of persons who internalize them in their own personal narratives. These communal narratives also function to sustain the community itself by preserving the culture of the community and maintaining its values.

Story making within a community is a collaborative process. Thus, stories must be tested out: "The interpretation embodied in a story must be persuasive, for if it is not the story fails and the storymaker must either forsake his views or alter them to accommodate the views of others."[69] The process of collaborative story making leads to a "consensually validated interpretation and account of some event. Thus, narrative transactions are a primary procedure for producing mutual understanding and social cohesion."[70] Individual and community narratives become woven into a whole that is mutually meaningful and sustaining for both individual and community. The interaction of life experiences and community narratives tends to create the context for the construction of meaning and the development of identity.

Religious instruction provides an excellent opportunity for creating, exploring, and sustaining individual identity within community. The

---

[67]For a more detailed description of *Nkang'a*, see V. W. Turner, *The Drums of Affliction: A Study of Religious Processes among the Ndembu of Zambia* (Oxford: Oxford University Press, 1968), pp. 198–268.

[68]Julian Rappaport and Ronald Simpkins, "Healing and Empowering through Community Narrative," *Prevention in Human Services* 10 (1991): 39.

[69]Robinson and Hawpe, "Narrative Thinking as a Heuristic Process," p. 117.

[70]Ibid.

Christian story and the church's many rituals may function as archetypes that initiate and bind individuals into the Christian community.[71] At the core of the Christian story is the archetypal death and resurrection of Jesus, into which all Christians are invited to participate. The Gospels and Epistles are replete with images of rebirth and resurrection. By embracing these stories and participating in such rituals as baptism and communion, the individual is assimilated into the larger Christian community. Religious instruction can create an environment rich with the stories, symbols, and rituals of the Christian story and can offer opportunities for learners to participate in these stories and to bring their own personal stories into dialogue with these archetypal stories. For example, a religious educator may wish to schedule a learning session for adult learners around a baptism in the church. The religious educator may offer some background on the history and meaning of baptism and may then invite adults to share the stories of their own baptisms.

Religious instruction is also a significant context in which learners may learn the community's own collection of stories and participate in the community's story making. As a little girl in Shorter Avenue Baptist Church in Rome, Georgia, I learned not only the biblical stories that shape the identity of the larger Christian community, but I also learned the stories of Lottie Moon, Annie Armstrong, Ann and Adoniram Judson—people who had significant roles in shaping Baptist identity. Later, as a seminary student, I learned the stories of Martha Stearns Marshall, an early American Baptist preacher, and then of the women of Woman's Missionary Union, who, during the antilynching movement of the 1930s, became a powerful force against the racist murder of black men in the South. These stories, and many others, played an important role in defining the community with which I identified and suggesting the shape of the identity I was constructing as a Southern Baptist woman preparing to enter full-time ministry.

This process of shaping individual identity within the community continues in the community's story making, and religious instruction can offer one context for this story making to happen. Within religious instruction, learners can struggle with the meaning of the lives of

---

[71]Robert L. Browning and Roy A. Reed, *The Sacraments in Religious Education and Liturgy* (Birmingham, Ala.: Religious Education Press, 1985), p. 77.

learners, with the lives of world leaders, with current events. How does the church tell the story of Martin Luther King Jr. or the civil rights movement? How does the church recount the story of the Holocaust, in which the church was both complicit and resistant? How does the church tell the stories of the complex social issues of the contemporary world? Where do individuals' stories fit within the church's grappling with these issues?

For example, when I was in seminary, I was a member of Shalom Baptist Church in Louisville, Kentucky. One of the major emphases of this church was racial reconciliation. On Holocaust Remembrance Sunday, I planned a religious instruction activity around the experiences both of victims of the Holocaust and the members of the church. Learners participated in an activity in which they were accorded privilege based on skin color. African-American learners were allowed to speak and move freely throughout the learning space and to eat the donuts I had brought that morning. White learners were confined to one area of the learning space, could not speak without the permission of an African-American learner, and could not have a donut unless given one by an African-American learner. After about fifteen minutes of this activity, the group came together and debriefed the experience. After learners talked about their feelings about the experience, I introduced stories of the Holocaust and then invited learners to tell stories of their own personal experiences of discrimination. We then talked about biblical views on discrimination and privilege and concluded with discussion of ways we could work to end discrimination.

In religious instruction, learners can engage in a number of important story processes. They can learn of archetypal patterns and how to identify these patterns operative in their own lives. They can participate in the healing process of being brought into the community through participation in the church's stories. They can learn the stories of the church's tradition and add their own stories to the community's historical sense of itself. They can participate in the ongoing story making of the community. In so doing, they find places to construct meaning of their own experiences and to continue to fashion their identities within the community context.

Stories and Meaning

The tendency of human beings to tell stories suggests a need to make sense of the events of their lives, to place them in a context that suggests meaning beyond mere reporting of random experiences. Stories are a way humans impose structure on the flow of experience.[72] Narratives help people understand human actions and imbue them with meaning. Donald Polkinghorne suggests that narrative is a way people give meaning to their experience of temporality and personal actions. Narrative meaning gives form to the understanding of a purpose to life and joins everyday actions and events into episodic units. It provides a framework for understanding past events and planning future actions and is a primary means by which human existence is rendered meaningful.[73]

From the perspective of depth psychology, Jung suggests that not only do humans construct meaning of experiences through narratives but also that myths give meaning to existence. He argues that humans need ideas and convictions that give meaning to life and enable them to find a place for themselves in the universe. For example, he cites the Pueblo Indians, who believe they are the children of Father Sun. "This belief endows their life with a perspective (and a goal) that goes far beyond their limited existence. It gives them ample space for the unfolding of personality and permits them a full life as complete persons."[74] They experience more satisfaction in life than do people in European culture who know they are and will remain underdogs with no inner meaning to life.[75] Without a sense of wider meaning to their existence, Jung contends, people are lost and miserable.[76]

Jung points to Jesus and Paul as examples of persons who were seized by myths that lifted them out of their narrow lives and made them more than mere craftspeople. Religious instruction can provide a context in which learners experience the sacred and encounter the myths that provide a meaningful framework that can help lift them out of the confines of their narrow lives and compel them to act in ways congruous with the larger story within which they create meaning. Millard Fuller, founder of Habitat for Humanity, found in the Gospel stories a framework for understanding wealth and poverty in such a way

---

[72]Sarbin, "The Narrative as Root Metaphor for Psychology," p. 9.

[73]Donald Polkinghorne, *Narrative Knowing and the Human Sciences* (Albany, N.Y.: State University of New York Press, 1988), p. 11.

[74]Jung, "Approaching the Unconscious," p. 76.

[75]Ibid.

[76]Ibid.

that he took his considerable fortune and began a program that builds houses for economically disadvantaged people throughout the world.

The stories people live, together with the stories they hear, give meaning to their existence and provide a foundation for identity. The fragments of experience and the tales of individuals' communities become linked in meanings that are integral to the shape of personal identity. This identity is a personal myth that gives cohesion to experiences and provides an organizing principle for self-creation.

Stories and Identity

Identity development begins in the personal experiences that give rise to persons' stories. Personal experiences are linked together and given meaning in the context of a particular community. As these experiences are linked, people construct a personal myth, an identity that embodies their personal histories and includes their biological histories, which reach back to the beginnings of life and take in the larger histories of their communities and the human race itself.[77]

From a Jungian perspective, the process of therapy, for example, involves "restorying" the psyche, which has not been able to construct its own healthy narratives and hence its own healthy identity. James Hillman writes, "Perhaps our age has gone into analysis not to be loved or get cured, or even to Know Thyself. Perhaps we go to be given a case history, to be told into a soul story and given a plot to live by."[78]

Self-constructive narrative begins in memory. Experiences are recalled, from which learners sort out the ones that are laden with emotion and recalled ritually. These experiences become ingested as they are told, retold, and edited, moving from outer history to inner history to soul. The plot of an ingested story is mythic; it connects the individual to the larger experiences of the human race. This process that turns event into soul is a religious process requiring faith and involving powers and lives beyond the ego's grasp.[79]

---

[77]James P. Carse, "Exploring Your Personal Myth," in *Sacred Stories: A Celebration of the Power of Stories to Transform and Heal*, ed. Charles Simpkinson and Anne Simpksinson (San Francisco: HarperSanFrancisco, 1993), pp. 224–232.

[78]James Hillman, *Healing Fiction* (Barrytown, N.Y.: Station Hill, 1983), p. 49.

[79]James Hillman, *Insearch: Psychology and Religion* (London: Hodder and Stoughton, 1967).

The storied psyche contains the scripts or the metanarratives that influence human lives.[80] These scripts involve the narratives of people's own experiences as well as the stories of others that give shape to their narratives. These scripts are the guiding myths of people's lives, their identities.[81] As stories are ingested, they form the myths that people come to embody in their ways of being in the world. They may be unaware of their myths or even of the many episodes that have formed them. "In other words, we live out of curious scripts according to stories that even we ourselves may hide so well from ourselves that we need help identifying the essence or troublesome heart of the story, or myth, that guides our unhappiness or incompetencies."[82] In fact, people are often not only ignorant of their own guiding myths but also of the guiding myths of their culture. For religious instruction, this lack of awareness implies the need for an abundance of stories. Religious instruction can provide opportunities for learners to explore their personal myths and to come to know the myths of their culture. This transformation of consciousness of the individual within a community setting can be a healing or "soul making" process as personal stories are identified, recovered, and deepened in interaction with the great archetypal stories.[83]

Anthropologist Mary Catherine Bateson calls this process of identity development "composing a life."[84] For Bateson, composing a life involves weaving a life history that can accommodate discontinuous and conflicting accounts of self while providing threads of continuity. Identity is not a single, consistent narrative, but a collection of multiple versions of one's life story. The version one tells depends on context. At particular times, one interpretation of a life event may be more

---

[80]George S. Howard, "The Stories We Live By: Confessions by a Member of the Species *Homo Fabulans (Man the Storyteller)*, in *Life and Story, Autobiographies for a Narrative Psychology*, ed. D. John Lee (Westport, Conn.: Praeger, 1994), p. 247.

[81]Sam Keen, "Our Mythic Stories," *Sacred Stories: A Celebration of the Power of Stories to Transform and Heal*, ed. Charles Simpkinson and Anne Simpkinson (San Francisco: HarperSanFrancisco, 1993), p. 33.

[82]Sarah Dubin-Vaughn, "Stories from World Mythology and the Growth of Individual Consciousness," *The Humanistic Psychologist* 18 (Summer 1990): 189.

[83]Ibid., pp. 191–192.

[84]Mary Catherine Bateson, "Composing a Life," in *Sacred Stories: A Celebration of the Power of Stories to Transform and Heal*, ed. Charles Simpkinson and Anne Simpkinson (San Francisco: HarperSanFrancisco, 1993), p. 39.

psychologically appropriate or more important. At another time, the same event may be interpreted in another way. According to Bateson, the availability of multiple interpretations provides great advantages in developing identity and in communicating lives as they are actually lived. Multiple versions of a life history allow both the expression of the discontinuities of human experience and the recognition of continuity within those discontinuities. In other words, stories provide ways of organizing experiences, interpreting events, and creating meaning while maintaining a sense of continuity.[85]

Recently a colleague and I did a series of interviews with women doctoral graduates of a seminary that had been embroiled in a controversy over fundamentalism during their time there. One of the key issues of the debate was the role of women in ministry. As these women told us their stories five to fifteen years after their graduation, many acknowledged that their version of the story now is different than their version of the story would have been five years ago or during their time at seminary. That controversy resulted in most of these women's leaving the denomination; some have even left the church. During the interviews, they all talked about their sense of calling to ministry before going to seminary. Despite the difficulties and discontinuities created by the controversy, they still see themselves in terms of that calling, though for most the shape of their acting on that calling changed as a result of the controversy. Interestingly, even those who left the church are still in some form of a helping profession.

CONCLUSION

Stories are essential in the development of the human psyche. In fact, stories may characterize the structure and formation of the psyche. Humans experience life narratively and construct narratives of their experiences. The structure of sequences of lived action seems to be quite similar to the structure of a traditional narrative plot.[86] Because people live in time, they experience events as a sequence of

---

[85]Adital Tiorsh Ben-Ari, "It's the Telling That Makes the Difference," *Interpreting Experience: The Narrative Study of Lives*, ed. Ruthellen Josselson and Amia Lieblich (Thousand Oaks, Cal.: Sage, 1995), 3:155.

[86]Richard L. Ochberg, "Life Stories and Storied Lives," in *Exploring Identity and Gender: The Narrative Study of Lives*, ed. Amia Lieblich and Ruthellen Josselson (Thousand Oaks, Calif.: Sage, 1994), 2:116.

actions. Stories, then, become a way of encoding time in human existence. In the process of narrative construction, events are narrated relative to time and are imbued with meaning. As particular stories are ingested, they become part of people's personal myth. This process occurs within the context of community—including the particular cultural community of the individual, the wider community of the human race, and even the prehistoric forms of life to which humans are related.

The development of rich and deep personal stories that make contact with the world stories of human existence is essential for the healthy growth of the psyche, and, as Hillman suggests, this process may in itself be religious—the making of the soul. This suggests profound importance for storytelling in religious education. As those concerned with the religious life of humanity, religious educators should be storytellers and story facilitators. As religious educators help deepen learners' stories, they will participate in a cocreative process of soul making, thus enabling persons to live richer, more meaningful lives in the world.

6

Storytelling as an Educational Form

I became a Hasid because in the town where I lived there was an old man who told stories about the great masters. He told what he knew and I heard what I needed.[1]

—Rabbi Menahem Mendel of Kotsk

During his one year as a school teacher on the South Carolina coastal island of Yamacraw, Pat Conroy attempted to use a number of innovative teaching approaches to engage his young and apathetic students in the learning process. His efforts were met by skepticism and even hostility from the older and more traditional teacher, Mrs. Brown: "We run this school here for education's sake. Give them seat work. Keep them busy. We're not here to have fun. We're here to educate. We got rules to follow."[2]

Mrs. Brown had the notion that education was not meant to be enjoyable. Enjoyable activities such as storytelling, acting, and dancing surely were meant for playtime and were not to be considered legitimate parts of the academic experience. Yet Pat Conroy's discovery was that these activities invited learners into the education experience. As he engaged their imaginations, he also elicited their interest and attention.

---

[1]Martin Buber, *Tales of the Hasidim*, (New York: Schoken, 1947), 2:270.
[2]Pat Conroy, *The Water Is Wide* (New York: Bantam, 1972), p. 102

114

Even now imaginative teaching procedures remain suspect in some places in both academe and religious education. Those who dichotomize content and method often believe content is sacrificed to technique when learner-centered, active procedures are used in an educational setting. This fear seems particularly prevalent in the college and university arena in which education is often seen as transmission of course content from professor to student. In the church, this fear becomes embodied in didactic transmission of theological propositions from religious educators to learners. As James Michael Lee has argued, however, content and procedure are not two separate components of religious education but are inextricably linked as what Lee terms substantive content and structural content.[3] The development of each is determined by educational goals. So, for example, transmissive techniques work well if the goal is simply the transfer of information from the teacher to the learner. Rarely, however, especially in religious education, should the acquisition of bald information be the primary goal. In religious education in particular, the goal is religious living. Religious living is not brought about by the acquisition of information but by engagement in religion.[4] Religious education, then, must structure the learning environment so that this engagement may happen. This means the substantive and structural contents must be selected in order to bring about the desired goal of religious living.

Storytelling can provide one means of achieving educational goals on a number of levels, including lifestyle. Storytelling organically unites substantive and structural content and can bring a holistic way of learning into the religious educational setting. Storytelling can bring together experiential, intuitive, imaginative knowing and rational, analytic knowing in ways that engage the whole being of the learner.

Rabbi Jacob Joseph was bitterly averse to the Hasidic way of life. One summer morning, a man whom no one knew came to town. He called to the first person to pass him by and began to tell a story to the stranger. The listener was so captivated that he could not break away. A second person passing caught a few words of the story, and so he stayed and listened. Soon a whole group of people were gathered

---

[3]James Michael Lee, *The Content of Religious Instruction*, (Birmingham, Ala.: Religious Education Press, 1985), pp. 106–107.
[4]Ibid., pp. 97–102.

around the storyteller. Among them was the man whose job it was to unlock the doors of the house of prayer each morning for the rav. When the rav arrived and found the doors locked, he flew into a rage and went to find the servant. Just then the servant arrived, having been signaled by the storyteller to go. When Rabbi Jacob Joseph demanded to know why the servant was late, he explained that a man was telling stories in the marketplace, and he had been captivated by the story.

"Bring him to me," the rav demanded, "and I'll have him beaten up."

In the meantime, the storyteller, the Baal Shem, had finished his story and had gone to the inn. The servant found him there and delivered the rav's message.

The Baal Shem followed him to the rav, who began to berate him, saying, "Who do you think you are to keep people from prayer!"

"Rabbi," the Baal Shem replied, "it does not become you to fly into a rage. Rather, let me tell you a story."

And so the Baal Shem told: "Once I drove in the country with three horses, a bay, a piebald, and a white horse. And not one of them could neigh. Then I met a peasant coming toward me, and he called, 'Slacken the reigns.' So I slackened the reigns, and all of the horses began to neigh."

The rav was overcome with emotion.

"The peasant gave good advice," said the Baal Shem. "Do you understand?"

"I understand," said the rabbi, and he burst into tears.[5]

In a number of Eastern cultures, storytelling has been essential educational practice, communicating the paradoxical understandings of the great teachers of these cultures. The Taoist sage taught through the use of parable, anecdote, and poetry, encouraging learners to live in harmony with the Tao, which itself is paradox that cannot be fully grasped by logical, analytical thinking.[6] The awakening in Zen Buddhism is achieved through the use of stories. The Zen story destroys

---

[5]Martin Buber, *Tales of the Hasidim: Early Masters* (New York: Schocken, 1947), pp. 56–57.

[6]For more information on Taoist stories, see Raymond Van Over, *Taoist Tales* (New York: Mentor, 1973). See also Lao-tzu, *Tao Te Ching*, trans. Stephen Mitchell (New York: Harper and Row, 1988); Lao-tzu, *The I Ching*, trans. Cary F. Baynes (Princeton, N.J.: Princeton University Press, 1977).

illusions and brings about an awareness of reality as it truly is.[7] Likewise, Sufi stories intend to lead the learner to mystical perception by calling ordinary understandings of reality into question. Storytelling is an important procedure in Sufi religious education, and Sufi stories are considered to be primarily teaching materials. The Sufi teacher tells stories in response to questions posed by learners. These stories illustrate the question in such a way that learners are better able to answer the question for themselves.[8]

Stories also hold a place of central importance among the Hasidim. In Hasidic tradition, the story is a transformative vehicle that transmits the light of God. The Hasidim consider storytelling the best procedure for introducing their beliefs and practices to the children of the community. Many Hasidic stories date to the time of the Rabbi Baal Shem Tov (c. 1700–1760 C.E.), the founder of the Hasidim, and many of these stories have him as their central character.[9]

Once the Baal Shem came to a certain town and asked the people who read the prayers there. They told him that this was done by the rav of the town. "And what is his manner of praying?" the Baal Shem asked.

"On the Day of Atonement," they replied, "he recites all the confessions of sin in the most cheerful tones."

The Baal Shem sent for the rav and asked him the reason for his curious manner of praying on such a solemn day. The rav explained, "The least among the servants of the king, whose task it is to sweep the forecourt free of dirt, sings a merry song as he works, for what he does, he does to gladden the king."

The Baal Shem responded, "May my lot be with yours."[10]

Storytelling has also been an important part of Western educational tradition. Both Plato and Aristotle advocated the use of stories in the

---

[7]John Daido Loori, "The Zen Koan: Lancet of Self-Inquiry," in *Sacred Stories: A Celebration of the Power of Stories to Transform and Heal*, ed. Charles Simpkinson and Anne Simpkinson (San Francisco: HarperSanFrancsico, 1993), pp. 192–207.

[8]Anne Pellowski, *The World of Storytelling*, rev. ed. (New York: Wilson, 1990), p. 64. For more information on Sufi storytelling, see Idries Shah, *Learning How to Learn: Psychology and Spirituality in the Sufi Way* (London: Octagon, 1982).

[9]Ibid., p. 56. For more information on Hasidic storytelling, see Martin Buber and Jerome R. Mintz, *The Legends of the Hasidim: An Introduction to Hasidic Culture and Oral Tradition in the New World* (Chicago: University of Chicago Press, 1968).

[10]Buber, *Tales of the Hasidim*, p. 70.

educational process to provide models of virtue for children.[11] Quintillian suggested that learners paraphrase Aesop's *Fables* in order to express themselves simply.[12] In medieval society, stories were one means of socializing children into adulthood. Children heard the same stories as adults, from the *Iliad* and *Odyssey* to the Arthur legends to the *Canterbury Tales*. Because of the illiteracy of the masses, the early Church found many ways to tell its stories in nonwritten forms. Church architecture, stained-glass windows, paintings, and statuary have often been used by the church to tell its stories.[13] The vestments of the liturgical ministers, drama, and even the Mass itself have all been important means for conveying the church's stories. In fact, one of the most powerful ways in which the church has passed on its stories is through its hymnody.[14] For centuries, churchgoers, young and old alike, have learned biblical stories through the hymns they have sung in public worship.

Although interest in storytelling has waxed and waned among adults since the Middle Ages, it has consistently been a part of the education and entertainment of children. In the nineteenth century, Friedrich Froebel connected the hearing of stories to the development of the child, and, as his principles were incorporated into the kindergarten, storytelling found a permanent place there.[15] Froebel did not feel children heard enough stories, and he felt the stories they did hear were too moralistic and didactic. Rather, he preferred folktales as the means to develop the spiritual life of the child. For Froebel, growth occurred naturally and incrementally as the life of the child was

---

[11]Plato, *The Republic*(trans.. Benjamin Jowett) bk. 2; Aristotle, *Politics* (trans. Benjamin Jowett) 7.1336.

[12]Quintillian, *Institutio Oratoria* (James J. Murphy) 1.9.2.

[13]For more on church architecture, see Rudolf Schwartz, *The Church Incarnate: The Sacred Function of Christian Architecture*, trans. Cynthia Harris (Chicago: Henry Regnery, 1958) and Richard Krautheiemer, *Early Christian and Byzantine Architecture* (Baltimore: Penguin, 1965). For more on religious art, see Doug Adams and Diane Apostolos Cappadona, eds., *Art as Religious Studies* (New York: Crossroad, 1987); and Walter Lowrie, *Art in the Early Church* (New York: Pantheon, 1947).

[14]See Patrick Henry, "Singing the Faith Together: The Stories of God's Household," *The Christian Century*, May 21, 1997,: pp. 500–501.

[15]Friedrich Froebel, *The Education of Man* (New York: Appleton, 1896). See also James L. Hughes, *Froebel's Educational Laws for All Teachers* (New York: Appleton, 1897).

nurtured by the educational process, which included the hearing of folktales without any moralizing addendum. These stories, according to Froebel, had the power to refresh the mind, exercise the intellect, and test judgment and feeling without adult explanation or interpretation. Froebel's basic trust in the story itself came to characterize educators who emphasized storytelling in education.

In the twentieth century the efficacy of stories as an educational tool for adults found renewed recognition. An interesting story comes from the days shortly before the United States entered World War I. A number of relief efforts, such as the British War-Orphan Relief, the Fund for French Wounded, and the fund for the fatherless Children of France, were having difficulty raising money in many places in America. Often Americans did not see the problems as their responsibility. So a storytelling campaign was begun. Storytellers visited afternoon teas given by society women; they went to schools, churches, public libraries, city parks and told their stories of suffering. And wherever they visited, dollars were put into the relief funds.[16]

Storytelling's long history of educational effectiveness suggests its potential significance for the contemporary religious instruction setting. Stories have the power to effect change and to help bring about the desired goals of religious instruction. In Barbara Robinson's children's story, *The Best Christmas Pageant Ever*, the five Herdman children, the meanest in the neighborhood, come to church just before the holidays and get involved in the Christmas pageant.[17] The Herdmans had never heard the Christmas story before Imogene Herdman ends up as Mary, Ralph becomes Joseph, and Gladys is the Angel of the Lord. In dramatizing the Christmas story, with their own special touches (for example, when Imogene explains she would have slugged anyone who tried to hurt the baby and Ralph says the wise men were a bunch of dirty spies), the Herdmans experience the reality of Christmas, as do the other children in the pageant and the people in the audience who watch the spectacle. Stories are a powerful religious educational form, and their demonstrated effectiveness in the past certainly seems to point to the desirability of their continued use in the future.

---

[16]Katherine D. Cather, *Religious Education through Story-Telling* (New York: Abingdon, 1925), pp. 27–28.

[17]Barbara Robinson, *The Best Christmas Pageant Ever* (New York: Harper and Row, 1972).

THE VALUES OF STORYTELLING
IN EDUCATION

Stories teach much about reality. Myths and folktales provide frameworks for experiencing, understanding, and interpreting the world. Stories stimulate the imagination and encourage creativity. Even more specifically, stories play a role in a variety of educational tasks from language acquisition to critical thinking to lifestyle choices. In fact, research indicates that children who do not hear stories during their early years suffer a deprivation of mind and spirit.[18]

Contemporary goals of education reflect a movement away from passive memorization of compartmentalized content areas, which are often irrelevant to the learners' world, toward more active participation in self-directed and collaborative learning experiences which are connected to learners' daily lives. These goals reflect an awareness of the need for education to be connected to learners' lives and for content areas to be integrated in ways that reflect learners' experiences of the world. In current practice, these goals are greatly facilitated by self-directed learning projects and by cooperative and collaborative learning experiences, such as small group discussions or group projects.[19]

---

[18]Kathryn Farnsworth, "Storytelling in the Classroom—Not an Impossible Dream," *Language Arts* 58 (February 1981): 163.

[19]For more on self-directed learning, see Philip C. Candy, *Self-Direction for Lifelong Learning: A Comprehensive Guide to Theory and Practice* (San Francisco: Jossey-Bass, 1991); Jane Pilling- Cormick, "Transformative and Self-Directed Learning in Practice," *New Directions for Adult and Continuing Education* 74 (1997): 69; Rivka Glaubman, Hananyah Glaubman, and Lea Offir, "Effects of Self-Directed Learning, Story Comprehension, and Self-Questioning in Kindergarten," *The Journal of Educational Research* 90 (July–August 1997): 361. Irving H. Buchen, "Continuous Quality Improvement and Adult Education," *Adult Learning* 7 (September–October 1995): 11–12. For an application of self-directed learning, see Mark P. Silverman, "Self-Directed Learning: A Heretical Experiment in Teaching Physics," *American Journal of Physics* 63 (June 1995): 495–508; For more information on collaborative and cooperative learning, see Dennis M. Adams and Mary Hamm, *Cooperative Learning, Critical Thinking, and Collaboration across the Curriculum*, 2d ed. (Springfield, Ill.: Thomas, 1996); John R. Magney, "Working and Learning Together," *Techniques* 72 (September 1997): 57; Yiping Lou, et al, "Within-class Groupings: A Meta-analysis," *Review of Educational Research* 66 (Winter 1996): 423–458; Kimberly D. Williams, "Cooperative Learning: A New Direction," *Education* 117 (Fall 1996): 39–42; Michelle G. Zachlod, "Room to Grow," *Educational Leadership* 54 (September 1996): 50–53; Alexis J. Walker, "Cooperative Learning in the College Classroom," *Family Relations* 45 (July 1996): 327–35.

These educational procedures seek to develop acting, feeling, and thinking persons who are able to direct their own lives while working in cooperation with others to make contributions to the global community. Such a process may be greatly facilitated by storytelling.

Through its imaginative and ambiguous nature, story creates, affirms, and challenges reality, offering learners an impetus for growth. Learners engaged in stories participate in the development of valuing processes, attitudes, lifestyles, communication skills, imagination, critical thinking, appreciation of diversity, and integration. These basic skills are essential components of the self-directed learners the religious instruction process seeks to develop. In its own unique way, story invites persons to grow, even though they may be unaware of story's pervasive effects. For religious educators, storytelling is an important tool toward the achievement of myriad religious educational objectives.

STORYTELLING IN THE AFFECTIVE DOMAIN

Although much of religious education focuses on cognitive content, cognitive content alone has little power to effect Christian living. Knowledge about Christian living does not of necessity lead to Christian living. Effective religious education must take into account another, more powerful form of content, affective content. Storytelling can provide one teaching procedure to address affective content.[20]

Affective content is characterized by feeling.[21] Its forms include feelings, emotions, attitudes, values, and love.[22] The feeling dimension of religious education is particularly important since the goal of Christian living is better facilitated by experiencing and feeling the presence of God in one's life than by knowing about God. Because stories reflect direct experiences and create vicarious experiences, they can be a significant medium for evoking affective responses in religious education. Part of the power of stories is their ability to tap

---

[20]For more information on affective learning, see Daniel Goleman, *Emotional Intelligence: Why It Can Matter More Than IQ* (London: Bloomsbury, 1996); Peter Salovey, *Emotional Development and Emotional Intelligence: Education Implications* (New York: Basic, 1997).

[21]Lee, *Content of Religious Instruction*, p. 196.

[22]Ibid., p. 210.

into the feeling dimension of human experience. When this happens in the religious education context, it can facilitate movement toward the goals of religious education.

Feelings, Emotion, and Storytelling

Feelings are mild forms of emotion, simple experiences of pleasantness or unpleasantness associated with various phenomena in human lives.[23] Emotion is a much more complex experience, involving psychological, cognitive, and physiological attributes, making a concise definition impossible at this time. James Michael Lee suggests that emotions fall into three major groupings: "(1) a consciously experienced affect, such as a feeling of anger, joy, or grief; (2) an observed overt activity, such as terrified flight or friendly vocalizing; (3) a physiological behavior, such as marked activity in the autonomic nervous system and viscera, blushing, and so forth."[24] The expression of emotion may be involuntary, as in sweating or blushing, or voluntary, as in speaking or hitting. These voluntary expressions are learned and shaped through socialization as persons mature. This suggests that religious education should concern itself with the facilitation of mature and appropriate expressions of emotion. One way this process may be enhanced is through storytelling.

Stories evoke powerful emotions. When I saw a stage production of Marsha Norman's "'Night, Mother" at Actors Theatre in Louisville, I found myself in the grip of anxiety as the play moved toward its inevitable conclusion. I remember how my heart pounded, my palms sweated, and my jaw clenched as I waited for the gunshot offstage that signaled the protagonist's suicide, and I remember squelching the desire to shout out, "No! There has to be another way!" A few years later, I saw the film version, thinking that because I knew the ending the emotional impact would be lessened. I was wrong. Even though the different medium distanced me somewhat from the story, I still found myself hoping against hope that the protagonist would change her mind this time and not kill herself. This story of a woman's final encounter with her mother still haunts me. In it I experience my own anguish of failed dreams and seemingly endless despair; and yet in it I also struggle to find hope, to find the strength to hold on to something

---

[23]Ibid., p. 211.
[24]Ibid., pp. 212–213.

through the darkness. It is the same conflict I feel every time I see Willy Loman leave for his fatal drive. Because I have felt the despair and hopelessness of these characters, I am forced to confront my own despair and hopelessness and weight it against suicide on the one hand and the will to survive on the other. I recognize that for each of these stories to work they must end in suicide, but I still find myself coming away from the experience with each of them affirming life.

Stories can provide religious educators with one medium for the facilitation of emotional development and expression. On the one hand, because stories evoke powerful emotions, they can become a way to help people feel. Stories may allow people to feel emotions they have shut off from their own life experiences or they may evoke sympathetic responses toward persons or situations that were formerly objects of apathy or hostility. For example, a person who harbors racist attitudes may hear the story of Rosa Parks and be able to feel the injustice and indignity of discrimination. A person who has not developed a relationship with God may watch a Christmas pageant and be struck, like Imogene Herdman, with the wonder of God.

On the other hand, stories may also facilitate emotional expression. First, stories can provide models for appropriate emotional expression. Second, stories may be told as a means of emotional expression. A learner who may not be able to name or define an emotion may yet be able to tell a story. For example, an abused child may not be able to say, "This is what I'm feeling," but she may be able to say, "This is what happened to me" or to act out the story of the abuse with dolls or drawings. Third, storytelling experiences may provide debriefing times during which learners can talk about their emotional responses to the stories they have heard.

In itself, the emotional impact of stories is significant for religious education as it brings the important affective aspect of the self into play. At another level, the impact of emotions is important because of the influence the emotions have on attitudes and lifestyle. Religious educators should not use stories to manipulate learners' emotions, but they should be aware of the power of stories in the emotional realm and should use stories to facilitate reaching the affective goals of religious education.

Attitudes and Storytelling

According to James Michael Lee, an attitude is "an affective, acquired, and relatively permanent disposition or personality-set to respond in a consistent manner toward some physical or mental stimulus."[25] An attitude directs a person either for or against a stimulus in the individual's perceptual field. Thus, attitudes are extremely important in defining a person's response to almost everything. This makes attitudes a highly significant factor in the process of religious education. Attitudes help shape responses toward persons, situations, and doctrines; they influence conduct and lifestyle; and they interact with beliefs, opinions, preferences, prejudices, and values.[26]

Attitudes are formed from a number of sources, including two particularly relevant to storytelling—experiences and group influences.[27] Research indicates that direct experiences tend to shape and modify attitudes.[28] Lee suggests that the impact of these direct experiences is related to the quality and forces of the experiences rather than the simple accumulation of experiences. As argued earlier in the present volume, stories can create powerful experiences for learners. Although these experiences are not direct, they are vicarious experiences that may be enactive, iconic, or symbolic, depending on the medium of storytelling.[29] Stories provide experiences that can assist in the formation of attitudes as defined by the goals of religious instruction. For example, children may experience the conflicts of Dr. Seuss' *The Butter Battle Book* or *Old Turtle* in such a way that they form attitudes toward peace and tolerance and against violence and bigotry. Or an adult may experience the horror of the Holocaust by hearing and seeing its story through the displays of the national Holocaust Museum in Washington, D.C. or the Museum of Tolerance in Los Angeles in such a powerful way that they develop attitudes toward diversity and against prejudice.

Attitudes are also shaped by group influences. The early influence of the family is the most pervasive in attitude formation, whereas both the broad culture and particular subculture of the individual play an important role in shaping attitudes.[30] As suggested earlier, stories are an important part of a community's identity; to be part of a community

---

[25]Ibid., p. 217.

[26]Ibid., pp. 219–220.

[27]Ibid., pp. 223–225.

[28]Ibid., p. 224.

[29]Jerome Bruner, *Beyond the Information Given: Studies in the Psychology of Knowing*, ed. Jeremy M. Anglin (New York: Norton, 1973).

[30]Lee, *The Content of Religious Instruction*, p. 225.

is to have its stories. Thus, the stories of a group are a factor in the cultural milieu that gives shape to individuals and attitudes. This means that the stories of a faith community are significant in the development of religious attitudes by its members. For example, an important part of the Quaker story is its peace testimony, exemplified in the lives of George Fox and John Woolman, among many others. The pervasiveness of their stories in the identity of the Quaker community shapes attitudes toward peace and against war. Religious educators, therefore, should be aware of the milieu created by the stories they tell and should select with intentionality stories that shape attitudes along desired religious lines.

Values and Storytelling

Valuing has to do with worth as it has come to be internalized by a learner. James Michael Lee defines values as "the worth of a reality."[31] Values arise as attitudes are consistently evidenced in a learner's behavior in such a way that the behavior is not motivated by the desire to comply or to obey but by commitment to the underlying value itself. Valuing involves ascribing worth to a phenomenon, choosing to pursue the value, and making a commitment to the value.[32] This process, as Lee contends, is primarily affective, though it does contain a number of cognitive components.[33] Value has to do with a person's affective attachment to a reality. These values, however, are not innate but are learned. Thus, the teaching of values is an important task for religious educators.

Because stories are value-laden, they are an excellent tool to assist learners in creating, discovering, exploring, and acting upon their values. Stories point, first of all, to values that the storyteller implicitly or explicitly holds. A story itself is a value system in which some ideas, actions, or objects assume more worth than others. As a result, stories may bring to light hitherto unexplored values, or they may hold up values that are in conflict with the learner's own values. For example, the story in the Gospel of the widow's mite may conflict with

---

[31]James Michael Lee, *Principles and Methods of Secondary Education* (New York: McGraw- Hill, 1963), p. 179.

[32]David R. Krathwohl, Benjamin S. Bloom, and Bertram Masia, *Taxonomy of Education Objectives, Handbook II: Affective Domain* (David McKay, 1964), p. 7.

[33]Lee, *Content of Religious Instruction*, p. 227.

materialistic values that learners have learned from the dominant American culture. Or the story of Jesus and Mary and Martha may challenge certain sexist values. Such encounters with stories can lead learners to reflection on their own values by comparison or contrast.

A learner's own stories may reveal to her the degree to which her life is characterized by particular values. One's own stories will reflect one's orientation toward life and may in turn also critique that orientation. In some sense, each personal story is a microcosm of the self story. In each story is reflected something of the teller's worldview, his philosophy of life. At the center of reflection on these stories is the criterion of consistency. A person characterized by a value will exhibit that value in her behavior with a fair degree of consistency. Thus, exploration of personal stories may provide an important means for developing and examining values.

Values are exhibited in consistent patterns of behavior that indicate a commitment to a particular phenomenon. Religiously significant stories issue a call to commitment. These stories demand choices—to accept or reject certain values, to assimilate or accommodate particular ideas, to explore and to modify ways of being in the world. As values are embodied in stories, stories call for learners to embody these values in their lives. What is externalized in stories may become internalized in the lives of learners.

Love and Stories

According to James Michael Lee, love is the fulfillment of human being and doing.[34] Because God is love, love is central in religious instruction. The ultimate goal of religious living itself is love—being in love and acting in love toward God, self, others, and all of creation. Love is a function, a way of behaving in the world. More than a feeling, love is a lifestyle in which one behaves in good and loving ways toward all that is. In this sense, love is a commitment, a choice people make in the ways they behave toward others.

Stories, then, can have a significant impact on human ability to act in love. Stories can evoke love. Often people who read C. S. Lewis's *The Lion, the Witch, and the Wardrobe* feel love for Aslan, the noble and good Lion. Certainly, the gospel itself is intended to evoke love for God. Stories also can model loving behavior. The Good Samaritan shows people how they ought to love their neighbors.

---

[34]Ibid., p. 229.

In J. D. Salinger's *Franny and Zooey*, Franny, a brilliant college student has a spiritual crisis that leads to a nervous breakdown. As she is recuperating, her brother Zooey reminds her of something their older brother Seymour once told them when they were on a radio show called *Wise Child*. Before they went on the air, especially when they were not feeling like giving their best to do the show, Seymour had told them to do their best "for the Fat Lady." Both Franny and Zooey had constructed stories for Seymour's Fat Lady—a woman with cancer whose only joy was listening to "Wise Child" on the radio. Franny remembers the Fat Lady, and Zooey explains, "There isn't anyone out there who isn't Seymour's Fat Lady," and the secret is that the Fat Lady is Christ. With this revelation, Franny is filled with joy and is at last able to sleep.[35]

The story Franny has created for Seymour's Fat Lady becomes the means by which she is able to feel love for all humanity. Doing her best for the Fat Lady is doing her best for all people. And, ultimately, what she does for all people, she does for Christ.

STORYTELLING IN THE COGNITIVE DOMAIN

In their taxonomy of educational objectives, Benjamin Bloom and colleagues have developed a hierarchical classification system of cognitive educational objectives. The cognitive goals of religious instruction may include, for example, knowledge of biblical material, comprehension of Christian ideals, analysis of ethical situations, synthesis of ideas from theology and other disciplines, and evaluation of new trends in Christian thought. Storytelling provides one teaching procedure that may facilitate the achievement of numerous cognitive religious instruction objectives. Religious educators may turn to stories as a means to teach basic content or as a means to develop critical thinking skills. Although storytelling is not the only way to achieve cognitive educational objectives, it does provide another tool for religious educators to select as they determine the most appropriate ways to achieve the goals of religious instruction.

---

[35]J. D. Salinger, *Franny and Zooey* (New York: Bantam, 1961).

Knowledge through Storytelling

The lowest level of cognitive educational objectives is "knowledge," which Bloom defines as "the recall of specifics and universals, the recall of methods and processes, or the recall of a pattern, structure, or setting."[36] Essentially, knowledge objectives emphasize remembering.

One of the earliest forms of knowledge learned by children is language. Although the complexities of language acquisition defy simple classification into one form of knowing or one method of learning, one facet of language acquisition is the learning of words and structure.[37] No one theory adequately explains how children acquire language skills, but research does tend to indicate that storytelling facilitates the process. Stories help children build vocabulary, understand sequencing, reinforce concepts, and foster the art of communication.[38]

Storytelling experiences provide opportunities for optimum language development by creating situations in which children can use a more elaborate vocabulary as well as practice other language skills, such as beginnings and endings and description. Most children are oral language experts by age five.[39] They are able to tell stories using the conventions of beginnings, endings, plot, and character. One study that compared children's stories in response to a picture and children's original stories found that the telling of original stories led to the use of more descriptive vocabulary, more conventional beginnings and endings, past tense, mature narrative structures, and more spontaneous use of language functions, such as reasoning, imagining, and projecting than the picture tasks.[40] The consequence for religious education here is the importance of providing experiences for children to tell their own stories. For example, in the home, parents may create

---

[36]Benjamin S. Bloom et al., *Taxonomy of Educational Objectives, Handbook I: Cognitive Domain* (New York: David McKay, 1956), p. 25.

[37]For more information on language acquisition, see Lev Vygotsky, *Thought and Language* (Cambridge: MIT Press, 1962); Noam Chomsky, *Language and Mind*, ext. ed. (New York: Harcourt Brace Jovanovich, 1972); Hilary Putnam, *Mind, Language, and Reality* (Cambridge: Cambridge University Press, 1975).

[38]Farnsworth, "Storytelling in the Classroom," p. 163.

[39]Diane N. Bryan, *Inquiries into Child Language* (Boston: Allyn and Bacon, 1982), p. 96.

[40]Ruth A. Hough, Joanne R. Nurss, and Dolores Wood, "Tell Me a Story: Making Opportunities for Elaborated Language in Early Childhood Classrooms," *Young Children* 43 (November 1987): 11.

specific opportunities for children to tell stories about their experiences of the world. These storytelling experiences facilitate for children the very basic acquisition of language, the element upon which all more complex forms of cognition are built.

Another way storytelling may achieve the educational objective of knowledge is through conveying information. On a very simple level, stories teach information. Stories may teach specific facts—dates, events, persons, places—and ways of organizing, studying, judging, and criticizing this information, or stories may teach abstractions—the overarching structures, theories, and generalizations of a field of knowledge. Studies indicate narrative may provide a useful framework for learning and recall by facilitating the initial storage of material and aiding learners in establishing a system for retrieval of information.[41] Stories provide a context for remembering facts that may be more difficult to recall when isolated. Narrative sets this information in a situation that provides cues for retrieval, connecting through character and plot one piece of information to another. Thus, narrative may serve well in a context in which a religious educator wishes learners to learn a series of interrelated facts.

When the Herdmans first came to church, they had never heard the Christmas story. During the first meeting for the Christmas pageant, the director had no choice but to tell the story. "Begin at the beginning," they demanded. This, of course, worried the other children. They figured this meant starting the story with "in the beginning," which meant the story would take awhile. But the pageant director began the story with Mary and Joseph and the announcement of the angel. Along the way, the Herdmans stopped her to explain something like what a manger was or swaddling clothes or to offer their own unique interpretation of the story: "You mean they tied him up and put him in a feedbox?" The Christmas story gave the Herdmans their first basic knowledge of what the season and the church were all about.

Comprehension through Storytelling

The second level of Bloom's taxonomy is comprehension. Comprehension is "a type of understanding or apprehension such that the

---

[41]Fernald L. Dodge, "Tales in a Textbook: Learning in the Traditional and Narrative Modes," *Teaching of Psychology* 16 (October 1989): 24; Fernald L. Dodge, "Of Windmills and Rope Dancing: The Instructional Value of Narrative Structures," *Teaching of Psychology* 14 (December 1987): 216.

individual knows what is being communicated and can make use of the material or idea being communicated without necessarily relating it to other material or seeing its fullest implication."[42] Comprehension can further be divided into translation (the ability to paraphrase or render from one form of communication to another, i.e., understanding metaphor and symbol or translating verbal mathematical material into symbolic statements), interpretation (explanation of material), and extrapolation (determination of implications, consequences, corollaries, and the like). The very nature of stories, as discussed earlier, make storytelling an effective procedure for addressing comprehension objectives.

Storytelling itself demands each of these skills of comprehension. Storytelling requires translating experience into verbal material within a particular structure of established conventions. Storytelling also functions as an interpretation of experience, and stories usually call on the listener to draw conclusions. For religious educators, this means that storytelling (both by religious educators and by learners) may be used to facilitate comprehension of an incredibly wide variety of material. One college professor's experience with storytelling in a large introductory biology course may be instructional for religious educators. He created a tale of a prince and frog that acted as an allegory of active transport, the vehicle by which cells acquire certain necessary molecules. This allegory allowed students to understand the material presented.[43] Religious educators may also invite learners to create stories of their own in order to understand and interpret material. As learners move from material organized around discipline structures to narrative, they begin to understand the symbolic and interrelated aspects of the material through its development in narrative. Stories created by learners demand a basic understanding and ability to utilize the material being taught. Thus, the educational objective of comprehension may be achieved as learners both hear and tell stories that call for them to translate and interpret the material covered and to determine its implications, consequences, and corollaries.

---

[42]Bloom, *Taxonomy of Educational Objectives*, p. 204.

[43]John A. Sperling, "Let Me Tell You a Story," *Journal of College Science Teaching* 18 (May 1989): 361.

Application through storytelling

The third level of Bloom's taxonomy is application. Application is the use of abstractions in concrete situations.[44] It involves the ability to utilize general ideas, principles, theories, procedures, or methods in practice.[45] This knowledge is in a form that can be used by learners in specific and appropriate situations.

Storytelling may facilitate the achievement of this objective by providing a model of application for learners. Characters in stories may act out the behaviors being taught. Stories may also present a challenge to learners to discover methods of application of the material. Through plot, characters, and theme, stories may suggest possible avenues of action through which learners may address issues raised by the stories. Learners may also explore possibilities for application by creating stories in which characters try out different options and confront their consequences. In these ways, stories create a context for the use of abstractions in particular and concrete situations.

In religious education, stories offer an especially useful means for helping learners apply Christian principles to life situations. For example, a story may help learners apply the principle of loving one's neighbor. Jesus certainly used this technique when he told the story of the Good Samaritan. Stories may also be especially helpful in applying abstract theological notions, such as salvation, redemption, and sanctification, in learners' lives. Given religious education's primary goal of religious living, application through storytelling seems a particularly apt way to facilitate the desired learning outcomes.

Analysis through storytelling

Analysis is the fourth level of Bloom's taxonomy. It involves breaking down material into its constituent elements so that the relationships between ideas are made explicit.[46] Analysis is composed of elements, relationships, and organizational principles. Again, storytelling is an appropriate tool for achieving the cognitive objective of analysis. Storytelling requires a variety of levels of analytical skills. In storytelling, analysis of elements occurs as learners identify component parts of narratives. Storytelling also calls for exploration of the connections and interactions among elements, as well as of the structure or pattern

---

[44]Bloom, *Taxonomy of Educational Objectives*, p. 205.
[45]Ibid.
[46]Ibid.

that holds stories together. In literature, literary analysis explores narratives in this way as a means to understand a work of art. For hundreds of years, the church has used religious literature as a means of inspiring, edifying, and educating. Beginning in the 1970s and 1980s, theology rediscovered narrative as one appropriate mode for theological discourse, as noted in chapter 3, in which theological ideas are generated in the creation and exploration of narratives.

Storytelling develops analytical skills by challenging learners to explore meanings that are created in the relationships of the narrative elements of stories. Because stories are not simply illustrations of propositions, analysis of stories necessitates dealing with ambiguity and complexity in the many issues and ideas that stories raise. This process calls for an understanding of the variables that interact in narratives. Thus, religious educators who desire to achieve the educational objective of analysis may find storytelling an excellent means for challenging learners to discover the elements and their relatedness in a given topic.

For example, in the children's story *Old Turtle*, all of creation begins to squabble about who God is.[47] The mountains argue that God is high and above all. The fish argue that God is in the sea. The stars argue that God is far away, and the ants argue that God is very near. The arguing increases until Old Turtle steps in and explains that God is all of these things—near and far, high above and far below, in the wind and in the rocks—and more. Then the people come, and they begin to argue about who God is and who knows God and who does not. And they begin to hurt one another and the earth, until one day a voice comes from the mountains saying that God is in the sea. The sea says that God is in the mountains, the stars say that God is very near, and the ants say God is far away. At last, the people listen, and they begin to see God in one another and in the earth. Then Old Turtle smiles, and so does God. This story contains messages about the environment, animals, God, humans, and peace. Within the story, learners come to see the interrelatedness of these elements. As learners explore the story in terms of its elements, relationships, and organizational principles, they may begin to see connections between theology, environmental ethics, and human relationships.

---

[47]Douglas Wood, *Old Turtle* (Duluth, Minn.: Pfeifer-Hamilton, 1992).

Synthesis through storytelling

The fifth level of Bloom's taxonomy is synthesis. Synthesis is the process of putting elements together to form a whole.[48] The effective telling of an original story is an example of synthesis at its most basic level. In telling an original story, learners demonstrate the ability to take the elements, relationships, and organizational principles of the given content and weave them into a narrative whole. This arrangement of elements constitutes a unique pattern or structure that did not exist clearly in the same way apart from the story. Thus, the story created is always more than the sum of its parts. The story tells more than did the individual items in isolation from the narrative whole. A narrative that achieves this level of synthesis will demonstrate a complexity and unity that transcend the mere linking of particular facts in some related form.

Synthesis may also include the derivation of a set of abstract relations from a story. This skill involves the ability to deduce propositions and make generalizations from the material. In religion, for example, this form of synthesis might occur in the abstracting or formulating of ethical principles from learners' narratives. This process combines the assorted ideas and factors generated in stories into an integrated whole that expresses some generalized idea about the issue being explored. Thus, storytelling may facilitate synthesis in either of two ways: through the creation of an original story or through the formulation of generalizations as integrated expressions of particulars created from the analysis of stories.

Evaluation through Storytelling

The highest level of Bloom's taxonomy is evaluation. Evaluation moves beyond understanding or grasping material to making judgments about the value of ideas, solutions, methods, or material for a given purpose.[49] This process involves the ability to evaluate material both in terms of internal evidence such as logical accuracy and consistency and in terms of external criteria such as theories or standards of excellence within the field. Because the religious life calls for making crucial decisions in many complex, controversial, and significant areas of life, the skill of judgment or evaluation is especially

---

[48]Bloom, *Taxonomy of Educational Objectives*, p. 206.
[49]Ibid., p. 207.

important. Critical and divisive issues such as physician-assisted suicide, abortion, and abuse demand critical religious responses.

Storytelling may provide one way to help learners learn to evaluate issues and ideas by allowing them to explore values, particularly their own unexamined assumptions by which they make judgments. The evaluative process in religious instruction, therefore, involves more than eliciting subjective responses from learners; it also includes the scrutiny of responses up against other stories, texts, ideas, and experiences. Because stories embody particular values or systems of value that may affirm or challenge the values held by learners, they are particularly useful in teaching evaluation. Stories inform the experiences and values of learners and allow them to engage in critical reflection. Stories expose problems, raise difficult issues, and challenge implicitly held assumptions. Thus, stories may facilitate the process of critical thinking, and as learners engage in critical thinking they become able to make judgments about the value of arguments, theories, works, and even stories themselves.

Conclusion

As an instructional tool, stories may provide one means by which religious educators may facilitate the achievement of any number of educational objectives. Stories allow religious educators to bring together lifestyle, affective, and cognitive domains, as well as experiencing, thinking, and feeling ways of knowing. In his essay on the metaphysical poets, T. S. Eliot bemoans the "dissociation of sensibility," in which, for example, falling in love and reading Spinoza have nothing to do with each other. He says the dissociation of thinking and feeling have made English poetry since the metaphysical poets incomplete. His advice to poets is also perhaps good advice to religious educators:

> Those who object to the 'artificiality' of Milton or Dryden sometimes tell us to 'look into our hearts and write.' But that is not looking deep enough; Racine or Donne looked into a good deal more than the heart. One must look into the cerebral cortex, the nervous system, and the digestive tracts.[50]

---

[50]T. S. Eliot, "The Metaphysical Poets," in *Selected Prose of T. S. Eliot*, ed. Frank Kermode (New York: Harcourt Brace Jovanovich, 1975), p. 66.

Storytelling calls religious educators and learners to look into a good deal more than the substantive content. Like the poets, they must look into the cerebral cortex, the nervous system, and the digestive tracts.

STORYTELLING AS
STRUCTURED EXPERIENCE

Structured experiences offer one especially useful model for designing teaching/learning sessions using storytelling. A structured experience is an inductive learning activity through which learners create meanings and knowledge within a community context. In a structured experience, learners engage in an activity, look back on the activity critically, abstract some useful insights from the analysis, and put the results to work through a change in behavior.[51] This model is composed of five movements: experiencing, publishing, processing, generalizing, and applying.

Experiencing
The experiencing stage is the data-generating phase of the structured experience. This stage develops a common database for the processing discussion that follows. Whatever happens in the experiencing stage becomes the basis for critical analysis. Even an unexpected turn of events becomes part of the learning data in a structured experience. As John Hendrix, one of my seminary professors, often used to say, "Nothing never happens." Whatever happens in the experiencing stage is examined in the debriefing process, and learning can occur in surprising ways.

The experiencing stage in a storytelling structured experience is the storytelling event itself. This may be the telling of a story by the religious educator, or it may be the telling of stories by participants. A storytelling experience may also include dramatizing a story, reading or writing a story, drawing or painting a story, using puppets to tell a story, or watching a video. Whatever the particular mode of storytelling used, this activity becomes the basis for group exploration in the following movements of the cycle. If the storytelling experience

---

[51]"Introduction to the Structured Experiences Section," in *The 1983 Annual for Facilitators, Trainers, and Consultants* (San Diego: University Associates, 1983), p. 3.

occurs in isolation from exploration, a great deal of learning may not be facilitated. The debriefing stages of the structured experience provide an opportunity to move from the story itself to Christian living. Without the debriefing stages, religious educators must assume that learners move from experience to application themselves and that exploration in a community does not enhance overall learning. Obviously, discussion of the storytelling experience is necessary to maximize potential learning. Discussion can raise new and relevant issues and enrich the learning experience by the input of a variety of perspectives from the learning community. Thus, the educational task of the religious educator is not only to prepare an excellent storytelling experience but also to guide discussion and exploration of the experience.

Publishing

Publishing involves the sharing of individual experiences of the activity. The purpose of this stage is to make the individual's experience available to the group. This means finding out what was happening affectively and cognitively inside the individual while the activity was in progress. Publishing may be accomplished through a number of techniques: listing adjectives to describe feelings during the experience, free associating on various topics related to the experience, double-entry listing of what learners saw or felt. Publishing questions might include: What happened? How did you feel about that? Were there any surprises? What did you observe? What were you aware of? What are you feeling about the experience now?

For a storytelling event, publishing involves the sharing of individuals' experiences of the storytelling experience. If the group has heard a story, for example, this means discussing their reactions to the story and to the telling of it. What did they feel in connection with the story? What was happening inside them as they listened to the story? What did they observe happening in the group during the storytelling? What did they observe about the storyteller? How did they experience the storytelling?

If the group has told stories, publishing involves discussion of learners' experiences of telling stories, as well as of hearing the stories told. How did they feel telling their stories? What were they aware of while telling their stories? Such questions can also be adapted to fit situations in which stories are dramatized, read, or viewed. The significant task is to engage learners in sharing their personal experiences of the activity so that the group is aware of each individual's perspective on what happened in the storytelling event.

Processing

The processing phase involves the systematic exploration of commonly shared experience by participants in the group. This movement deals with the dynamics of the experience. It reconstructs the patterns and interactions of the activity from the published individual experiences. Techniques for processing include identifying and discussing recurring themes in individual reports, creating a list of key terms raised during publishing, identifying roles and behaviors of group members during the activity. Questions during this phase may include: What dynamics did you observe? What struck you about the published experiences? What did the interaction suggest to you about the group? What do you understand better about yourself? About the group?

In a storytelling experience, this phase involves exploring the dynamics of the storytelling event. How did learners interact with the storyteller? How did they interact with the story? With one another? What common experiences did they have of the storytelling event? Different experiences? The point of this movement is to name the dynamics of group interaction. Thus, this stage does not move on to creating meaning. The religious educator needs to be careful during this phase to guide discussion away from questions of meaning and keep it focused on exploring and expressing dynamics. This movement brings to awareness the dynamics of human relations, an important part of the learning process. Thus, thorough examination of this component should be made before the discussion moves to the next stage.

Generalizing

During this movement, learners begin to infer from the experience general ideas that are relevant to everyday life outside the religious instruction context. The task of this stage is to abstract principles that can be applied in similar situations. This movement is also an appropriate place for the religious educator to bring in relevant theoretical and research findings to supplement the experiential learning activity. Some techniques for developing generalizations include guiding learners to imagine realistic situations and how what they have learned in the discussion may be applicable there, writing statements from the discussion about what holds true in their experiences in the world, and completing sentences about what they have learned.

Questions for discussion may include: What did you learn? What does that suggest in general? What principle do you see operating? How does this relate to other experiences?

For the storytelling experience, this stage includes discussing and exploring the meanings of the story, as well as bringing the story into dialogue with learners' personal stories and the larger Christian story. As stories and the Christian story are placed in dialogue, learners may infer basic principles for Christian living. Questions for discussion may include: How are the themes of this story related to themes of the Christian story? Are these themes significant in your life? Are these themes significant in the life of this group? Does the story challenge or affirm this community's interpretation of what it means to be Christian? Does the story challenge you to struggle with your own lifestyle, values, or theology? Where does God speak to you in this story? Once general principles for Christian living have been named and explored, the religious educator may bring the discussion to the final movement.

Applying

The crucial question for the final stage and for the entire learning cycle is: Now what? Once generalizations have been made, learners need to identify ways to apply these principles in their lives. Religious instruction may truly become a laboratory for Christian living as learners are provided with opportunity to experiment with new behaviors (which then lead back into the learning cycle as new behaviors become concrete experiences for critical reflection). This stage makes learning most useful for participants; it pulls all the learning forward and applies it in a way that helps enable Christian living. Techniques for application may include role plays of everyday situations as learners apply generalizations, goal setting, and contracting. Questions for exploring application may include: How might these principles be applied in real world situations? What are the options? What would be possible consequences for each option? What modifications can you make work for you? What could you imagine in that situation?

Here participants apply what they have learned from the story and the storytelling experience. Because the goal of religious instruction is religious living, this stage is essential for an effective religious instruction experience. Learners should explore ways this experience may help them live better Christian lives in the world and should try out those behaviors in the religious instruction laboratory, even if only through their imaginations.

The religious educator may wish to add one additional step to the experience and process the process. This step explores the entire storytelling experience as a complete learning experience. Questions for discussion may include: How was this learning experience for you? What did you like? dislike? What would you do differently? What would you continue? What suggestions do you have? This phase should elicit feedback that may be used by the religious educator in structuring new storytelling experiences.

TWO EXAMPLES OF STORYTELLING STRUCTURED EXPERIENCES

Example 1: Telling a Story
Title: Washing Feet: A Story for Christian Living
Goals: To allow learners to evaluate servanthood as a model for Christian living

To facilitate valuing of servanthood as a model for Christian living

To enable internalization of servanthood as a model for Christian living

To facilitate lived servanthood

Group size: 5–10
Time required: 1½ hours
Materials needed: Basin, pitcher of water, towel, chalkboard or flip chart, paper and pens for each participant
Physical setting: Chairs in a semicircle facing the performance area
Process
I. Experiencing
    A. Have participants remove shoes and socks and sit in the chairs around the semi-circle.
    B. Beginning with the first participant on the left, pour some of the water from the pitcher over her feet into the basin and then dry the participant's feet with the towel. Move then to the next participant and repeat the process until each person's feet have been washed.
    C. Put aside the towel, basin, and pitcher in a place still in view of the participants and then tell the story of Jesus' washing the disciples' feet (John 13:1–7).

II. Publishing
   A. On the chalkboard or flip chart create two columns: "What we saw" and "What we felt." Record participants' responses to these two headings.
   B. Ask: What did you feel in connection with the story as told and enacted? What was happening inside you as your feet were washed? As you watched others' feet being washed? As you heard the story of Jesus' washing the disciples' feet? What did you experience in this telling of the story?
III. Processing
   A. Ask participants to identify recurring themes of their experiences of the story. List these on the chalkboard or flip chart.
   B. Ask: What struck you about the published experiences? What dynamics did you observe? What do you understand better about yourself? The group?
IV. Generalizing
   A. Ask learners to imagine and to share similar situations in which these recurring themes may be applicable.
   B. Ask: What did you learn from this storytelling experience? What does this story mean to you? What does this story imply about Christian living? How adequate is a servanthood model for Christian living? Does your experience as a Christian validate the story's implications? Is servanthood a significant theme in your life? In the life of this group? Does this story challenge or affirm your interpretation of what it means to be Christian? Does the story challenge you to struggle to live as a servant in the world?
V. Applying
   A. Ask: How might the principle of servanthood be applied in your own life situations? What are the options? What do you think the consequences would be? What could you imagine about living as a servant in the world?
   B. Ask participants to write goals for themselves toward lived servanthood.
   C. Conclude with a time of silence in which learners may commit themselves to carrying out their goals of lived servanthood in the world.

Variations

I. During the generalizing stage, the religious educator may present a brief lecture on the nature of Christian servanthood.

II. In the application phase, the religious educator may ask participants to role-play a situation facing them in which they may practice lived servanthood.

I have used this structured experience several times in a college classroom in a course on Christian teaching. Each time, the experience has been incredibly powerful, both for the learners and for myself as the facilitator. The combination of the enacted and the told story contributes a heightened level of awareness and participation to the entire learning experience. In such powerful experiences, adequate debriefing is essential. Learners need to talk about powerful learning experiences. These meaningful conversations then become the basis for even deeper learning which may have been missed had the experience not been thoroughly processed.

Example 2: Facilitating Storytelling

Title: "Celebration: Forgetting in Order to Remember"[52]

Goals: To foster understanding of the role of celebration in Christian living

To facilitate valuing of celebration in Christian living

To heighten awareness of spiritual experiences in celebration

Group size: A maximum of five groups of four

Time required: 1–1 1/2 hours

Materials needed: chalkboard, paper and pens for each participant

Physical setting: A room large enough to accommodate five discussion groups and movable chairs for participants

Process

I. Experiencing

A. Divide participants into groups of four.

B. Guided imaging: Ask participants to close their eyes and remember a particularly meaningful celebration in their lives— a holiday, wedding, birthday. Then ask the following

---

[52]This definition of celebration is drawn from Matthew Fox, *Whee! We, Wee: A Guide to the New Sensual Spirituality* (Wilmington, N.C.: Consortium, 1976), p. 10.

questions: Where are you? What are you doing? Who is there with you? What are you wearing? What is the general atmosphere of the celebration? What are you feeling? What happens?

C. Ask participants to open their eyes and to share the story of that celebration within their groups.

II. Publishing

A. On the chalkboard create three columns: Remembering, Telling, Listening. Ask participants to list adjectives describing their feelings as they participated in each part of the experience. Write responses on the chalkboard in the appropriate column.

B. Ask: What happened as you remembered your story? As you told it? As you heard the stories of others?

III. Processing

A. Ask participants to identify recurring themes and key terms from the publishing stage. List these on the chalkboard.

B. Ask: How did you respond to one another as you told your stories? What did your interaction suggest to you? What do you understand better about yourself? The group?

IV Generalizing

A. Ask: What do you think your stories suggest about celebration? Do you see a connection between celebration and Christian living?

B. Give a brief lecture on celebration as a spiritual experience, using Matthew Fox's *Whee! We, Wee* as a primary resource. Focus particularly on the importance of forgetting oneself, getting outside of one's self, in celebration in order to share communion with others. Fox writes, "A celebration is a sharing of common memory and, therefore, a forgetting of private memory."[53]

C. Ask: Recall the story of celebration you told. Are there ways you can understand that experience as a spiritual experience? Does your experience validate Fox's understanding of celebration as an experience of God's presence? Can you think of other celebrations in which you have forgotten yourself and experienced communion with God and with others? What is a biblical understanding of celebration? What have you learned

---

[53]Ibid., p. 42.

from this experience about celebration as a facet of Christian living?

V. Applying

   A. Ask learners to imagine times in the next year when they will be involved in a celebration. Have them list ways they can raise their own awareness of the spiritual value of these celebrations.

   B. Ask each group to plan a celebration for some occasion in the life of the church and allow groups time to share their plans with the large group.

   C. Close the session with a common element of celebration for the church's life, such as a joyful song, a dance, or prayer.

PART II

TYPES OF STORY IN
RELIGIOUS EDUCATION

7

Myth and Parable

Earth Magician shapes this world.
Behold what he can do!
Round and smooth he molds it.
Behold what he can do![1]

Language is the means by which people perceive and interpret experiences.[2] Psychologist Jerome Bruner adds that language also transforms experience.[3] Just as language creates and transforms experience, stories, as a form of language, can both create and destabilize a person's constructions of the world. John Dominic Crossan suggests that myth and parable are opposite points on a continuum of stories; myths are the stories that establish the world, and parables are the stories that subvert the world.[4] Myths are sacred stories that tell how things came to be; parables are surprising stories that challenge the ways things are.

---

[1]Hartley B. Alexander, *North American Mythology* (New York: Cooper Square, 1963), p. 229.

[2]For in-depth discussion of language and identity development, see Jacques Lacan, "The Function and Field of Speech and Language in Psychoanalysis," in *Ecrits: A Selection*, trans. Alan Sheridan (New York: Norton, 1977), pp. 30–113; and Jacques Derrida, *Writing and Difference*, trans. Alan Bass (Chicago: University of Chicago Press, 1978).

[3]Jerome S. Bruner, "The Course of Cognitive Growth," *American Psychologist* 19 (January 1964): 1–15.

[4]John Dominic Crossan, *The Dark Interval: Towards a Theology of Story* (Niles, Ill.: Argus, 1975).

MYTH

The Mono myth of the earthdiver tells the story of creation in this way. Prairie Falcon and Crow were sitting on a log above the water that covered the world. Prairie Falcon told Duck to dive into the water and bring up some sand from the bottom. Duck tried, but before he reached the bottom, he died. He then floated to the surface, and Prairie Falcon brought him back to life. Next Coot tried to reach the bottom and suffered the same fate as Duck. Finally, Prairie Falcon sent Grebe. He reached the bottom and secured some sand in each hand, but, on the way to the surface, he died, and the sand slipped from his hands. Prairie Falcon brought Grebe back to life. At first Prairie Falcon and Crow did not believe Grebe had reached the bottom, but then they looked at his hands and found sand under his fingernails. They took the sand and threw it in every direction. This was the way in which they made the world.[5]

Myths are stories that establish the world for people,[6] or as James Michael Lee suggests, myths are tales of beginnings, accounts, and interpretations of origins.[7] They are stories that give order to an individual's or a society's experiences of the world. Myths make the world coherent by imposing a narrative order on natural phenomena and human experiences.[8] In other words, myths are narrative expressions of realities so deeply felt that they can be expressed in no other linguistic way.[9]

One could assume that because mythic tales are themselves created symbols, the realities to which they point are false. After all, if there are no gods on Mount Olympus, then perhaps humans are left to themselves, and there are no standards of right and wrong in the universe. This results, as Friedrich Nietzsche suggests, in nihilism.

---

[5]Adapted from Susan Feldman, "The Earthdiver," in *The Storytelling Stone: Traditional Native American Myths and Tales* (New York: Dell, 1965), pp. 59–60.

[6]Mircea Eliade, *Myth and Reality*, trans. Willard R. Trask (New York: Harper and Row, 1963), pp. 1–6.

[7]James Michael Lee, *The Content of Religious Instruction* (Birmingham, Ala.: Religious Education Press, 1985), p. 330.

[8]Stephen C Ausband, *Myth and Meaning, Myth and Order* (Macon, Ga.: Macon University Press, 1983), p. 2.

[9]Foster R. McCurley, *Ancient Myths and Biblical Faith: Scriptural Transformations* (Philadelphia: Fortress, 1983), p. 1.

On the whole, for contemporary humans, nihilism is not practical. Yet the unquestioning acceptance of a mythical world is no longer possible. As many existentialist philosophers suggest, human existence in the post-Enlightenment, scientific, and technological world is primarily characterized by alienation from the sacred.[10] Drawing from the mythic language of the Genesis story, Mircea Eliade calls this situation of contemporary humanity, a second Fall.[11] Theologian Thomas Altizer argues that modernity arose out of the dissolution of the sacred brought about by the rationalization of Western culture. Knowledge about religion came into existence in contrast to participation in the sacred in all of life. In the modern world, then, myth has become a mode of religious response, a "mode of encounter with the sacred which makes possible the continuous re-presentation, or re-evocation of a primal sacred event."[12] In other words, myth recreates primeval realities by distracting people from their ordinary, historical existence. In so doing, "myth dissolves the profane world of reality and opens its participants to the transcendent world of the sacred Reality."[13]

In the decentered or deconstructed world, postmodernity's emphasis on the role of the reader/listener as mythmaker provides a means of avoiding the pitfall of nihilism through playful exploitation of the potentials of linguistic expression.[14] Linguist Jonathan Culler explains, "to deconstruct a discourse is to show how it undermines the philosophy it asserts, or the hierarchical oppositions on which it relies, but identifying in the text the rhetorical operations that produce the supposed ground of argument, the key concept or premise."[15] In the

---

[10]For example, see Martin Heidegger, *The Question of Being*, trans. William Kluback and Jean T. Wilde (New York: Twayne, 1958); and Jean-Paul Sartre, *Existentialism and Human Emotions,* trans. Bernard Frechtman and Hazel E. Barnes (New York: Wisdom Library, 1957).

[11]Mircea Eliade, *The Sacred and the Profane*, trans. Willard Trask (New York: Harcourt, Brace and World, 1959), p. 213.

[12]Thomas J.J. Altizer, "The Religious Meaning of Myth and Symbol," *Truth, Myth, and Symbol*, ed. Thomas J.J. Altizer, William A. Beardsless, and J. Harvey Young (Englewood Cliffs, N.J.: Prentice-Hall, 1962), pp. 92–93.

[13]Ibid., pp. 93–94.

[14]William G. Doty, *Mythography: The Study of Myths and Rituals* (Tuscaloosa, Ala.: University of Alabama Press, 1986), pp. 191.

[15]Jonathan Culler, *On Deconstruction: Theory and Criticism after Structuralism* (Ithaca, N.Y.: Cornell University Press, 1982), p. 86.

decentered cosmos, humans must grapple with multiple perspectives, competing truths, multiple identities. In the postmodern world, myths allow humans to go on making meaning.[16] At the same time, in their attempt to represent origins, myths also remind of language's inability to signify ultimately.[17] Myths, then, establish, not literal meanings, but patterns of relationships between things.[18]

In the contemporary world, myth and order are human realities. Because myth and order are created by humans, they are not unchanging and infallible. Instead, they reflect the complexities of multiple perspectives and competing experiences of the world. Nonetheless, because humans must live and act in the world along with other humans, the standards created by myths are just as real as the pronouncements of the gods.[19] In other words, even (and maybe especially) in the postmodern world, people still create meaning through myths and still create and participate in social orders that are supported and explained by those myths. For example, a great deal of American culture rests on the myth of the American Dream. For good or ill, many Americans continue to order their lives and participate in the American social order based on their appropriation of this myth. The American Dream suggests the possibility that each American is free to build a good life based on hard work. For many Americans, the dream may be realized. For many others, it may not.

Myths, however, are not false in the way, say, an incorrect statement about a historical event is false. The truth of myths is judged, not by standards of rationality, but as James Michael Lee suggests, in accordance with myths' accuracy in portraying extrarational, subjective reality.[20] Myths are true in the sense that they provide satisfactory representations of a personally or socially perceived order in the world.[21] Altizer offers this example. He says that Christians participate in the reality of Jesus through the mythical symbol of Christ and through the ritual action of Christian worship. He argues that for Christians, there is no "historical" Jesus but only a "mythical" Jesus because for

---

[16]Eric Gould, *Mythical Intentions in Modern Literature* (Princeton, N.J.: Princeton University Press, 1981), p. 180.

[17]Doty, *Mythography*, p. 245.

[18]Gould, *Mythical Intentions in Modern Literature*, p. 186.

[19]Ausband, *Myth and Meaning*, p. 3.

[20]Lee, *Content of Religious Instruction*, p. 152.

[21]Ausband, *Myth and Meaning*, p. 5.

Christians, Jesus is wholly a sacred reality and not, in any sense, a profane being. Thus, he contends, to have a consciousness of Jesus as a "historical" being is to live apart from faith; to understand Jesus primarily as a historical or objective phenomenon is to live in unbelief. The preservation and renewal of Christian faith has been made possible, according to Altizer, not because of concrete historical memories, but because of the mythical form of the Christ event and the living reality of Christian worship.[22]

Myths offer a way of seeing the world, a lens of perception into deep, sacred realities of human experience. As scholars have sought to explore and explain myths, three understandings or perspectives on myth have emerged that may be of help to religious educators: (1) the literary, (2) the comparative religious, and (3) the depth-psychological.[23]

Myth as a Literary Genre

As a literary genre, myth is generally defined as a story about gods[24] or suprahuman entities.[25] Mythologist Joseph Campbell defines the gods as personifications of motivating powers or value systems that function in human lives and in the world, such as the powers of the human body or of nature.[26] According to literary critic Northrop Frye, myth is the archetype for all literary works. He suggests that myth relies on the fundamental element of design offered by nature—the cycle of the seasons—and applies it to the human cycle of life, death, and rebirth.[27] Thus, myth and narrative are, for Frye, coterminous; the structural principles of mythology become the structural principles of literature.[28] Literary critic Eric Gould notes, however, that myth and fiction should not be confused. Fiction, he argues, is always potentially mythic, but all fictions are not necessarily myths.[29]

---

[22]Altizer, "Religious Meaning of Myth and Symbol," p. 95.

[23]My thanks to James Michael Lee for identifying, categorizing, and naming these various perspectives in the wealth of source material on myth.

[24]McCurley, *Ancient Myths and Biblical Faith*, p. 1.

[25] Doty, *Mythography*, pp. 33–34.

[26]Joseph Campbell, *The Power of Myth* (New York: Doubleday, 1988), p. 22.

[27]Northrop Frye, *Fables of Identity: Studies in Poetic Mythology* (New York: Harcourt, Brace and World, 1963), p. 32.

[28]Ibid., pp. 33–34.

[29]Gould, *Mythical Intentions in Modern Literature*, p. 113.

Joseph Campbell sees myths as instances of one constant story—the monomyth, the story of the hero.[30] Generally, the pattern of the hero's adventure in the monomyth is separation—initiation— return. The hero leaves the common, ordinary, everyday world and ventures into a realm of supernatural wonder. There, the hero encounters significant struggle and wins a decisive victory. Thereupon, the hero returns to the ordinary world, bringing some life-enhancing gift to share with others.[31] For example, in the Hebrew Bible, Moses leaves the people to ascend Mount Sinai. There, he encounters God and receives the tables of the law, which he takes back down the mountain to the people. Of course, there are variations on the monomyth: the hero attempts to flee from the gods, the gods provide the hero with supernatural aid, the hero tries to trick the gods, or the hero meets with misunderstanding and disregard upon return.

The hero is generally a person of exceptional ability who undertakes the adventure because of a deficiency in personal or societal life. During the adventure, the hero discovers that the godly powers sought were in the heart of the hero all along. The result of the successful adventure is the unlocking of a renewed flow of life into the world.

This story comes from the Northern Cheyenne. Long ago, the people did not know how to live. They had no laws or rules of behavior. They barely knew enough to survive. A young girl began to have dreams, hearing a voice saying to her, "Sweet Root is coming—woman's medicine that makes a mother's milk flow." Soon the young girl found herself to be pregnant, even though she had not been with a man. When she began to feel birth pangs, she left the camp and gave birth to a baby boy in the prairie. Knowing that a baby without a father would be scorned in her village, she left him there. Soon an old woman came by and found the baby. All around him grew sweet root, and so she named him Sweet Medicine. She took him to live in her humble tipi, and the child grew to be wise beyond his years. When the boy killed his first buffalo and was skinning it, a harsh old chief happened by and demanded the hide from Sweet Medicine. Sweet Medicine reminded him that he could not give away his first hide, but he offered the old man half of the meat. The old man refused and tried to

---

[30]Joseph Campbell, *The Hero with a Thousand Faces* (New York: Pantheon, 1949), p. 3.
[31]Ibid., pp. 30, 35.

grab the hide and walk away with it. Sweet Medicine grabbed the other end, and they began a tug-of-war. Soon the old man began to beat Sweet Medicine with his whip. Sweet Medicine grabbed a buffalo leg bone and hit the old man over the head with it. The people in the village became angry that a young boy would fight an old chief, and so they began to say, "Let's whip him, let's kill him." And so Sweet Medicine fled. Wandering across the prairie, Sweet Medicine saw a huge mountain, standing alone, like a tipi. He found a secret opening into the mountain and entered it. There he found a sacred lodge filled with powerful spirits, who looked like ordinary men and women. The spirits began to teach him the Cheyenne way to live so he could return to the people and give them this knowledge. The spirits gave him four arrows with great powers, and they taught Sweet Medicine how to pray to the arrows, how to keep them, and how to renew them. Sweet Medicine listened respectfully and learned well. Finally, he put his bundle of arrows on his back and set out on the long journey to return to his people. When he found them, he called them all together and all night he taught them the ways to live which he had learned from the spirits. For many nights after that, Sweet Medicine instructed the people in the sacred laws, and from him they learned the Cheyenne ways.[32]

Campbell enumerates four functions of myth: (1) mystical, (2) cosmological, (3) sociological, and (4) pedagogical. The mystical function of myth is to inspire awe and wonder before the universe. The cosmological function illuminates the shape of the universe in such a way that mystery permeates it. The sociological function supports and validates particular social orders (e.g., in the United States, the frontier myth supports the notion of rugged individualism that supports the nation's capitalist economic system). And finally, the pedagogical function teaches people how to live as humans under any circumstances.[33] Campbell concludes, "The way to become human is to learn to recognize the lineaments of God in all of the wonderful modulations of the face of [humanity]."[34] For Campbell, this commonality is most powerfully expressed in human symbols, rituals, and myths.

---

[32]adapted from Richard Erdoes and Alfonso Ortiz, eds., "The Life and Death of Sweet Medicine," *American Indian Myths and Legends* (New York: Pantheon, 1984), pp. 199–205.

[33]Campbell, *Power of Myth*, p. 31.

[34]Campbell, *Hero with a Thousand Faces*, p. 390.

Myth in Comparative Religions

Historian of religions Mircea Eliade is particularly concerned with myth's etiological function. According to Eliade, myths narrate sacred history. They relate events that took place in primordial time, the time of "beginnings."[35] Because humans understand themselves as constituted by primal events, recollected myths and reenacted rituals allow people to become reunited with the powerful time of beginnings. The implication is that by knowing something's origins, one has power over it.[36] Therefore, people enter the time of beginnings in order to heal or to gain control over natural or humanly made objects.[37] According to Eliade, by ritual retelling of the primal creative acts, societies believe they can again make present the power of creation and so reenergize the present.[38]

People live their myths in the sense that they are seized by the sacred power of the recollected events. Living a myth, claims Eliade, is a genuine religious experience in that it differs from ordinary, everyday experiences. In living a myth, persons reenact significant events, again witnessing the fabulous deeds of the supernatural beings; they cease to exist in the everyday world and enter a world filled with the presence of the sacred. Eliade argues that what happens is not a commemoration of mythic events but a reiteration of them. People enter primordial time, and the protagonists of the myths are made contemporary. Myths, then, suggest that the world, humanity, and all of life have a supernatural origin and history, which is important, valuable, and exemplary.[39]

Myths also offer models for human values and behaviors. By suggesting standards of morality, myths affirm meaningfulness in the world and remind humans that the glorious past is partly recoverable. Because great deeds have been done before, they can be done again. Myths, thus, create an opening between this world and the world of the sacred; they become the vehicle through which consciousness to a sacred world is awakened and through which commitment to its realities, truths, and values is maintained.[40]

---

[35]Eliade, *Myth and Reality*, pp. 1–6.
[36]Ibid., pp. 18–19.
[37]Doty, *Mythography*, p. 64.
[38]Ibid., p. 141.
[39]Eliade, *Myth and Reality*, pp. 18–19.
[40]Ibid., pp. 139–142, 144–147.

Myth in Depth-Psychology

Depth psychologists have identified myth as an integral part of the human psyche. Beginning with Sigmund Freud and continuing through Carl Jung, an emphasis on the role of myth in psychic health has been an important part of depth psychology. For Freud, dreams represent earlier traumas that have not been satisfactorily resolved.[41] In dreams, latent thoughts are transformed into manifest contents so that dream symbols are not what they appear to be. Rather they are expressions of these earlier traumas. According to Freud, the mechanisms at work in the transformation of latent contents into manifest contents are the same sorts of mechanisms operative in the formation of myths. Two especially relevant mechanisms identified by Freud are condensation and visual representability. Condensation involves the compression of an extensive amount of content into a brief expression or fragment. Visual representability refers to the symbolic mechanism by which latent contents are given visible representations. Thus, according to Freud, myths are probably "distorted vestiges of the wish-phantasies of whole nations—the age-long dreams of young humanity."[42] Myths are societies' attempts to return to realities which have been repressed, yet are present and active in the unconscious. Myth allows these realities to be brought to consciousness.[43]

Whereas Freud brings the language of myth into psychology, his one-time student Carl Jung offers a more profound and inclusive approach to mythology in psychology. Unlike Freud, Jung sees dreams as a positive means toward wholeness. The contents of dreams and myths are not purely personal but share in the psychic material and mythic imagery of all people.[44] Thus, Jung suggests, myths and dreams reveal the structure and contents of the human psyche. Myths

---

[41]For a more thorough discussion of Freud's understanding of dreams, see Sigmund Freud, *The Interpretation of Dreams*, trans. A. A. Brill (New York: Modern Library, 1978).

[42]Sigmund Freud, *Sigmund Freud on Creativity and the Unconscious, Papers on the Psychology of Art, Literature, Love, Religion*, ed. Benjamin Nelson (New York: Harper and Row, 1958), p. 53.

[43]Lee, *Content of Religious Instruction*, p. 350.

[44]Carl G. Jung, *Civilization in Transition*, trans. R. F. C. Hull, in *The Collected Works of C. G. Jung*, ed. Herbert Read et al. (Princeton, N.J.: Princeton University Press, 1964), 10: 144–145.

represent projections from the unconscious, and the similarities in myths provide representations of typical psychic phenomena.[45]

For Jung, then, myths are an integral part of religions, for myths provide a connection with the transpersonal and the eternal. Myths allow a connection with energies represented in past myths in a way that leads to affirmation of one's own personal mythic system and therefore to a meaningful universe.[46] For Jung, myth is the best and most natural language for dealing with psychic processes. Psychic processes are concerned, Jung claims, with primordial images, and these images are best expressed in mythic language.[47]

More recently, psychologist Rollo May has claimed that myths are persons' self-interpretation of their inner selves in relation to the outside world, and these myths are the narratives by which a society is unified.[48] Thus, although each person has a myth around which she patterns life, these individual myths are generally variations on some central theme of classical myths.[49] May suggests four functions of myth: to give persons a sense of personal identity, to make possible a sense of community, to undergird moral values, and to provide a way of dealing with the mystery of creation.[50]

May sees myth as essential to the human enterprise; myths provide significance in human existence, and without myths humans are not healthy. Similarly, Jerome Bruner argues that when myths fail to fit the situations of human existence, people experience frustration, loneliness, and fragmentation.[51] May, in fact, attributes the overwhelming proliferation of psychotherapy in the contemporary world to the disintegration of myths.[52] The loss of myth in the twentieth century left people without a means for making sense of existence. Reliance on science and technology destroyed myths, relegating them to the realm of fantasy or delusion, while in reality diminishing the very spark of

---

[45]Doty, *Mythography*, pp. 150–151.

[46]Ibid., p. 52.

[47]Carl G. Jung, *Psychology and Alchemy*, trans. R. F. C. Hull, in *The Collected Works of C. G. Jung*, ed. Herbert Read et al. (Princeton, N. J.: Princeton University Press, 1953), 12: 25.

[48]Rollo May, *The Cry for Myth* (New York: Norton, 1991), p. 20.

[49]Ibid., p. 33.

[50]Ibid., pp. 30–31.

[51]Jerome Bruner, "Myth and Identity," in *Myth and Mythmaking*, ed. Henry A. Murray (New York: Braziller, 1960), p. 285.

[52]May, *Cry for Myth*, p. 15.

mystery that makes people human. May argues that people understand one another by identifying the subjective meaning of their language, by experiencing what words mean to them in their world. Without myth, people are unable to go beyond the word and hear the person who is speaking. He contends that the strongest proof of the impoverishment of contemporary culture is the popular, but profoundly mistaken, definition of myth as falsehood.[53] Rather, he says, myths are narrative patterns that give significance to existence. They are dramas that begin in historical events, eventually becoming a way of orienting people to reality, a vital mode of perception by which people create order out of chaos and sense out of the many mysteries of human life.[54]

MYTH IN RELIGIOUS INSTRUCTION

As sacred stories, myths should have a significant place in religious instruction. For learners, myths provide ways of constructing the world; they offer lenses of perception; they inspire awe and wonder at the mystery of the universe; they provide a sense of personal identity; and they offer models for behavior. Jung contends that people who think they can live without myth have no true link to the sacred past or contemporary human society.[55]

Myths, then, have a vital role to play as part of the verbal content of religious instruction. In religious instruction contexts, myths can be shared, created, and critiqued in ways that help achieve desired learning outcomes. If, as Eliade argues, living myth is a genuinely religious experience, then certainly religious educators should emphasize myths in the planning and implementing of teaching/learning situations.

Myth as Verbal Content

James Michael Lee suggests that myth has cognitive, affective, and lifestyle functions as verbal content in religious instruction.[56] First, myth, according to Lee, is a fundamental way of knowing. Myths provide answers and explanations, reveal insights, and awaken

---

[53]Ibid., p. 23.
[54]Ibid., p. 26.
[55]Jung, quoted in May, *Cry for Myth*, p. 63.
[56]Lee, *Content of Religious Instruction*, pp. 331–332.

consciousness. Second, myths evoke feelings, express attitudes, name basic needs, suggest deeply felt beliefs, and create patterns of beliefs and attitudes. And finally, myths present models for human conduct. Myths suggest directions for living, encourage commitment and involvement, promote the integration of society, and provide a basis for a way of life. Thus, as a form of verbal content, myth can be utilized to facilitate desired learning outcomes in each of the religious education domains.

Sharing Myths

A primary task for religious educators is the sharing of appropriate myths. Christians have inherited a wealth of tradition that has given shape and meaning to experience. One task of religious educators is to hand on to others the mythic constructions of the world that have come down to them through the faithful transmission of those who have gone before. Timothy Arthur Lines also contends that religious educators should be mythologists, offering comparative studies of myths from many different cultures and religions to learners.[57]

Sharing myths demands a certain amount of reverence from religious educators and learners because myths are sacred histories. Thus, traditional myths should not simply be discarded when new ones arise. Rather, religious educators and learners should value and utilize myths, old and new, even those that are not from their own tradition, for they too have much to teach. Religious educator Maria Harris warns that Christians often too easily critique traditions that are not their own and deal with fundamental issues of life and death with an arrogant certainty.[58] Likewise, James Michael Lee contends that religious educators should take seriously the myths they teach and should choose to teach the best myths that various cultures and religions have to offer.[59]

In sharing myths, religious educators should seek to present the myths as dramatically as possible—to make the myths live for learners. The telling or enacting of myths ought to be filled with the very suspense, wonder, and sometimes even humor that the mythic stories

---

[57]Timothy Arthur Lines, *Functional Images of the Religious Educator* (Birmingham, Ala.: Religious Education Press, 1992), pp. 234–236.

[58]Maria Harris, "From Myth to Parable: Language and Religious Education," *Religious Education* 73 (1978): 390.

[59]Lee, *Content of Religious Instruction*, p. 351.

themselves convey. Learners may then be able to connect with myths in such a way that they are truly transported into the powerful time of beginnings and there find new power to return to the everyday world energized by their encounter with myth.

Creating Myths

Beyond sharing traditional myths, a second task of religious instruction is to create myths. To the traditions handed down in the old myths, learners add their own unique experiences; they continue to establish the world. James Michael Lee describes this task as structuring the learning situation so that learners live their own myths in the present.[60] When learners are immersed in an environment rich with the great mythic stories of tradition, they may begin to hear the resonances of their own personal stories with these sacred stories. Historian of religion James Carse suggests four ways the practice of listening for resonance may produce new insights: (1) it brings into clearer focus the fact that life is an unfolding story, and it helps learners understand where they are in that story; (2) it exposes the wide range of possible paths lying before each learner; (3) it helps bring about greater intimacy with others who are also participants in learners' stories; and (4) it opens learners to the possibility of experience with the divine.[61]

In the religious instruction context, religious educators may facilitate the development of personal myths by introducing learners to traditional myths and having them identify places in which they feel a resonance with those myths in their own lives. They may even retell the myths with themselves as the central character and with others in their lives appearing as supporting characters in the mythic cast. Or learners may recall certain significant events in their lives and then explore similar stories in myths. They may write out their life stories in mythic form.[62] James Michael Lee suggests that learners keep a personal journal that records the deep, significant moments on their human journey.[63]

---

[60]Ibid., p. 352.

[61]James P. Carse, "Exploring Your Personal Myth," in *Sacred Stories: A Celebration of the Power of Stories to Transform and Heal*, ed. Charles Simpkinson and Anne Simpkinson (New York: HarperSan Francisco, 1993), pp. 228–229.

[62]Ibid., pp. 230–231.

[63]Lee, *Content of Religious Instruction*, p. 352.

A second way learners may create myths is through the development of new rituals. Psychologist Rollo May claims that celebrations are a form of people's contemporary embodiment of myths. He contends that across the years, these holy days gather around them a mythic quality of eternity, providing a sense of union with the distant past and the far-off future.[64] Similarly, ritual is myth expressed bodily. Or, put another way, myth is that which is spoken, whereas ritual is that which is acted out.[65] Eliade claims that every ritual has a divine model and that across cultures religions hold their ritual acts to have been founded by the gods, civilizing heroes, or mythic ancestors. For example, the aborigines of southeastern Australia practice circumcision with a stone knife because that is what their ancestors taught them to do; the hako cremony of the Pawnee was given to them by Tirawa, the supreme god, at the beginning of time;[66] Jews practice circumcision because God commanded it of Abraham; Christians re-enact Christ's passion in communion. Religious educator Randolph Crump Miller summarizes: Myth is a traditional way of telling a story of beginnings that provides grounds for ritual actions which help contemporary people live in the world.[67]

Recently Jewish women have begun to develop feminist forms of the Haggadah. Feeling that women's history and women's experiences had been left out of the traditional Haggadah, Jewish women have rewritten the Haggadah to include the experiences of the women of Jewish tradition—Sarah, Miriam, Rachel, to use a feminine name for God, Shekinah, to change the four sons to four daughters, and to express experiences of contemporary Jewish women in their struggle for ethnic and gender justice.[68] These new forms of Haggadah allow

---

[64]May, *Cry for Myth*, p. 50.

[65]Jane Ellen Harrison, *Themis: A Study of the Social Origins of Greek Religion*, 2d ed. (Cleveland, Ohio: World, 1957), p. 378.

[66] Mircea Eliade, *The Myth of the Eternal Return*, trans. Willard R. Trask (Princeton, N.J.: Princeton University Press, 1954), pp. 21–23.

[67]Randolph Crump Miller, "Empirical Theology and Religious Education," in *Theologies of Religious Education*, ed. Randolph Crump Miller (Birmingham, Ala.: Religious Education Press, 1995), pp. 160–161.

[68]For example, see E. M. Broner, *The Women's Haggadah* (New York: HarperSan-Francisco, 1994); Jane S. Zones, ed., *San Diego Women's Haggadah* (La Jolla, Calif.: Woman's Institute for Continuing Jewish Education, 1986); Aviva Cantor, "Jewish Women's Haggadah,"in *Womanspirit Rising*, ed. Carol P. Christ and Judith Plaskow (New York: HarperSanFrancisco, 1979), pp. 185–192.

Jewish women to position their struggles for justice within the ancient story of the Hebrew people's struggle for freedom in such a way that they emerge from the practice renewed for daily life.

Critiquing myths

Finally, religious instruction has the task of challenging and critiquing myths. Although myths are sacred histories that carry eternity within them, myths are also only partial reflections of human truths and therefore are susceptible to falsehoods that are part of human cultures. For example, the biblical story of the Fall purports to explain the subordination of women to men and is still in many conservative circles used to justify continuation of that practice. Although that piece of the story reflects the cultural norm of the society which created it, it does not reflect the overarching theme of the Good News of God's inclusive love in which there is neither male nor female, Jew nor Gentile, slave nor free.

Myths have been used to justify wars, to contaminate the environment, to enact prejudices. Unexamined acceptance of myths, from the rape of Leda to Manifest Destiny, have allowed many destructive elements to continue in individual and cultural practices. Religious instruction should provide a context for critiquing myths in the light of the Good News. These critiques of myths may also function as critiques of learners' own lives. They may perhaps discover ways in which their own behaviors have reflected destructive elements, and they may find new models in other myths to help create new, more appropriate behaviors.

Religious instruction can also provide a forum for examining the images of God that learners have constructed from myths. Any myth can only partially represent the unrepresentable nature of God. Unfortunately, learners sometimes take these partial representations to stand for the whole. Particularly through comparative studies of myths in interaction with learners' own personal stories of their experiences with God, fuller representations of God may be created, and, even more importantly, the infinite and ultimately indescribable nature of God may be more fully underscored, creating an openness to experience God in new ways.

PARABLE

If myths are stories that establish the world, parables are stories that subvert it. Parables challenge conventional notions of being in the world; they encourage learners to examine their way of living and to explore alternative and more authentic lifestyles. Theologian C. H. Dodd suggests that parables are common images used in uncommon ways in order to tease learners into new ways of seeing and being in the world.[69] When Jesus told the parable of the Good Samaritan, he used a common experience of a traveler running into trouble, coupled with an uncommon hero in the form of a good Samaritan, to challenge narrow, conventional, and stereotypical notions about who is a neighbor and who is not. The story, of course, was a response to a question of lifestyle—how does one go about loving one's neighbor.

Metaphors and parables are not identical, but relationships between the two do exist. Although both are comparisons, metaphoric comparisons are most often expressed in single images, and comparisons in parables arise from the stories themselves.[70] At its semantic level, however, parable functions similarly to metaphor, and therefore metaphor becomes an appropriate model by which to explore parable.[71] Rhetorician Philip Wheelwright suggests that metaphors can be characterized by two elements: epiphor and diaphor. Epiphor is the expression of similarity between something well known and something less well known. It is what allows the extension of meaning through comparison. Diaphor is the aspect of juxtaposition that allows the creation of new meaning through the combining of the particulars.[72] As a model for parables, Wheelwright's description of metaphor suggests two movements in parables: one epiphoric, which builds within the story an implied comparison, and the other diaphoric, which juxtaposes the narrative against its immediate context.[73]

---

[69]Charles H. Dodd, *The Parables of the Kingdom* (New York: Scribners, 1961), p. 5.

[70]Mary Ann Tolbert, *Perspectives on the Parables: An Approach to Multiple Interpretations* (Philadelphia: Fortress, 1979), p. 43.

[71]Ibid., p. 44.

[72]Philip Wheelwright, *Metaphor and Reality* (Bloomington: Indiana University Press, 1962), p. 72.

[73]Tolbert, *Perspectives on the Parables*, p. 44.

A parable thus sets up an implicit comparison, leaving the story open-ended and therefore generative of new meanings.[74] Rather than convey a message, a parable is itself the message. Therefore, a parable cannot be reduced to a single point or translated into an abstract concept. Rather, parable's resistance to flattening reduction is precisely the characteristic that creates an opening for mystery. In other words, a parable itself is more than any single interpretation of it. And its open-endedness allows the parable to work on learners and to interpret them to themselves.[75] Again, the parable of the Good Samaritan points irrefutably toward its hearers' own prejudices, preconceptions, and shortcomings in regard to their neighbors. In this way, the story is much more than a statement about prejudice; it is a direct challenge to the lifestyle of its hearers. This parable puts its hearers in a very uncomfortable position. They had been taught to despise Samaritans and to see them as inferior. Yet this story allows hearers to identify either with the victimized man, the religious hypocrites who walked by, or the Samaritan, none of whom would have seemed a good choice to the hearers. In this way, the parable created a crisis, a confrontation for those listening and a challenge for them to broaden their notion of neighbor and to act accordingly.

Philosopher Søren Kierkegaard often uses parables, not only to make his complex philosophical contentions plain but also to challenge his readers to change.[76] For Kierkegaard, parables can draw learners into more profound self-awareness and can introduce new possibilities of self. Parables, he suggests, communicate to learners their own capacity to reach into their own experiences with heightened self-awareness.[77] In other words, Kierkegaard uses parables in particular to facilitate development of selfhood. He tells this parable: When Philip threatened to lay siege to Corinth, all of its inhabitants busied themselves, polishing weapons, gathering stones, mending the walls of the city. Seeing all of this activity, the philosopher Diogenes quickly wrapped his mantle around him and began zealously to roll his tub back and forth through the streets of the city. When asked why

---

[74]Sallie McFague, *A Study in Metaphor and Theology* (Philadelphia: Fortress, 1975). P. 72.

[75]Ibid.

[76]Thomas C. Oden, introduction to *Parables of Kierkegaard* (Princeton, N.J.: Princeton University Press, 1978), p. xiv.

[77]Ibid., p. xvi.

he did so, he replied that he wanted to be busy like all the rest and rolled his tub lest he be the only idler among so many industrious citizens.[78]

In any discussion of the value of parables for religious instruction, three dimensions of the nature of parables are especially important: their literary form, their historical setting, and their hermeneutical purpose.[79] The parables of Jesus, in particular, stand as excellent examples for religious instruction of the power of parable to subvert the world and call learners to new ways of living. By understanding the form, settings, and hermeneutical purposes of the parable of Jesus, religious educators can utilize these parables to challenge learners to examine their lives and try out new behaviors in light of the parables' call to authentic existence.

The parables of Jesus were originally oral events, addressing learners in their ongoing lives and demanding personal response. The defining characteristic of these parables is their internal juxtaposition. The word "parable" derives from a Greek preposition and verb that mean "to throw alongside." Theologian Sallie McFague, drawing on the work of Paul Ricoeur, suggests that two ways of being in the world interact in parables—one is the conventional way and the other, the way of God's realm.[80] Parables hold these two ways of being in tension in such a way that they effect a shock that upsets the conventional way of seeing and being in the world. For example, in Luke 12, Jesus tells the parable of the rich fool: Once a very rich man grew an especially abundant crop of grain, and he wondered to himself how he would store such an abundance. Then an idea came to him. He would tear down his existing barns and build even bigger ones and there would store his grain, saying to himself, "Self, you have ample grain stored for years to come. Relax now. Eat, drink, and be merry." But at that very moment, at the height of his satisfaction with himself, God said to him, "You fool. This very night your life will be demanded of you. And then who will have all of those things you have prepared?"

---

[78]Søren Kierkegaard, "The Busy Philosopher," in *Parables of Kierkegaard*, ed. Thomas C. Oden (Princeton, N.J.: Princeton University Press, 1978), p. 5.

[79]Peter Rhea Jones, *The Teaching of the Parables* (Nashville: Broadman, 1982); Norman Perrin, "Historical Criticism, Literary Criticism, and Hermeneutics: The Interpretation of the Parables of Jesus and the Gospel of Mark Today," *Journal of Religion* 52 (October 1972): 361–375.

[80]Sallie McFague, *Metaphorical Theology* (Philadelphia: Fortress, 1982), p. 45.

In this parable, the conventional wisdom, of course, is to plan for the future, to store the extra, to put something away for a rainy day. But the way of God's realm recognizes the futility of relying on wealth. In this way, this parable puts the gaining of wealth into perspective. As the parable asks, what is the value of hoarding riches if it means losing one's soul?

Ricoeur suggests that parables work on a pattern of orientation, disorientation, and reorientation. A parable begins in the ordinary world with its conventional standards and expectations, but in the course of the story a radically different perspective emerges and disorients learners. As the competing viewpoints interact, a tension is created that finally results in a redescription of life in the world.[81]

Parables achieve the aim of self-confrontation by overriding learners' immediate defenses through narrative expression. As narratives, parables are less threatening than direct confrontations. Learners generally find hearing a story about other people easier than hearing direct attacks on their own behaviors. Thus, parables are able to move past defenses and draw learners into these stories, which contrast new ways of being in the world with learners' conventional ways of being. In this way, parables may introduce learners to new ways of life that in a more directly didactic form may never have received a hearing. In Matthew 18, Peter asks Jesus how often he should forgive those who sin against him. Jesus responds with a parable. A slave owed his king ten thousand talents, but he could not pay. So the king ordered him, his wife, his children, and his possessions to be sold for payment. But the slave fell on his knees and begged the king for patience. Out of pity, the king released him and forgave him the entire debt. The slave left the king, and on his way out he met a fellow slave who owed him a hundred denarii. The slave seized him by the throat and demanded that he pay what he owed. The other slave fell on his knees and begged for patience. But the first slave refused and had him thrown into prison until he could pay the debt. When the other slaves heard what had happened, they were horribly upset and told the king. The king summoned the first servant and said to him, "You wicked servant. I forgave you the immense debt you owed me, but you did not forgive the tiny debt your fellow servant owed you. Should you not

---

[81]Paul Ricoeur , "Biblical Hermeneutics," *Semeia* 4 (1075): 122–128.

have shown mercy as I had shown mercy?" And so the king imprisoned him until he could pay his debt.

The pronounced contrast of conventional and unconventional ways of being presented in parables evoke self-confrontation in learners. By witnessing a new way of being in the world in a parable, learners must confront their own conventional ways of existing. Thus, parables subvert the comfortable structures that learners have built for themselves and suggest that perhaps their way of being in the world is not necessarily God's way. This disorienting effect of parables then creates space for the possibility of reorientation—ordering learners' lives in accordance with the new way of being they have glimpsed. As Sallie McFague suggests, the security of learners' everyday life is shaken because they have seen another way of being; they have seen another mundane life like their own moving by a different logic, and they begin to realize that another way of living may well be a possibility for them.[82]

The historical dimension of the interpretation of the parables of Jesus involves learners' exploring the *Sitz im Leben Jesu*, or life setting of the parables. The parables of Jesus were an integral part of his life and religious education ministry. Discovering the life setting of a parable often offers clues to meanings of the parable to the generation who first heard them told. Although the actual occasion for every parable is not possible to recover, many arose out of situations that may be classified by life setting. For example, a number of parables came out of conflicts in which Jesus was criticized for his lifestyle and religious education activity. Other parables grew from scholarly debates and teaching/learning situations. Biblical source and form criticism offer fruitful tools for the exploration of the historical dimension of the parables. Biblical source criticism facilitates the study of parables by assessing sources such as Mark, Q (*Quelle*, a source of common material in Matthew and Luke), M (material unique to Matthew), and L (material unique to Luke).[83] Biblical form criticism recognizes both the life setting of Jesus and of the early church (*Sitz im Leben Kirche*), which applied the parables to new situations the church

---

[82]Sallie McFague, *Speaking in Parables: A Study in Metaphor and Theology* (Philadelphia: Fortress, 1975), p. 79.

[83]The seminal work on source criticism of the parables is Alexander B. Bruce, *Parabolic Teaching of Christ: A Systematic and Critical Study of the Parables of our Lord* (London: Hodder and Stoughton, 1882).

encountered. Biblical form criticism traces the development of the parables during the period of oral tradition to discover their various stages prior to their final form in the written text.[84] Essentially, historical study of the biblical parables focuses on their meaning and significance in their original context as oral events and their development and incorporation into the written text.

The hermeneutical or educational purpose of Jesus's parables is to explore the meaning of the kingdom of God for Christian living. This image of the kingdom of God is central in Jesus's parables. No single parable defines the kingdom of God, but each parable illuminates some aspect of the kingdom. Even taken together, however, the parables do not describe the totality of the kingdom of God. Nonetheless, these parables do give us a glimpse of the meaning of God's kingdom and the kingdom way of living.

Four primary characteristics of Jesus's parables summarize their educational purpose. First, the parables are eschatological; they are about the imminence of God's kingdom. They describe an immediate rather than a coming realm of God. The eschaton is present rather than future.[85] Thus, there is a definite sense of urgency about the parables. Now, the parables seem to say, is the time for decision. This urgency is probably because the parables were told in a time when Jesus was announcing that the kingdom of God was bursting into history. Change had come. A new way of being in the world was now possible. Second, the parables have existential import; they illumine existence. In them, Jesus exposes inauthentic existence and extols authentic existence in light of the kingdom way of living. Third, the parables are ethical; they are concerned with persons' relationships with others. The kingdom way brings with it a new set of values that are to be lived out in relationships with all other people. Finally, the parables are evangelistic; they invite people to participate in the kingdom of God.[86] As religious educator Joseph S. Marino suggests, the parables of Jesus demand decision. Those who hear the parables cannot remain

---

[84]Two seminal works in form criticism of the parables are Charles H. Dodd's *The Parables of the Kingdom* (New York: Scribner's, 1961); and Joachim Jeremias, *The Parables of Jesus*, trans. S. H. Hooke (New York: Scribner's, 1963).

[85]For an in-depth examination of the eschatological implications of the parables, see William R. Herzog II, *Parables as Subversive Speech: Jesus as Pedagogue of the Oppressed* (Louisville, Ky.: Westminster, 1994).

[86]Jones, *Teaching of the Parables*, pp. 44–45.

neutral but must make a judgment on the situation the parable narrates. From this judgment, learners are no longer mere listeners; they
are also actors.[87]

PARABLES IN RELIGIOUS INSTRUCTION

Just as Jesus told parables to subvert the comfortable world of his followers, religious educators can use parables, both biblical and nonbib-
lical, to shatter conventional ways of being in the world and to create
spaces for learners to experience God at the edges of their existence.
Because parables are a powerful means of challenging the status quo
of learners' lives, they make an especially appropriate companion to
myths in religious instruction. Myths can provide a foundation of
identity within community for learners, but parables can facilitate
learners' continued growth by helping learners discover new ways of
living.

Parables as Verbal Content
Like myths, parables also have cognitive, affective, and lifestyle functions as verbal content in religious instruction. Parables challenge
learners' ways of thinking; they offer new ways of seeing the world,
new perspectives, possible new worldviews. Parables also can evoke
strong feelings. Because parables are confrontational, they can point
out problematic attitudes and suggest new ones. Most importantly,
parables call for decision and change in conduct. Parables contend that
different ways of living are possible and that learners should respond
by trying out these new ways.

Sharing Parables
Religious educators can read, tell, or dramatize parables to achieve a
number of learning goals. Through parables, religious educators can
announce the presence of God's kingdom and invite learners to participate. In Matthew 25, Jesus says that the kingdom of God is like ten
bridesmaids who took their lamps and went to meet the bridegroom.
The five wise bridesmaids took extra oil for their lamps, but the five

---

[87]Joseph S. Marino, *Biblical Themes in Religious Education* (Birmingham, Ala.:
Religious Education Press, 1983), p. 69.

foolish bridesmaids did not. Later that night, when the five foolish bridesmaids ran out of oil, they had to leave to go and buy more. While they were gone, the bridegroom came. The five wise bridesmaids went into the banquet with the bridegroom, and the five foolish bridesmaids were locked out of the celebration. Martin Buber relates this parable from Hassidic tradition. Rabbi Barukh's grandson was playing hide-and-seek with a friend. The young boy hid himself well and waited for his friend to find him. After he had waited for quite a long time, he came out of his hiding place, but his friend was nowhere around. Suddenly, the young boy realized his friend had not been looking for him at all. He began to cry, and he ran crying to his grandfather to complain about his friend's behavior. The wise old rabbi listened with tears in his eyes and replied, "God says the same thing: I hide, but no one wants to seek me."[88]

Religious educators can also use parables to remind learners that the way of God's kingdom is possible and that a new way of living is within their grasp. Parables can disrupt learners' complacency and their assumptions that theirs is the only right way of living. Parables can call people to authentic existence. Religious educators can use parables to encourage learners to try out new behaviors and to affirm ways in which learners are already living out God's kingdom. For example, a religious educator may have learners act out the parable of the Good Samaritan using contemporary characters. Or characters may act out other possible responses to the wounded man's plight. Or characters may pick up the story where the biblical parable leaves off. Discussion following the dramatization could center on why characters behaved as they did, how those behaviors should be evaluated, and what alternative behaviors might have been possible.

Through parables, religious educators can also address ethical issues. Many parables are concerned with how people live out their faith through their personal relationships. Often these parables invite learners to form a moral verdict, and over and over again they encourage learners to embrace a new set of values. Often, as in the parables of the Good Samaritan and the two debtors (Luke 7:41–43), Jesus asked those around him to make a judgment about the behavior of the characters in the parable, and often their judgments pointed to

---

[88]Martin Buber, *Tales of the Hasidim: The Early Masters* (New York: Schocken, 1947), p. 97.

inadequacies in their own lives. Likewise, religious educators can use parables to help learners examine ethical dilemmas in both the parables and in their own lives. Parables can become case studies for ethical decision making.

Because parables subvert the ordinary and the conventional, they create space for the extraordinary and the unconventional.[89] Used skillfully by religious educators, parables can make room for faith; they can open the door for learners to experience the presence of God in a new way and to respond in faith to their experience. Jesus said a sower went out to sow seed. As the sower sowed, some seed fell on the path and was trampled or eaten by birds. Some seed fell on rocks, and it grew only to wither for lack of moisture. Still other seed fell among thorns that eventually choked it. Finally, some seed fell into good soil, grew, and produced a hundredfold.

---

[89]See Jerry H. Stone, "Narrative Theology and Religious Education," in *Theologies of Religious Education*, ed. Randolph Crump Miller (Birmingham, Ala.: Religious Education Press, 1995), pp. 281–285.

8

Folktales

Because grandmothers looking like spiders
want to enchant the children
and grandfathers need to convince us
what happened happened because of them

and though we listen only
haphazardly, with one ear,
we will begin our story
with the word and[1]

—Lisel Mueller

Folktales, traditional stories that are passed orally from generation to generation,[2] can assist religious educators in facilitating a number of goals of religious instruction. Folktales can reach into the human psyche to foster, explore, and allay emotion; they can invite learners into mysterious and wonder-filled worlds in which vision can be renewed so that learners come to see anew the mystery and wonder in their own worlds. Many folktales provide powerful models of ethical behavior and offer harsh judgments of immoral and unethical characters; they espouse virtues of compassion, humility, and altruism over the vices of greed, selfishness, and pride. These stories can raise

---

[1]Lisel Mueller, "Why We Tell Stories," in *Favorite Folktales from Around the World*, ed. Jane Yolen (New York: Pantheon, 1986), p. 16.

[2]Joanna Cole, *Best-Loved Folktales of the World* (Garden City, N.Y.: Doubleday, 1982), p. xvii.

171

learners' awareness, enlarge their vision, and motivate their actions. What happened "once upon a time" can lead to envisioning what can happen here and now.

Educator Bette Bosma suggests that folktales have four especially relevant educational characteristics. First, the magic in the tales comes from the characters as they really are, not as the result of wishes or dreams. In fact, wishes are often shown to be foolish. Second, goodness and intelligence generally outwit evil. Third, magical power can only change outward conditions; it cannot change a person's heart or the state of the world. Fourth, evil does not triumph; it is exposed or it receives its just recompense.[3] These characteristics affirm learners' agency and encourage them to lead good and moral lives.

Folktales are part of living traditions. And as they are passed down, they have changed with each successive telling. A single tale may exist in hundreds of variations, each containing elements peculiar to the culture that produced it.[4] The term "folktale" encompasses a number of subgenres: fairy tales, fables, legends, tall tales, simpleton tales, pourquoi tales, and cumulative tales. Each form offers religious educators unique tools for creating effective teaching/learning situations.

Two theories offer possible explanations of the origins of folktales. The mongenesis theory suggests that these stories originated in a single source and then were disseminated throughout the world. The polygenesis theory contends that similar tales emerged independently throughout the world as the result of common human experiences and fundamental similarities in the human psyche.[5] Possibly some combination of the two processes most adequately explains the existence of similar tales in quite dissimilar cultures.

Students of folktales take a number of different approaches in studying and interpreting these tales. Literary scholars explore the history, structure, style, and meanings of folktales. Folklorists seek traces of old customs and rites and explore the place of the tales in their community of origin. Sociologists examine folktales as expressions of

---

[3]Bette Bosma, *Folktales, Fables, Legends, and Myths: Using Folk Literature in Your Classroom* (New York: Teachers College Press, 1987), p. 3.

[4]David L. Russell, *Literature for Children: A Short Introduction* (New York: Longman, 1991), p. 54.

[5]Ibid.

social contexts. Historians of religion look to folktales as evidence of humans' connection to the divine, and psychologists analyze folktales as expressions of human development.[6] My examination of folktales draws from each of these areas.

Folktales have probably served a variety of functions from education to reinforcement of cultural practices and social norms to entertainment, and many folktales continue to serve these functions today.[7] However, religious educators who want to use folktales for educational purposes should be aware that these tales, like many other forms of stories, can be used to reinforce norms that oppose the desired goals of religious instruction. For example, some folktales may present and reinforce stereotypical images of women and men or various racial groups.[8] When these elements (such as associating dark skin or age with evil) are not integral to the story, they may be altered. In other instances, religious educators may choose to select an alternative story that does not rely on negative stereotypes. Religious educators can also address issues of stereotypes by making efforts to dis-

---

[6]Max Lüthi, "Aspects of the Märchen and the Legend," in *Folklore Genres*, ed. Dan Ben-Amos (Austin: University of Texas Press, 1976), p. 19. For examples of various forms of the study of folktales, see (literary) Pierre Maranda and Elli Kongas Maranda, eds., *Structural Analysis of Oral Tradition* (Philadelphia: University of Pennsylvania Press, 1971); (psychological) Alan Dundes, *Interpreting Folklore* (Bloomington: Indiana University Press, 1980); (sociological) Richard Bauman, "Differential Identity and the Social Base of Folklore,"in *Toward New Perspectives in Folklore*, ed. Americo Paredes and Richard Bauman (Austin, Tex.: University of Texas Press, 1972); (folklorist) Simon J. Bronner, ed., *Creativity and Tradition in Folklore* (Logan: Utah State University Press, 1992).

[7]For example, Jack Zipes notes that in the development of the literary fairy tale in the seventeenth century there was an overwhelming tendency for fairy tales to provide models of behavior for upper-class children. "Setting Standards for Civilization through Fairy Tales: Charles Perrault and His Associates,"in *Fairy Tales and the Art of Subversion: The Classical Genre for Children and the Process of Civilization* (New York: Wildman, 1983), p. 14.

[8]For examples of feminist criticism of folktales, see Kay F. Stone, "Things Walt Disney Never Told Us," *Women and Folklore* 88 (1975): 42–50; Rosemary Minard, "Introduction," *Womenfolk and Fairy Tales* (Boston, Mass.: Houghton-Mifflin, 1975); Ethel Johnston Phelps, introduction to *Tatterhood and Other Tales* (New York: Feminist Press, 1978); Marcia R. Liebermann, "Some Day My Prince Will Come: Female Acculturation through the Fairy Tale," *College English* 34 (December 1972–73): 383–395.

cover and utilize tales that present contrasting images.[9] For example, the tale "Tatterhood," is the story of an unconventional young girl who refuses to conform to expected norms of dress and behavior. Her conventional, docile, and gentle sister is bewitched by trolls, and Tatterhood sets off with her to sail for the kingdom of the trolls. Tatterhood sails the ship unaided, defeats the trolls, saves her sister, and meets a prince who accepts her individuality.[10] By careful and intentional selection of folktales, religious educators may address both primary goals for a teaching/learning situations (learning to do the right thing in a difficult situation, for example) and secondary goals (challenging stereotypes that may prevent learners from feeling and believing they can do the right thing in a difficult situation).

FAIRY TALES

And then the marriage of the King's son with Briar-rose was celebrated with all splendor, and they lived contented to the end of their days.[11]

—Little Briar-Rose

Marvelous things happen in the realm of *faerie*. Animals speak; enchantresses cast spells; peasants outwit kings; frogs turn into princes. Fairy tales are stories about the realm in which magical and marvelous things happen.[12] *Faerie* is an Old French word that means enchantment, and fairy tales are stories that take place in this enchanted realm. "Faerie contains many things besides elves and fays, and besides dwarfs, witches, trolls, giants, or dragons: it holds the seas, the sun, the moon, the sky; and the earth, and all things that are in it: tree and bird, water and stone, wine and bread, and ourselves . . . when we are enchanted."[13] Fairy tales are actually about people, about their

---

[9]Marni Schwartz, "Storytelling—A Way to Challenge Stereotypes," *English Journal* 74 (March 1985): 91–92.

[10]Ethel Johnston Phelps, ed., "Tatterhood," in *Tatterhood and Other Tales* (New York: Feminist Press, 1978), pp. 1–6.

[11]"Little Briar-Rose," in *The Complete Grimm's Fairy Tales* (New York: Pantheon, 1972), p. 241.

[12]James M. McGlathery, *Fairy Tale Romance: The Grimms, Basile, and Perrault* (Urbana: University of Illinois Press, 1991), p. 2.

[13]J. R. R. Tolkein, *Tree and Leaf* (Boston: Houghton Mifflin, 1964), p. 9.

adventures in the realm of Faerie, and ultimately about their lives in the world.[14]

Faerie's enchantment is not an end in itself. Rather, faerie serves to satisfy a primordial human desire to survey the depths of space and time and to have communion with other living things by allowing learners to glimpse other worlds.[15] Enchantment produces a secondary world in which learners are allowed to regain a clear view of their own world, to see things as they ought to see them.[16] Fairy tales primarily deal with fundamental issues that are rendered luminous by their setting. Fairy tales simplify situations. Their figures are clearly drawn, and details, unless absolutely essential, are eliminated. Characters are typical rather than unique.[17] The effect, then, is that fairy tales create a new world in which learners see themselves and their world in a new light; they escape into faerie to recover their vision, and there they may find things not at all as they thought them to be.[18] Fairy stories "may open your hoard and let all the locked things fly away like cage-birds. The gems all turn into flowers or flams, and you will be warned that all you had (or knew) was dangerous and potent, not really effectively chained, free and wild; no more yours than they were you."[19]

Beyond the fulfillment of primordial desires fairy tales offer the consolation of the happy ending, or what J. R. R. Tolkein calls "Eucatastrophe."[20] The consolation of fairy tales is the happy ending or the felicitous catastrophe, the sudden, joyous turn that overcomes crisis. This sudden turn in fairy tales is a "miraculous grace: never to be counted on to recur. It does not deny the existence of dyscatastrophe, or sorrow and failure: the possibility of these is necessary to the joy of deliverance; it denies . . . universal final defeat."[21] It is the moment when the tears of Rapunzel touch the blinded eyes of the king's son

---

[14]Joyce Thomas, *Inside the Wolf's Belly: Aspects of the Fairy Tale* (Sheffield, U.K.: Sheffield Academic, 1989), p. 17.

[15]Tolkein, *Tree and Leaf*, p. 13.

[16]Ibid., p. 57.

[17]Bruno Bettelheim, *The Uses of Enchantment: The Meaning and Importance of Fairy Tales* (New York: Knopf, 1976), p. 8.

[18]Thomas, *Inside the Wolf's Belly*, p. 274.

[19]Tolkein, *Tree and Leaf*, p. 59.

[20]Ibid., p. 68.

[21]Ibid.

and his sight is restored; or when the prince approaches the hedge of thorns around the castle of Rosamond and it changes into a hedge of flowers that allows him to pass and wake the sleeping princess with a kiss; or the moment when Tatterhood turns her goat into a fine steed and her ragged hood into a circlet of gold and pearls. When this moment comes, it can give to the learner "a catch of the breath, a beat and lifting of the heart, near to (or indeed accompanied by) tears."[22] That moment in the story has a more marvelous, a more enchanted quality than the event described. In that return, learners receive "a piercing glimpse of joy, and heart's desire, that for a moment passes outside the frame, rends indeed the very web of story, and lets a gleam come through."[23] By extending beyond possibility, by reaching for the wondrous, fairy tales set learners to wondering and enlarge learners' daily horizons.[24] These tales remind learners of who they are, who they were, and who they might be.[25]

Obviously, then, fairy tales have an important role to play in religious instruction for learners of all ages. The realm of faerie can open up learners to new experiences, feelings, meanings, and understandings throughout their lives. As psychologist Bruno Bettelheim suggests, fairy tales have meanings on many different levels.[26] Fairy tales are not just for children; the tales themselves often offer complex adult situations. Unfortunately, however, in the contemporary world fairy tales are often relegated to the nursery and considered irrelevant to the lives of adult learners.[27]

A more helpful approach to fairy tales for religious educators mines the potential for the tales to connect to learners at all stages of life— childhood, adolescence, young adulthood, midlife, and senior adulthood. As religious educator Catherine Leary suggests, fairy tales are stories told to children by adults who at the same time speak to the child in themselves.[28] Tolkein concurs. If, he argues, a fairy tale is

---

[22]Ibid., p. 69.

[23]Ibid., p. 70.

[24]Iona Opie and Peter Opie, *The Classic Fairy Tales* (New York: Oxford University Press, 1974), p. 16.

[25]Thomas, *Inside the Wolf's Belly*, p. 285.

[26]Bettelheim, *Uses of Enchantment*, p. 169.

[27]Tolkein, *Tree and Leaf*, p. 34.

[28]Catherine Leary, "Parables and Fairy Tales," *Religious Education* 81 (Summer 1986): 489.

worth anything, it is worth adult attention because adults will put more in and get more out of the encounter than children.[29]

From the perspective of depth psychology, fairy tales reveal learners to themselves, whatever their stage of life. Although Sigmund Freud excluded fairy tales from consideration in his own work, many of his followers have developed a tradition of Freudian interpretation of fairy tales. These Freudians have suggested that fairy tales express themes of the Oedipal crisis, mirror childhood conflicts and anxieties (and hence alleviate them) and reflect children's unconscious and infantile sexuality.[30]

Carl Jung placed a great deal of emphasis on fairy tales, unlike his teacher. Jung had observed that mythical elements and images existed in the stories of people who could have had no knowledge of them from other cultures; in other words, these images emerged from the indigenous culture itself.[31] These images, common across cultures, he called archetypes, inherent structures in both the psyche of individual people and the inherited, collective psyche (the collective unconscious) of all people.[32] These archetypes, according to Jung, emerge in myths and fairy tales.[33] They provide the assurances and spiritual and moral force needed for the protagonists of the tales to succeed. Jungian Marie-Louise von Franz contends that fairy tales are the purest and simplest expressions of the psychic processes of the collective unconscious. She suggests that fairy tales demonstrate basic patterns of the human psyche, perhaps even more clearly than myth, because in myth the basic patterns are rendered through an overlay of cultural material. Fairy tales, on the other hand, contain much less

---

[29]Tolkein, *Tree and Leaf*, p. 45.

[30]For example, see Kate Friedlaender, "Children's Books and Their Function in Latency and Prepuberty," *The American Imago* 3 (1942): 129–150; Geza Roheim, "Psycho-Analysis and the Folk-Tale," *The International Journal of Psycho-Analysis* 3 (1922): 180–186; Ernest Jones, "Psychoanalysis and Folklore," in *The Study of Folklore*, ed. Alan Dundes (Englewood Cliffs, N. J.: Prentice-Hall, 1965).

[31]Carl G. Jung, "The Psychology of the Child Archetype," in *The Archetypes and the Collective Unconscious*, 2d ed., trans. R. F. C. Hull, in *The Collected Works of C. G. Jung*, vol. 9, pt. 1 (Princeton, N.J.: Princeton University Press, 1968), p. 154.

[32]Ibid., p. 155.

[33]Carl G. Jung, "The Phenomenology of the Spirit in Fairy tales," in *The Archetypes and the Collective Unconscious*, 2d ed., trans. R. F. C. Hull, *in The Collected Works of C. G. Jung*, vol. 9, pt. 1 (Princeton, N.J.: Princeton University press, 1968), p. 155.

culturally specific material and thus mirror the anatomy of the psyche with greater clarity.[34]

In religious instruction, the effective fairy tale addresses the psychic experiences of human beings through its simple correspondence with the conflicts and anxieties of learners' lives. Adults can explore this reality in depth on a cognitive level, but for children fairy tales offer empowering experiences of Eucatastrophe. Tolkein, for example, argues that children should experience fairy tales, even if they are beyond the children's immediate cognitive grasp.[35] These enchanting stories touch emotions and imagination long before learners are able to analyze them. Because fairy tales are primarily affective, children can be drawn to stories generally considered to be too advanced for them intellectually.[36] Tolkein adds that fairy stories, like clothes, should allow for growth and, indeed, should encourage it.[37] Bruno Bettelheim agrees. He contends that for fairy tales to hold children's attention, they must entertain them and arouse their curiosity. To enrich children's lives, however, they must stimulate the imagination, help children clarify emotions and develop intellect, be attuned to children's anxieties and aspirations, give recognition to children's difficulties and at the same time suggest solutions to the problems children face.[38]

Fairy tales afford religious educators an excellent opportunity to address childhood fears and anxieties. Faith development theorist James Fowler notes the role that fear plays in children's lives. Drawing on Bettelheim's work, Fowler suggests that fairy tales provide indirect yet effective ways of helping children externalize their anxieties.[39] Through identification with fairy tales, children can gain

---

[34]Marie-Louise von Franz, *The Psychological Meaning of Redemption Motifs in Fairy Tales* (Toronto: Inner City, 1980), pp. 1–2.

[35]Tolkein, *Tree and Leaf*, p. 45.

[36]Isabelle Jan offers an enlightening discussion regarding the ways in which fairy tales have been told for children or for adults relative to the historical context in which they were told. See *On Children's Literature* (New York: Schocken, 1974), pp. 30–44.

[37]Tolkein, *Tree and Leaf*, p. 45.

[38]Bettelheim, *Uses of Enchantment*, p. 5. For an in-depth examination of children and fairy tales, see Maria Tatar, *Off with Their Heads! Fairy Tales and the Culture of Childhood* (Princeton, N.J.: Princeton University Press, 1992).

[39]James W. Fowler, *Stages of Faith* (San Francisco: Harper and Row, 1981), p. 130.

comfort from knowing that their distressing or violent fantasies are common experiences. In fact, fairy stories can provide meaningful sources of strength for useful sublimations.[40] Fairy tales address children's deepest fears and suggest that solutions do exist for their anxieties, offering reassurance for the children's private concerns. Through their experience in faerie, children can distance themselves from the content of the unconscious and experience it as something external in order to gain control over it. The fairy tale mode removes the anxieties from connections to the children's present day home and reality.[41] This externalization of present, real inner conflicts provides a safe means whereby children can deal with developmental issues of childhood. Furthermore, fairy tales create a world that is not actually obtainable by children but is nonetheless reassuring to them as their experiences teach them the often harsh realities of the world in which they live.[42]

Religious educators can use fairy tales in both formal and informal settings to address children's anxieties. For example, if tragedy touches children, for example a kidnapping or an abandonment, fairy tales can provide a way for religious educators to help children deal with the tragedy. The fairy tale of Hansel and Gretel tells the story of young children abandoned by their parents in the woods and held captive by an evil witch. The children, however, turn the tables on the witch, destroy her, escape with great riches. In the meantime, the stepmother who had convinced the father to leave the children in the woods has died, and the children are reunited with their father, who has not had one happy hour since he had left them.[43] This story may allow children temporarily to leave behind the immediate crisis and enter for a while a more stable, predictable, and familiar world embodied in the tale.[44] By enclosing anxiety or even terror in a fictional frame, the tale reminds children that no matter how powerful evil may

---

[40]Julius E. Heuscher, *A Psychiatric Study of Fairy Tales: Their Origin, Meaning, and Usefulness* (Springfield, Ill.: Thomas, 1963), p. 291.

[41]Martin J. Lubetsky, "The Magic of Fairy Tales: Psychodynamic and Developmental Perspectives," *Child Psychiatry and Human Development* 19 (Summer 1989): 246.

[42]F. Andre Favat, *Child and Tale: The Origins of Interest* (Urbana, Ill.: National Council of Teachers of English, 1977), pp. 52–54.

[43]"Hansel and Gretel," trans. Margaret Hunt and James Stern, *in The Complete Grimm's Fairy Tales* (New York: Pantheon, 1972), pp. 86–94.

[44]Favat, *Child and Tale*, p. 60.

seem to be, its time is limited. The fictional frame puts the anxiety in such a faraway time and place that children are reassured that the terror is far from them.[45]

Fairy tales probably have a smaller role to play in the religious instruction of adolescents. Generally, children outgrow fairy tales and even become contemptuous of them.[46] Whereas children find the fairy tale to be a safe place into which to retreat from the harshness of reality, adolescents are often ready to face that reality. They see the fairy tale as not being like their world; instead of looking back to a mystical, magical world, they look forward to the world to which they are acclimating.[47]

One potential use of fairy tales in the religious instruction of adolescents may be in the area of identity development. Psychologist Erik Erikson has suggested that during adolescence people begin to create identity and develop a sense of self.[48] Psychologist Ronald Koteskey adds that identity is developed through culture, community, church, and family. When no positive identity is offered by these groups, adolescents develop a negative identity by rejecting the forms of identity society offers.[49] Fairy tales may offer a way to strengthen adolescents' sense of self by providing models of youth who are establishing themselves in the world. In fairy tales, often youth leave home, struggle through great ordeals until they prove victorious, and then live "happily ever after."[50]

For example, in "Rapunzel," an enchantress takes a young girl from her parents. When the girl turns twelve, the enchantress shuts her up in a tower in a forest. The tower has no doors or stairs, only a window at the very top. When the enchantress wants to enter the tower, she calls to Rapunzel who lets down her long hair, which the enchantress climbs to the window. After a year or two, the king's son happens to ride through the forest past the tower. He hears Rapunzel's song and

---

[45]Simon O. Lesser, *Fiction and the Unconscious* (New York: Vintage, 1957), p. 185.

[46]Favat, *Child and Tale*, p. 54.

[47]Ibid., p. 55.

[48]Erik Erikson, *Identity: Youth and Crisis* (New York: Norton, 1968).

[49]Ronald L. Koteskey, "Adolescence as a Cultural Invention," in *Handbook of Youth Ministry*, ed. Donald Ratcliff and James A. Davies (Birmingham, Ala.: Religious Education Press, 1991), pp. 52–56.

[50]Allan B. Chinen, "Middle Tales: Fairy Tales and Transpersonal Development at Mid-Life," *Journal of Transpersonal Psychology* 19 (1987): p. 124.

wants to climb up to her but can find no way into the tower. Each day, he returns to the tower to listen to her beautiful song. One day, as he stands behind a tree listening, the enchantress comes to the tower and cries out for Rapunzel to let down her hair. The next day, the king's son calls out for Rapunzel to let down her hair, and she does. The king's son climbs up, and they fall in love and make plans to flee the tower. One day, however, Rapunzel mistakenly mentions the king's son to the enchantress. Enraged, she cuts Rapunzel's hair and casts her out into a desert. When the king's son comes, the enchantress lets down Rapunzel's braids. The young man climbs into the tower only to find the enchantress, who tells him that Rapunzel is lost to him forever. He is so overcome with grief that he throws himself out of the tower and lands in a briar patch, which blinds him. For years, he roams around in misery until one day he comes to the desert and hears a familiar voice. There he finds Rapunzel and the twins to which she has given birth. Rapunzel recognizes him and falls on his neck, weeping. Her tears wet his eyes, and he regains his sight. He then takes Rapunzel and the children to his kingdom, where they are joyfully received and live a long time afterward in great contentment.[51]

Religious educators can use fairy tales such as this to enhance adolescents' developing sense of self. These stories can underline adolescents' ability to cope with the world they are confronting and can strengthen their sense of self-construction. In particular, fairy tales may offer models of adolescent will, strength, and ability to deal positively with the numerous moral and ethical dilemmas youth face each day. As psychologist Allan Chinen suggests, heroes and heroines dominate the fairy tales of youth. Struggle characterizes this time of life and these fairy tales, and triumph is the outcome.[52]

These themes of struggle and triumph and growth into maturity continue in young adulthood, a time during which religious educators may find fairy tales to be more effective in facilitating the goals of religious instruction. Despite the loss of interest in fairy tales in adolescence, a resurgence of interest occurs in young adulthood and continues throughout life.[53]

---

[51]Adapted from "Rapunzel," trans. Margaret Hunt and James Stern, in *The Complete Grimm's Fairy Tales* (New York: Pantheon, 1972), pp. 73–76.

[52]Chinen, "Middle Tales," p. 125.

[53]Favat, "Child and Tale," p. 56.

The Yiddish word for fairy tale is *vunder-mayses*, literally "wonder tales." By far the majority of Yiddish wonder tales deal with young men and women who leave home and have many adventures. These tales dramatize the problems and complexities of young adulthood and chart a course toward maturity.[54] Erik Erikson suggests that young adulthood is a time during which learners deal with issues of intimacy and face the task of finding people with whom they can be intimate.[55] A prominent strand of many wonder tales is the search for a partner. In many of these stories, young adults must overcome numerous difficulties in order to marry the ones they love. In "The Princess and Vanke, the Shoemaker's Son," the princess must face death in order to be with her true love, Vanke, when her father, the king, tries to marry her off to a man he finds more socially acceptable. With the help of a magic ring given to Vanke by a sorcerer, the two are able to outwit the king and at last be married to live happily ever after.[56]

A smaller group of fairy tales deals with the developmental realities of middle adulthood. In what Chinen terms "middle tales," the trickster takes center stage, and transformation, not triumph, is the challenge.[57] The trickster is the character who rebels against authority and breaks taboos. Part imp and part hero, the trickster is the character most people at times secretly would like to be.[58] In Europe, Reynard the Fox is the trickster in folktales. In Native American culture, the primary trickster is Coyote, though Raven, Mink, Rabbit, Blue Jay, and other animals also occasionally play pranks and make trouble. Coyote represents spontaneity and creativity; he is a reminder of celebration in life, and he invites learners to join him.[59] Sometimes the trickster represents the "little person" fighting against the odds, struggling against a bully or unjust authority and winning.[60] Issues of justice and power are at the heart of these tales, such as the African Fan

---

[54]Beatrice Silverman Weinreich, *Yiddish Folktales*, trans. Leonard Wolf (New York: Schocken, 1988), pp. 65–66.

[55]Erik Erikson, *Childhood and Society*, 2d ed. (New York: Norton, 1963), p. 263.

[56]Weinrich, *Yiddish Folktales*, pp. 105–106.

[57]Favat, "Child and Tale," p. 56.

[58]Richard Erdoes and Alfonso Ortiz, *American Indian Myths and Legends* (New York: Pantheon, 1984), p. 335.

[59]Ibid.

[60]Cole, *Best-loved Folktales*, p. xxiii.

Tribe's tug-of-war story in which a clever tortoise triumphs over two larger animals.[61] At other times, however, the trickster may be a greedy fool who fails in the end and serves as an object lesson demonstrating the folly of selfishness and greed.[62] As Erik Erikson has pointed out, middle adulthood, in particular, is a time during which adults focus on issues of generativity and creativity.[63] Thus, religious educators can utilize fairy tales with adults to encourage transformation through celebration, spontaneity, creativity, and justice.

Older adults are at the center of another group of fairy tales. In these elder tales, the figure of the sage predominates, and transcendence is the theme. These stories often deal with poverty, self-reformation, worldly wisdom, emancipated innocence, and mediation with the supernatural.[64] Erikson suggests that the tasks of older adulthood include developing a sense of ego integrity and wisdom.[65] Religious educators can use fairy tales to help older adults deal with issues of aging and death. Through fairy tales, for example, older learners can explore eschatology, by examining their own feelings and beliefs about death through the experiences of the characters in the tales. These tales can help affirm tenets of faith that suggest hope for people beyond this life. As Chinen suggests, "In more familiar fairy tales, the young Prince and Princess marry and live happily ever after. Elder tales tell us what ideally happens in that ever after."[66]

Across the lifespan, fairy tales have an essential role to play in religious instruction. Fairy tales provide one means of facilitating the goals of religious instruction in the cognitive, affective, and lifestyle domains. In the cognitive domain, fairy tales allow learners to explore the human psyche and to discover common experiences of the self. These tales help learners understand themselves; fairy tales often clarify problems and offer a means of dealing with inner conflicts. They affirm progress through life, and they stimulate the imagination and creativity in addressing the situations that learners face. Religious educators can, for example, use fairy tales for religious instruction in the

---

[61]Ibid., pp. 658–660.

[62]Ibid., p. xxiii.

[63]Erikson, *Childhood and Society*, p. 267.

[64]Allan B. Chinen, "Fairy Tales and Psychological Development in Later Life: A Cross-Cultural Hermeneutic Study," *Gerontologist* 27 (June 1987): 344.

[65]Erikson, *Childhood and Society*, pp. 268–269.

[66]Chinen, "Fairy Tales and Psychological Development in Later Life," p. 345.

cognitive domain by having learners discuss the meanings of the tale and suggest ways to apply the meanings to their own lives.

Fairy tales are especially powerful in the affective domain. For this reason, fairy tales are effective learning tools with children as well as with adults. The tales can be felt long before they can be understood. In the affective domain, fairy tales can engulf learners in a whirlwind of emotions and provide ways in which learners can find comfort from the fears and anxieties of their own lives. Furthermore, fairy tales can challenge and affect attitudes through the simple but powerful systems of morality that learners experience in the world of faerie. Religious educators can utilize fairy tales in the affective domain, for example, by telling a tale and then asking learners to relate events in their own lives that have evoked similar feelings. Or religious educators may have learners explore attitudes expressed in a fairy tale and compare those attitudes with their own.

Finally, fairy tales are an effective tool for religious instruction in the lifestyle domain. Fairy tales often provide models for living. They offer examples of good women and men who struggle against incredible odds, do the right things, and triumph in the end. These stories encourage learners in their own daily struggles to be the people of God by showing them and reminding them that good wins in the end.

Tolkein contends that the Gospels themselves contain a fairy tale or a story of a larger kind that embraces the essence of fairy tales. He calls the birth of Christ humankind's eucatastrophe, and the resurrection the eucatastrophe of the story of the incarnation. Nonetheless, he adds, the "Evangelium has not abrogated legends; it has hallowed them, especially the 'happy ending.'"[67] Theologian Jurgen Moltmann suggests that in the stories of Israel and the early church, all events are experienced with a view to the future. God's activity in human history guides humanity toward a future that is open. Faith that God is, according to Moltmann, includes hope that someday God's kingdom will come.[68] The happy ending of fairy tales is a microcosm of the hope of the happy ending of the Christian story. Like the protagonists of fairy tales, learners can be the recipients of a miraculous grace; they can experience triumph, transformation, and transcendence.

---

[67]Tolkein, *Tree and Leaf*, pp. 71–73.

[68]Jürgen Moltmann, "Theology as Eschatology," in *The Future of Hope: Theology as Eschatology,* ed. Frederick Herzog (New York: Herder and Herder), p. 10.

FABLES

An Athenian once found Aesop joining merrily in the sports of some children. He ridiculed him for his want of gravity, and Aesop good-temperedly took up a bow, unstrung it, and laid it at his feet. "There, friend," said he: "that bow, if kept always strained, would lose its spring, and probably snap. Let it go free sometimes, and it will be the fitter for use when it is wanted. "[69]

—Aesop

Because of their overt concern with morality, fables are especially suited to use in religious instruction. A fable is a short tale with a moral. Animals serve as the primary characters, portraying human virtues and vices while retaining their animal traits. These stories are obviously exhortative, many concluding with a stated moral. The oldest surviving fables come from Greece and India. The oldest collections are those associated with Aesop, who was a slave in Ionia in the sixth century B.C.E. Probably Aesop's fables circulated orally for almost three centuries before they were written down by Demetrius Phalereus around 320 B.C.E. A Latin version of the tales was created by Phaedrus around the time of Christ.[70] The fables, like many books, disappeared during the Dark Ages but reappeared in a fourteenthth century collection by Planudes, a monk in Constantinople. One of the first books printed in England by William Caxton was *The Subtyl Historyes and Fables of Esope*.[71] Even Martin Luther began a translation of Aesop's fables because he regarded them quite highly. Finally in 1610, a Swiss scholar, Nevelet, compiled what became the standard text for the fables.

The oldest Eastern collection of fables is the *Panchatantra*, a textbook of the wise conduct of life, which begins with this guarantee of the effectiveness of storytelling in awakening intelligence:

Whoever learns the work by heart,
Or through the story-teller's art
    Becomes acquainted,

---

[69]Aesop, "Aesop at Play," in *Aesop's Fables* (London: Cassell, 1893), p. 60.

[70]*Babrius and Phaedrus*, trans. Ben Edwin Perry, (Cambridge, Mass.: Harvard University Press, 1965).

[71]J. B. R. editor's preface to *Aesop's Fables* (London: Cassell, 1893), p. iv-v.

His life by sad defeat—although
The king of heaven be his foe—
Is never tainted.[72]

Some of these tales were ascribed to Bidpai, a scholar in the court of an Indian prince. As the story goes, Bidpai produced the collection in order to reform an evil king. The tales became known as the *Fables of Bidpai*, which were translated from the original Persian into Arabic, then into Latin, and finally into the vernacular languages of Europe.[73]

In the Middle Ages, fables were used in sermons and *exempla* books. In 1688 Jean de la Fontaine's collection of fables appeared in France,[74] and Russian storyteller Ivan Andreevich Krylov's fables were published in 1843.[75]

Fables are a development of the animal tale, which in its earliest form attempted to explain some characteristic of an animal (why the rabbit has a short tail, for example). Fables, as a more developed genre, use the animal tale to teach moral precepts or satirize human behavior, not to explain characteristics.[76] Fables, however, do carry over some of the characterizations of animals already developed in animal tales (the fox as sly, for example). Most fables have two parts: the narrative, which exemplifies the moral, and often an epigram appended to the story explicitly stating the moral. Although animal characters may attract children, fables actually require abstract thinking and are probably more suited to religious instruction with adults.

Jean de la Fontaine contends that fables are all the more penetrating and effective in teaching because they are familiar and usual. He

---

[72]*The Panchatantra*, trans. Arthur W. Ryder (Chicago: University of Chicago Press, 1925), p. 16.

[73]For example, see *Les Fabulistes latins depuis le siècle d'Auguste jusqu'a la fin du Moyen Age*, vol. X, trans. Hervieux Leopold (Paris: Firmin-Didot, 1890).

[74]Jean de la Fontaine, *The Fables of La Fontaine*, trans. Marianne Moore (New York: Viking, 1954).

[75]Ivan Andreevich Krylov, *Kriloff's Fables*, trans. Charles Fillingham (London: Dutton, 1920).

[76]For more information on moral development, see Andrew Garrod, *Approaches to Moral Development: New Research and Emerging Themes* (New York: Teachers College Press, 1993) and Carol Gilligan, *Mapping the Moral Domain: A Contribution of Women's Thinking to Psychological Theory and Education* (Cambridge: Harvard University Press, 1988).

continues, "Anyone who offered us none but master minds to imitate would be affording us an excuse for falling short; there is no such excuse when ants and bees are capable of performing the tasks we are set."[77]

Fables offer religious educators an effective tool for exploring moral issues with adults. They can use them to teach morality by sharing the fables of Aesop, Krylov, Bidpai, or La Fontaine with learners. Religious educators may also have learners create their own fables to address contemporary issues of moral concern. These simple tales can provide a means to fruitful experience in religious instruction.

A crow was ready to die of thirst. He spied a pitcher and flew to it with joy, hoping to find water in it. There was water there, but to his dismay, it was only a small bit at the bottom, far from his reach. The crow tried to overturn the pitcher, but it was too heavy. So he began to gather stones from the ground nearby. Taking them in his beak, one by one, he dropped them in the pitcher. In this way, the water gradually reached the top, and the crow was able to drink.[78]

LEGENDS AND TALL TALES

The old country wives . . . who are the best judges of these matters maintain to this day that Ichabod was spirited away by supernatural means; and it is a favorite story often told about the neighborhood round the winter evening fire.[79]

—Washington Irving

Legends

Legends are traditional stories that are supposedly based on historical facts and are told as if they are true.[80] Whereas myths focus on gods and goddesses, legends focus on mortal heroes.[81] The Bible itself

---

[77]La Fontaine, La Fontaine's Preface to *The Fables of La Fontaine*, p. 7.

[78]Adapted from Aesop, "The Crow and the Pitcher," in *Aesop's Fables*, p. 217.

[79]Washington Irving, "The Legend of Sleepy Hollow," in *Legends Every Child Should Know*, ed. Hamilton Wright Marbie (New York: Grosset and Dunlap, 1906), p. 260.

[80]Bosma, *Folktales, Fables, Legends, and Myths*, p. 6.

[81]Russell, *Literature for Children*, p. 60.

contains many legends, stories about heroic people, that were once rooted in facts but grew to serve larger ethnological, etymological, and ceremonial purposes (explaining tribal relations, the origins of names, and the origins of festivals) for the Jewish people.[82] Many early Western legends were about religious people or places with religious association. On the whole, these stories were concerned with saints and martyrs. The church used them to provide religious instruction. Hagiography, the study of the lives of the saints, focuses on the idealized biographies of the saints which picture them as exemplary leaders and models of Christian virtue.[83] These legends usually have a single protagonist and celebrate that hero's ideal experiences.[84] The structure of the legends of saints' lives is fairly common among the tales— childhood, adulthood, and death, with emphases on religious, theological, and ethical themes. The hero turns from the world, gains experience and depth of judgment, brings about miracles, and ultimately transcends human life through death.[85] The early tales of the saints' lives were written in Latin but were quickly adapted into the vernacular languages of Europe as a recognition of the value of the lives of extraordinary characters for ordinary people. These vernacular versions often sought to make the legends available to an uneducated and unsophisticated audience. Depending upon the audience the tales were adapted with appropriate cultural conventions.[86] The success of vernacular hagiographers depended on their ability to combine the exceptional with the plausible, the extraordinary with the ordinary.[87]

---

[82]Laura H. Wild, *A Literary Guide to the Bible: A Study of the Types of Literature Present in The Old and New Testaments* (London George Allen & Unwin, 1922), p. 64. See also James George Frazer, *Folk-lore in the Old Testament*, 3 vols. (London: Macmillan, 1919); Theodor H. Gaster, *Myth, Legend, and Custom in the Old Testament* (New York: Harper and Row, 1969).

[83]Gordon H. Gerould, *Saints' Legends* (Boston Houghton Mifflin, 1916), p. 5.

[84]Paul Maurice Clogan, *Medievalia Et Humanistica* (London: Cambridge University Press, 1975), p. ix.

[85]Charles W. Jones, *Saints' Lives and Chronicles in Early England* (Ithaca, N.Y.: Cornell University Press, 1947), p. 73.

[86]Phyllis Johnson and Brigitte Cazelles, *Le Vain Siecle Cuerpir: A Literary Approach to Sainthood through Old French Hagiography of the Twelfth Century* (Chapel Hill, N.C.: North Carolina Studies in the Romance Languages and Literatures, 1979), pp. 13–18.

[87]Ibid., p. 19.

And, as most stories do, these stories continued to change in response to social and cultural changes and needs. In the thirteenth century, Jacobus de Voragine collected a number of stories of the saints' lives into the *Legenda Aurea, The Golden Legend*, which became one of the most popular books during the Middle Ages.

Originally, legends had some basis in fact, though often it was slight. As time progressed and legends were handed down through generations, the element of fact grew smaller and smaller. Finally, the term has come to apply to any story supposedly based on fact, intermingled with imagination and traditional materials, told about a person, place, or incident. These imaginative tales provide religious educators with useful examples of moral and ethical behavior. Legends can be taught in religious instruction settings in many ways. Children can make puppet characters and then perform a legend, or they can draw or paint scenes to tell the story. Adults may tell the story as a readers theater piece and follow the reading with a discussion of the relevance of the legend to contemporary life. Legends are especially useful in the lifestyle domain, since they offer models of exemplary character and behavior.

Tall Tales

A special group of heroic tales has grown up around fictional characters whose exploits belong to the genre of tall tale. A tall tale is a humorously exaggerated story of impossible feats. More than any other story form, the tall tale is a peculiarly American tale, born out of the vastness and fertility of the land.[88] Tall tales are characterized by larger-than-life characters, vast exaggeration, and local color.[89] This genre flourished particularly in the oral tradition of the nineteenth century American frontier.[90] The most popular and enduring character of American tall tales was that amazing lumberjack, Paul Bunyan. Paul Bunyan could spin a log till the bark came off and then run ashore on the bubbles created in the water by the spinning log. Once, when he was in Washington, he got into an argument with Billy Puget (whose

---

[88]Carolyn S. Brown, *The Tall Tale in American Folklore and Literature* (Knoxville: University of Tennessee Press, 1987), p. 2.

[89]Norma J. Livo and Sandra A. Rietz, *Storytelling: Process and Practice* (Littleton, Colo.: Libraries Unlimited, 1986), p. 251.

[90]Brown, *The Tall Tale*, p. 3.

construction company was building Puget Sound and moving record levels of dirt) about who had shoveled the most dirt. Paul got mad and said he would show Billy Puget who could move the most dirt. He started shoveling dirt back, and before Billy could stop him, he had piled up the San Juan Islands.[91]

In American literary history, Mark Twain is perhaps the most prolific and excellent writer of tall tales. Twain is able to combine the characteristics of the oral yarn spinner and the literary writer in producing humorous tales that affirm processes of dialogue and interpretation, satirizing behavior and dramatizing the interaction of competing voices.[92] In his tales, the reader is invited to experience new understandings of the world and to join in the fun of comic exaggeration.[93]

Tall tales are excellent resources for religious instruction in the affective and lifestyle domains. The humor of tall tales is evocative of powerful, positive emotions. Learners are able to laugh at ridiculous situations in the tales, which may be quite similar, despite their exaggerations, to situations in learners' lives. These tales may help learners laugh at themselves as well. These tales also often point out inconsistencies and hypocrisy, encouraging honest and decent behavior. A religious educator may use a tall tale, for example, Mark Twain's "The Story of the Bad Little Boy," to explore hypocrisy in the church and in society. In this tale, Twain tells of a bad little boy, who, unlike the bad little boys in the Sunday school literature, does terrible things and has nothing bad happen to him. He grows up to be a scoundrel, a cheat, and a respected legislator.[94] Or religious educators can have learners tell their own tall tales to expose some facet of human behavior. Tall tales use their exaggeration to make points about the absurdity of human behavior. Religious educators can use these tales to help learners examine their own behavior and the absurdities of their own lives.

---

[91]*Paul Bunyan and His Big Blue Ox: Their Marvelous Exploits*, 30th anniversary ed. (Westwood, Calif.: Sugar Pine, 1944); see also Daniel Hoffman, *Paul Bunyan: Last of the Frontier Demigods* (Lincoln: University of Nebraska Press, 1980).

[92]Henry B. Wonham, *Mark Twain and the Art of the Tall Tale* (New York: Oxford University Press, 1993), pp. 68–69.

[93]Brown, *The Tall Tale*, p. 121.

[94]Mark Twain, "The Story of the Bad Little Boy," in *The Complete Short Stories of Mark Twain* (Garden City, N.Y.: Hanover House, 1957), pp. 6–9.

DROLL, CUMULATIVE, AND POURQUOI TALES

Droll Tales

Droll tales, also known as simpleton or noodlehead tales, rely on ridiculous situations or lovable fools to create humor. Chelm, a mythical town in Yiddish folklore, is filled with fools, affectionately and ironically dubbed "the wise men of Chelm." The Chelmites have a penchant for misunderstanding the laws of nature and misinterpreting the laws of the Torah.[95] According to one tale, Chelmites became fools when a new Torah reader misread the Scripture. Instead of reading, "In the beginning, God created the heavens," he read, "In the beginning, God created fools," and the inhabitants of Chelm have been fools ever since. Another story suggests that when the angel carrying the jar of foolish souls passed by Chelm, he lost his footing and slipped, spilling the entire contents of the jar near Chelm, and since that time the Chelmites have been fools.[96] According to author Isaac Beshevis Singer, the pious believe that God said, "Let there be Chelm," and there was Chelm. Other scholars, he explains, believe Chelm came about as the result of an eruption. Before Chelm, they contend, there was chaos, fog, and mist. Then there was a great explosion, and Chelm appeared.[97]

Once the Chelmites decided to make money by selling the lumber from a mountain overlooking the town. The men chopped down the trees and then began the slow, laborious process of carrying the huge tree trunks down the mountain. On the last day of their work, a stranger arrived in town and watched the men carrying the trees down the mountain. He asked why they had not rolled the trees down the mountain instead. The wise men of Chelm thought it such a good idea that they carried the logs back up the mountain so they could roll them down.

The Chelmites were troubled by the dark. At night they would run into things, fall down, and injure themselves. One day they overheard a man from another city say that even the nights in his city were bright. So the Chelmites held a meeting and developed a plan. They

---

[95]Weinreich, *Yiddish Folktales*, p. 204.

[96]Ibid., pp. 222–223.

[97]Isaac Bashevis Singer, *The Fools of Chelm and Their History* (Farrar, Strauss, and Giroux, 1973).

waited for a moonlit night, and it was such a fine night that they blessed it in proper form. Then, seeing the moon's reflection in a barrel of water, they quickly nailed a board over the barrel. Later, when the moon was new again and the night was dark, they opened the barrel to take their moon out of storage. But when they looked into the barrel, there was no moon. "Alas," they cried, "Someone has stolen our moon."[98]

The appeal of droll tales is often rooted in the learners' sense of superiority over the fools, but many times the triumph of the good-hearted simpleton over craftier evil characters attracts learners to the tales. Often, the fool or simpleton is indeed wiser than anyone else, affirming the paradox that the wise may actually be simple and the simple truly wise.[99]

In the Swedish tale "The Old Woman and the Tramp," a tramp stayed the night with a stingy old woman. Now, this was a very clever tramp. When he asked for food, she claimed to have none, and so he offered to make a pot of broth from a nail. As he boiled the water and dropped the nail in, he commented that the broth might be a little thin because he had been using the same nail all week. "If only I had a scrap of flour to put in," he lamented.

"Well, I think I have a scrap of flour," the old woman said, and the tramp added it to the mixture.

"Now, if only I had a bit of beef and potatoes, this broth would be fit for company," the tramp then said. And the old woman found a bit of beef and a few potatoes.

"Now, if I only had a little barley and a drop of milk, this broth would be fit for a king," and the old woman found some barley and milk, which the tramp added to the broth.

Then the tramp took out the nail. "Now it's ready. But when the king and queen have this kind of soup, they always have a drink or two and a sandwich with it."

By now, the old woman was feeling quite fine, and so she found a bottle of brandy and bread, meat, cheese, and butter for sandwiches. And they had a fine meal.

The old woman was amazed with the marvelous feast the tramp had made from only a nail. The next day when the tramp went on his way, she gave him a dollar coin and thanked him for what he had taught

---

[98]Ibid., p. 225.
[99]Russell, *Literature for Children*, p. 55.

her. "Now I will live in comfort," she said, "since I have learned to make broth from a nail."

"Well," the tramp replied, "it isn't very difficult if you only have something good to add to it."

The tramp left, and the woman stood at her door, staring after him. "Such people don't grow on every bush," she said.[100]

In this tale, the tables are turned on the selfish old woman, the real noodle in the story, who thanks the tramp for creating a broth for which she has actually supplied all of the ingredients. This tale, like many droll tales, focuses on a seemingly innocent hero who profits from the greed of his victim.[101] Such stories provide a means for religious educators to help learners explore such paradoxes as the wisdom of fools and the wealth of the poor. These stories can affirm biblical truths that the wise of this world are truly foolish, that the way to gain one's life is to give it away, and that the way to be filled is to hunger for righteousness. A number of novels particularly appropriate for religious instruction also deal with this theme. Henry Morton Robinson's *The Cardinal* and Georges Bernanos's *Diary of a Country Priest* are excellent resources for religious instruction.[102]

In some cultures, the simpleton takes on the role of the sacred clown, who inserts levity and foolishness in the midst of solemn ritual. Generally, the aim of the sacred clown or ceremonial fool is a ritual withdrawal from social norms and taboos, resulting in foolish or contrary behavior, in order to reinforce social traditions for observers.[103] These buffoons often engage in such activities as backward speech, contrary behavior, and revolting acts such as throwing manure. Hopi clowns got into tussles and tormented each other with cactus branches. Papago clowns visited people's houses and upset things. Miwok clowns pried into people's houses and wrecked them. The Huichol

---

[100]Adapted from Atelia Clarkson and Gilbert B. Cross, *World Folktales: A Scribner Resource Collection* (New York: Scribner's, 1980), pp. 370–374.

[101]Ibid., pp. 374–375.

[102]Henry Morton Robinson, *The Cardinal* (New York: Simon and Schuster, 1950); Georges Bernanos, *The Diary of a Country Priest*, trans. Pamela Morris (New York: Macmillan, 1937).

[103]Anton C. Zijdervedl, *Reality in a Looking-Glass: Rationality through an Analysis of Traditional Folly* (London: Routledge and Kegan Paul, 1982), p. 141. For more information on court fools, see Dr. Doran, *The History of Court Fools* (New York: Haskell, 1966).

clowns of Mexico prevented people from sleeping by shaking rattles near their ears or by tugging at their clothing.[104] In a Lent ceremony in Southern Sonora, Mexico, ceremonial clowns staged a passion play, which became an opportunity for mocking facets of everyday life, particularly sexuality and sickness.[105] During a New Year's festival in Lhasa, Tibet, one man from the lower social strata was chosen to be ruler for a week. During this week, he mocked the sacred Buddhist foundations of his society; he could eat and drink and do whatever he liked. For a week, he held a reign of complete license. But, at the end of the week, he was sent into the desert as a kind of scapegoat. This one-week ruler represented the hidden, negative, and evil sides of Tibetan society. His banishment represented Tibet's rejection of his values and reinforced the ascetic and deeply spiritual values of the community.[106]

The actions of these fools are quite similar to the buffoons of the medieval Feast of Fools. This festival flourished primarily in the cathedral towns of France, although there is evidence of it in other countries. The celebration involved a complete reversal of the ordinary. During this time, the authority of the clergy was transferred to the subdeacons who burlesqued the Mass. Although the Church tried to eradicate the Feast, it persisted until the end of the fifteenth century, with some traces of it remaining as late as the seventeenth century.[107] This feast offered an opportunity for the fools to offer critiques of the Church and probably helped develop the medieval idea of the Fool as social critic.[108]

Stories of fools remind learners of their own human fallibility. They offer social critiques and provide a new lens on the world. Droll stories help learners laugh at themselves and suggest that learners should not always take everything in life too seriously. Sometimes everyone plays the fool, but noodlehead stories affirm the truth that sometimes the foolish is truly wise.

---

[104]Julien H. Steward, *The Ceremonial Buffoon of the American Indian*, vol. 14 of *Papers of the Michigan Academy of Science, Arts, and Letters* (Ann Arbor: University of Michigan Press, 1931), p. 194.

[105]Zijdervedl, *Reality in a Looking-Glass*, pp. 139–140.

[106]Ibid., p. 132.

[107]Enid Welsford, *The Fool: His Social and Literary History* (Gloucester, Mass.: Peter Smith, 1966), pp. 202–203.

[108]Ibid., p. 204.

Cumulative Tales

Cumulative tales are brief, rhythmical stories that rely entirely on repetition for their total effect. As each new detail is added to earlier details, the entire list is repeated, creating a sort of chorus and a challenge to the memory of the learner.[109] In these tales, the structure controls the movement of the plot through its formulaic repetition.[110] In the cumulative story of "The Cat and the Mouse," the mouse lost her tail to the cat, who refused to return it until the mouse went to the cow and brought the cat milk. The cow refused milk until the mouse went to the farmer to get hay. The farmer refused the hay until the mouse went to the butcher to get him some met. The butcher refused to give her the meat until she went to the baker to get him some bread. The baker gave the mouse some bread, which she took to the butcher, who gave her some meat, which she took to the farmer, who gave her some hay, which she took to the cow, who gave her some milk, which she took to the cat, who gave her her tail.[111]

Cumulative tales are especially appealing to young children because often they allow them to join in the storytelling. These types of stories are especially entertaining, and they also teach children to use their imaginations. Many present children with the consequences of silly, selfish, and arrogant behavior. Religious educators can use cumulative tales with young children to encourage participation, to develop a sense of church as an enjoyable place to be, and to boost self-confidence. Since cumulative tales can be told in ways that invite learner participation, religious educators can use these stories to help children be active participants in teaching/learning situations. Because these tales are funny and entertaining, they can create positive energy, helping children feel welcome and happy in church. Because children can successfully participate in telling these tales, their use in religious instruction can help boost self-confidence in children who need encouragement. For example, a dramatization of "Henny Penny" can allow learners to participate in active storytelling, enjoy themselves, and feel valued by adults and their peers.[112]

---

[109]Russell, *Literature for Children*, p. 56.
[110]Clarkson and Cross, *World Folktales*, p. 221.
[111]Adapted from Ibid., pp. 237–238.
[112]Ibid., p. 395.

Pourquoi Tales

Like myths, pourquoi tales offer religious educators an excellent resource for exploring the ways the world has come to be constructed. These tales, which attempt to explain the natural world and the peculiarities and incongruities that are part of the way the world is, can be used in religious instruction to help learners see examples of good and bad behavior, sympathize with characters and develop appropriate attitudes toward characters' actions, and to think through the ways in which learners construct the world around them. The name of the tales derives from the French word for why.[113] Pourquoi stories differ from myths in that the characters are almost all animals, and rarely do any divine or higher powers intervene. These stories are thus much less profound than myths, though they do suggest systems of morality in which good characters succeed and wicked characters are punished.[114] These stories explain such things as cracks in Tortoise's shell, the sea's saltiness, chipmunks' stripes, and why the sun and moon live in the sky.

A Sukuma tribe tale from Africa explains how frog lost his tail. Frog knew he was ugly, but his chief complaint was that he had no tail. The other animals swished their tails at Frog and jeered. At last Frog went to the Sky God and begged for a tail. Sky God agreed and gave Frog the assignment of watching over Sky God's special well that never dries up. Frog began to show off his tail to everyone, and his new position made him unbearably conceited. He remembered how unkind the other animals had been to him, and when all the other water holes dried up and the animals came to the Sky God's special well, Frog sent them away. The Sky God heard of Frog's behavior. He came to the well and received the same unkind treatment that Frog gave the other animals. The Sky God was so angry that he took away Frog's tail and drove him from the well. The Sky God still reminds Frog of the misery he caused. Each spring, when Frog is born as a tadpole, he has a long, beautiful tail. But as he grows, his tail shrinks until it disappears. The Sky God takes Frog's tail away because Frog was once spiteful and unforgiving.[115]

---

[113]Russell, *Literature for Children*, p. 56.
[114]Clarkson and Cross, *World Folktales*, p. 345.
[115]adapted from Cole, *Best-loved Folktales of the World*, pp. 626–627.

CONCLUSION

Folktales can carry learners away from the mundane world to wonder-filled worlds in which their vision can be renewed to see the mystery and wonder in their own world. Forces of good and evil do battle; the weak defeat the strong, and the foolish confound the wise in the realms of wonder. The themes of folktales touch on significant themes of human existence—overcoming obstacles, finding a place in the world, escaping enemies, creating identity. Folktales extol the virtues of compassion, humility, persistence, creativity, and wisdom. Through folktales, religious educators can help learners challenge and transform their visions and their lives.

9

Life Stories

Maybe we ought to take a trip, he says. Didn't I use to want to?
But I tell him no. I don't see the need, I say. We have been
traveling for years, traveled all our lives, we are traveling still.
We couldn't stay in one place if we tried.[1]

—Anne Tyler

This is how I remember it. I grew up in the church. Southern Baptists
have something called "cradle roll," the Sunday school membership
list for "bed babies," those infants still too young walk. Now, Southern Baptists love to count things, especially people, and so the cradle
roll is important because it allows Southern Baptists to count all the
inhabitants of the church nursery in their numbers for Sunday school
enrollment and Sunday school attendance. It does not help in the
"Bible brought" and "lesson prepared" columns of the weekly report,
but it does set a life pattern for Southern Baptist children of knowing
that it is important to be counted. After I was born, my parents took
me home from McCall Hospital to our little house on Nanellen
Street. The next place they took me was church, and my name was
entered into the cradle roll.

As far back as I can remember, I loved church. I loved my Sunday
school teachers and my missions education leaders. I loved the songs
we sang about the B-I-B-L-E and Jesus and the little children of the
world. I loved the child-sized chairs and the flannelgraph boards and

---

[1]Anne Tyler, *Earthly Possessions* (New York: Berkeley, 1977), p. 222.

arts and crafts. Early on, I knew that Jesus loved me and wanted me for a sunbeam to shine for him each day. And I knew that if the devil did not like the fact that I had joy down in my heart, he could sit on a tack. For me, church was a place of warmth, acceptance, belonging, nurturing, and growth.

I have two especially vivid memories of church from my preschool years. The first is of my mother's baptism. I must have been only three or four years old because my sister had not been born yet. Baptists practice baptism by immersion, and so every Baptist church that can afford one has a baptismal pool in the front of the sanctuary. The baptistry at Shorter Avenue Baptist Church in Rome, Georgia was especially impressive to a preschooler because on the back wall of the baptistry was painted a picture of a river bank leading down into the baptismal pool. When my mother walked down into that pool to be baptized, I was sure she was walking into the River Jordan. Sometime afterward, while I was still a child, the church built a new sanctuary and remodeled the old one, tearing out the baptismal pool and its river scene backdrop. And I am glad. I imagine if I saw that painting now, I would probably think it was pretty tacky. But in my mind I can forever see my mother coming up out of the baptismal waters onto the bank of the Jordan River.

My other vivid memory of my preschool years in church is of one of our pastor's Sunday rituals. Every week, the pastor, Brother Corby Yother, would enter the worship service from the back of the church. He would stop and shake hands with people in the pews, sitting along the aisle. Each Sunday, I eagerly awaited Brother Corby's entrance so he could shake my hand, call my name, and say hello. When Brother Corby took my hand, I knew I belonged. I was important. After all, the preacher paid attention to me. One Sunday, Corby was making his way down the aisle, and somehow he missed my outstretched hand. By the time he reached his chair on the podium, I was distraught. Knowing there would be no peace until I had shaken the preacher's hand, my father took me from our pew in the back of the church up to the front and onto the podium. With one hand around my feet and the other supporting my torso, my father sort of thrust me at the pastor. With determination I stuck out my hand. Corby looked up in surprise, and with a grin on his face, gave my hand a proper shake. Satisfied, I allowed my father to take me back to my seat, content in having secured my place in the congregation of faith for another week.

Life stories are the narratives that people tell out of their personal experiences. Formalized, they become literary biography and autobiography. In daily life, however, life stories are the anecdotes, illustrations, sagas, and legends that people create from the raw data of personal experiences. Life stories reflect personal histories and constitute personal myths. Personal myths are the stories about themselves that individuals have amassed, which to some extent become who the individuals are.[2]

Life stories, however, are not formed in isolation. The narratives of people's lives are inextricably interwoven with the narratives of the lives of their communities, their families, and those individuals who participate and have participated in those communities. Individuals' histories and the histories of their communities and of other individuals are connected. Thus, to engage in one's own life stories is to engage in the life stories of others. As learners create narratives of their life experiences, therefore, they always do so in the context of other stories that preceded theirs and which continue alongside theirs.

In telling life stories, people often recreate powerful experiences, which may be humorous or sad, exciting or heartrending. Used in religious instruction, the recounting of these experiences can facilitate learning in the cognitive, affective, and lifestyle domains. Life stories can engage learners in vicarious experiences, evoke powerful emotions, provide models of exemplary behavior, or challenge conventional attitudes or modes of thinking.

In religiously significant stories (those narratives that have particular import for the religious lives of learners) learners may even experience the presence of God. In these stories, learners find God at work in the lives of other people, in communities, and even in themselves. These powerful stories plumb the depths of human experiences of the divine and offer the possibility of recreating those experiences in learners. In religiously significant life stories, learners experience something of God in the particulars of one person's or one community's story. In experiencing life stories, learners can feel compassion for those different from themselves by entering into the Other. They can come to new attitudes and values. They can find paradigms of Christian identity, love, meaning, and action.

---

[2]William Lowell Randall, *The Stories We Are: An Essay on Self-Creation* (Toronto: University of Toronto Press, 1995), p. 67.

AUTOBIOGRAPHY AND BIOGRAPHY

Autobiography and biography represent formal versions of life stories. Both autobiography and biography claim to be true to life—true to the actual lives of the persons whose histories are told. Because of this connection to the lives of actual persons, autobiography and biography are especially well suited for use in religious instruction. These types of stories can provide learners with glimpses of God at work in the lives of people like themselves and thus affirm their own intimations of God at work in their lives. Autobiographies and biographies can touch learners' emotions, inviting them to respond to God in love. These life histories can provide significant models of behavior as learners discover how others have lived out their faith; through these stories learners can experience embodied faith and can be challenged to live their own faith as God's people in the world.

Autobiography

Autobiography is a process of self-creation.[3] In writing autobiography, the author both recalls past experiences and reorders them into a unified whole. Yet experience itself is not seamless, and the autobiographer's reconstruction of self ultimately results in a fiction that more or less reflects the standpoint of the author at the time of writing.[4] The effect of autobiography is to reveal the self the author has created through the broad patterns and details of the events and circumstances of life. Autobiography, then, evokes a self that readers see, not directly, but elliptically through the experiences recounted by the author.

---

[3]James Olney, *Metaphors of Self: The Meaning of Autobiography* (Princeton, N. J.: Princeton University Press, 1972); William C. Spengemann, *The Forms of Autobiography: Episodes in the History of a Literary Genre* (New Haven: Yale University Press, 1980).

[4]Shari Benstock, "Authorizing the Autobiographical," in *The Private Self: Theory and Practice of Women's Autobiographical Writings*, ed. Shari Benstock (Chapel Hill: University of North Carolina Press, 1988), p. 11; Karl J. Weintraub, "Autobiography and Historical Consciousness," *Autobiographical Acts: The Changing Situation of a Literary Genre*, ed. Elizabeth W. Bruss (Baltimore, Md.: Johns Hopkins University Press, 1976), p. 827. See also Paul John Eakin, *Fictions in Autobiography: Studies in the Art of Self-Invention* (Princeton, N. J.: Princeton University Press, 1985).

Autobiographical criticism is fraught with debate over the definition of the genre itself.[5] Central to the debate is the question of the
subject of autobiography. In traditional definitions of autobiography,
which focus on the centrality of the self as a witness to his own being,
the subject becomes an object of investigation, and the first-person
voice of the account masks the actual third-person object of the narrative.[6] These definitions have generally excluded writings that do not
present a coherent self or which do not foreground the "I."[7] Traditional definitions have also excluded more personal forms of writing
such as diaries, letters, and journals, forms typical of women's autobiographical writings. Feminist critics, in particular, have noted the
links, especially the etymological link, between "genre" and "gender."[8] Often in women's autobiographical texts, the self is de-cen-
tered, perhaps even absent.[9] Thus, feminist Nancy Miller argues that
genre is more accurately a context for reading rather than a prescrip-
tion for writing.[10] Limiting autobiography to its more traditional definition has also often excluded the autobiographical writings of women
and men of color. As Anne Goldman points out, for ethnic Americans,
writing a distinctive "I" often means writing against the grain.[11]

---

[5]See, for example, James Olney, ed., *Autobiography: Essays Theoretical and Critical* (Princeton, N. J.: Princeton University Press, 1980).

[6]Benstock, "Authorizing the Autobiographical," p. 19.

[7]Anne E. Goldman, *Take My Word: Autobiographical Innovations of Ethnic American Working Women* (Berkeley, Calif.: University of California Press, 1996), p. xv.

[8]Benstock, "Authorizing the Autobiographical," p. 20; Laura Marcus, *Auto/bio-
graphical Discourses: Theory, Criticism, Practice* (Manchester, U.K.: Manchester
University Press, 1994), p. 230; Nancy K. Miller, "Women's Autobiography in
France: For a Dialectics of Identification," *Women and Language in Literature and
Society*, ed. S. McConnell-Ginet, R. Borker, and N. Furman (New York: Praeger,
1980), p. 267. For a comprehensive discussion of the relationship between genre and
gender, see Jacques Derrida, "Lo Loi du Genre/The Law of Genre," trans. Avital Ron-
nell, *Glyph* 7 (1980): 202–232.

[9]Benstock, "Authorizing the Autobiographical," p. 20.

[10]Miller, "Women's Autobiography in France," p. 267.

[11]Goldman, *Take My Word*, p. xvi. See also Joanne M. Braxton, *Black Women
Writing Autobiography: A Tradition within a Tradition* (Philadelphia: Temple Univer-
sity Press, 1989). For an excellent example of writing the "I" against the grain, see
Audre Lorde, *Zami: A New Spelling of My Name: A Biomythography* (Freedom,
Calif.: Crossing, 1982).

Adopting a broad definition of autobiography can enrich the practice of religious instruction. A greater diversity of forms can allow learners to experience a wide variety of the multitudinous ways in which people experience the world. Equally important, experiencing a wide variety of forms of autobiography can also affirm the vast variety of experiences that learners bring to the religious instruction context. As social learning theory suggests, the stronger the learner's identification with the model, the more effective the teaching.[12] Thus, as religious educators provide a wider variety of models with which learners can identify, more effective teaching/learning situations can be created. Frederick Buechner's *The Sacred Journey* and Gloria Anzaldua's *Borderlands: La Frontera: The New Mestiza* offer two exceptional examples of very different styles of autobiography.

The Sacred Journey, Frederick Buechner's autobiographical narrative of his early life, is an especially powerful and moving tale of a man who comes to recognize the grace and mystery that permeate and transform every moment of his existence. In recounting his life from his earliest childhood memories though his calling into ministry, Buechner recreates key experiences couched in an awareness of the presence of God at every turn. *The Sacred Journey* offers religious educators a wealth of material to use in religious instruction. Buechner deals with themes from family relationship to vocation to grace. On a cognitive level, *The Sacred Journey* invites learners to explore religious and theological themes, such as grace and immanence. It also offers an excellent model to help learners reflect on their own life histories. Religious educators may suggest that learners read *The Sacred Journey* and then write their own life stories as sacred journeys. On an affective level, *The Sacred Journey* evokes potent emotions and suggests particular approaches to valuing in the world. After learners have read the book, religious educators may ask them to share times in their own lives when similar emotions were present or when similar values were created or challenged. Finally, *The Sacred Journey* offers a model for religious living. Buechner's approach in this book suggests a mode of living by which learners come to contextualize their lives within the presence of God. In *The Sacred Journey*, Buechner sees God at work in every facet of his life. This model can help learners

---

[12]Albert Bandura, *Social Learning Theory* (Englewood Cliffs, N.J.: Prentice-Hall, 1977).

begin to live their lives with a sense of themselves living and having their being in God.

Borderlands: La Frontera: The New Mestiza, an autobiographical work by Chicana feminist Gloria Anzaldua takes a form that is very different from Buechner's book. Written in both English and Spanish, prose and poetry, *Borderlands: La Frontera* traces the author's childhood along the Texas-Mexico border and describes her experience of being caught between two cultures, at home in neither.[13] Anzaldua contextualizes her story in the larger story of mestizos and mestizas. Key to her story is the image of *Coatlalopeuh*, the Indian name for *La Virgen de Guadalupe*. Like many Chicano families, Anzaldua's family practiced a folk Catholicism that incorporated many elements from the indigenous religions that preceded Catholicism in Central and South America.

Coatlalopeuh is descended from earlier Mesoamerican fertility and earth goddesses, the earliest being *Coatlicue*. *Coatlicue* had a human skull or serpent for a head, a necklace of human hearts, and a skirt of twisted serpents. She was a creator goddess. Her other aspect was *Tonantsi*, the holy mother. *Coatlicue*, like other Mesoamerican goddesses, was eventually driven underground by a patriarchal Aztec-Mexican culture. She was vilified and split from *Tonantsi*, who became the good mother. After the conquest, the Spaniards and the Catholic Church continued to split *Tonantsi* and *Coatlicue*. *Tonantsi* was completely desexed and grafted into the chaste protective mother, *la Virgen de Guadalupe*. In 1660, the Roman Catholic Church made her synonymous with *la Virgen Maria*, and she became the patron saint of Mexicans. During the Mexican revolution, Emiliano Zapata and Miguel Hidalgo used her image to motivate the people toward freedom.

In *la Virgen de Guadalupe*, Anzaluda sees a powerful image for Chicano and Mexican peoples. She represents the synthesis of cultures, the mestizo, the oppressed, and the rebellious. For Anzaldua, she represents the struggle of the mestiza to survive. She is the coming together of the many forces that make up mestiza life, and she acts as a symbol of the power of the mestiza to resist all attempts to divide any part of her from herself.

---

[13]Gloria Anzaldua, *Borderlands: La Frontera: The New Mestiza* (San Francisco: Aunt Lute, 1987).

Borderlands: La Frontera offers religious educators an amazing opportunity to explore the many contradictory forces at work in learners' lives. It can create an opportunity for non-Chicano learners to experience something of another culture. For Chicano and Chicana learners it can offer a powerful experience of identification. *Borderlands: La Frontera* challenges learners to examine their notions of normative ideas, attitudes, values, and behaviors. Most powerfully, it calls for learners to take a look at the ways in which their lives are forces toward liberation or toward oppression.

Religious educators may ask learners to identify a central image, like *la Virgen de Guadalupe*, in their own tradition and write a part of their personal life history in relation to that image. This activity may have a twofold result. Learners may explore in depth some little known aspect of their tradition, and learners may engage in deep self-reflection, assessing their own beliefs, convictions, and behaviors. *Borderlands: La Frontera* is filled with Anzaldua's poetry about her experiences as a mestiza. Religious educators can ask learners to write poems of their own to reflect their spiritual struggles and personal triumphs.

Autobiography, especially among traditionally marginalized groups, offers one possibility for what educator Paulo Freire calls *conscientization*.[14] In this view, autobiography provides learners with the opportunity of seeing the construction of subjectivity in the context of power relations and repositioning themselves in ways that may allow them to effect change.[15] As educator Robert Graham suggests, autobiography in education plays a significant role both in the construction of subjectivity as a collective and social enterprise and in the emancipation of voices that may have been silenced by dominant discourses and modes of representation.[16] Religious educators can use these liberatory functions of autobiography to create learning contexts that allow learners to participate actively and intentionally in the creation of their own subjectivity and voice. The use of personal autobiographical stories in

---

[14]Paulo Freire, *Pedagogy of the Oppressed* (New York: Continuum, 1970).

[15]Henry A. Giroux, *Schooling and the Struggle for Public Life: Critical Pedagogy in the Modern Age* (Minneapolis: University of Minnesota Press, 1988); Jennifer Nias, *Primary Teachers Talking: A Study of Teaching as Work* (London: Routledge, 1989).

[16]Robert J. Graham, *Reading and Writing the Self: Autobiography in Education and the Curriculum* (New York: Teachers College Press, 1991), p. 144.

religious instruction will be discussed in greater detail in the section of this chapter on personal stories.

The Sacred Journey and Borderlands: La Frontera are two very different examples of the wide variety of types of autobiography available to religious educators. Formal autobiographies such as these can act as catalysts for learners to do their own autobiographical work. For learners, autobiography offers opportunities to explore ideas, feelings, emotions, attitudes, values, and behaviors. Perhaps most importantly, autobiography offers a means for conscious and intentional work in the ongoing creation of self in all its linguistic, psychological, physical, cognitive, affective, behavioral, and spiritual wonder.

Biography

Like autobiography, biography encompasses a wide range of styles or types. Biography critic Leon Edel suggests three types of biography: chronicle, pictorial, and narrative-pictorial (or novelistic). The chronicle is the more traditional documentary biography in which the subject's voice is central. The pictorial biography is akin to a painter's portrait, a creation of words. And the novelistic biography reflects the ever present voice of the biographer as omniscient narrator.[17] Biography critic James Clifford offers five categories of biography: the so-called objective, the scholarly-historical, the artistic-scholarly, the narrative, and the fictional. The so-called objective biography, which consists almost entirely of facts, is nonetheless subjective because the inclusion of some facts and exclusion of others represents a subjective decision on the part of the biographer. The scholarly-historical is closely akin the Edel's chronicle, and the artistic-scholarly approximates the novelistic type in Edel's schema. The narrative is highly imaginative but not pure fiction, and the fictional is about real characters about whom few facts are known.[18] Obviously, biographies, like autobiographies, are not simply forthright and objective statements of the facts of someone's life. Instead, biography is an intimate and collaborative activity between subject and biographer that results in the creation of a life history.[19]

---

[17]Leon Edel, *Literary Biography* (Bloomington: Indiana University Press, 1973), p. 125.

[18]James L. Clifford, *From Puzzles to Portraits: Problems of a Literary Biographer* (Chapel Hill: University of North Carolina Press, 1971), pp. 83–95.

[19]Marc Pachter, "The Biographer Himself: An Introduction," *Telling Lives: The Biographer's Art*, ed. Marc Pachter (Philadelphia: University of Pennsylvania Press, 1981), pp. 3–15.

Certain lives present models of faithful living that call learners to embody their faith in their ways of being in the world. Biographies of these people can serve as a valuable tool in facilitating the goals of religious instruction.

In the cognitive domain, biographies can provide an impetus for theological, moral, and ethical reflection. Biographies provide learners with ways to explore lived convictions, to understand what a life lived out of a particular worldview and its attendant convictions looks like. These lives can challenge the theological reflection and ethical action of learners' lives.[20] Furthermore, biography can lead learners to self-knowledge. In reading biographies, learners find themselves. From the stories of others, learners learn who they are.[21] The story of a single life calls learners to reflect on their own stories, and, ultimately, these stories challenge learners to look at their own lives and assess their own embodiment of their beliefs and convictions. Biographies also are valuable tools for theological reflection. Biographical theology challenges propositional theology by holding it accountable to the actual lives and experiences of persons in the world. These lives present data that propositional theology must explore and order. Thus, biographies present a means by which learners can examine, challenge, and recreate their theological beliefs.

In the affective domain, biographies can invite learners to enter into the lives of people who are different from themselves and can help them to develop empathy, tolerance, and compassion. Biographies invite learners to respond affectively to the lived experiences of others. Japanese feminist Takayo Mukai writes about her experience of befriending photographer Diane Arbus as Mukai read Arbus's autobiography. Mukai writes that the biography "allowed me to jump in anywhere in Diane's life, whenever and wherever I wanted to talk to her, to hug her, to cry with her." Through her interaction with Diane's biography, Takayo was at last able to come to terms with her own experience of anorexia.[22]

---

[20]James William McClendon Jr., *Biography as Theology: How Life Stories Can Remake Today's Theology* (Nashville: Abingdon, 1974), p. 40.

[21]Michael Goldberg, *Theology and Narrative: A Critical Introduction* (Nashville: Abington, 1981), p. 111.

[22]Takayo Mukai, "Learning from Women's Biography," in *All Side of the Subject: Women and Biography*, ed. Teresa Iles (New York: Teachers College Press, 1992), pp. 152–161.

In the lifestyle domain, biographies offer models of behavior. In these life histories, learners experience the ways others have lived faithful lives and find examples of ways they can live their own faith. In Crisogono de Jesus's biography of John of the Cross, learners discover that John became a close friend of Teresa of Avila and with her worked to reform the Carmelites. Eventually, John was thrown into prison, tormented, and ordered to forsake his commitment to the reform movement. For nine months, John suffered his dark night of the soul, which is a spiritual rather than a physical condition. Finally, John escaped and rejoined a community of Reformed Carmelites. Many years later John fell out of favor with a vicar general and was sent to an isolated monastery as punishment. There he became very ill, and the prior of the monastery treated him poorly. Realizing that he was about to die, John asked the prior to forgive him for the inconvenience he had caused. John's gentleness and compassion melted the prior's heart, and he confessed his sorrow at his shabby treatment of John. Shortly after midnight, John heard the ringing of the bells for Matins. He asked why the bells were ringing and was told they were ringing for Matins. He exclaimed, "Glory be to God for I shall say them in heaven." He put his crucifix to his lips and said, "*In manus tuas Domine, commendo spiritum meum*," (into your hands, O Lord, I commend my spirit). After John uttered these words, he died.[23] John's story offers a powerful model of commitment and compassion. His life provides moving examples of faithful behaviors and challenges learners likewise to live the faith that they profess.

Conclusion

Biographies and autobiographies furnish religious educators with excellent tools for creating teaching/learning situations in which learners can make significant connections with the lives of other people through narrative. Biographies and autobiographies provide learners with glimpses into the lives of others as well as into their own lives. In many biographies and autobiographies, learners can identify God at work in the lives of people like themselves and thus affirm learners' intimations of God at work in their own lives. Biographies and autobiographies can help learners experience the Other, calling learners to empathy, concern, compassion, and love for an extended circle of

---

[23]Crisogono de Jesus, *The Life of St. John of the Cross*, trans. Kathleen Pond (London: Longmans, Green, 1958), pp. 303–304.

human beings. And biographies and autobiographies can demonstrate a wide variety of forms of religious living.

Most importantly, many biographies and autobiographies can invite learners to respond to God. In these stories, learners can experience the presence and voice of God. As these narratives reveal God at work in the lives of others, they suggest the work of God in the lives of learners. In so doing, biographies and autobiographies call learners to live in faithful response to their experiences of the love of God.

PERSONAL STORIES

Because learners experiences their lives narratively, each learner has stories that not only communicate the events of their lives but also embody the wisdom, passion, and meaning that learners ascribe to those events. Created from the raw data of learners' ordinary (and sometimes extraordinary) experiences, these personal stories are the deeply felt, personally significant accounts of learners' daily lives. In telling and retelling personal stories, learners create new experiences and meanings of the events, which may not have been readily available in the midst of the experiences themselves. These stories, then, become an important part of learners' self-concept.[24]

This is the story of the day I became a feminist. It was my first semester at seminary, and I was enrolled in a course entitled "Formation for Christian Ministry." I was one of three women in a class of twenty students. Also in that class were three men who had come to the seminary directly from the coal mines of Kentucky to earn a diploma through the seminary's program for ministerial students who did not have a bachelor's degree. Now, I came to seminary from a very conservative church, in which women did not preach or pray in public worship; nor did they teach men in Sunday school or discipleship training. So I reached the hallowed halls of The Southern Baptist Theological Seminary in a definitely prefeminist state.

One day the professor announced that we were to have a guest speaker in the next class—a woman hospital chaplain. The professor had participated in her ordination service when he was her pastor. "This should be interesting," I thought, never having met an ordained

---

[24]Robyn Rivush, "The Social Construction of Personal Narratives," *Merrill-Palmer Quarterly* 37 (January 1991): 59.

woman. After all, the ordination of women was quite a controversial issue among Southern Baptists. In Southern Baptist life, ordination is entirely a local church issue; local churches supportive of ordination for women are free to ordain women in whom they sense a calling to ministry. In the early 1980s, however, very few Southern Baptist women had been ordained by their local churches. But the number of women attending Southern Baptist seminaries was on the rise, and the issue of the ordination of women was rapidly moving to the forefront of Southern Baptist life.

At the next formation for Christian ministry class meeting, the professor introduced our guest. Suddenly, the room shook with the sound of a slamming briefcase. One of the coal miners, who was as big as a Kentucky mountain, noisily backed his chair away from the table, stood up, grabbed his briefcase, stormed out of the classroom, and slammed the door. Without a word, he had conveyed his opinion on the issue of women in ministry.

The next class session was the regularly scheduled small group meeting, which was a required part of all formation for Christian ministry classes. I was the only woman in our group of ten, and, you may have guessed it, all three coal miners were in my small group. The topic for discussion that day was women in ministry. No sooner had the graduate teaching fellow announced the topic than the mountain-sized coal miner repeated his briefcase slamming routine. Something inside me snapped. Until this moment, I had not even spoken in class, being a quiet and shy student. But this coal miner had upset me with his rudeness to our guest, and so when he started his routine again, it was more than I could stand. Before I knew what I was doing, I had slammed my fist down on the table and shouted at him, "You can't just walk out every time you disagree with something. How will you ever do ministry like that?"

The room fell silent. I figured I was about to die. He turned, glaring at me, and said, "I can do anything I want." Then he stormed out of the room, waving his Bible above his head and shouting about the in-errant, infallible Word of God.

But that was not the day I became a feminist. It was the next day. I was walking down the hall in the seminary's academic building when I ran into the other two coal miners who stopped me to chat. "Don't take him too seriously," they suggested. But then one of them, meaning well, I am sure, said to me as they resumed their walk down the hallway, "I'll be praying for you that you won't get messed up in this women in ministry thing." That did it. I became a feminist on the spot.

Personal stories help learners explore those events that have been seminal in their development. These stories become religiously significant when learners become aware of the presence of God in their stories. Four types of religiously significant personal stories may be delineated, although they do often overlap and flow into one another: self-discovery stories, mystical stories, conversion stories, and revelatory stories.[25]

Self-discovery Stories

In self-discovery stories learners find out something about themselves and also discover God at work in their lives through the events they narrate in self-discovery stories.[26] Religious educators can use stories of self-discovery to help learners discern and respond to God's presence in their lives. Pulitzer Prize-winning author Annie Dillard tells the story of watching a single-winged maple seed fall from a tree. She picked the seed up and threw it into the wind. It flew off again "like a creature muscled and vigorous, or a creature spread thin to that other wind, the wind of the spirit which bloweth where it listeth, lighting, and raising up, and easing down." She writes, "And the bell under my ribs rang a true note, a flourish as of blended horns, clarion, sweet, and making a long dim sense I will try at length to explain. Flung is too harsh a word for the rush of the world. Blown is more like it, but blown by a generous, unending breath."[27] For Dillard, the simple, unremarkable experience of watching a maple seed fall helped her to discover the Spirit of God gently at work in herself and in the world. Self-discovery stories allow learners to extract from very ordinary experiences the extraordinary felt awareness of self and God. These stories can reinforce learners' feelings, values, attitudes, ideas, and behaviors as they see God at work in their lives in the past, experience God's presence in their lives in the present, and anticipate God's continued work in their lives in the future. Self-discovery stories can help

---

[25]These four types of personal stories are drawn from William J. Bausch, *Storytelling: Imagination and Faith* (Mystic, Conn.: Twenty-Third, 1984) and John Shea, *An Experience Named Spirit* (Chicago: Thomas More, 1983).

[26]Bausch, *Storytelling*, p. 174.

[27]Annie Dillard, *Pilgrim at Tinker Creek* (Toronto Bantam, 1974), p. 275.

religious educators achieve cognitive goals by facilitating self-knowledge and knowledge of God. Affective goals can be facilitated as self-discovery stories evoke powerful feelings and reinforce values and attitudes, and lifestyle goals can be achieved as these stories also reinforce behaviors by which learners define themselves.

Mystical Stories

A mystical story is a story that expresses a mystical experience, an experience of heightened feeling and awareness of Mystery and of the unity of all that is.[28] It is a holistic experience involving the spirit, the body, and the mind. Episcopalian priest Matthew Fox calls these experiences "ecstasies."[29] Ecstasies are experiences of getting outside of oneself and being one with Mystery.

Trappist monk Thomas Merton tells of a day when he was watching a group of myrtle warblers playing and diving for insects in the low pine branches over his head. They were so close he could almost touch them, and he was awed at their beauty, their quick flight, their chirpings, and the yellow spot on their backs that was revealed as they flew. He experienced, he writes, "a sense of total kinship with them as if they and I were all of the same nature and as if that nature were nothing but love."[30]

In this mystical experience, Merton felt himself at one with Mystery. He became aware of his connectedness with all that exists, and he named the unity of all things love. James Michael Lee enumerates eight characteristics of mystical experience: (1) in mystical experience, learners sense that what is transpiring is essentially given to them; (2) mystical experience is overpowering; (3) mystical experience confers a sense of conviction of the significance of the experience; (4) in mystical experience, learners are caught up in the unity of all that is; (5) mystical experience conveys an overwhelming awareness of Divine presence; (6) mystical experience brings a deep sense

---

[28]Ralph W. Hood Jr., "The Facilitation of Religious Experience," *Handbook of Religious Experience*, ed. Ralph W. Hood Jr. (Birmingham, Ala.: Religious Education Press, 1995), p. 575. See also Walter T. Stace, *Mysticism and Philosophy* (Philadelphia: Lippincott, 1960).

[29]Matthew Fox, *Whee! We, Wee, All the Way Home: A Guide to the New Sensual Spirituality* (Wilmington, N.C.: Consortium, 1976), p. 3.

[30]Thomas Merton, *Vow of Conversation: Journals 1964–1965*, ed. Naomi Burton Stone (New York: Farrar, Strauss, Giroux, 1988), p. 95.

of joy and well-being; (7) mystical experience alters sense of time so that everything is present; and (8) mystical experience is impossible to convey completely through words.[31] Stories about mystical experiences cannot fully capture the experience, but they can provide a narrative frame for continuing to live in the experience. Psychologist Ralph W. Hood Jr. suggests that language affects the reporting of religious experiences in four major ways: (1) it can facilitate awareness of foundational realities; (2) it can provide the necessary mediation whereby experience becomes reflexively conscious; (3) it can facilitate the reporting of experiences within a particular language context; and (4) it can lead learners to reject some experiences as not being legitimately religious ones.[32]

Annie Dillard describes a mystical experience of watching for muskrats: "I wait on the bridges and stalk along banks for those moments I cannot predict, when a wave begins to surge under the water, and ripples strengthen and pulse high across the creek and back again in a texture that throbs. It is like the surfacing of an impulse, like the materialization of fish, this rising, this coming to a head, like the ripening of nutmeats still in their husks, ready to split open like buckeyes in a field, shining with newness. 'Surely the Lord is in this place; and I knew it not.' The feeling shreds I see, the back parts, are a gift, an abundance. When Moses came down from the cliff in Mount Sinai, the people were afraid of him: the very skin on his face shone."[33]

Religious educators can use mystical stories to help learners develop an attentiveness to the Mystery in which they live and which lives in them. In narratizing their own mystical experiences or in hearing the mystical experiences of others, learners can become more attuned to the presence of God in their lives and their place in the unity of all that is. Furthermore, mystical stories can encourage learners to practice spiritual disciplines, such as prayer and meditation. James Michael Lee points to considerable empirical evidence showing that religious experience, which includes mystical experience, can be facilitated.[34] Mystical stories can offer learners models of mystical experience from which they may learn ways to engage themselves with Mystery.

---

[31]James Michael Lee, *The Content of Religious Instruction* (Birmingham, Ala.: Religious Education Press, 1985), pp. 664–665.

[32]Hood, "Facilitation of Religious Experience," p. 577.

[33]Annie Dillard, *Pilgrim at Tinker Creek*, pp. 209–210.

[34]Lee, *Content of Religious Instruction*, p. 668.

Revelatory stories

Revelatory stories describe experiences in which learners are struck by some insight and receive some truth about the ultimate Mystery of life.[35] The word "revelation" literally means an unveiling, the disclosure of something previously hidden. Theologically, revelation refers to Divine self-disclosure. Theologian John Baille contends that from a biblical perspective what is revealed in Divine revelation is God, not information.[36] Theologian John Macquarrie suggests that the word "revelation" points especially to the cognitive elements of the Divine initiative which makes faith possible. This initiative, he argues, brings people to new understandings of themselves and the wider being within which they have their being.[37] He explains that revelation reverses the familiar epistemological situation. Typically, learners attain truth when what was concealed is brought out into the light. In religious revelation, the initiative lies with what is known. Learners do not bring the Divine into the light, but rather the Divine provides the light by which it is known and by which learners in turn know themselves.[38]

The Bible is full of examples of revelatory stories. Abraham, Moses, Isaiah, Mary, all had direct encounters with the Divine in which something of God's self was revealed to them. The greatest revelatory story of all, the story of God in Jesus, fills the pages of the New Testament.

Revelatory stories provide an "aha!" of understanding. Something becomes clear all at once. Something makes sense in an instant. Although the following story is drawn from a fictional work, it serves as an example of a revelatory story. Porter Osborne Jr. left Brewton County, Georgia, to attend a Southern Baptist college. Having been "Raised Right," Porter firmly believed every word in the Bible and firmly believed that he completely and rightly understood every word the Bible said. Then Porter ran into the college Religion Department. Every notion of truth he had been taught in his Baptist church back

---

[35]Shea, *An Experience Named Spirit*, p. 99.

[36]John Baille, *The Idea of Revelation in Recent Thought* (New York: Columbia University Press, 1956), p. 28.

[37] John Macquarrie, *Principles of Christian Theology*, 2d ed. (New York: Scribner's, 1977), p. 85.

[38]ibid., p. 86.

home was challenged by a group of religion professors who did not believe Moses had written the Pentateuch or that the world had been created in six days. Upset by this perceived heresy, a group of students protested the unorthodoxy of the religion faculty in a treatise mailed to several local newspapers. During the formal proceedings that followed, Porter eavesdropped from the bough of a tree just outside the conference room window. Struggling with the religion faculty's reconciliation of religion and science, Porter listened carefully to the arguments inside. Then a line from Tennyson came to him: "By faith and faith alone embrace / Believing where we cannot prove." Faith! That was the answer for Porter Osborne Jr. With faith, he could have science and Genesis at the same time. With that revelation, he aligned himself squarely on the side of the faculty.[39]

Frederick Buechner tells this story of the day he signed the contract for his first novel. As he was leaving the publisher's office, he ran into a man he had known slightly at college. The man told Buechner he was working as a messenger boy. Instead of feeling pride or a sense of superior accomplishment, Buechner felt something like sadness, almost like shame. The pleasure he could have taken in what had just happened to him was lost in the realization that nothing comparable had happened to his acquaintance. He said nothing to the man about the contract he had just signed. Instead, they said good-bye and went their separate ways. Buechner writes, "All I can say now is that something small and unforgettable happened inside me as the result of that chance meeting—some small flickering out of the truth that, in the long run, there can be no real joy for anybody until there is joy finally for us all—and I can take no credit for it. It was nothing I piously thought my way to. It was no conscious attempt to work out my own salvation. What I felt was something better and truer than I was, or than I am, and it happened, as perhaps all such things do, as a gift."[40]

Revelatory stories are important in religious instruction because they emphasize the ongoing nature of human relationship with God. God continues to reveal God's self to humans. James Michael Lee suggests that religious instruction represents an intentional effort to

---

[39]Ferrol Sams, *The Whisper of the River* (New York: Penguin, 1984), pp. 259–260.
[40]Frederick Buechner, *The Sacred Journey* (San Francisco: Harper and Row, 1982), p. 97.

heighten revelation in the lives of learners.[41] Religious educators can use revelatory stories as a means to facilitate learners' continuing engagement with the communication and disclosure of the divine Self.

Having become seriously ill at the age of thirty, Julian of Norwich received sixteen dramatic revelations of God's love. She called these revelations, "showings." Soon after her health improved, she wrote a short version of the showings. Many years later, she wrote an extended version of these sixteen revelations. In her writings, Julian combines originality, imagination, and biblical spirituality to create a theology centered on her own experiences of the love of God.[42] Learners in our era may not have equally dramatic revelations, but religious educators can encourage learners to keep journals to record the ways in which God reveals God's self to them each day. These journal entries can then be shaped into stories to be read or told to a group of learners in a religious instruction setting.

Conversion Stories

Conversion stories are narratives that emphasize the process of change. Bailey Gillespie suggests that to study religious conversion is to study its stories. For Gillespie this study is no simple cognitive activity; rather it involves engagement in the very essence of religious living itself.[43]

I grew up in a climate of racism. Of course, being situated in it, I did not really recognize it at the time. Racial epithets and jokes were simply an accepted and expected part of the language of daily life. The irony, I suppose, is that the same people who taught me racism also taught me that Jesus loved the little children of the world—red and yellow, black and white. And they encouraged me to save money to give each year to the Lottie Moon Christmas Offering for Foreign Missions so that our missionaries could carry the good news of God's

---

[41]James Michael Lee, *The Shape of Religious Instruction* (Birmingham, Ala.: Religious Education Press, 1971), p. 232.

[42]Gloria Durka, *Praying with Julian of Norwich* (Winona, Minn.: Saint Mary's, 1989), pp. 15–21. For more on Julian, see *Julian of Norwich: Showings*, trans. Edmund College and James Walsh (New York: Paulist, 1978). Learners may also be interested in the revelatory experiences of Hildegard of Bingen. See *Hildegard of Bingen, Scivias*, trans. Mother Columba Hart and Jane Bishop (New York: Paulist, 1990).

[43]Bailey Gillespie, *The Experience of Faith* (Birmingham, Ala.: Religious Education Press, 1988), p. 16.

love to all the people of the world. As a child I lived easily with the two messages, side by side, with no apparent need to resolve the contradiction. But the contradiction became clear when I became an adolescent. I remember the day I told the last racist joke ever to cross my lips. As soon as the punch line left my mouth, than I was struck by the great moral agony of having committed a terrible transgression. Racism and all its manifestations were wrong. I knew it. I felt it with every fiber of my body. On the spot, I resolved never to tell another racist joke again. Instead, I would commit myself to working on behalf of racial justice for all of God's children—red and yellow, black and white.

Religionist Walter Conn defines conversion as a radical turning or a redirection of one's life.[44] Drawing from developmental studies, Conn suggests four types of conversion: moral, affective, cognitive, and religious. Moral conversion refers to the shift from a radically egocentric orientation, in which decisions are made by self-interest, to a social orientation in which decisions are made by conventionally defined value. Conn characterizes this shift in perspective as the ability to distinguish the valuable from the valuable-for-me.[45] Affective conversion comes when learners can make their actions consistent with their judgments, and, Conn argues, this happens only when learners fall in love. Love, Conn contends, allows learners to escape the persistent force of egocentrism and act in accordance with their best judgment.[46] Cognitive conversion is the critical recognition of one's own role in constituting reality and therefore value. It is coming to realize the self as knower. Consequently, the self ceases to look to an external authority for the real or the valuable.[47] Finally, religious conversion is a radical reorientation of life that occurs when God becomes central rather than peripheral in learners' lives. It is total surrender of self to God and can occur only when learners have completely and totally fallen in love with God.[48]

---

[44]Walter Conn, *Christian Conversion: A Developmental Interpretation of Autonomy and Surrender* (New York: Paulist, 1986), p. 5.
[45]Ibid., p. 28.
[46]Ibid.
[47]Ibid., p. 29.
[48]Ibid., pp. 30–31.

Isabella was born a slave in New York. She served several masters before Isaac Van Wagener emancipated her in 1827. One day Isabella had a vision in which she realized that there was no place where God was not, and she became conscious of how she had forgotten God. She was stricken by the weight of her sin and longed for someone to intercede between herself and God. She felt that her vileness prevented her from talking to God directly. Eventually a friend appeared to stand between her and God. "Who are you?" she asked the radiant form. "I know you—and I don't know you." She longed to know who this figure was. At last it came to her. "It is Jesus. Yes, it is Jesus." She had heard of Jesus before, but now she saw how lovely he was, and she realized that he loved her, had always loved her, and she had not known it. Now, he would stand between her and God, and God would no longer be a terror to her. Her heart was full of joy and gladness. As the years passed, Isabella had more religious visions and mystical experiences. Following one of these divine encounters, she changed her name—to Sojourner Truth. Sojourner Truth became a powerful voice for abolition, women's suffrage, and women's rights.[49]

Not all conversions are dramatic and sudden; often conversion is a slow, gradual process. C. S. Lewis calls himself "the most dejected and reluctant convert in all England." Lewis was an avowed and happy atheist who longed for nothing more than to call his soul his own. He could not, however, escape the Spirit, whom he found at every turn. At last, he gave in and admitted that God was God. "Kicking, struggling, resentful, and darting his eyes in every direction for a chance of escape," he knelt to pray. This conversion, however, was only to theism, not to Christianity. That came later. Lewis writes, "I know very well when, but hardly how, the final step was taken. I was driven to Whipsnade one sunny morning. When we set out I did not believe that Jesus Christ is the Son of God, and when we reached the zoo I did."[50]

Religious educators can use conversion stories to facilitate cognitive, affective, and lifestyle objectives. According to William James,

---

[49]*Narrative of Sojourner Truth; A Bondswoman of Olden Time . . . Drawn from Her "Book of Life,"* (Battle Creek, Mich. 1878), pp. 64–71. Excerpted in *Conversions*, ed. Hugh T. Kerr and John M. Mulder (Grand Rapids, Mich.: Eerdmans, 1983), pp. 113–117.

[50]C. S. Lewis, *Surprised by Joy* (New York: Harcourt, Brace, 1955), pp. 211–224.

conversion is the collapse of a cognitive schema by an emotive occa-sion.[51] From this collapse, a new schema must be built. By asking learners to recall their own conversion experiences, religious educators can help learners explore the assumptions that form the schemas by which they now live. This process may reinforce or challenge the identity that learners have constructed out of their conversion experiences.

Conversion is often likened to falling in love.[52] This powerful affective experience is centered on relationship, and the discovery of a new truth is usually indistinguishable from the discovery of a new relationship.[53] Religious educators can use conversion stories to help learners reconnect with the feelings experienced in conversions. Furthermore, these stories offer useful models of potent affective experiences, which can help learners develop religious attitudes and values, as well as emotions. Religious educators can also use conversion stories to help learners open themselves to being converted to a deeper way of life.

Finally, conversion stories provide religious educators with models of renewed religious living. Conversion stories document people's reorientation, not only toward thought and emotion but also toward life. Albert Schweitzer's conversion marked the beginning of his journey toward the hospital at Lambarene. Dorothy Day's conversion led to her cofounding the Catholic Worker Movement. Thomas Merton's conversion led to a Trappist monastery in Kentucky. The changes brought about by conversion lead people to make choices to align their living with their reorientation. Stories of these life-changing experiences can act as catalysts for learners to reorient their own lives.

At the age of fifteen, William Booth attended a service at Wesley Chapel in Nottingham. There, he writes, he "was wrought upon quite independently of human effort by the Holy Ghost, who created within me a great thirst for a new life." Immediately he felt that he must make restitution to a friend whom he had cheated. He found the young man, confessed his sin, and made his restitution. At that moment, his guilt rolled away, and he determined to serve God from that hour on.

---

[51]William James, *The Varieties of Religious Experience: A Study in Human Nature* (New York: Modern Library, 1902), p. 166.

[52]Chana Ullman, *The Transformed Self: The Psychology of Religious Conversion* (New York: Plenum, 1989), p. xvi.

[53]Ibid.

Eventually, he organized the East London Revival Society, later known as the Christian mission, and finally as the Salvation Army.[54]

FAMILY STORIES

A family story is an incident that has been told and retold within a family over a period of years. Based on real incidents, these stories usually become embellished over the years. Often they are about eccentric rather than conventional family members and extraordinary rather than ordinary events.[55] These stories often become part of the learners' psyche long before learners even have the words to explain the stories.[56]

Individual incidents that characterize a particular family member are especially remembered in family tradition. These single incidents often come to represent the whole of the individual's personality, and the tales remembered tend to be about heroes, rogues, mischief makers, survivors, and innocents. Events included in family tradition tend to be the ones that mark some transition in the family's life, such as courtships, great fortunes lost, migrations, catastrophes, and family feuds.[57]

Within the family, telling family stories serves a number of essential functions. It stimulates healthy family interaction. It provides a means for influencing family members. It passes family tradition and culture from one generation to the next and integrates the disturbing and tragic events of the family into the ongoing life of the family.[58] Telling family stories can also serve a religious instruction function within the family. Families can tell stories of the faithful lives of

[54]George Scott Railton, *The Authoritative Life of General Booth: Founder of the Salvation Army* (New York, 1912), pp. 9–12. Excerpted in *Conversions*, ed. Hugh and Mulder, pp. 140–143.

[55]Steven J. Zeitlin, Amy J. Kotkin, Holly Cutting Baker, *A Celebration of American Family Folklore: Tales and Traditions from the Smithsonian Collection* (New York: Pantheon, 1982), pp. 3–5, 10.

[56]Nancy J. Napier, "Living Our Stories: Discovering and Replacing Limiting Family Myths," in *Sacred Stories: A Celebration of the Power of Stories to Transform and Heal*, ed. Charles Simpkinson and Anne Simpkinson (New York: HarperSanFrancisco, 1993), p. 153.

[57]Zeitlin et al., *A Celebration of American Family Folklore*, pp. 15–16.

[58]Ibid., p. 19.

family members, which can model behavior and shape identity. Family members can learn what religious living means from the stories of family members who went before and lived lives of faith despite adversity or temptation.

In many ways, the church that I currently attend is a family. Recently an elderly member of the congregation died, and her memorial service became a celebration of her life within our church family. Hazel Motley was a driving force in Ainsworth United Church of Christ. During the service, member after member of the Ainsworth family stood to tell a story about Mrs. Motley. Over and over again, people told of their experiences of her wagging her finger and demanding the best of them. Her special passion and gift was raising money for the church's Cambric Scholarship for church members to attend college. At the most recent fund-raising banquet for the scholarship fund, we all felt Mrs. Motley's presence, and we made sure we did things just as she would have wanted them done.

Family stories are dynamic, changing with each telling to meet the needs of the current generation. Additionally, each new generation adds its own stories to the family's lore. These stories are part of a stream that both shapes the family and is shaped by it. Family stories reveal not only the family's past but also those who tell family stories, what these people think about themselves, and what they need to think about their families and their pasts.

Telling family stories in religious instruction involves a great deal of self-disclosure and creates a context for loving, valuing, and understanding the one telling the story. Telling family stories, through photographs or scrapbooks or diaries, adds a significant element of engagement by providing visual or tactile links with the subject of the story. Interactions around recounting family stories promote the building of community and affirm the risk taking of self-disclosure. Family stories allow learners a new experience of one another and can encourage the growth of empathy and compassion as learners enter into the lives of one another.

CONCLUSION

Autobiography, biography, personal stories, family stories—all of these life stories can connect learners more closely to the human family. In these stories, learners can find the many experiences they share with others, even those whom they consider different from themselves. Many life stories allow learners to explore the activity of God in the experiences of individual persons and communities. Often these stories energize learners to experience and identify the activity of God in their own lives. These stories are important for religious instruction because they can reach learners in cognitive, affective, and lifestyle ways that invite learners to participate fully in the depth and breadth of religious living.

This is what happened, and I know because I was there. I was kneeling at the front of the church One by one, each of the congregants was coming forward to lay hands on me and to whisper a blessing in my ear: Wes, Jane, Tisa, Karen, Ann, Dawn, Ronelle, Nancy, the people I had come to hold dear during my seminary and early ministry experience. At last the Bernards came forward. James came first, an eighty-two year old African-American man with a third grade education and a heart of gold. He put his hands on my shoulders and, leaning over, whispered, "I love you, and I sure hope you live as long as I have." A smile and tears. Then Mary Anna, his wife, followed. Seventy-two years old, with experiences I could never imagine written in the lines of her face. She touched me. "Oh, I wish I was as young as you. If I was as young as you and if I was born in times like these, I think I'd be a preacher." *You already are*, I thought. She returned to her seat, and I rose, knowing I would never again be the same.

10

Children's Stories

No book is really worth reading at the age of ten which is not equally (and often far more) worth reading at the age of fifty.[1]
—C. S. Lewis

The first stories many learners heard were the ones read to them by their parents from a children's storybook. Although children's literature has much in common with adult literature, children's literature can be defined as written and/or illustrated narrative created specifically for children with regard to their experiences, abilities, and life-stage needs. Like literature for adults, good children's literature reveals human existence; it is of aesthetic quality and it gives its readers pleasure. Like many other kinds of stories, children's literature has its roots in the oral storytelling tradition. Ancient tales were told for the delight of the entire community and were not specifically intended for children. Not until the late seventeenth century was childhood considered a distinct developmental period. Children were simply regarded as miniature adults.[2] Only with the advent of childhood as its own developmental stage did literature for children begin to emerge.

---

[1]C. S. Lewis, "On Stories," in *Of Other Worlds: Essays and Stories*, ed. Walter Hooper (New York: Harcourt Brace Jovanovich, 1966), p. 15.

[2]Jane Bingham and Grayce Scholt, *Fifteen Centuries of Children's Literature: An Annotated Chronology of British and American Works in Historical Context* (Westport, Conn.: Greenwood, 1981), p. 53.

Children's literature offers a vast array of narrative forms and stories that can be of value in religious instruction for both children and adults. For children, both in the family and in formal religious instruction settings, children's literature can help address numerous personal, social, psychological, and religious issues. Because children's literature is generally targeted toward the specific needs of particular ages, religious educators should be sure to select age-appropriate works. In many bookstores the children's literature section is divided into age-appropriate sections.[3]

In the cognitive domain, the stories of children's literature can teach information and facilitate understanding. For older children, children's literature can work to facilitate the ability to use ideas in particular situations, analyze ideas, and develop syntheses from a variety of ideas. Children's literature can help children deal with difficult and important issues, such as divorce, death, racism, sexism, and injustice. For example, Dr. Seuss's *The Butter Battle Book*, which is especially appropriate for children ages 5-8, addresses issues of conflict, violence, and nuclear armament. The Yooks and the Zooks are pretty much alike, except for the fact that they butter their bread on opposite sides. Based on this difference, each group begins to amass more and more powerful weapons until they end up in a standoff, directing bombs with the capability of annihilating both sides at one another. The story concludes there, leaving the ending open for speculation. Does one side drop the bomb? Do they find a way to deescalate the crisis? For children, *The Butter Battle Book* provides an opportunity to explore conflict and violence and to look toward a future in which they may have the opportunity to find new ways for people to resolve disputes without resorting to war.

In the affective domain, children's literature is especially useful in facilitating the goals of religious education. Carefully selected children's stories can help children deal with their feelings and emotions. Particularly important is the potential for children's literature to allow children to confront their fears and insecurities within the security of the family and faith community. Children's literature can also

---

[3]Masha Kabakow Rudman, *Children's Literature: An Issues Approach*, 3d ed. (White Plains, N.Y.: Longmans, 1995) is an excellent resource for religious educators. This textbook divides children's literature into relevant issues, such as family, divorce, and sexuality, and suggests appropriate readings for each issue.

facilitate the development of attitudes and values. Many works of children's literature contain either implicit or explicit religious morals, values, and expressions of faith.[4] These stories, such as *Old Turtle* and *The Giving Tree*, are especially useful to parents and religious educators.

Children's literature also offers a helpful tool for religious instruction in the lifestyle domain. Many children's books point to the possibility of positive ways of being in the world. Many of these stories offer models of religious living. E. B. White's *Charlotte's Web*, which is appropriate for children age nine and up, provides a classic example of a children's story in which the protagonist provides a model of faithful religious living. Wilbur the pig is slated to be slaughtered when he gains enough weight. So his friend Charlotte the spider sets out to save him by making him so famous that the farmer will not kill him. She gives so much of herself in spinning her webs to save Wilbur that in the end she gives her own life as well. As a result, Wilbur repays her friendship by caring first for the sac of eggs left by Charlotte and then by caring for the young brood of spiders, Charlotte's offspring.

Children's literature also has a place in adult religious instruction because children's stories may also address adult needs. Children's literature invites adults into imaginary worlds they may have abandoned long ago and may open doors to possibilities accessible only through imagination. In opening adults to these worlds, children's literature may also again open for them doors to childlike faith.

While waiting in a train station, the atheist C. S. Lewis picked up a copy of George MacDonald's *Phantastes, a Faerie Romance*. On the train, he began to read his new fairy story, and the experience transformed him. "But now I saw the bright shadow coming out of the book into the real world and resting there, transforming all common things and yet itself unchanged. Or, more accurately, I saw the common things drawn into the bright shadow. . . . That night my imagination was, in a certain sense, baptized; the rest of me, not unnaturally, took longer. I had not the faintest notion what I had let myself in for by buying Phantastes."[5]

---

[4]Miriam J. Johnson, *Inside Twenty-Five Classic Children's Stories: Discovering Values at Home or in School* (New York: Paulist, 1986), p. 2.

[5]C. S. Lewis, *Surprised by Joy: The Shape of My Early Life* (New York: Harcourt Brace Jovanovich, 1955), p. 181.

A BRIEF HISTORY OF
CHILDREN'S LITERATURE

The history of children's literature as a distinctive written form of narrative actually begins two centuries before the genre itself came into being. With the development of the printing press in the fifteenth century, books in Europe became somewhat more accessible, and oral tales found their way into printed texts.[6] The earliest books for children were intended to teach manners, morals, the alphabet, and numbers. Hornbooks were 2 ¾-by-5-inch pieces of wood cut in the shape of a paddle on which were pasted lesson sheets of vellum or parchments protected by a piece of transparent horn.[7] Hornbooks, usually consisting of the alphabet, a syllabary, numerals, and the Lord's Prayer, were introduced to teach reading and writing and were used until the eighteenth century when they were replaced by battledores, which were printed lesson books made of folded paper or cardboard and contained the alphabet, numerals, and prayers or proverbs.

The earliest books printed for children consisted primarily of instruction in morals and manners. Printed by William Caxton in 1477, Caxton's *Book of Curtesye*, for example, contained exhortations toward a life of virtue and away from a life of vice. By far the majority of books printed by Caxton were not intended for children, although now three of his publications are considered classics in children's literature: *Reynard the Fox* (1481), *The Book of the Subtyl Historyes and Fables of Esope* (1484), and *Le Morte d'Arthur* (1485). Even so, in the fifteenth century, Caxton's books remained too expensive for most of the few people who could read. These people relied instead on chapbooks such as *The Pleasant and Delightful History of Jack and the Giants* or *The Most Lamentable and Deplorable History of the Two Babes in the Wood*, which sold for pennies. Quite popular during that time, chapbooks included a number of types of literature (although they did not by any means attain the literary quality of

---

[6]Mary F. Thwaite, *From Primer to Pleasure: An Introduction to the History of Children's Books in England from the Invention of Printing to 1900* (London: Library Association, 1963), p. 1.

[7]Margaret C. Gillespie and John W. Conner, *Creative Growth through Literature for Children and Adolescents* (Columbus, Ohio: Merrill, 1975), p. 55.

Caxton's books): religious instruction, supernatural interpretation, romantic legends, ballad tales, and historic narratives.[8]

In the seventeenth century, Puritan influence on children's literature in England and North America was profound.[9] Puritans objected to stories of witches, giants, and fairies, insisting that children read morally edifying material. The titles of books produced for children during this period are particularly revealing: *Spiritual Milk for Boston Babes in Either England, Drawn from the Breasts of Both Testaments for their Souls' Nourishment* (1649) and *A Token for Children, Being an Exact Account of the Conversion, Holy and Exemplary Lives, and Joyful Deaths of Several Young Children* (1671), for example.[10] Probably the most significant work of Puritan literature during this period was John Bunyan's *Pilgrim's Progress* (1678), which combined moral edification and an adventure story. *Pilgrim's Progress* was not intended for an audience of children, but it quickly became a children's classic. Pilgrim's adventure through snare and pitfalls, his encounters with giants and fiends, and his rewards for bravery and endurance captivated children much more than the edifying manuals that had been written for them.[11]

In colonial New England, *Spiritual Milk* and *Pilgrim's Progress* were required reading for children, along with *The New England Primer*. The purpose of the primer was to teach the alphabet and Puritan ideals.[12] Originally published in 1690, the primer appeared in various editions until 1830.

Changes in children's literature in the eighteenth century came about in great part because of the educational influence of John Locke's philosophy. Locke suggested that the mind was a tabula rasa, a blank slate, on which impressions were made as a result of experiences.[13] Locke argued that children should read books geared toward

---

[8]Donna E. Norton, *Through the Eyes of a Child: An Introduction to Children's Literature* (Columbus, Ohio: Merrill, 1983), p. 41.

[9]John Rowe Townsend, *Written for Children: An Outline of English-language Children's Literature* (New York: Lippincott,1983), p. 20.

[10]Mary Lystad, *From Dr. Mather to Dr. Seuss: 200 Years of American Books for Children* (Cambridge, Mass.: Schenkman, 1980), pp. 6–7.

[11]Thwaite, *From Primer to Pleasure*, pp. 26–27.

[12]Ibid., p. 247.

[13]John Locke, *An Essay Concerning Human Understanding*, ed. John W. Yolton (London: Dent, 1965).

their capacities based on the impressions made thus far by their experiences. Few existing books met his criteria, but he did recommend *Aesop's Fables* and *Reynard the Fox*, which he considered both entertaining and rewarding for children.[14]

In France, Charles Perrault's *Contes de ma Mere l'Oye* (*Tales of Mother Goose*) appeared in 1698. This collection of tales included stories from French oral tradition, such as Cinderella, Sleeping Beauty, and Little Red Riding Hood, not the Mother Goose rhymes learners know today. Although Perrault did not create original stories for children, he did recognize the relevance of fairy tales for children and thus created one of the earliest collections of stories for children's enjoyment.[15]

In the eighteenth century, books written specifically for children with regard to their developmental level began to appear. In England in 1744, John Newberry demonstrated the possibilities for publishing children's literature with *A Little Pretty Pocket Book*, a collection of songs, moral tales, and woodblock illustrations. It was the first children's book that aimed both for edification and enjoyment. [16] *A Little Pretty Pocket Book* embedded its lessons and morals in letters from Jack the Giant Killer, admonishing readers to be good girls and boys. Newberry's publishing company became very successful and opened the market for other publishers of children's literature.

Later in the eighteenth century, Jean Jacques Rousseau advocated a possibility other than Locke's method of formal discipline for educating children. Rousseau argued that education should return to nature and that children should be allowed to unfold naturally.[17] The literary work that Rousseau recommended as providing worthwhile reading for children approaching adolescence was Daniel Defoe's *Robinson*

---

[14]John Locke, *Some Thoughts Concerning Education, The Educational Writings of John Locke: A Critical Edition with Introduction and Notes*, ed. James L. Axtell (London: Cambridge University Press, 1968), pp. 259–260.

[15]John Goldthwaite, *The Natural History of Make-Believe: A Guide to the Principal Works of Britain, Europe, and America* (New York: Oxford University Press, 1996), pp. 47–55.

[16]David L. Russell, *Literature for Children: A Short Introduction* (New York: Longman, 1991), p. 5.

[17]Jean-Jacques Rousseau, *Emile*, trans. William Boyd (New York: Teachers College Publications, 1965).

Crusoe. In *Robinson Crusoe* Rousseau saw the self-sufficient, solitary man who uses his intelligence to develop practical solutions for his problems.[18]

The eighteenth century also saw the production of various redac-tions of the Bible for children. *The Holy Bible in Verse* (1724) included a number of crude pictures to go along with the text and a set of questions and answers. *The Children's Bible* was first printed in London and then in the United States in 1763. This edition attempted, in prose, a more detailed account of the entire Bible than did the earlier works. In 1770, *The Holy Bible Abridged; or, The History of the Old and New Testament for Children* was published with crude, though bountiful, illustrations. The 1783 *A Curious Hieroglyphic Bible: or Select Passages in the Old and New Testament, Represented with Emblematical Figures for the Amusement of Youth* attempted to illustrate individual verses rather than stories.[19]

In the nineteenth century, the Grimm Brothers collected a number of traditional tales that were not published expressly for children but children did nonetheless read and enjoy. *Kinder und Hausmärchen* (*Nursery and Household Tales*) are filled with violence, and children's reading of them ignited debate among adults about the appropriateness of the collection for children. Scottish folklorist Andrew Lang created the yellow, blue, green, and red fairy books (1889-1894) in which he compiled old and modern tales, and Dane Hans Christian Andersen became the first writer to create his own original fairy tales, including *Ugly Duckling, Wild Swan.*

Lewis Carroll's *Alice in Wonderland* appeared in 1865, beginning a new era in children's literature. Alice's adventure was the first significant literary work for children that was offered purely for children's enjoyment.[20] Other significant fantasy stories followed Carroll's work, including *The Wizard of Oz* (1900) and *The Wind in the Willows* (1908). Adventure stories, such as *Treasure Island* (1881 and 1883), *The Adventures of Tom Sawyer* (1876) and *The Adventures of Huckleberry Finn* (1884), were also popular in the nineteenth century. For girls, domestic stories such as *Little Women* (1868) and *Anne of Green*

---

[18]Ibid., p. 84.

[19]Ruth K. MacDonald, *Literature for Children in England and America from 1646 to 1774* (Troy, N. Y.: Whitson, 1982), pp. 21–22.

[20]Russell, *Literature for Children*, p. 6.

Gables (1908), which focused on home and family life, were popular. Not until the 1970s did children's literature really begin to challenge Victorian ideas about the role of women.

The twentieth century saw the realization of the potential for quality children's literature. In the early part of the century, the work of Beatrix Potter (*The Tale of Peter Rabbit*) and Wanda Gag (*Millions of Cats*) laid the groundwork for the picture storybook for children. (The first picture book for children, *Orbis Pictus*, had been written by Johann Amos Comenius and published in 1658.) Gag's *Millions of Cats* (1927) is considered the first American picture book for children. In the 1930s publications of numerous high-quality picture books for children began, and in 1936 the American Library Association began awarding the Caldecott Medal for the most distinguished American picture book for children.

Fantasy stories have remained a mainstay in children's literature as evidenced by the continuing popularity of such works as *Winnie-the-Pooh* (1926), *Mary Poppins* (1934), *The Chronicles of Narnia* (1950–1956), *Charlotte's Web* (1952) and *A Wizard of Earthsea* (1968). Modern realistic literature for children encompasses both historical realism and contemporary realism. *The Little House* (1932-1945) series represents the best of historical realism; *The Chocolate War* (1974) and *The Great Gilly Hopkins* (1977) offer outstanding examples of contemporary realism. Considerable work has also been done in children's nonfiction—biography, history, art, and science, such as *Cheer the Lonesome Traveler: The Life of W. E. B. DuBois* (1970), *Only the Names Remain: The Cherokees and the Trail of Tears* (1972), *Cathedral: The Story of Its Construction* (1973), and *Tales Mummies Tell* (1985).

One of the most striking characteristics of contemporary children's literature is its sophistication. Few topics are taboo. Contemporary children's literature deals with issues ranging from sexual preference to divorce to violence. Because issues such as these are inescapable aspects of contemporary American society, many authors of children's literature have chosen to deal explicitly with these issues. Many of the children's books dealing with contemporary issues have been highly controversial. For example, *Heather Has Two Mommies* (1991), for children ages 4–6, presents the story of a young girl growing up parented by two lesbians. The late twentieth century saw the disruption of traditional values. Although enduring values of the past continue to be reflected in children's books, so are the values of a more diverse contemporary society.[21]

Contemporary children's books present protagonists who reflect the diversity of children in contemporary society: persons with disabilities (*The Bells of Christmas*, 1989), persons who do not fit sex role stereotypes (*Amazing Grace*, 1991), and persons from a variety of cultural and ethnic backgrounds (*The Paper Crane*, 1985). Two significant trends in nonfiction have also emerged in recent years. One is the inclusion of subjects that were once thought to be of interest only to adults—the environment (*Careers in Conservation*, 1980), immigration (*Coming to North America from Mexico, Cuba, and Puerto Rico*, 1982), and war (*Nobody Wants a Nuclear War*, 1987), for example. The other is the careful attempt to produce accurate and authoritative books, complete with sources and appendices.[22]

Writing children's literature has also undergone a transformation in recent years, becoming a valued and validated form of work.[23] Like writers of literary tales for adults, writers for children must possess a gift for writing. Contrary to an attitude held by some readers and writers of children's books, children's literature is not easy to write. Just as great adult literature requires highly talented authors, great children's literature is produced by committed and talented writers who have an understanding of children's psychosocial development as well as aesthetics. A good children's story will be as well drafted, as entertaining, and as enlightening as any good story for adults. Thus adults, as well as children, can enjoy children's literature. C. S. Lewis explains: "When I was ten, I read fairy tales in secret and would have been ashamed if I had been found doing so. Now that I am fifty I read them openly. When I became a man I put away childish things, including the fear of childishness and the desire to be very gown up. . . I now enjoy Tolstoy and Jane Austen and Trollope as well as fairy tales and I call that growth. If I had to lose the tales in order the acquire the

---

[21]Zena Sutherland and May Hill Arbuthnot, *Children and Books*, 7th ed. (Glenview, Ill.: Scott, Foresman, 1986), p. 7.

[22]For an in-depth discussion of children's non-fiction, see *Beyond Fact: Nonfiction for Children and Young People*, ed. Jo Carr (Chicago: American Library Association, 1982).

[23]For more on writing for children, see Catherine Woolley, *Writing for Children* (New York: New American Library, 1989); and Jane Yolen, *Writing Books for Children*, rev. ed. (Boston: The Writer, 1983).

novelists, I would not say that I had grown but only that I had changed. A tree grows because it adds rings; a train doesn't grow by leaving one station behind and puffing on to the next."[24]

GENRES OF CHILDREN'S LITERATURE

Children's literature shares a number of genres with adult literature, but puts a spin on them that makes them uniquely suited to an audience of children. Children's literature also has unique genres that belong solely to the realm of children's books. This section briefly explores the variety of genres of children's literature, their distinguishing characteristics, and their relevance for religious instruction.[25]

Picture Storybooks

In picture storybooks, which are generally created for younger children, the pictures tell the story in conjunction with the text. The picture storybook differs from an illustrated text—one in which the text is primary—in that the pictures assume a role equal to or even greater than the text in telling the story. In fact, some picture storybooks, such as the *Carl* series, are essentially wordless and yet do tell stories with themes, characters, setting, atmosphere, and point of view. In a picture storybook, pictures and text extend each other, reinforcing concepts, attitudes, and models, and forwarding the movement of the story line so that neither eye nor ear senses an interruption in the flow of the story.[26]

Picture storybooks tend to be brief. Character development occurs partially through illustration and often through emphasis on a particular trait or behavior pattern or through individual relationships in the story. For example, in *Old Turtle*, the main character is developed through her sparse use of words. Since Old Turtle rarely speaks, the other creatures believe Old Turtle to be very wise; when she does speak, they listen carefully. The plot of a picture storybook may be

---

[24]C. S. Lewis, "On Three Ways of Writing for Children," in *Of Other Worlds: Essays and Stories*, ed. Walter Hooper (New York: Harcourt Brace Jovanovich, 1966), pp. 25–26.

[25]An excellent and practical resource for religious educators is Sharron L. McElmeel, *Educator's Companion to Children's Literature* (Englewood, Colo.: Libraries Unlimited, 1995).

[26]Sutherland and Arbuthnot, *Children and Books*, p. 81.

very simple, but, as in any good story, it presents some sort of conflict and resolution. Action, humor, originality, and information are also important elements that make picture storybooks appealing to children. These key elements are conveyed through the interaction of text and illustrations.

Picture storybooks themselves include a wide variety of genres: folktales, legends, and myths, modern fantasy stories, realistic stories, and anthropomorphic stories.[27] Folktales, legends, and myths are traditional stories and have been discussed in detail in chapters 7–8. An interesting trend in the 1990s was the contemporary adaptation of traditional tales to reflect modern culture. For example, *The Frog Prince Continued* (1991) begins where the older fairytale ends. The story finds the Frog Prince dealing with the realities of marriage, and all is not happily-ever-after bliss. Other especially well-done adaptations include *Cinder-Elly* (1994), *The Three Little Wolves and the Big Bad Pig* (1990), and *The True Story of the 3 Little Pigs* (1989).

Modern fantasy picture book stories are defined by their use of magic as a principal feature of the story (*Jumanji*, 1981). Realistic picture book stories depict reality much as it is actually experienced by children, and these stories may be historical or contemporary (*Sam, Bangs, and Moonshine*, 1966). Anthropomorphic picture book stories are defined by their characters. In anthropomorphic picture book stories, the characters are nonhuman characters (animals or toys, for example) that are endowed with human traits (*Do You Want to Be My Friend?* 1987).[28]

Besides providing enjoyment for children, picture storybooks serve a number of other general educational functions. They stimulate language development, increase aesthetic capacity, expand intellectual development, facilitate observational skills and descriptive vocabularies, and develop appreciation for language style.[29] Research indicates that six aspects of children's literature are important in influencing young children's experiences of a story: appealing illustrations, interesting story content, useful information, broad humor, surprise

---

[27]Russell, *Literature for Children*, p. 26.

[28]For an in-depth discussion of children's toy literature, see Lois Rostow Kuznets, *When Toys Come Alive: Narratives of Animation, Metamorphosis, and Development* (New Haven: Yale University Press, 1994).

[29]Norton, *Through the Eyes of a Child*, p. 137.

elements, and appealing, recurring refrains.[30] Young children exposed to picture storybooks generally have positive and rewarding experiences that may shape later attitudes toward reading. In both formal and informal educational settings, sharing picture storybooks with children provides time for meaningful experiences and interactions between children and adults. A good picture storybook enriches children's reading experiences and provides pathways for meaningful development in a number of areas of children's lives.

Children's picture storybooks can also serve a number of functions in religious instruction for young children. In a formal religious instruction setting, for example, a picture storybook can help teach religious values. *Who Is the Beast?* is a children's picture storybook that explores similarities among the animals of the jungle and suggests the commonality of all creatures, including human beings. In working with children who cannot yet read, religious educators can use picture storybooks in a traditional story time setting with children sitting in a circle with an adult reader who reads the text and shows the pictures to the children. Readers can also involve children by having them point out characters, actions, or emotions in the pictures.

In the family, picture storybooks can be an important part of informal religious instruction. One of my very earliest memories is of my mother reading to me from picture storybooks that contained Bible stories. Every night, she would read a story and show me the pictures. Apparently, by the time my sister was born when I was four and a half years old, I had memorized many of the stories and insisted on "reading" them to my sister.

Children are particularly adept at expressing their emotions, and the potential for using picture storybooks to teach in the affective domain with children is immense. Children are quite able to pick up on emotional cues in stories and formulate appropriate emotional responses.[31] In fact, Horace Bushnell suggests that children should be taught feeling rather than doctrine. He contends that religious educators, especially parents, should "bathe the child in their own feeling of love to God."[32]

---

[30]Gillespie and Conner, *Creative Growth through Literature*, p. 58.

[31]Daniel O. Aleshire, *Faithcare: Ministering to All God's People through the Ages of Life* (Philadelphia Westminster, 1988), p. 105.

[32]Horace Bushnell, *Christian Nurture* (Grand Rapids, Mich.: Baker, 1979), p. 51.

An especially important facet of using picture storybooks in religious instruction is the creation of a sense of belonging for children. When parents and religious educators share story time with children, they create a time for meaningful, child-centered interactions, that emphasize the importance of the child in the family or community. Furthermore, since children tend to have positive experiences with picture storybooks, the pleasure derived from picture storybook times at church can create a sense in children that church is an enjoyable place to be. Children's experiences in the faith community should be positive, creating a climate of warmth and acceptance so that they have good feelings about going to church.[33] Sharing times with picture storybooks can facilitate this experience.

Picture storybooks can also be used effectively in adult religious instruction. Religious educator Jerome Berryman argues that the child within each adult promotes an opportunity for adult growth in religion. He explains that many adults have grounded themselves in a false self and that a return to the child within them allows them a way to begin anew to create an authentic self.[34] Picture storybooks can offer one way for adults to reawaken their child selves in religious instruction, while facilitating cognitive, affective, and lifestyle goals of religious instruction. For example, *The Three Little Wolves and the Big Bad Pig* reverses the roles of the traditional tale in which the Big Bad Wolf tries to gobble up the three little pigs and is finally destroyed when he climbs down their chimney into a pot of boiling water. In this modern adaptation of the story, the three little wolves build stronger and stronger houses to protect themselves from the Big Bad Pig who destroys each house with greater and greater destructive powers. Then comes a twist to the story. The three little wolves at last build a house of flowers. When the Big Bad Pig breathes in the sweet fragrance of the flowers he is transformed, much as the Grinch in Dr. Seuss' *How the Grinch Stole Christmas* is transformed by the singing of the Who's in Whoville. The three little wolves invite the pig to join them for tea and games, and they all become fast friends. This story has profound possibilities for the religious instruction of adults. On the cognitive level, the story can challenge beliefs and understandings

---

[33]Aleshire, *Faithcare*, p. 112.
[34]Jerome W. Berryman, *Godly Play: A Way of Religious Education* (New York: HarperSanFrancisco, 1991), p. 158.

of difference and conflict. On the affective level, the story can suggest alternative feelings, attitudes, and values toward difference, conflict, and violence, and on the lifestyle level the story can challenge adults to live peace-making lives. To teach the story, religious educators can use the traditional children's story-time format, which will likely appeal to adults' memories of childhood and invite the presence of the child within each adult learner. Religious educators can also present the story through a dramatic reading in which different adult readers read the parts of the narrator, wolves, and Big Bad Pig. The reading of the story should then be followed by a discussion of the characters and themes of the story and the story's implications for learners' religious living.

Traditional Stories

Traditional stories—folktales, fables, myths, and legends—have been considered in some detail in previous chapters. Thus, this section focuses particularly on the values of traditional stories for children and their uses in religious instruction.

As noted depth psychologist Bruno Bettelheim has argued, traditional stories help children cope with their psychological struggles.[35] Myths and folktales allow children to learn about human problems, discover possible solutions, and realize that they are not alone in their dilemmas. In the cognitive domain, traditional tales enrich children's lives by offering them new ways of understanding the world. Traditional tales provide information about different countries and cultures. Through traditional tales children can better understand cultures other than their own and develop an appreciation for various cultural manifestations in music, art, literature, dance, and customs. Traditional tales help children understand story forms and discover the relatedness and distinctions of various story forms and motifs from around the world.

In the affective domain, traditional tales provide ways for children to address their emotional needs. Traditional tales suggest that good triumphs over evil, that scary forests give way to cozy cottages, that people care for one another in a sometimes cruel world. In the lifestyle domain, traditional tales provide models of heroes and heroines who display goodness, compassion, courage, and industry. From

---

[35]Bruno Bettelheim, *The Uses of Enchantment: The Meaning and Importance of Fairy Tales* (New York: Knopf, 1976), p. 5.

these models, children can learn ways to become good people in the world.

Religious educators can use traditional tales in children's literature to teach appreciation for other cultures, to facilitate children's emotional growth, and to encourage children to act in loving, courageous, and industrious ways. A number of traditional tales have been captured in especially well-done picture story books—*Anansi the Spider* (1973), *Why Mosquitos Buzz in People's Ears* (1976), *Saint George and the Dragon* (1985), and *Raven, a Trickster Tale* (1994), for example.

If the goal of a teaching/learning situation with younger school children is to help children feel safe and welcomed, the religious educator may choose to read aloud a traditional tale, such as *Hansel and Gretel*, in which children face a frightening situation and succeed in overcoming adversity. Following the story, the religious educator may ask the children to create illustrations for the story, focusing on Hansel and Gretel's feelings in each scene. As the children draw, the religious educator may ask them to talk about their own feelings of fear and safety and may offer assurances of safety and welcome.

Modern Fantasy Stories

A fantasy story is a story of events that can never really happen, people or creatures who do not exist, or another world that differs from the real world. Children's fantasy stories differ from traditional tales in that they are originally literary rather than oral narratives. Successful fantasy stories require a believable (albeit impossible) world and once the fantasy world is established, the story must operate within that world. The setting and the action within the story must be credible for the fantasy to work. The fantasy must also be maintained. For example, if the reader discovers at the end that the fantasy was a dream, the reader experiences a sense of betrayal or treachery. Thus the fantasy world must be presented as an actual world, with its own laws and limitations.

An excellent example of a successful fantasy world that is especially appropriate for utilization in religious instruction is Narnia. Narnia was created by C. S. Lewis in his seven-volume series, *The Chronicles of Narnia*. Four English schoolchildren first enter Narnia through a wardrobe in an old English castle. Narnia is ruled by the White Witch, who maintains a never-ending winter in which Christmas never comes. There the children meet a faun, talking animals, and the great lion, Aslan, the rightful ruler of Narnia. When one of the children commits an act by which his life is forfeit to the White Witch, Aslan takes his place and is killed. But the witch does not know of a deeper magic by which Aslan is restored to life. Aslan then leads the forces of goodness in a battle in which the White Witch is destroyed and Narnia is returned to a peaceful and prosperous existence. In subsequent volumes, readers experience many adventures in Narnia and learn of both Narnia's creation and its fate. These books can be used in a number of ways in religious instruction, from providing opportunities to explore cognitively various religious and theological ideas embodied in the stories to helping learners feel the great weight of Aslan's sacrifice for Edmund to offering models of religious living through the actions of many of the books' characters.

Fantasy stories can be divided into a number of classifications: articulate animals (*Charlotte's Web*), dolls, toys, and inanimate objects (*Winnie-the-Pooh*); eccentric characters, preposterous situations, and exaggerations (*Harold and the Purple Crayon*); little people (*The Borrowers*); friendly presences, ghosts, and goblins (*The Ghost of Thomas Kempe*, 1973); time warps (*A Wrinkle in Time*, 1962); and science fiction (*Dolphin Island*, 1963).[36] Although each classification represents a different possibility for fantasy stories, each classification shares a common experience of enchantment and entrance into a mysterious world different from the real world. Although fantasy stories take place in impossible worlds, they do teach learners about real possibilities in learners' real worlds. The situations, settings, and characters of fantasy stories may not be real, but their depictions of human existence is. Fantasy stories work as educational tools because they take readers out of the ordinary and into the extraordinary. Readers can experience fresh perspectives on the realities in which they participate, and, when these perspectives have religious relevance, fantasy stories can be used in religious instruction. For example, Susan Cooper's quintet—*Over Sea, under Stone* (1965), *The Dark is Rising* (1973), *Greenwitch* (1974), *The Grey King* (1975), and *Silver on the Tree* (1977)—explores the eternal struggle between good and evil by reworking legends, myths, and material from the Arthurian cycle.

---

[36]Norton, *Through the Eyes of a Child*, p. 249.

Fantasy stories are especially fruitful tools in the realm of imagination. Through fantasy stories, learners can discover ways to imagine what might be. Since religious living is characterized by hope that is rooted in the possibility of what might be, development of imagination is an integral part of religious instruction. In the world of fantasy, learners can experience a different world that allows them to develop a new viewpoint on the ordinary, real world.

In a teaching/learning situation with older children, for example, a religious educator may help facilitate appropriate religious attitudes by utilizing a children's fantasy story, such as Dr. Seuss's *The Sneetches*. An animated version of this story may be found on video. In this story, difference defines power and privilege for the Sneetches. But by the end of the story, both the Sneetches with a star on their belly and the Sneetches without learn that they have a great deal in common and that having a star on one's belly or not does not make one Sneetch better than another. The religious educator may show the videotape and then use a talk show format to help children explore the story. With children acting the various parts, characters from the story who serve as the talk show's guests and audience members can be interviewed by the host about their experiences of being the same or different. Audience members may also be allowed to ask questions of the characters. Following the talk show, the religious educator may lead the children in a discussion of their own experiences of being the same and being different.

Realistic Fiction

Realistic fiction is defined by its adherence to the experience of real life. Realistic stories take place in the world as learners know it, and the events of the stories are events that could actually happen in the real world. The plots and characters are plausible, and the conflicts are resolved in natural and not supernatural ways. Realistic fiction is geared toward the various developmental periods of childhood and take into account the needs and capabilities of children in various stages. Thus the appeal of realistic fiction for children is the children's ability to identify closely with the characters in the stories. Often the characters in realistic fiction are the same age as their audience members, with similar interests, concerns, and problems. In realistic fiction, children discover that they are not alone in facing their problems or struggling with their situations. Often realistic stories provide options for children, showing them ways they can deal constructively and creatively with their problems. These stories can also help children cope with their own emotions, as well as providing insight and empathy for the feelings and lives of others.[37]

For example, in *The Cat Ate My Gymsuit* Marcy Lewis is bored to tears by her experience of the ninth grade. She hates her life and her tyrannical father. But then she encounters a new English teacher, Miss Finney, whose care and concern begin to have a positive impact on Marcy. When Miss Finney is suspended because of her controversial teaching methods, Marcy moves outside the protective shell she has built around herself and organizes a protest, upon which she finds herself suspended from school. Despite her father's pressure, Marcy stands by her principles and learns that she is capable of dealing successfully with adversity.

Realistic fiction can be subdivided into a number of categories. Domestic realism (*The Secret Garden*, 1909) deals with stories of home and family. Social realism (*Roll of Thunder, Hear My Cry*, 1976) examines important social issues facing the contemporary world. Problem novels (*Are You There, God? It's Me, Margaret*, 1970) focus on issues of concern to young people, such as divorce, drugs, and puberty. Adventure stories (*The Adventures of Huckleberry Finn*, 1884) are characterized by fast-moving plots that follow the adventures of often unusual or bizarre protagonists, often in exotic settings. Survival stories (*Julie of the Wolves*, 1972) pit people against nature in an effort to survive. Multicultural realism (*Yentl the Yeshiva Boy*, 1962) introduces readers to the variety of culture groups so that they might better understand and appreciate them.

The success of realistic fiction depends on the story's faithfulness to reality and its adherence to literary standards. Realistic fiction allows children to deal with issues of importance to them, and, in fact, has often spawned a great deal of controversy because of the concern of writers of realistic fiction for relevancy. For example, the appearance of *Heather Has Two Mommies* in 1991 generated conflict because of its accepting portrayal of a lesbian relationship. Perhaps realistic fiction's most valuable contribution in education is its ability to allow children to explore their own experiences in the world, process their feelings about these experiences, and come to an understanding of the issues that confront them.

---

[37]Russell, *Literature for Children*, pp. 111–119.

In religious instruction, realistic fiction can help children develop religious understandings of contemporary issues, religious attitudes and values, and religious lifestyles. For example, young children are characterized by egocentrism, but older children are beginning to differentiate self from the world and to develop an awareness of self and relationships. Although children do not move from egocentrism into a fully developed altruism, they are learning love for others in ways that are different from the self-serving love of earlier periods.[38] As James Michael Lee suggests, love is learned.[39] Being loved, participating in loving behaviors, and observing loving behaviors are powerful and important ways religious educators can teach love to children. In the religious instruction context, religious educators can and should love children and should model loving behaviors for them. Religious educators can also invite children to engage in loving behaviors, such as sharing toys, giving someone a hug, or helping someone who is ill. Using a narrative from realistic fiction, such as *A Gift for Mama* (1987), religious educators can provide another model of loving behavior. In this story for eight-to-ten-year olds, a young girl in Poland, wanting to be like the adults, flouts tradition and buys her mother a Mother's Day gift instead of making one. At first her mother is disappointed but then she sees the sewing the young girl did for family members and friends in order to earn the money to buy the gift. On considering all the hard work her daughter put into her gift, the mother is touched and appreciative. This story may be especially appropriate for a teaching/learning session shortly before Mother's Day. The religious educator may tell the story and then have children discuss their feelings for their mothers and their plans for making or buying a Mother's Day gift.

Historical Fiction

Children's historical fiction is set in the past and attempts to portray the historical period as accurately as possible. These stories allow children to enter the world of the past and experience a time gone by, as in *Caddie* Woodlawn (1936), *Thy Friend, Obadiah* (1965), and *Sarah, Plain and Tall* (1985).

---

[38]Aleshire, *Faithcare*, pp. 106-107.

[39]James Michael Lee, *The Content of Religious Instruction* (Birmingham, Ala.: Religious Education Press, 1985), p. 238.

Because it attempts to be faithful to the past, historical fiction presents a number of special demands. The setting for the story is particularly important. The author of historical fiction must convince the reader that the story is integrally related to its setting or, in other words, that the conditions of the historical period have a specific impact on the characters and actions of the story. For example, the stories of the Ingalls family in *The Little House* series grow out of the family's experiences of American frontier life. Character development, which is usually partially achieved through dialogue, can be problematic because the author must find a balance between the language of the time and language that children can understand. Likewise, plot must emerge from the time period and be consistent with the experiences of the time.

Historical fiction allows children to experience another time in human history. In these stories, children can discover their own heritage as well as the commonalities and differences of human experiences across time. Thus, while learning information about other historical eras, children are also learning about the human family in general.

In religious instruction, historical fiction can help children learn the heritage of people of faith, both from their own and from other traditions. Many religious educators suggest that one's religious heritage is a significant piece in one's developing identity within the faith community.[40] Furthermore, learning about the religious heritage of groups other than their own may help children develop an appreciation for the diversity of religious expression throughout the world and in their own neighborhoods.

Who Came with Cannons (1992) is the story of a Quaker girl in North Carolina who learns that her family is operating a station for the Underground Railroad. Targeted toward ten-to-twelve-year-old children, this story can be used in religious instruction both to introduce learners to Quakerism and Quaker values and to help children to take

---

[40]C. Ellis Nelson, *How Faith Matures* (Louisville, Ky.: Westminster/John Knox, 1989), pp. 42–59; Charles R. Foster, *Teaching in the Community of Faith* (Nashville: Abingdon, 1982), pp. 16- 19; John H. Westerhoff III, *Will Our Children Have Faith?* (New York: Seabury, 1976), p. 69; Mary Elizabeth Moore, *Education for Continuity and Change: A New Model for Christian Religious Education* (Nashville: Abingdon, 1983), pp. 59–85.

right actions even in difficult situations. Likewise, *Number the Stars* (1989) can be used with eight-to-ten-year-old children to explore the Holocaust, Judaism, and justice. The protagonist of the story, ten-year-old Annemarie, learns bravery from the people around her who are involved in the effort of the Danish resistance to smuggle Jews to Sweden.

CONCLUSION

Not long ago, I preached a memorial service for a hospice in Portland, Oregon. Every six months, the hospice invites all of the family members of patients who have died in that six month period to return for a service of remembrance and celebration of the lives of those whom they loved. Instead of preaching a traditional sermon, I read a children's story, *The Last Dance*. In this story, Ninny and Bessie learn from Ninny's grandfather, Oppa, that every human being has the right to three things: to dance, to sing, and to tell stories. After Oppa dies, Ninny and Bessie sneak away at night to his grave and dance for him. There they make a bargain. When one dies, the other will come to the graveyard and dance on the other's grave. When they grow up, Bessie and Ninny marry, and soon Ninny is sent off to fight in World War II. Bessie longs for Ninny to return home to dance with her. At last she receives word: Coming home. Put on your dancing shoes. Bessie and Ninny grow old together, surrounded by family and friends. And Ninny reminds Bessie when his time comes to save the last dance for him. Eventually, Ninny does die, and Bessie keeps her promise, sneaking away to the graveyard to dance for him there.

Although they may be simple in language and plot, children's stories are powerful narratives for both children and adults. Because these books are written with children's developmental abilities and needs at the center, they are especially helpful for religious educators in addressing age-appropriate issues in age-appropriate ways. Children's literature used in religious instruction can help facilitate children's cognitive, affective, and behavioral growth by teaching information, by evoking emotions, and by exemplifying behaviors, for example.

Ramona Quimby, (*Ramona the Pest*) age five, was having the best day of her life. Today was the day she was starting school. "Hurry!" Ramona urged her mother. Ramona was a girl who could not wait.

Life was so interesting that she simply had to find out what happened next. At last, when she arrived at school, her teacher took her by the hand and led her to a little chair. "Sit here for the present," the teacher said with a smile. "A present!" thought Ramona. No one had told her that she was going to get a present the very first day.

Children's literature is a gift to children and adults alike. Children and the children within adults respond to the humor, actions, emotions, characters, and situations of children's literature. Used in religious instruction settings, children's literature can reach the child in each learner and facilitate the holistic goals of religious instruction.

11

Literary Tales

Love is one of the great enlargers of the person because it re-
quires us to "take in" the stranger and to understand him, and to
exercise restraint and tolerance as well as imagination to make
the relationship work. If love includes passion, it is more explo-
sive and dangerous and forces us to go deeper. Great art does the
same thing.[1]

—May Sarton

Literary tales are written to be read.[2] They differ from the stories of
oral tradition primarily in their modes of composition and reception.
Because the tale is not intended to be told orally, the author has freedom to create a narrative with greater complexity, utilizing all of the
elements of literary tradition. In literary tales, the narrator is not the
author, but a persona created by the author for the express purpose of
conveying the story. This ironic distance, the discrepancy between
the author and the narrator, would be highly unusual in oral storytelling, but in literary storytelling, ironic distance adds to the richness
and meaning of the narrative.[3]

---

[1]May Sarton, *Journal of a Solitude* (New York: Norton, 1973).

[2]Literary critic Northrop Frye distinguishes between "naive" and "sophisticated"
literature. By naive, he means primitive or popular literature. This chapter deals with
sophisticated literature—tales of literary merit—rather than naive literature. Northrop
Frye, *Anatomy of Criticism: Four Essays* (Princeton, N.J.: Princeton University Press,
1957), p. 35.

[3]Robert Scholes and Robert Kellog, *The Nature of Narrative* (London: Oxford
University Press, 1966), p. 53.

245

The literary tale is an event rather than an object. Learners participate in the construction of the narrative as they read it or as it is read
to them.[4] The tale, then, is a coming together of a learner and a literary narrative. The learner brings to this experience her past experience
and present personality and out of the words and images of the literary
text creates a new experience that she perceives as the literary tale; it
becomes part of her ongoing stream of experience. This transaction
between learner and literary narrative is a lived relationship that may
become an object of thought but should not be confused with an object
as an entity existing apart from the learner.[5] In other words, the literary tale exists as an event only in the actual moment of its reading or
being heard. Thus, each learner, based on his past experiences and present personality, will experience the literary tale differently. This diversity of experiences with a literary narrative can add a rich dimension to discussion of a literary tale in religious instruction.

Two forms of literary tales predominate American and British literature—the novel and the short story. Although each category may be
subdivided into yet other genres, this chapter focuses on the larger categories (novel and short story) and the commonalities of literary tales.

Literary tales can play an important role in religious instruction for
older adolescents and adults. Because of the complexity of literary
tales, the cognitive abilities of older adolescents and adults are better
suited to grappling with experiencing, interpreting, and applying literary narratives. Probably the best setting for utilizing literary tales in religious instruction is a reading group in which learners read the works
on their own and then come together on a regular basis for discussion.
The length and complexity of literary tales essentially precludes their
usefulness in settings in which learners do not have time to read the
works before they come to the group. Occasionally, however, an especially concise short story or a short passage from a novel may be read
aloud or distributed for learners to read in the group setting.

An especially useful instructional tool for assisting learners in reading literary works and preparing for discussion is the double-entry

---

[4]Alan C. Purves and Dianne L. Monson, *Experiencing Children's Literature*
(Glenview, Ill.: Scott, Foresman, 1984), p. 9.

[5]Louise Rosenblatt, *The Reader, the Text, and the Poem: The Transactional Theory
of the Literary Work* (Carbondale, Ill.: Southern Illinois University Press, 1978), pp.
12–13.

journal.[6] The double-entry journal allows learners to interact with the narrative and explore the possible meanings they may construct from the story. On the left side of a notebook, the learner takes notes on the reading, collects direct quotations, makes observations, and writes images, symbols, and ideas. On the right side of the notebook, the learner records notes about the notes, summaries, formulations, comments, editorial responses, feelings, revisions. Thus the facing pages are in dialogue with one another. The double-entry journal facilitates learners' ability to approach literary tales holistically, responding to the narratives cognitively and affectively. The contents of the double-entry journal then can provide a fruitful resource for group discussions of literary tales.

Literary tales provide for learners experiences of the depth and breadth of human existence. In the novel, in particular, the combination of the individual and the archetypal engages learners in the journey of the protagonist, in whom learners find themselves. At the core of the protagonist's story is a concern for reality as humans experience it. A good novel will be true to this reality, and this truth will draw learners into the story.[7]

In many novels, learners may experience cognitive, affective, and behavioral possibilities for authentic religious living. Novels often deal with important religious and theological themes, such as grace, forgiveness, and redemption, as in the works of Flannery O'Connor or Graham Greene. On a cognitive level, many novels appropriate for religious instruction call learners to believe rather than to beliefs. In

---

[6]Diane Wrobleski, "Finding Meaning: Reading, Writing, Thinking Applications: Double-Entry Notebooks, Literature Logs, Process Journals," ERIC Document Reproduction Service, 1985, p. 2.

[7]In selecting literary texts for inclusion in religious instruction, religious educators should be aware of the dynamics of power and privilege that are at work in literature and the literary publishing enterprise. Thus religious educators should seek works that reflect the diversity of human experience, intentionally including works by and about both women and men, people of color, people of all ages and abilities, and people of a wide variety of religious persuasions. Religious educators should also be aware of the possible ways some literary works may reinforce stereotypes and patterns of dominance and should help learners bring their religious experiences and convictions to bear on the ways these characters and stories are experienced, interpreted, and evaluated.

other words, novels can challenge learners to engage in critical theological reflection without specifying the doctrinal content of that reflection. The world of a novel can disrupt the comfortable worlds
learners have created, and the credibility of a novel's action may cause
learners to question their own assumptions about the realities they
have constructed. A novel can disrupt equilibrium, a necessary pre-
condition for cognitive growth, according to Jean Piaget.[8] In so doing,
a novel can invite learners to look at the world in a new way, from a
fresh perspective, and can provide learners with a model of an alternative way of seeing the world. Learners' experience in a novel can facilitate new awareness, new levels of understanding, and new abilities
to analyze and synthesize experiences and ideas.

For example, one of the themes of Herman Hesse's *Journey to the
East* is servant leadership. In the course of the novel, the reader discovers that Leo the servant is actually the leader of the organization.
In a culture that tends toward hierarchical leadership and top-down
administration, especially in the church, Leo's story may be challenging and disruptive to established ways of understanding leadership.
Leo's life suggests that the way to lead is to serve, and his example
may lead learners to develop new ideas about authority and control.

In the affective domain, novels can be powerful learning tools, affecting emotions, attitudes, and values. Novels have the power to speak
to the heart. Because of their form as written narrative, novels have the
luxury of dealing in complex ways with human emotions. A well-written novel can recreate emotion in its readers. Through a novel, learners
can enter into the emotional lives of others, even, and maybe most importantly, those who are quite different from themselves.

For example, in Alice Walker's *Possessing the Secret of Joy*, learners
can experience the emotions of an African woman, Tashi, who has been
genitally mutilated because of the traditional religious practices of her
community. Through Tashi learners can participate in emotions not
available to them probably in any other way than story. Although most
learners have no connections with Tashi's experience of female genital
mutilation, they do have experiences of fear, pain, sadness, and triumph
that allow them to identify with Tashi and possibly to enlarge their
hearts to include her (and others like her) in their circle of concern.

---

[8]Jean Piaget, *The Development of Thought: Equilibration of Cognitive Structures*
(New York: Viking, 1977).

In the lifestyle domain, many novels provide outstanding models of religious living. These models, unfortunately, are typically not found in most of the books published as "Christian novels" by Christian publishing companies. Rarely do "Christian" novels stand up to the scrutiny of real-life experience. Rather, models of religious living are found in the literary works that grapple with the human condition. Often, at first glance, these models are not what learners would consider ideal. They may be drunken priests, avowed agnostics, or hell-raising college students, but under the surface learners will find characters struggling to live authentic lives, like Jacob wrestling with God.

In Graham Greene's *The Power and the Glory*, a drunkard priest who has fathered an illegitimate child has the opportunity to flee a Mexican state during a anticleric purge as the police begin executing priests who will not renounce their vows. The police believe, and rightly so, that the priests, who lived extravagantly at the expense of the people, are partly to blame for the sorry state of affairs that typifies the region. As he hides from the police, the alcoholic priest has a self-awakening in which he sees himself as he really is. He becomes convinced that he is a horrible priest, but because he still has the ability to say the Mass he is of some use to the people, who still believe despite attempts by the police to stamp out religion. At last, when given the opportunity to escape, the priest chooses to stay and minister to the people. Eventually, he is caught and executed, but a young boy who has been watching the priest all along comes to believe in God because of the priest's actions. For the boy and for the novel's readers, the priest becomes an example of religious living because of his determination to stay and minister to those who needed him, including a wounded enemy, in spite of sure risk of his own life. The priest is not especially brave, not especially likable, not even an especially good priest. But, in the end, he chooses to do what is right, to live up to his calling and his ordination.

In many ways, short stories can likewise help facilitate the cognitive, affective, and behavioral goals of religious instruction. Because of its length, however, the short story relies on an economy of words, and at its core is an epiphany, a moment of revelation that suggests realities beyond the story itself.[9] This epiphany perhaps provides the

---

[9]John Bayley, *The Short Story: Henry James to Elizabeth Bowen* (New York: St. Martin's, 1988), p. 9.

short story's most important contribution to religious instruction. The epiphany of the short story may allow the story's use in religious instruction to create a space for learners to encounter Mystery. A short story suggests much that is beyond itself and in so doing may open learners to the possibility of experience with Mystery beyond the story. The "aha" (or epiphany) of the story can catch the learner up into the Mystery of Being to which the story may only point.

In Eudora Welty's "A Worn Path," an elderly grandmother must make her way through the countryside for several miles to reach the physician's office in town. A snide, judgmental nurse gives her medicine for her ailing grandson. The epiphany of the story comes when the reader learns that the worn path of the title is the path through the countryside that the old woman has literally worn with so many trips to the physician's office for her grandson. When that realization dawns, learners can be overwhelmed with the grandmother's love. At great risk to herself and with great difficulty, time and time again, out of love, she has made the trip that has allowed her grandson to survive.

Literary tales, both novels and short stories, have a place in religious instruction because they insist that behind the mundane and ordinary experiences of everydayness lurks the Mystery that learners may not look in the face but may glimpse, though only fleetingly. Literary tales can help learners stalk this Mystery, which permeates the world and learners' experiences, and learn to live in it with all of their bodies, hearts, and minds. The movements and epiphanies of literary tales echo learners' own experiences and constantly call learners to continue to become more than they are.

ELEMENTS OF LITERARY TALES

Because of the vast numbers of novels and short stories in publication, religious educators need some background in literary criticism in order to aid them in selection of appropriate literary tales for religious instruction. Furthermore, because of the complexity of literary tales, understanding of the elements of literary tales can aid religious educators in assisting learners in their experiences and interpretations of literary tales. Learners' past experiences and background knowledge are an important dimension of the transaction between learner and literary tale, and some understanding of the elements of literary narrative can therefore enhance the quality of this transaction. Literary critic Robert Scholes suggests that reading a literary narrative requires looking in two directions. One direction, he claims, is looking back toward the source and original signs of the narrative being read, and the other direction is forward, based on the textual situation of the person doing the reading.[10]

Significant elements of stories—point of view, meaning, character, and plot,—have been briefly mentioned earlier. But because these elements become more elaborate in literary tales, this section explores each of these elements in more detail. As religious educators are better able to understand these elements of literary tales, they will be better prepared to select appropriate literary tales for religious instruction and to aid learners in experiencing and exploring literary tales.

Point of View

In the literary tale, the storyteller or narrator is a persona assumed by the author. The narrator tells the story from a particular point of view, and learners should be aware of the narrator and how the narrator's point of view affects the way the story is told. Narrators of literary tales may be first-person, omniscient, or limited.

The first-person narrator is himself a character in the story. He may be a minor character, but he is nonetheless somehow involved in the plot of the story. The way the story is narrated is then defined by the persona of the first-person narrator. For example, the vocabulary used to relate the narrative must be appropriate to the narrator, and the information related must be within the narrator's credible grasp. Learners should be aware of the perspectives and biases that the first-person narrator brings to the narration; they become part of the story. Not all first-person narrators are reliable, and learners should read or listen to first-person narratives carefully in order to notice how the narrator's perspective has affected the narration. For example, Binx Bolling is the narrator of Walker Percy's *The Moviegoer*. One morning, Binx, who has spent most of his life sunk in "everydayness," woke up to the possibility of a search, for God, for meaning, for something more than everydayness. "To become aware of the possibility of the search is to

---

[10]Robert Scholes, *Protocols of Reading* (New Haven: Yale University Press, 1989), p. 7.

be onto something. Not to be onto something is to be in despair."[11] The rest of the narrative is Binx's story of his search. From Binx's perspective, learners follow his journey through movie theaters in search of a cure for his malaise. Because Binx narrates the story, learners watch his journey through his eyes, and his perceptions give shape to learners' experience of his narrative. Thus learners should be aware that they are experiencing only Binx's side of the story. On the one hand, learners are afforded an intimate look into Binx's life, and, on the other, they are also guided through his experiences by his perceptions of them.

Unlike the first-person narrator, the omniscient narrator is outside the action of the story. This narrator is able to see all the events of the narrative and to know the interior life of all of the characters. Thus an omniscient narrator can reveal the thoughts and actions of all the characters to learners. In *Wise Blood*, the narrator tells the story of Hazel Motes, a man running from God. In addition to Motes' thoughts, learners are privy to the interior lives of the other main characters—Enoch Emery and Mrs. Flood. By offering glimpses into the thoughts and feelings of all of the primary characters, the narrator allows learners to see the powerful interconnections among the three, thus complicating and deepening the meaning of the story itself.

A limited narrator tells the story from outside the action but describes the perceptions, thoughts, and feelings of a single character rather than every character. Ferrol Sams's *The Whisper of the River* is an excellent example of a novel that utilizes a limited narrator. The novel is the story of Porter Osborne Jr.'s experiences in a Baptist college in Georgia. Although numerous characters people the novel, learners know the interior life of Porter alone. Sams's use of the limited narrator focuses the story solely on Porter Osborne Jr. and allows learners to watch the internal as well as the external changes that occur as his faith, family, and ideals are challenged.

The choice the author makes about point of view will affect the narration of the story and, for learners, will affect the ways they experience and interpret the story. Thus learners should begin interaction with the narrative by asking who is narrating the story and why. The answer to these questions then provides clues as to how learners should pay attention to the story the narrator is offering. In teaching

---

[11]Walker Percy, *The Moviegoer* (New York: Avon, 1961), p. 18.

with literary tales, religious educators may want to lead learners in a discussion of the narrative's point of view. As learners are better able to explore how the narrator's point of view affects the relating of the story, they will be better able to develop more sophisticated analyses and interpretations of the story.

Meaning

Meaning occurs in the correlation learners make between the world of the narrative and the real world in which they live. This meaning arises through the actions of the characters and the subsequent consequences of those actions. Thus meaning is not a thematic statement about a story but rather the story's statement about the nature of reality, contextualized within the learner's framework. In other words, one correct meaning does not exist. Rather, meaning is created in the encounter between the learner and the tale; the learner's standpoint has a direct effect upon the meanings the learner constructs from the tale. Scholes suggests that reading almost always encompasses two times (the time of the narrative and the time in which the learner reads the text), two places (the world of the narrative and the world of the reader), and two consciousnesses (the consciousness of the narrator and the consciousness of the reader).[12] On the one hand, this transaction between learner and literary text means religious educators can not assume that all learners will derive the same meaning from tale. On the other, this transaction opens up the possibility of multiple interpretations, fruitful dialogue, and meaningful self-disclosure.

For example, in Graham Greene's *Brighton Rock*, Pinkie, the central character, personifies evil. Throughout the story, he pursues evil and rejects grace; at the very last, he plummets over a cliff. Throughout the book, however, a refrain has echoed: "Between the stirrup and the ground, he mercy sought and mercy found." On the surface, the ending of the book would leave learners certain of Pinkie's damnation, but this echoing phrase suggests the smallest of possibilities that Pinkie sought mercy as he plunged to his death. This ambiguity leaves an openness for learners in a religious instruction setting to explore themes of evil, damnation, mercy, grace, and salvation.

Exploring meaning in literary tales brings a unique problem to religious educators and learners that does not exist in oral tradition. The

---

[12]Ibid.

learner and the writer of the literary work may come from two very different times, cultures, and worldviews. The real world of the author, including language, becomes fixed in the literary tale, whereas in oral tradition the teller and listener live in the same world. Even traditional tales are altered in the retelling to make them relevant and comprehensible to a contemporary audience. Furthermore, in oral cultures, the tales themselves act as a means of preserving traditions and worldviews. In literary tales, however, the fixed text finds itself in new surroundings in which its language may be archaic and its worldview outdated, as in Geoffrey Chaucer's *Canterbury Tales*, for example. Nonetheless, such literary works can be valuable tools for religious instruction, and therefore religious educators need to be prepared to assist learners in understanding the historical and linguistic context of the writing of literary tales. Granted, some meaning may be derived from a literary narrative with no knowledge of its background, but a thorough reading necessitates some grasp of the milieu from which the narrative emerged. An understanding of the historical context of a literary tale can help bring the world of the author and the world of the learner into a close alignment which then assists the learner in exploring the narrative.

Character

The meanings of literary tales are conveyed and constructed primarily through characters and their actions. In a well-written story, characters act because of the kind of people they are, and the kind of people they are is shown through their actions.[13] For example, Mrs. Turpin in Flannery O'Connor's short story "Revelation" is a self-righteous, self-satisfied hypocrite. Because this is the kind of character she is, she volunteers for her church and gives to the poor, all the while judging them as "trash." She believes herself to be better than they—until one day in a doctor's office, an acne-faced girl throws a book at her, calls her an old warthog, and tells her to go back to hell where she came from. This revelation sets Mrs. Turpin on a path of self-examination that leads to the story's final revelation.

Ancient literature focused primarily on heroic action and hence the external attributes of characters. With the influence of Christianity, focus shifted to the character's inward development. The public

---

[13]Cleanth Brooks and Robert Penn Warren, *Understanding Fiction*, 3d ed. (Englewood Cliffs, N.J.: Prentice-Hall, 1979), p. 107.

concept of heroic excellence, as in Odysseus, was supplanted by the soul's private and personal relationship with God, as in Parzival, and literature took up this concern with the interior life. Such a shift called for growth or change on the part of the characters, which had not been demanded in earlier tales. [14]

Participating in a character's interior life and its concomitant development in the literary tale is an especially important means by which learners construct experience from the narrative transaction. Generally, the interior life is revealed through narrative analysis of the character's thoughts, which are filtered and commented upon by the narrator and through interior monologues, direct, immediate presentation of the unspoken thoughts of the character without the intervention of the narrator's interpretation or commentary.[15] According to novelist E. M. Forster, characters become real to learners when they are convincing. Characters are convincing when learners have a sense that the narrator knows everything about the characters, even though she may not choose to tell everything she knows. One factor that contributes to the realness of characters is the revelation of their interior lives. Forster claims this factor allows learners to know characters in a way that is impossible to know other people. Human relations are always approximate. People do not know each other's interior lives, but in a literary tale learners can know characters fully, their interior lives exposed. Access to the interior lives of characters make literary tales compelling because they offer to learners a way of experiencing other human beings that is not possible in the real world.[16]

This access to the interior life and development of literary characters is an important factor in using literary tales in religious instruction because it can provide a means by which learners can enter into the Other. Through encounters with these characters, learners may experience aspects of other humans that are usually hidden in real life, or they may find aspects of their own lives embodied in ways that may lead them to new levels of self-knowledge. In teaching with literary tales, religious educators can facilitate learners' exploration of characters by helping learners do close readings of interior monologues or

---

[14]Scholes and Kellogg, *Nature of Narrative*, pp. 160–170.

[15]Ibid., pp. 177, 193.

[16]Edward Morgan Forster, *Aspects of the Novel* (New York: Hacourt, Brace, 1927), pp. 74, 97– 99.

the narrator's interpretive comments. Or religious educators can ask learners to identify with characters and imagine how they would feel or react in the character's situation. Empathy grows out of learners' basic capacity for human relatedness. This capacity allows learners to perceive another's affective cues in such a way that learners respond to these cues as if the cues were learners' own, thus producing a temporary identification with the other's emotional state.[17] Experiencing empathy with another, then, tends to produce a more differentiated and articulated image of the other, a greater appreciation of the' Other.[18] Perhaps as learners are able to empathize with the Other whom they encounter in literary tales, they will become better able to develop empathy with those in the real world who are Other.

Plot

Like other kinds of stories, the literary tale relies on movement, or a plot. Something happens and something changes. Reading fiction involves seeing, following, and interpreting these movements.[19] Plot is a sequence of causally linked interrelated events.[20] Within the story world, the plot must be credible, given the nature of that world, and the characters must behave in accordance with their personalities and environment. The events of the story must be logically and causally related, and the plot should not rely on coincidence or some *deus ex machina* to carry the story. Rather, the plot should depend on actions and consequences credible in the given situation of the story. For example, in Leo Tolstoy's short story, "The Forged Coupon," a young boy's forgery of a two-and-a-half-ruble bond coupon sets off a chain of events, leading from one disaster to another, until an innocent man is willing to absorb the evil done him and not pass it on.

Plot, probably more than any other narrative element, elicits the desire for the learner to read or hear a literary tale. This desire is the

---

[17]Judith V. Jordan, "Empathy and the Mother-Daughter Relationship," in *Women's Growth in Connection: Writings from the Stone Center*, ed. Judith V. Jordan et al. (New York: Guilford, 1991), p. 29.

[18]Judith V. Jordan, "Empathy and Self Boundaries," *Women's Growth in Connection*, p. 73.

[19]Robert Scholes, *Elements of Fiction* (New York: Oxford University Press, 1968), p. 15.

[20]David L. Russell, *Literature for Children: A Short Introduction* (New York: Longman, 1991), p. 92.

impetus that carries learners onward through the literary narrative.[21] Thus religious educators should give careful consideration to the plot of a literary tale as they make selections for religious instruction. The plot should be relevant and engaging enough to elicit learners' desire to finish the tale, to complete the literary transaction. An excellent example of an engaging plot is found in Elie Wiesel's *Dawn*. In this novella, Elisha, a young Holocaust survivor who is now an Israeli freedom fighter, has been ordered to kill an English officer in reprisal for Britain's execution of a Jewish prisoner. The time frame for the story encompasses twilight of one day and dawn of the next; within that time Elisha must struggle with his principles and decide whether or not to follow through with his orders. As Elisha progresses toward his decision, learners are swept along with him, always wondering if he will or will not carry out the execution.

The sense of plot is found in what literary critic Barbara Hardy terms "the narrative motions of human consciousness," referring to the narrative structure of human experience, which perceives human actions in terms of a plot. Furthermore, she argues that plot in literary narrative not only represents life as activity but also incites action. People tell stories in order to change, to propel themselves toward purposive activity.[22] The relation between plot or narrative motion in literary tales and the narrative motions of human consciousness suggest that literary plots can be intimately related to the problems and possibilities of actual human lives. Thus as learners study the plots of literary tales, they are simultaneously engaged both in the process of exploring plot as a literary element and plot as a possible path for life.[23]

The implications of plot for religious instruction are significant. If plot can suggest potential life paths, then the exploration of plot in religious instruction may facilitate lifestyle goals for learners. For example, Gail Godwin's *Father Melancholy's Daughter* follows the

---

[21]Peter Brooks, *Reading for the Plot: Design and Invention in Narrative* (New York: Knopf, 1984), p. 37.

[22]Barbara Hardy, "Towards a Poetics of Fiction: An Approach Through Narrative," *Novel* 2 (1968): 5–14; Barbara Hardy, *Tellers and Listeners* (London: Athlone Press, 1975), pp. 3–4.

[23]Robert L. Caserio, *Plot, Story, and the Novel: From Dickens and Poe to the Modern Period* (Princeton, N.J.: Princeton University Press, 1979), pp. 8–9.

vocational struggles of the daughter of an Episcopalian rector as she attempts to come to terms with her calling to ministry. The novel ends with her commitment to enter ministry. In religious instruction, *Father Melancholy's Daughter* can be used to suggest a life path for learners that involves their finding, exploring, and committing to their own vocations, whether that calling is to ordained ministry or to the ministry of reconciliation that all Christians share.[24]

Design

The design or construction of a literary tale is built on two primary components—juxtaposition and repetition.[25] Juxtaposition occurs in the ways in which elements are put next to other elements in the story. Juxtaposition becomes especially important in a story that is not arranged chronologically, as in Margaret Atwood's *Alias Grace*. When events are related out of sequence, as in flashbacks, learners should pay close attention to the scenes surrounding the event that give it a context within the story. Learners should look for the reason the event occupies that particular place in the sequence of the narrative.

Repetition as a component of design occurs with repeated similar images, ideas, situations, or actions throughout the narrative. Repetition helps to tie the story together and solidify its structure. Repetition also creates significant patterns that help learners construct meaning from the narrative. As images or actions are repeated, they take on meaning beyond their literal value. As these images or actions amass levels of meaning, they enrich the complexity and deepen the meaning of the story. For example, in Alice Walker's *The Color Purple*, learners see a repeated pattern of the abuse and mistreatment of black women and the resiliency of these women who support one another and survive despite beatings, servitude, separation, and imprisonment. The cumulative effect of this pattern of survival and resiliency is a sense of the strength and sisterhood that emerges as these women overcome discrimination and oppression to love themselves and others and to thrive despite adversity.

Religious educators can use explorations of juxtaposition and repetition in teaching literary tales in religious education. For example,

---

[24]John Macquarrie, *Principles of Christian Theology*, 2d ed. (New York: Scribner's, 1977), pp. 420–428.

[25]Scholes, *Elements of Fiction*, p. 35.

learners may be asked to identify instances of juxtaposition and repetition in a tale and then discuss how these design components affect the narrative's structure and meaning. As with the previously mentioned elements of literary tales, juxtaposition and repetition provide important clues to assist learners in reading literary narratives, and a thorough exploration of these elements can help learners have more sophisticated and complex experiences with literary tales.

Conclusion

In the transaction between learners and a literary text, learners bring their past experiences and present personality to the construction of the literary tale, the event that occurs as they read or listen to the narrative. What learners bring to the transaction will affect the ways they experience, construct, and interpret the literary tale. Because literary tales are a fairly sophisticated form of narrative, learners' experiences with literary tales may be more demanding. If learners can bring to the literary transaction some background in literary criticism (e.g., some understanding of the elements of literary tales), they may be assisted in having more meaningful experiences with the narrative. Religious educators can help provide this background for learners both before they approach a literary tale and during their subsequent discussions of the tale. In a brief lecture, accompanied with handouts, religious educators can introduce learners to the elements of literary tales and the general process of literary criticism. Religious educators may also wish to analyze a short story with learners as an example of how to read literature critically. As learners are able to have more sophisticated experiences with literary tales, religious educators may be better able to use these tales to help achieve the cognitive, affective, and behavioral goals of religious instruction.

THE NOVEL

Most Western literary forms were created by the ancient Greeks and codified through the centuries,[26] but the novel did not develop as a distinct literary form until the eighteenth century, when English writer Daniel Defoe developed the modern novel. Defoe was the first

---

[26]Scholes and Kellogg, *Nature of Narrative*, p. 57.

English writer to use fiction to create an illusion of literal authenticity.[27] Defoe's creation sparked an aesthetic controversy that was resolved only as novelists perfected their techniques near the end of the nineteenth century and the novel became recognized as a legitimate art form.

From its beginnings, the novel emerged in two different forms: romanticism and realism.[28] Eighteenth-century literary critics saw literary art as a medium of rhetorical beauty whose purpose was to create an ideal world that would depict the goals of human life. Their tradition came to be known as romanticism, and it implied the writer's duty to represent the ideals of human existence in the world of their story rather than the reality of human experiences.

Opposing the romanticists were the realists, who contended that the writer's task was to reflect authentic human experience, both the good and the bad, the beautiful and the ugly. The resolution of this battle sparked by Defoe was brought about at last when American novelists and critics became engaged in the debate in the 1890s. During this period, critics began their first exhaustive study of the problems of the novel and discovered that realism and romanticism were not the real issues. Rather, the subject matter and form of the literary work had to be considered in related to the intentions and skills of the writer.[29] In the preface to his *House of the Seven Gables* Nathaniel Hawthorne weighed in: "The novel is presumed to aim at a very minute fidelity, not merely to the possible, but to the probable and ordinary course of [human] experience. The Romance—while as a work of art, it must rigidly subject itself to laws, and while it sins unpardonably so far as it may swerve aside from the truth of the human heart—has fairly a right to present that truth under circumstances, to a great extent, of the writer's own choosing or creation."[30]

The form of the novel that evolved in the eighteenth and nineteenth centuries gave rise to the contemporary novel, which suggests the tri-

---

[27]Eugene Current-Garcia and Walton R. Patrick, *Realism and Romanticism in Fiction: An Approach to the Novel* (Chicago: Scott Foresman, 1962), p. 5.

[28]R. G. Collins, "Divagations on the Novel as Experiment," *The Novel and Its Changing Form*, ed. R. G. Collins (Winnipeg: University of Manitoba Press, 1972), p. viii,

[29]Current-Garcia and Patrick, *Realism and Romanticism in Fiction*, p. 36.

[30]Nathaniel Hawthorne, *The House of the Seven Gables*, Riverside ed. (Boston: Houghton Mifflin, 1964), p. 3.

umph of realism's emphasis on accounts of real life. Elements of romanticism's focus on the fantasies, hope, and dreams of the private soul, however, remain.[31] Defining the contemporary novel is a difficult task. Common usage tends to connect the term with any book-length work of fiction. As a literary form, however, the novel does have particular defining characteristics which set it apart from, for example, satire or allegory. Structurally, novels construct actions around a unifying center of incident. Although novels have a distinct beginning, middle, and ending, the elements of the novel are presented in such a way that the work has coherence, continuity, and wholeness, achieved to a great extent through tensions and anticipations regarding the central characters which are carried through the entire length of the novel to be resolved only at the end.[32]

Some attempts have been made to describe novels by their subject matter. One critic has suggested that the subject matter of novels is human relationships in which the directions of human souls are made manifest.[33] Another critic has written that the subject of novels is the experience of reality as process rather than as a fixed, a priori set of beliefs.[34] Yet another critic claims that the novel deals with the movement from ignorance to maturity and with the distinction between appearance and reality.[35]

Novelist Joseph Conrad has described the novel as "the creation of the world."[36] He explains that the novelist begins by creating a believable world which is his own and yet resembles something already familiar to his readers. The task of the novelist is to create an imagined real world. By way of contrast, the person who narrates facts tells what she believes has happened to actual people, whereas the novelist

---

[31]Collins, "Divagations on the Novel as Experiment," p. viii.

[32]Philip Stevick, introduction to *The Theory of the Novel*, ed. Philip Stevick (New York: Free Press, 1967), p. 4.

[33]Dorothy Van Ghent, *The English Novel: Form and Function* (New York: Holt, Rinehart, Winston, 1953), p. 3.

[34]Albert S. Cook, *The Meaning of Fiction* (Detroit, Mich.: Wayne State University Press, 1960), pp. 298–302.

[35]Maurice Z. Shroder, "The Novel as Genre," in *The Theory of the Novel*, ed. Philip Stevik (New York: Free Press, 1967), p. 14.

[36]Joseph Conrad, "Novel as World," in *Theory of the Novel*, p. 29.

tells what she believes happened to imagined people. As one critic suggests, fiction is concerned with the real, not the actual.[37]

The novel may also be described perceptually (the novel expresses a rich sensory texture), sociologically (the novel is a middle-class genre, emerging as a response to the middle class and concerned with the middle class), mythically (the novel deals with those heroes who are like real humans in their capabilities), philosophically (the novel arose in the intellectual milieu shaped by the philosophical thought of Rene Descartes and John Locke), and culturally (the novel is the product of and deals primarily with the content of Western culture).[38] One critic suggests that every novel is an experiment. The novel, of all art forms, is the most versatile because the author can draw from words, and all material things have a name and a mental existence as words. Thus the novelist has available all the possibilities of reordering experience to create new and meaningful worlds. Each novel, then, is an experiment, the expression of the particular consequences of particular actions for the first time, but valid because of the capacity for infinite experiences, emotions, and meanings within each human being.[39]

Collins's description of novel as experiment suggests the unlimited possibilities for novels and for the utilization of novels in religious instruction. Because of the incredible variety of human experiences expressed in novels, religious educators can seek out and discover novels relevant to almost any theme or aspect of religious instruction. Because each novel is unique, each has the potential to introduce novelty to learners. Theologians John B. Cobb Jr. and David Ray Griffin contend that present processes are not determined by past ones, but rather that novel (as in new) elements can also be incorporated into present experience.[40] Because novels actualize new experiences, they provide a tool by which religious educators can introduce new possibilities into learners' experiences. These novel experiences hint at the efficacy of learners' decisions and suggest that learners can make positive changes in their own lives. Thus religious educators can use novels as a means of helping learners explore possibilities for new ways

---

[37]Katherine Lever, *The Novel and the Reader: A Primer for Critics* (New York: Appleton- Century-Crofts), p. 21.

[38]Stevick, introduction to *The Theory of the Novel*, pp. 3–10.

[39]Collins, "Divagations on the Novel as Experiment," p. x.

[40]John B. Cobb Jr. and David Ray Griffin, *Process Theology: An Introductory Exposition* (Philadelphia: Westminster, 1976), p. 27.

of religious living in the world. For example, in Zora Neale Hurston's *Their Eyes Were Watching God*, Janie Crawford, a poor black woman, evolves into a self-determining, self-efficacious woman through her refusal to accept any treatment that makes her less than human. At the end of the novel, Janie says, "Two[41] things everybody's got tuh do fuh theyselves. They got tuh go tuh God, and they got tuh find out about livin' fuh theyselves."

THE SHORT STORY

Even more recent on the literary scene is the short story, which developed at the end of the nineteenth century. The short story, like the novel, is difficult to define and is better described. A number of writers have offered these possibilities: any piece of short fiction that can be read in half an hour, a story that is not long, a record of things happening that moves swiftly through suspense to a climax and satisfying denouement.[42] Edgar Allen Poe claims that "in the whole composition there should be no word written, of which the tendency, direct or indirect, is not to one pre-established design."[43] Perhaps the overarching characteristic of the short story, and the one that makes it impossible to define satisfactorily, is its elasticity. The novel is based on movement—development across time. But the short story does not need to move in the same way. In fact, the movement of a short story may be infinitesimal. There may be no characters, or the characters may never speak. Sometimes the characters may not even be named; they may simply be labeled as "boy" or "girl," and the setting may be "the street" or "the room."[44]

The economy of the short story requires a suggestive precision. Each word must be focused toward the reality that the story suggests. The core of the short story is epiphany. This is the moment which the short story writer describes with the story. This significant moment is both the completion of the short story and the affirmation of the reality that lies beyond the story. In Flannery O'Connor's "Revelation,"

---

[41]Zora Neale Hurston, *Their Eyes Were Watching God* (New York: Harper and Row, 1965), p. 183.

[42]Herbert Ernest Bates, *The Modern Short Story: A Critical Survey* (Boston: The Writer, 1972), p. 16.

[43]Edgar Allen Poe, quoted. in Bates, *Modern Short Story*, p. 16.

[44]Bates, *Modern Short Story*, pp. 19–20.

the epiphany comes when Mrs. Turpin has a vision in which she sees herself as an old warthog from hell. She sees a bridge extending to heaven up through a field of living fire. On the bridge, a vast horde of people is moving toward heaven. Leading the way are "white trash," clean for the first time in their lives, blacks in white robes, freaks and lunatics shouting and clapping and leaping. Behind them is a tribe Mrs. Turpin recognizes as those like herself, the righteous people who always did the right thing. They are marching behind the others, marching with great dignity, respectable as they have always been. Yet Mrs. Turpin can see by their shocked and altered faces that even their virtues are being burned away.

The better the short story, the greater its capability of arousing in learners speculation about the reality that the story only suggests. This speculation can never be completely answered because the reality to which it points can never be fully known.[45] For this reason, the short story is often unsettling; it is not quite finished for learners but is suggestive of realities beyond its own narrative. The short story ends and is complete but leaves learners with a sense that there is something more. Learners do not know what happened to Mrs. Turpin after her vision. Perhaps she changed her life to reflect her new experiential understanding of grace; perhaps she did not. "Revelation" leaves learners to grapple with the efficacy of Mrs. Turpin's experience of revelation and, likely, with their own. Most people tend to struggle with the implications of the inclusivity of God's grace. Even the early church in the book of Acts did not always want to include those whom God chose to include. "Revelation" may assist learners in examining their own lives, attitudes, and beliefs in regard to those whom they include and exclude. It may also help learners ask themselves how their own revelatory experiences have exerted impact on their lives and how they may better reflect those experiences in their ways of being in the world.

CONCLUSION

Literary tales offer religious educators a particularly appropriate and effective means of facilitating the goals of religious instruction. Fiction is experiential. Literary tales are grounded in experience, and the

---

[45]Bayley, *Short Story*, p. 9.

reading and hearing of literary tales narratively recreates those experiences for learners who bring their own sets of lenses, experiences, and possibilities to the narrative transaction, in which they actively construct their own narrative experiences from all of these elements. When the central elements of literary tales are concerned with subject matter relevant to religious living, then learners' experiences with these tales can bring about cognitive, affective, and behavioral change and growth.

Literary tales offer images of the world humans live in and suggest possibilities for the world humans might create. Literary tales have the potential to disrupt established patterns of thinking, awaken perception, revise the usual way of looking at things, evoke powerful emotions, challenge implicitly held attitudes, and propose alternative ways of being in the world. Literary narratives do not allow learners to close their eyes to the side of life in which things do not always work together for good, God does seem absent, and bad things do happen to good people. Conversely, in many literary works (such as Flannery O'Connor's, for example) nonreligious persons may encounter the possibility that mystery and grace do exist in the world. Try though they might (like Hazel Motes in O'Connor's *Wise Blood*) to flee from grace, grace still pursues, even in their experience of the story.

12

Bible Stories

*I couldn't understand the Herdmans. You would have thought
the Christmas story came right out of the F.B.I. files, they got so
involved in it—wanted a bloody end to Herod, worried about
Mary having her baby in a barn, and called the Wise Men a
bunch of dirty spies.*

*And they left the first rehearsal arguing about whether Joseph
should have set fire to the inn, or just chased the innkeeper into
the next county.*[1]

—Barbara Robinson

I first heard the Bible stories in the context of a community that believed and appropriated those stories and lived its life in response to
them. This community encouraged me to allow those stories to shape
my life as a response to the truths I heard proclaimed in them. In fact,
somehow, those stories were told and lived by that community in
such a way that they became for me part of the cluster of images that
constitutes my own life myth. The authority of those stories in my
life came, not as a result of some intrinsic claim of Scripture about its
own nature, but as a result of my participation in a community that
valued those stories in a particular way. Thus, for me, the authority of
Scripture came through its salvific and religious educational functions rather than its theological description. In other words, biblical

---

[1]Barbara Robinson, *The Best Christmas Pageant Ever* (New York: Harper and
Row, 1972), pp. 47–48.

authority derived not from its own claims but from its role in the life of my faith community.[2]

THE RELIGIOUS EDUCATIONAL FUNCTIONS OF SCRIPTURE

The religious educational function of Scripture is twofold. First, Scripture communicates religion and, second, Scripture facilitates religious living.[3] In the first instance, Scripture bears witness to the events and faith history of the Christian community. In the second, Scripture teaches learners what it is to be Christian.

Scripture as Communication of Religion

In communicating the substance and structure of religion, Scripture functions as a witness both to the events that are constitutive of the Christian community and to salvation history which its writers recognize in the experiences of God's people.

In the first instance, Scripture bears the record of those experiences in which faith communities affirmed the active presence of God. The authority of this record comes not from the way in which it was inspired but from the testimony that it offers to God's acts in human history.[4] In some cases, the writers were in close proximity to the events they reported; in many others, they preserved oral traditions, many of which seem to be firsthand reports. As a witness to the Christian community's constitutive events, Scripture calls for historical-critical investigation, which allows religious educators and learners alike to explore Bible stories in more depth. Religious educators, in particular, should be steeped in the Bible. Historical criticism, which I shall discuss in more detail shortly, can provide one immensely helpful perspective from which to investigate and participate in biblical texts.

---

[2]For more on biblical authority, see William Countryman, *Biblical Authority or Biblical Tyranny? Scripture and the Christian Pilgrimage* (Philadelphia: Fortress, 1981).

[3]James Michael Lee, "Religious Education and the Bible: A Religious Educationist's View," *Biblical Themes in Religious Education*, ed. Joseph S. Marino (Birmingham, Ala.: Religious Education Press, 1983), p. 4.

[4]For more information on inspiration, see Paul J. Achtemeier, *The Inspiration of Scripture: Problems and Proposals* (Philadelphia: Westminster, 1980).

The Bible, however, is much more than a chronicle of events. In addition to reporting what they had witnessed or heard, the biblical writers testified to the grace they had seen and experienced. Scripture, then, offers not an objective history of a set of particular events that led to the formation of the Christian community but rather a faith interpretation of experiences in which God's redemptive activity was recognized, with the specific intent of teaching people to be the people of God.[5] The goal of these stories is not to report facts but to call people to authentic religious living. The writers, then, were concerned that the stories be religiously true, not historically accurate.[6] Thus the historical events of the Christian story can best be understood in the context of the complete narrative in which their meaning is fully realized. In exploring this interpretive facet of Bible stories, religious educators can benefit from the process literary analysis, which can complement historical criticism. Both methods are actually necessary if religious educators desire to explore the Scriptures fully.[7]

Scripture as Facilitator of Religious Living

The second religious educational function of Scripture is the facilitation of religious living. Scripture accomplishes this task by shaping the identity of the Christian community and the individuals within that community.[8] The Bible provides the story that is central to the identity of the individual Christian and the Christian community. These identities are shaped and reshaped in interaction with biblical stories. Although many factors are significant in the development of Christian identity, the Christian story found in the Bible is an essential piece in identity formation for the Christian community. In other words,

---

[5] For example, see Robert Barone, "Reconciliation," in *Biblical Themes in Religious Education*, pp. 257–276.

[6] George W. Stroup, *The Promise of Narrative Theology: Recovering the Gospel in the Church* (Atlanta: Knox, 1981), p. 251.

[7] A helpful, simple, basic resource is Gordon D. Fee and Douglas Stuart, *How to Read the Bible for All It's Worth: A Guide to Understanding the Bible* (Grand Rapids, Mich.: Zondervan, 1982). See also Leland Ryken, *How to Read the Bible as Literature . . . and Get More Out of It* (Grand Rapids, Mich.: Zondervan, 1984).

[8] An excellent resource on teaching in the faith community that focuses on the importance of biblical identity in the formation of individual and community Christian identity is Charles R. Foster, *Teaching in the Community of Faith* (Nashville: Abingdon, 1982).

Christian identity does not develop apart from the Christian story.[9] In fact, Christian identity is unique because it is a response to a particular story. The Bible provides an interpretive grid, or a lens, by which many dimensions of Christian experience are given shape.[10] Without the Christian story, no identity is Christian. Thus if religious instruction ignores the biblical narratives that give shape to Christian identity, then Christian identity may become quickly confused with the narrative identities of other religious and secular communities and traditions.[11]

In interaction with the Bible, learners learn how to think, feel, and act as Christians. As a book of religious instruction, the Bible offers stories that teach in cognitive, affective, and lifestyle domains. Using Bible stories, religious educators can facilitate the growth of Christian beliefs, feelings, attitudes, values, and behaviors.

Christian beliefs. As religious educator Sara Little points out, belief is one significant facet of Christian identity.[12] To be Christian is to hold certain ideas as true (although there is great disagreement throughout the Christian community about some of those ideas). Nonetheless, belief is a part of learners' Christian faith experience. Beliefs are cognitive experiences by which learners interpret, reinterpret, and reappropriate the meanings of Christian experiences in ways that inform and shape Christian identity. Christian beliefs arise from participation in the Christian community, a community rooted in the biblical narratives central to its identity. In religious instruction, teaching Bible stories provides one means by which learners may be encouraged to develop Christian belief systems. Bible stories embody truths. Of course, how learners construct and appropriate these truths depends on their standpoint as interpreters.[13]

---

[9]Psychologist Rollo May contends that having a myth of one's past is crucial to the development of present identity. *The Cry for Myth* (New York: Norton, 1991), p. 48. The Christian story provides a larger past myth in which learners can construct their own personal myths and identities.

[10]Sallie McFague, *Metaphorical Theology* (Philadelphia: Fortress, 1982), p. 61.

[11]Stroup, *Promise of Narrative Theology*, pp. 252–253.

[12]Sara Little, *To Set One's Heart: Belief and Teaching in the Church* (Atlanta: Knox, 1983).

[13]See, for example, Edgar V. McKnight, *Postmodern Use of the Bible: The Emergence of Reader-Oriented Criticism* (Nashville: Abingdon, 1988). For more on faith and belief, see Douglas Alan Walrath, *Counterpoints: The Dynamics of Believing* (New York: Pilgrim, 1991); Daniel Taylor, *The Myth of Certainty: The Reflective Christian and the Risk of Commitment* (Waco, Texas: Word, 1986); Richard E. Creel,

As narrative, Bible stories offer an exceptional way for learners to form, reform, and wrestle with their beliefs. The Bible holds doctrinal authority in the Christian community as its constitutive story because of the intrinsic power with which it has spoken truth to people across time. The world of the Bible opens learners' eyes to possibilities beyond their immediate situation in the world by providing images of alternative ways of being in the world. Given the richness of the worlds created by biblical narratives, many interpretations are necessary to explore the truths suggested by these stories. In fact, the Bible not only bears many interpretations, but it demands them. To interpret the Bible in many different ways, then, is not a travesty but precisely what should happen given the nature of the text.[14]

For example, one of the fundamental statements of Christian belief is "I believe in Jesus Christ." But do most learners know what they are saying when they make that statement? What do they mean when they say they believe in Jesus Christ? What does it mean for them to say Jesus is the Christ? Religious educators can utilize Bible stories as one way to help learners explore this central Christian belief. The birth narratives, the miracle stories, the passion and resurrection narratives all offer a variety of perspectives of the Gospel writers' understandings of what it meant to them to say that Jesus was the Christ. The task of religious instruction in this instance is to help learners take those stories and, in concert with their own experiences of Jesus as the Christ, to construct an understanding of what it means for them to say that they believe in Jesus Christ. And for different learners, that statement may well and probably will mean different things.

Christian affect. As narrative, biblical stories are quite powerful in helping learners to develop Christian feelings, emotions, attitudes, values, and love. In fact, James Michael Lee argues that the affective contents of the Bible are much more important than the cognitive contents in helping learners learn to live religiously.[15] Bible stories can evoke feelings, emotions, attitudes, and most importantly love as learners encounter the love of God at work in these stories and in learners' lives. The Bible itself teaches that loving God and loving

---

Religion and Doubt: Toward a Faith of Your Own, 2d ed. (Englewood Cliffs, N.J.: Prentice Hall, 1991).

[14]McFague, *Metaphorical Theology*, p. 60.

[15]Lee, "Religious Education and the Bible," p. 21.

others is the supreme goal of human existence, and again and again the Bible itself offers narrative models of Christian love, particularly in the stories of Jesus—healing the sick, raising the dead, feeding the hungry, sacrificing self for others. Bible stories can also teach Christian attitudes and values. For example, in many stories in the book of Acts, learners discover the inclusivity of God's love and the demand that God's people break down and not erect barriers to others. Acts challenges prejudices and suggests that learners value diversity as God does.

I have often used the stories from Acts when I was leading discussions on Christian attitudes toward homosexuality.[16] In the contemporary world, the church, on the whole, has erected many un-Christian barriers toward gay and lesbian people and has often taught intolerance, if not outright hatred, toward homosexuals. In dealing with this controversial topic, I usually use the stories from Acts to create a context for developing new attitudes toward gays and lesbians. One of the overarching themes of Acts is that barriers of discrimination and prejudice fall before the gospel.[17] Christianity began as a small sectarian movement among Jews, but in Acts these first Christians begin to see that the gospel is for all people and reaches beyond the boundaries drawn by their own biases and prejudices, even when those prejudices are based on their interpretations of Scripture.

Acts begins with Jesus' command to the disciples to carry the gospel to Jerusalem, Judea, and the ends of the earth. In chapter 2, the Holy Spirit comes upon the disciples, and they preach the good news to Jews from every nation who are in Jerusalem. And they continue to preach only to the Jews until Stephen is martyred and persecution begins.

---

[16]For in-depth explorations of this very controversial topic, see Robert Goss, *Jesus Acted Up: A Gay and Lesbian Manifesto* (San Francisco: HarperSanFrancisco, 1993); Carter Heyward, *Speaking of Christ: A Lesbian Feminist Voice* (New York: Pilgrim, 1989); James B. Nelson, *Embodiment: An Approach to Sexuality and Christian Theology* (Minneapolis: Augsburg, 1978); Letha Dawson Scanzoni and Virginia Mollenkott, *Is the Homosexual My Neighbor? A Positive Christian Response*, rev. ed. (San Francisco: HarperSanFrancisco, 1994); John Spong, *Living in Sin?* (San Francisco: Harper, 1990).

[17]See Frank Stagg, *The Book of Acts: The Early Struggle for an Unhindered Gospel* (Nashville: Broadman, 1955).

The first barrier to fall is the barrier to the Samaritans (Acts 8:4–25). Samaritans were considered half-breeds deserving scorn and contempt. Yet when persecution scatters those first Christians, Philip goes to Samaria and preaches the gospel. Many Samaritans believe, and Peter and John confirm to the Jerusalem church that indeed Samaritans are becoming believers.

The second barrier to fall is the barrier to the God-fearing Gentiles. These people are Gentiles who already worship God. The falling of this barrier is exemplified in the stories of Philip and the Ethiopian eunuch (8:26–40) and Peter and Cornelius (10:1–11:18). The pivotal point in the eunuch story occurs in verse 37, as the eunuch asks, "What is to prevent me from being baptized?" The answer, of course, is nothing.

The story of Peter and Cornelius is quite telling about the church's difficulty in reaching out beyond itself. In this story, Peter has a vision of clean and unclean animals, which ends with Gods' words: "What God has made clean, you must not call profane." Even so, Peter is reluctant to take the gospel to the Gentile Cornelius but eventually does, and the story concludes with the Gentiles' receiving the Holy Spirit.

The final barrier to fall is the barrier to pagan Gentiles. These Gentiles worshiped gods other than the God of the Jews. As believers spread out through the Roman Empire, they began to preach to all the people they encountered, and many Gentiles believed (11:19–26). The church at Jerusalem was not completely comfortable with the inclusion of Gentiles in their number. One group in the church thought Gentiles should have to convert to Judaism first to become Christians. They wanted Gentile converts to be circumcised and keep Jewish law. The mounting tensions in the church led the Jerusalem Council to address the issue of Gentiles in the church (15:1–21). The council reached a compromise: They would not require Gentile converts to be circumcised, but they would require that these Gentile converts live in keeping with much of the Mosaic law. Even this compromise was eventually overridden as Paul and others saw that keeping certain prescriptions of the Mosaic law was not an essential component of Christian experience. Rather, as Paul later wrote to Christians under the influence of this more conservative faction, "For freedom Christ has set us free. Stand firm, therefore, and do not submit again to a yoke of slavery" (Galatians 5:1).

These stories from Acts can create a context in which learners can struggle with attitudes toward gay and lesbian people as part of the continued movement of the gospel in breaking down barriers. In contemporary society, gays and lesbians are among those who have often been kept outside the church, refused full participation in the body of believers because of barriers erected by un-Christian prejudice and hatred. The stories of Acts may provide a gripping affective experience for learners in which to struggle with the prejudices they have learned and to apply the biblical movement toward the breaking down of barriers in their own lives, church, and culture.

Christian lifestyle. Christian living is the primary goal of religious instruction, and Bible stories offer a significant way of teaching Christian living. Of course, teaching Christian living with the Bible does not occur through Bible study, which focuses on cognition. Memorization of Scripture passages, analysis of Bible stories, and examination of biblical themes may all be important cognitive procedures for achieving cognitive goals, but they do not bring about lifestyle development. Teaching Bible stories for lifestyle goals involves using teaching procedures demonstrated to bring about lasting behavioral changes.[18]

Experiential learning offers an excellent way to teach Bible stories for lifestyle outcomes.[19] Experiential learning begins in concrete life experiences and then moves to application, appropriately infused with both affective and cognitive processes. The experiential phase may involve direct experience such as volunteering in a soup kitchen, contrived experiences such as simulations and role plays, dramatic experiences such as a play or video, or verbal experiences such as listening to or reading a story.[20] The more direct and concrete the experience, the more powerful it is educationally. Reflection involves publishing and processing the cognitive and affective data generated in the experience phase. In this phase, learners explore what happened and how they felt about it. Generalizing allows learners to move from the teaching/learning situation to the larger context of their lives. This phase examines the principles at work in the experience. In teaching the Bible, this phase allows religious educators to bring in tools of

---

[18]Lee, "Religious Education and the Bible," p. 26.

[19]See David Kolb, *Experiential Learning: Experience as the Source of Learning and Development* (Englewood Cliffs, N.J.: Prentice-Hall, 1984); and John and Lela Hendrix, *Experiential Education: XED* (Nashville: Abingdon, 1975).

[20]See Edgar Dale, *Audio Visual Methods in Teaching*, 3d ed. (New York: Holt, Rinehart, and Winston, 1969).

biblical exegesis and literary analysis to help learners develop a more complex and full experiential understanding of Scripture. Finally, applying involves connecting the learning experience to learners' behavior in their every day lives. This phase helps learners try out and develop new ways of acting in the world (which can subsequently become new experiences for the experiential learning process).

For example, if the goal of a religious instruction event for young adults is to teach learners to live compassionately, religious educators may wish to use the story of the feeding of the five thousand (Matthew 14:13–21). The experience may begin with learners volunteering in a local soup kitchen. Then the learners should talk about their experience and their feelings. The religious educator may read or tell the biblical story of the feeding of the five thousand, inviting learners to then explore connections between their experience in the soup kitchen and the Bible story and draw out life principles along the way. Finally, learners should suggest ways they can apply what they have learned in their daily lives and make commitments to try these behaviors out in their own lives during the next few days

INTERPRETING BIBLE STORIES

The biblical stories are a mixture of traditional tales, realistic narratives, and fiction. Traditional tales include myths and legends which are part of the sacred history of the Jewish people. For example, the stories of the primeval history found in Genesis 1–11—the creation, the fall, the flood, the Tower of Babel—all properly belong to the genre of myth. As defined in chapter 7, myths are sacred stories that explain how things came to be; they are the stories which establish the world. The religious educational function of biblical myths is to give a particular kind of order or coherence to Jewish and Christian people's experiences of the world. The biblical accounts of the patriarchs are best classified as legends, stories about ancient heroes rooted in some historical occurrence. These stories served the educational purposes of explaining tribal relations, the origins of names, and the origins of festivals for the Jewish people.[21] In addition, the continuing religious ed-

---

[21]Laura H. Wild, *A Literary Guide to the Bible: A Study of the Types of Literature Present in the Old and New Testaments* (London: George Allen and Unwin, 1922), p. 64.

ucational function of legends is to provide useful examples of moral and ethical behavior. The fictional tales of the Bible include the book of Jonah and the prose prologue to Job.

The greatest number of Bible stories, however, fall into the category of realistic narrative. These stories are a mixture of history, religious education interpretation, theology, and fiction. The composers of these narratives were not content to report bare facts. Rather, these authors utilized their imaginations under the guidance of the Holy Spirit to give dramatic expression to the impact these events had on their lives and on the lives of their communities. For this purpose, only story would serve.

The narrative form of the Bible, then, is an indispensable part of what is being said.[22] The narrative form is indispensable because narrative is an excellent way to do religious education, illuminating the import of the facts as can happen only within the context of a story. The task of the biblical writers was to elucidate learners' experience of the meaning of the facts by placing them in a narrative framework that opens up a wide range of possibilities for an experiential understanding of the events and for a personal transformation initiated by encounter with God within the story. Thus biblical authors were religious educators, historians, theologians, and artists—recording truth and interpreting it for learners.[23]

To teach effectively using Bible stories, religious educators should be capable interpreters of the Bible. Informed biblical interpretation allows religious educators to be faithful to the biblical text in planning and implementing religious instruction experiences. Bible stories are certainly powerful enough to effect change in learners' lives apart from any historical or literary background about the text, but biblical interpretation allows a more complex experience of the stories and opens up greater possibilities for rich interaction with the text.

Two separate but complimentary tools of biblical interpretation are essential for religious educators—historical-critical investigation and literary criticism. Historical-critical study allows religious educators to investigate the historical background of a Bible story, its author, and

---

[22]Darrell Jodock, "Story and Scripture," *Word and World* 1 (Spring 1981): 132.

[23]For an interesting essay on the rhetorical nature of Scripture, see Stewart Sutherland, "History, Truth, and Narrative," in *The Bible as Rhetoric: Studies in Biblical Persuasion and Credibility*, ed. Martin Warner (London: Routledge, 1990), pp. 105–116.

its intended audience. This approach is useful but limited and provides only minimal help in a religious educational interaction with a Bible story. Thus religious educators should also turn to literary criticism. A Bible story should be read as a story that is inclusive of learners as active participants in the story.

Historical-Critical Study

The historical-critical approach to biblical interpretation has been an essential process by which to remove biblical interpretation from non-critical literalism.[24] The premise of historical criticism is that the meaning of a biblical passage is to be found in the history the text has recorded. Thus early historical-critical investigation focused on determining which events described in the Bible were historical and which were not. In the process of exploring the history behind the biblical stories, biblical scholars came to recognize the necessity of understanding the biblical text in its historical context as an essential part of the exegetical task. Because the biblical books were written in a specific historical setting with a particular audience in mind, the meaning of the historical events they recorded could only be discovered by exploration of the text in its historical context. Because the biblical text is distant from contemporary readers in terms of language, historical setting, worldview, and social setting, contemporary interpreters must understand the historical, social, and political backgrounds of biblical passages, investigate the language of the passages, and come to an understanding of what the authors of the passages meant to communicate to their original readers.[25]

Source criticism, the earliest of the historical-critical methods, grew out of a nineteenth century interest in the literary relationships of biblical texts.[26] In the Pentateuch, for example, biblical scholars began to examine the origins of duplicate accounts of the same event, such as the creation story.[27] In New Testament studies, scholars began careful

---

[24]R. Alan Culpepper, "Story and History in the Gospels," *Review and Expositor* 81 (Summer 1984): 468.

[25]Ibid., pp. 468–469.

[26]James King West, *Introduction to the Old Testament*, 2d ed. (New York: Macmillan, 1981), p. 29; Edgar V. McKnight, *What Is Form Criticism?* (Philadelphia: Fortress, 1969), pp. 4–10.

[27]For an example of Old Testament source criticism, see S. R. Driver, *Introduction to the Literature of the Old Testament*, rev. ed. (New York: Scribner's, 1913).

study of the origins of the materials in the Synoptic Gospels.[28] Relying primarily on internal clues such as language, literary style, and allusions to historical people and events, source criticism seeks to discover when, where, why, and by whom biblical passages were composed.[29] In a religious educational study of Scripture, source criticism can be an important tool in assisting religious educators and learners by providing a sense of the historical context and literary origins of a Bible story. For example, source criticism can help learners to identify and compare and contrast the two creation accounts of Genesis 1–2. Source criticism can also assist learners in understanding how the two accounts were written by people in different contexts with different educational goals. In so doing, source criticism may allow learners to see the stories, as complementary stories directed toward different instructional aims, not as competing accounts.

Biblical scholars discovered, however, that source criticism was quite limited in providing clues to the origins of many Bible passages because source criticism deals only with the biblical material in its written form. Many biblical narratives existed in oral tradition long before the biblical authors wrote them down. The tool needed to explore the narratives behind the written text was form criticism.[30] Form criticism seeks to isolate the individual oral units behind the written biblical passages, classify them according to their genre or form, and identify the life setting (*Sitz im Leben*) out of which they arose.[31] Identifying forms and life settings can offer religious educators and learners clues to deepen their experience with a biblical story.[32] For example, in the parables of Jesus, form criticism can assist religious educators and learners in identifying the situation in which Jesus used the parable in his teaching and the application that would suggest

---

[28]For example, see Burnett Hillman Streeter, *The Four Gospels: A Study of Origins*, rev. ed. (London: Macmillan, 1930).

[29]James King West, *Introduction to the Old Testament*, p. 29.

[30]For an example of Old Testament form criticism, see Hermann Gunkel, *The Legends of Genesis*, trans. W. H. Carruth (New York: Schocken, 1964); and for an example of New Testament form criticism, see Martin Dibelius, *From Tradition to Gospel*, trans. Bertram Lee Woolf (New York: Scribner's, 1934).

[31]West, *Introduction to the Old Testament*, p. 32.

[32]For an excellent summary of form criticism, see Edgar V. McKnight, *What Is Form Criticism?* (Philadelphia: Fortress, 1969).

itself to a learner in that particular situation.[33] This portion of interpretation of the story can provide clues as to how religious educators can help learners make appropriate applications of a parable in their own lives. For example, when Jesus heard religious leaders grumbling about the tax collectors and sinners who were coming to listen to him, he told the parables of the lost sheep, the lost coin, and the prodigal son (Luke 15). The context of these parables suggests that Jesus saw his role as expressing Divine concern for lost, helpless, sinful people. These parables, then, tend to stand in judgment of the harsh and exclusive attitudes of the Pharisees and scribes who condemned rather than loved those with whom Jesus associated. In a religious instruction setting, exploration of the life setting of these parables may help learners evaluate their own attitudes about and actions toward people whom they consider to be sinners and to make appropriate changes in their behaviors.

Unfortunately, source and form criticism tend to dissect the Bible into its smallest components, resulting in a loss of the unity of the biblical text. Using only source and form criticism, learners are left with only small segments of Scripture, unconnected to the larger biblical text. These passages, however, were included by the biblical authors as part of a larger work, and the ways the writers used the passages and included them in the biblical books is significant and necessitates another tool of biblical study—redaction criticism. Redaction criticism examines the intent of the writer by studying biblical passages within the context of the books of which they are a part.[34] In other words, redaction criticism focuses on the editorial functions of the biblical writers, exploring the arrangement, editing, and expansion of oral and written sources in the final formation of the biblical books.[35] For religious educators, redaction criticism provides a way for learners to explore the choices a biblical writer has made about inclusion of

---

[33]See C. H. Dodd, *The Parables of the Kingdom*, rev. ed. (New York: Scribner's, 1961).

[34]For example, see Willi Marxsen, *Introduction to the New Testament*, trans. G. Buswell (Philadelphia: Fortress, 1969); Gunther Bornkamm, *Tradition and Interpretation in Matthew*, trans. P. Scott (Philadelphia, Pa.: Westminster, 1963); Hans Conzelmann, *The Theology of St. Luke*, trans. G. Buswell (New York: Harper and Row, 1960). For an excellent introduction to redaction criticism, see Norman Perrin, *What Is Redaction Criticism?* (Philadelphia: Fortress, 1969).

[35]West, *Introduction to the Old Testament*, p. 34.

a particular story and to establish the writer's intention in using the story. For example, the evangelistic intent of the Gospel writers greatly influences their inclusion of material. Religious educators can use this piece of information to guide them in exploring the evangelistic intent behind the miracle stories of Mark, for example. Contextualizing these stories in evangelistic intent can then provide clues toward the ways religious educators may wish to use the miracle stories in religious instruction.

For example, the book of Mark is filled with miracle stories, but the intent of these stories is not to establish the actuality of miracles in the world.[36] Rather, they point toward the very nature of Jesus. In other words, the miracles seem more a natural consequence of who Jesus is, an overflowing of his very nature, than a supernatural interruption of the normal sequence of things. This understanding of the miracles in Mark is reinforced by the constant refrain of the miracle stories in which Jesus tells those who witness the miracles not to tell anyone. Herein lies the evangelistic intent of the writer. For the author, the revelation of Jesus as Messiah occurs in the crucifixion and resurrection. In his gospel, the secrecy surrounding the miracles of Jesus acts as a form of foreshadowing the revelation that comes in the resurrection. In religious instruction, then, religious educators may choose to lead learners away from discussions about the historicity of miracles and toward explorations of what particular miracle stories suggest about who Jesus is and how learners should respond to him.

Although historical-critical study does provide important clues about the interpretation of a biblical text, the process in itself falls far short of facilitating many of the goals of religious instruction. Historical-critical study provides information and knowledge about biblical texts and offers suggestions for interpretation, but it does not teach religious living. On the positive side, historical criticism does demonstrate the fallacies of some interpretations and points learners in the direction of viable options. If, however, in religious instruction, attention is focused away from the story itself and toward the historical events or the theology of the writer as the locus of meaning, then the story is robbed of its power to speak to learners as narrative.

---

[36]For a detailed discussion of scholarship on the Messianic Secret, see James L. Blevins, *The Messianic Secret in Markan Research, 1901–1976* (Washington, D.C. University Press of American, 1981).

The questions of historical-critical study are important to religious educators because these questions do open certain windows on the biblical narratives. Recognizing the worldview of a writer and the social setting of the narrative allows learners to appreciate more fully particular aspects of the story. Stories, however, create their own contexts, and learners can be caught up into a Bible story without knowing if it derives from the Q source,[37] if it harmonizes with duplicate accounts, or if it was intended for a Jewish or Hellenistic audience.

The task of exegetical study of Bible stories in religious education is to enhance learners' experience with stories. The tools of biblical criticism should be used by religious educators to help learners' readings of biblical narratives be more alert, appropriate, and intelligent while allowing the story to speak for itself with all the inherent power of narrative.[38] Historical criticism is not the interpretation of a Bible story; it only serves to expand the interpretation. The meaning of the story is to be found in the learner's experience with the story.

Story in Scripture

In essence, the Bible is a collection of stories, given for religious educational purposes, which reveal glimpses of the larger story of God. The Bible is not a single story, but each story in it points to some movement, some moment in the story of God. These stories cannot be distilled into theological propositions and dogmatic statements because the stories themselves are experiences. Early Christians experienced the risen Christ. Out of their experiences, they told stories. Christology, a theological concept, arose out of reflection on those stories, but the intent of the stories is not to teach Christology.[39] Bible

---

[37]The Q source (presumably an abbreviation for the German *Quelle*, "source") is the hypothesized source for the non-Marcan materials common to Luke and Matthew. See McKnight, *What Is Form Criticism?*, p. 6.

[38]Hans Frei, *The Identity of Jesus Christ: The Hermeneutical Bases of Dogmatic Theology* (Philadelphia: Fortress, 1975), p. xv.

[39]James Michael Lee labels theology's tendency to impose theological goals and methods on other disciplines, including literary criticism and religious education, "theological imperialism." In relation to teaching with Bible stories, theological imperialism assumes the primacy of the theological, rather than religious, content of the stories. For religious educators desiring to facilitate religious living, however, theological content is not particularly useful. Religious content facilitates religious living. See James Michael Lee, "The Authentic Source of Religious Instruction," in *Religious*

stories do not contain theological meaning. Rather, they contain an imaginative world in which learners participate and from which learners construct meaning.[40]

In order to take the narrative nature of much of Scripture seriously, religious educators should be proficient in using the tools of literary criticism—questions of narrator, plot, atmosphere, characters, theme, irony, motifs—in teaching Bible stories. Especially important is the recognition of the centrality of the reader/learner in the experience of the story.[41] Learners participate in Bible stories; they are not dispassionate observers. Rather, they enter into the story, and the story enters into them. They become involved in the story. Religious educators can help learners find themselves in Bible stories and make contact with the lives of biblical characters. The narrative nature of Scripture allows learners to enter another world and participate in its story. Learners are compelled to enter the Christian story, and the story works on them. The effects of the Christian story are evidenced in Christian lives. Learners live the story, and the story lives in learners. In Bible stories, learners glimpse a world that is possible, and they are challenged to respond by living transformed lives in the world.

To read the Bible as story, learners must distance themselves from questions of historicity. They must suspend disbelief long enough to hear the story itself. When learners enter the narrative world of the Bible, they open themselves up to challenge and transformation. The narratives invite learners to experience the world in new ways, to participate in life from a stance of faith. These stories allow learners to see responses to God, experiences of faith and commitment, a world that might be. The call of these stories is for learners to find their place in relation to God and to the world. As learners respond to this call, these biblical narratives mediate the healing, redemptive work of God in their lives.

Some of the most interesting literary biblical criticism in recent years has come out of the interpretation of biblical texts by historically marginalized persons (women, women and men of color) from their

---

Education and Theology, ed. Norma Thompson (Birmingham, Ala.: Religious Education Press, 1982).

[40]William A. Beardslee, *Literary Criticism of the New Testament* (Philadelphia: Fortress, 1970), p.13.

[41]For an overview of narrative criticism, see Mark Allan Powell, *What Is Narrative Criticism?* (Minneapolis: Fortress, 1990).

standpoint as oppressed people. The work of these scholars has suggested the need to read between the lines and in the margins of the
biblical narratives to find the presence of marginalized groups.[42] For
example, feminist Hebrew Bible scholar Judith Plaskow reminds
learners that women were present at the receiving of the law at
Sinai,[43] and New Testament scholar Elisabeth Schüssler Fiorenza
points out women's important presence in the early Christian community.[44] Feminist biblical scholars have also pointed out an androcentric
worldview that pervades a great deal of Scripture. Unfortunately,
some Christian leaders have used this worldview to maintain a mar-
ginalization and oppression of women in church, home, and society.
African-American biblical scholars have found a prototype for black
struggle in the stories of the Bible,[45] as have Latino *campesinos* in
base communities in Latin America.[46] The work of these scholars provides useful models of biblical interpretation for religious educators
and helps religious educators avoid the error of assuming that there is
only one correct experience of Scripture or that all people experience
Scripture from the same standpoint. For example, Judith Plaskow
points to the story of the Exodus, a favorite text of liberationists, and
notes that not everyone was liberated by the Exodus.[47] Women, she
points out, were invisible as a social class in the Exodus story. They
were barred from religious leadership and were valued differently in
the Hebrew community than were men. Her observations can remind
learners that even in the work of liberation and justice, well-

---

[42]For example, see Norman K. Gottwald and Richard A. Horsley, ed., *The Bible
and Liberation: Political and Social Hermeneutics*, rev. ed. (Maryknoll, N.Y.: Orbis,
1993).

[43]Judith Plaskow, *Standing Again at Sinai: Judaism from a Feminist Perspective*
(San Francisco: HarperSanFrancisco, 1990), p. 27.

[44]Elisabeth Schüssler Fiorenza, *In Memory of Her: A Feminist Theological Reconstruction of Christian Origins* (New York: Crossroad, 1983).

[45]For example, see Cain Hope Felder, ed., *Stony the Road We Trod: African American Biblical Interpretation* (Minneapolis: Fortress, 1991).

[46]For example, see Carlos Mesters, "How the Bible Is Interpreted in Some Basic
Christian Communities in Brazil," in *Conflicting Ways of Interpreting the Bible*, ed.
Hans Küng and Jürgen Moltmann (New York: Seabury, 1980), pp. 41–46; and Rigob-
erta Menchu, "The Bible and Self-Defense: The Examples of Judith, Moses, and
David," in *Feminist Theology from the Third World*, ed. Ursula King (Maryknoll,
N.Y.: Orbis, 1994), pp. 183–188.

[47]Plaskow, *Standing Again at Sinai*, pp. 41–49.

intentioned people can continue to perpetuate wrongs if they view an event from their own perspective only.

TEACHING BIBLE STORIES

Because the Bible provides the constituting stories of Christian identity, it has a significant role to play in religious instruction. The biblical story is for the Christian community the normative story by which learners construct and judge their own life stories. The biblical story is paradigmatic for the Christian life. It gives shape to Christian identity and, in turn, learners give shape to the ways the Christian story continues to be communicated. Religious instruction that truly enables Christian living will, of necessity, take the place of the Bible seriously in all its religious educational activities.

Communicating the story

A primary task of religious instruction is communicating the biblical story. Without the Christian story, learners do not form Christian identities. Only as the story is communicated, experienced, and appropriated are learners able to give shape to Christian lives. The Christian story teaches learners who they are as Christians. In addition to the many relevant contents of contemporary culture, religious educators should not overlook the necessity of the central story of Christian faith, which gives definition to the religious educational task and shape to Christian identity.

The biblical story allows learners to share in the continuity of the Christian community. The Bible offers the normative story for Christian identity and behavior. The Christian life is intimately connected to the Bible and especially to the Jesus of Scripture, who provides the ultimate model for Christian living. Often tension exists between the Jesus of learners' imagination and the Jesus of Scripture.[48] The Jesus of imagination may simply affirm learners' own preconceptions and prejudices. The image of Jesus propagated by the Ku Klux Klan serves as a chilling example of how notions of Jesus can be twisted and misshapen to reflect prejudice and hatred. Thus a connection between the Jesus of imagination and the Jesus of Scripture is essential

---

[48]John Navone, *Seeking God in Story* (Collegeville, Minn.: Liturgical, 1990), p. 86.

to safeguard against interpretations of Jesus that have no grounding in the biblical story. Although religious educators must and should make the Jesus of Scripture relevant to contemporary culture, contemporary images of Jesus should remain rooted in the biblical story of Jesus, for the biblical story of Jesus reminds learners that Christian living involves a lifestyle commitment to continue the work of Jesus in the world. As learners affirm the biblical narratives, they find their place in the Christ story and in the story of the Christian community, which has through the centuries lived in response to that story. For example, the biblical narratives often suggest a love for one's enemies, coupled with appropriate action, which is quite contrary to most contemporary norms. If those stories become central for learners, they may suggest ways of living that reflect love rather than hatred for enemies. And these biblical stories may be reinforced by the stories of others in the Christian community who have embodied love for enemies, such as George Fox or Martin Luther King Jr.

Religious instruction that communicates Bible stories will challenge learners to root themselves in the historic images that have given identity to the Christian community. Learners' experiences with Bible stories will remind them of the limitations of any one person's image of Jesus and will call them to assess their personal images of Jesus against the Jesus of Scripture in an ongoing dialogue that challenges and affirms learners' appropriation of the model of Jesus for Christian living. Finally, communicating Bible stories in religious instruction will remind learners that the kaleidoscope of Bible stories is necessary because no one story or image fully exhausts the reality of God. Each narrative simply leads learners deeper into the Mystery that is God.

Reading the Story

A second task of religious instruction in relation to Bible stories is to teach learners how to read the Bible. Bible stories can be read on a number of levels, from the devotional to the critical. The power of Bible stories is such that Mystery can reach out from the biblical text and grab learners in even the most cursory reading, but the richness and complexity of these stories demand closer attention in order for learners' to experience the depth of each story.

Reading Bible stories devotionally involves allowing the stories to speak directly to the spirit. Devotional reading may involve meditation on the story, listening for the word of God for the learner at that moment in the story. This form of reading Bible stories is more affective than cognitive, more spiritual than intellectual, although, of course, cognition is involved. Devotional reading of Scripture may be described in the words of James Michael Lee as a form of passive religious living in which the focus is on waiting attentively.[49] Reading Bible stories critically involves utilizing the tools of historical-critical and literary study. Religious educators should be well versed in these methods and should teach learners to employ these methods of Bible study in order to plumb the richness of the biblical narrative. Religious educators should help learners learn to read to catch the subtleties of the text, follow the plot, listen to the narrator's voice, make the inquiries and inferences the text requires, and relate to the characters the way the story demands. Religious educators should not try to give learners "the point" of a story, nor infer theological maxims for learners, nor tell learners how they ought to respond to a story or live in response to a story. Rather, religious educators should facilitate learners' experience with the story, helping them construct their own experiential truths and responses from their encounter with the narrative. In particular, by teaching learners to read Scripture for themselves, religious educators enable learners to have fuller and richer encounters with Bible stories throughout their lives.

Recasting the Story

A third task for religious instruction is to create ways to recast the old, old story in contemporary experience. Each new generation and each culture offers a new framework in which learners experience the Bible. Biblical stories continue to communicate existential truths throughout time and across cultures. Yet for each new generation, the Bible's stories must be experienced within the framework of their time and culture. The realities of the faith experiences expressed in the Bible must be complemented by their expression in the mythic patterns of the particular culture.[50] Mythopoesis is the process of reinterpreting an ancient story by historicizing it or making it relevant to contemporary situations. The New Testament is itself a mythopoetic reinterpretation of the Old Testament to explain the meaning of Jesus

---

[49]James Michael Lee, *The Content of Religious Instruction* (Birmingham, Ala.: Religious Education Press, 1985), p. 657.

[50]Navone, *Seeking God in Story*, p. 103.

Christ.[51] The task of religious instruction is to reinterpret the biblical narratives for contemporary times and situations, to make the old stories relevant to contemporary life.

An excellent example of New Testament mythopoesis is Clarence Jordan's *The Cotton Patch Gospels*. In the midst of the racial tensions of the 1960s, Jordan translated much of the New Testament into "Southern." Locating New Testament events in the South and making Jews and Gentiles into whites and blacks, Jordan reinterpreted the New Testament to speak directly to the racial prejudices, hatred, and violence of the civil rights era. *The Cotton Patch Gospels* can be used in contemporary religious instruction to help learners confront the prejudices and systems of discrimination that persist in society. Or learners may recast the *Cotton Patch Gospels* to reflect patterns of prejudice that exist in their own cultures, for example, casting Latinos or Asian Americans instead of blacks.

Feeling the Story

A fourth task of religious instruction is to assist learners in developing appropriate affective responses to biblical narratives. Bible stories evoke a wide range of feelings and emotions that can be utilized as powerful affective contents in religious instruction. Likewise, Bible stories can challenge implicitly held attitudes and values; most importantly, Bible stories can teach learners to feel and express love.

The Bible teaches that God is love and that all the people of God are called to express that love in both their relationship with God and their relationships with others. The Bible also offers numerous stories that embody the love to which God's people are called. For example, in the miracle stories of the New Testament, Jesus heals the sick, touching those considered to be unclean and untouchable. Jesus gathers children to him and weeps over Jerusalem. He washes the disciples' feet. Finally, he suffers and dies on a cross in an ultimate act of love. In religious instruction, these stories can both evoke and model love.

During a period of my own personal struggle with my Christian faith, the stories of Jesus became central in my choice to remain Christian. Having grown up as a fundamentalist Protestant, much of my seminary experience involved deconstructing the belief system

---

[51]Ibid., p. 106.

that had been handed down to me. With each lost belief, I seemed to have less and less to hold onto with confidence. At last I realized that for me there was no certainty about any of my beliefs. In fact, I realized how detrimental many of my fundamentalist beliefs had been to me and to others, and I realized that my newfound beliefs were tentative at best. Having come out of a tradition that prizes belief as a necessary and definitive part of Christian faith, I began to wonder if I was (or wanted to be) Christian at all. At that point, I remembered the stories of Jesus. Even now, no matter how many times I have heard those stories, I respond to them, not intellectually necessarily, but affectively. At the lowest point in my faith journey, the stories of Jesus touched me, not with beliefs but with love. I decided that, apart from Christology, soteriology, or eschatology, I loved the Jesus whom I knew from Scripture, and I wanted to stake my life with his—to love God, to love my neighbors as myself, to love even my enemies. That commitment became more important than any belief I had ever held, and to this day it causes me to continue to call myself Christian. The power of the biblical stories to reach the heart is immense.

Participating in the Story

A fifth task of religious instruction is to facilitate learners' participation in biblical stories. The very nature of Scripture demands participation as the appropriate and authentic response, and participation in biblical stories can bring about growth and wholeness. Biblical narratives show learners the way of authentic existence; they offer meaning and values, and they provide a myth by which to order identity. The biblical narratives show learners the love of God and can mediate encounter with the God who loves; they remind learners that they are invited to take up the yoke that is easy and the burden that is light, that they are to love as they have been loved, and that they are given the power to live as children of God. In this sense, biblical narratives can be redemptive for learners. They can open up a way for learners to find wholeness and new life in relationship with God.

In the biblical stories, learners can experience God in ways that transform their ways of being in the world and seeing it. Bible stories call learners to live differently, to live in authentic relationship with God and to express that relationship in every life choice. In Bible stories, learners can profoundly experience the myriad possibilities of life in Christ. Furthermore, encounter with God through biblical narratives can recreate learners' vision to see the possibilities of life in Christ in their own world. This vision, then, both unifies learners' experiences and mediates them. It unites the stories of learners' pasts into a single story understood through the eyes of faith, and it provides a means whereby learners process the experiences in which they are engaged. Thus, through biblical narratives, religious educators can assist learners in seeing, interpreting, and telling the stories of their lives through eyes of faith. Through Bible stories, learners can come to experience the world differently as they see their lives through the lens of the world-that-might-be, which they have encountered in the stories of Scripture.

Re-enacting the Story

A final task of religious instruction in relation to Bible stories is to teach learners to reenact the Christ story. Each Christian is called to respond preeminently to the Christ story by living it. The Word became flesh, and now the community inaugurated by Jesus is called to be a continuing incarnation in the world. Christians continue to communicate the Christian story by the Christian lives they lead. And as Christians live in response to the Christian story, they represent the reality of the Christian life through their living. For Christians, the Christ story is paradigmatic, and the life of Christ continues in their lives. This is a primary way in which the Good News continues to be communicated. Learners respond to the Christ story in its narrative form, but they also respond to it as it is embodied in the lives Christians lead. Christians retell the old story in their words and, more importantly, in their lives.

In Andre Dubus's short story "A Father's Story," a father covers up his daughter's hit-and-run accident in which a young man is killed.

> I say to Him: I would do it again. . . .
> And He says: I am a Father too.
> Yes, I say, as You are a Son Whom this morning I will receive; unless You kill me on the way to church, then I trust You will receive me. And as a Son You made Your plea.
> Yes, He says, but I would not lift the cup.
> True, and I don't want You to lift it from me either. And if one of my sons had come to me that night, I would have phoned the police and told them to meet us with an ambulance at the top of the hill.
> Why? Do you love them less?

I tell him no, it is not that I love them less, but that I could bear the pain of watching and knowing my sons' pain, could bear it with pride as they took the whip and nails. But You never had a daughter and, if You had, You could not have borne her passion.

So, He says, you love her more than you love Me.

I love her more than I love truth.

Then you love in weakness, He says.

As You love me, I say, and I go with an apple or carrot out to the barn.[52]

The Bible is filled with stories that challenge, comfort, shape identity, and provide ways of being in the world and seeing it. As the paradigmatic stories of the Christian community, biblical narratives deserve a central place in the religious educational life of the church and in the personal life of the learner. In these stories, learners can learn Christian beliefs, Christian identity, Christian affect, and Christian living.

This story was told by Rabbi Israel of Rizhyn:

All of the pupils of my ancestor, the Great Maggid, transmitted the teachings in his name—all except Rabbi Zusya. And the reason for this was that Rabbi Zusya hardly ever heard his teacher's sermon out to the end. For at the very start, when the maggid recited the verse from Scriptures which he was going to expound, and began with the words of the Scriptures: "And God said," or "and God spoke," Rabbi Zusya was overcome with ecstasy, and screamed and gesticulated so wildly that he disturbed the peace of the round table and had to be taken out. And then he stood in the hall or in the woodshed, beat his hands against the walls, and cried aloud: "And God said!" He did not quiet down until my ancestor had finished expounding the Scriptures. That is why he was not familiar with the sermons of the maggid. But the truth, I tell you—I tell you, the truth is this: If a man speaks in the spirit of truth and listens in the spirit of truth, one word is enough, for with one word can the world be uplifted, and with one word can the world be redeemed.[53]

[52]Andre Dubus, "A Father's Story," in *The Times are Never So Bad* (Boston: Godine, 1983), pp. 179–180.

[53]Martin Buber, *Tales of the Hasidim: The Early Masters* (New York: Schocken, 1947), pp. 236–237.

13

Original Stories

At its best, the sensation of writing is that of any unmerited
grace. It is handed to you, but only if you look for it. You search,
you break your heart, your back, your brain, and then—and only
then—it is handed to you.[1]

—Annie Dillard

Creating one's own stories is a process that comes partly as gift but
mostly as hard work. The flash of inspiration, a story idea, an image,
a place, or maybe a title is what is given. The narrative itself must be
nurtured, developed, and birthed as imagination and skill combine to
create a story. A religious educator who would tell an original story
must live inside it, learn from it, give it shape, and be shaped by it.
No one who creates a story is not changed by it.

Not all religious educators or learners will express their creativity
by making original stories. For those who wish to tell original narratives, desire to do so is a starting place; but desire alone is not enough
to create an effective story. An effective story is not simply the
chronological narration of an event; it is an expression of human experience. Creating an effective story involves more than the ability to
give sequence to actions. It requires talent and discipline to place
characters in a setting in which their actions and the consequences of
those actions express the theme of the story.

Flannery O'Connor's warning about writing fiction applies to creating oral stories as well: "I find that most people know what a story is

---

[1]Annie Dillard, *The Writing Life* (New York: Quality, 1989), p. 75.

290

until they sit down to write one. Then they find themselves writing a sketch with an essay woven through it, or an essay with a sketch woven through it, or an editorial with a character in it, or a case history with a moral, or some other mongrel thing."[2] The religious educator who creates a story should be good at story making, and good story making involves understanding what makes a story effective. O'Connor defines a story as "a complete dramatic action—and in good stories, the characters are shown through the action and the action is controlled through the characters, and the result of this is meaning that derives from the whole presented experience."[3] Creating a story, then, begins and ends with the story; the story itself is the meaning. Especially important for religious educators is a recognition that creating an effective story comes about not out of a desire to make a point or illustrate an abstraction but out of desire to tell a story. As O'Connor quips, creating stories is not a missionary enterprise.[4] It is a calling to give expression to human experience. The story is created to be a good story, and in being a good story it fulfills its task.

Thus the religious educator who wishes to create a story must begin where all stories begin, in the "foul rag-and-bone shop of the heart."[5] Stories begin in the concrete, in this person or that building or this shaggy dog. Stories deal with the reality of the senses. An effective story does not begin with an abstract notion but with the vision of some concrete reality. The religious educator who looks for a story idea should look for experiences, images, characters—not theological concepts. If the characters and the actions are expressed truthfully, the meaning will emerge.

THE STORY IDEA

The story idea, the inspiration, is the driving impetus that gives a story its shape. Story ideas can come from anywhere if religious educators keep their eyes open and watch for possibilities. A religious

---

[2]Flannery O'Connor, *Mystery and Manners* (New York: Farrar, Straus, and Giroux, 1969), p. 66.

[3]Ibid., p. 90.

[4]Ibid., p. 81.

[5]William Butler Yeats, "The Circus Animals' Desertion," in *Selected Poem and Two Plays of William Butler Yeats* (New York: Collier, 1962), p. 185.

educator's own everyday life experiences can provide a reservoir of story ideas. Other ideas may come from stories overheard at a party, from events reported in a newspaper, from an incident seen on television. Exploration of these ideas may suggest stories that religious educators may wish to develop for use in religious instruction.

Religious educators can plumb the possibilities of a story idea by raising a number of questions about it: What is the situation here? How did it come to be? What if . . . ? What might I title it?[6] At this point in the process, religious educators should allow their imagination to play with the idea, to see where it may take the story. Once the idea is firm, then the religious educator moves to the creation of characters and development of a plot.

CHARACTERS

Flannery O'Connor advises a storyteller to start with the characters. She writes, "If you start with a real personality, a real character, then something is bound to happen; and you don't have to know what before you begin. In fact, it may be better if you don't know what before you begin. You ought to be able to discover something from your stories. If you don't, probably nobody else will."[7]

The key to creating effective characters is to create believable characters. The characters need to invite the willing suspension of disbelief. Learners have to want to believe the characters. Thus characters need to be interesting and multidimensional. Flat characters do not invite empathy, and without empathy learners will not care what happens to the characters.

Religious educators can bring a character to life by representing the character's dominant qualities through the way the character looks, dresses, talks, and acts. In fact, characterization should be developed through action rather than explanation. On the other hand, religious educators want to avoid overloading the character with so many attributes that the story becomes a description rather than a narrative. One simple device for developing characterization is giving the

---

[6]Jack Maguire, *Creative Storytelling* (New York: McGraw-Hill, 1985), pp. 126–131.

[7]O'Connor, *Mystery and Manners*, p. 106.

character a symbolic name, such as Flannery O'Connor's Hazel Motes or William Faulkner's Joe Christmas.[8]

Religious educators should work with their characters for a while before placing them into a plot.[9] How would the characters respond in different situations? What habits would the characters have? How would they talk? What would their voices sound like? How would they relate to other characters? As religious educators become familiar with their characters, awareness of how the characters would act in the particular story taking shape develops. The more real the characters become to religious educators, the more believable the characters will be to the audience.

SETTING

The action of a story takes place somewhere—whether Beverly Cleary's Klikitat Street, Flannery O'Connor's Georgia, or C. S. Lewis' Narnia—and at some time.[10] And the shape of that setting will influence the action that takes place. The setting creates certain parameters of action, while at the same time stimulating responses from the characters that inhabit that setting. Fiction writers from the American South provide a particularly outstanding example of the function of setting.[11] Southern culture itself dictates parameters of action, what is possible within that context. Yet, a character placed in that setting can be imagined to respond in particular ways to it. Often the characters' attempts to defy the parameters of setting can provide an interesting and exciting conflict for a story. Nonetheless, setting must be inseparably entwined with characters and plot. Characters set down in Rome, Georgia, will respond differently than if they were set down in Riverside, California. A story set in Atlanta will be a different story if

---

[8]Flannery O'Connor, *Wise Blood, Three by Flannery O'Connor* (New York: Signet, 1962); William Faulkner, *Light in August* (New York: Modern Library, 1968).

[9]Nancy Kavanaugh, "5 Tips for Making Characters Real," *Yarnspinner* 16 (December 1992): 3.

[10]David L. Russell, *Literature for Children: A Short Introduction* (New York: Longman, 1991), p. 90.

[11]For a description of how place functions in a regional fiction writer's work, see Eudora Welty, "How I Write," in *Understanding Fiction*, ed. Cleanth Brooks and Robert Penn Warren, 3d ed. (Englewood Cliffs, N.J.: Prentice-Hall, 1979), pp. 310–317.

set in Portland, Oregon, or Beijing, China. A strong sense of place helps shape the characters and actions of a story.

In creating a setting, religious educators need to be especially aware of their senses. The setting should create an atmosphere, a sense of place. Yet it should not overwhelm the story by its description. Like character, setting is best revealed through the action of the story, though some description is necessary and appropriate for both. Keeping the setting relevant to the plot is essential for the development of an effective story. O'Connor writes that two qualities make fiction: "One is the sense of mystery and the other is the sense of manners. You get the manners from the texture of existence that surrounds you. The great advantage of being a Southern writer is that we don't have to go anywhere to look for manners; bad or good, we've got them in abundance."[12]

PLOT

Action is the element of story that most engages learners. They want to know what happened. The action carries the story and reveals the characters. Through action, the meaning of the story is created and conveyed. The plot begins as the character is plunged into a situation. Storyteller Jack Maguire offers these suggestions for developing plot:

1. Have the story unfold according to events, not explanations, descriptions or summations.
2. Organize individual scenes around separate confrontations or conflicts.
3. Remember that the story is the important thing, not any message that can be derived from the story.
4. Keep plot details simple and easy to remember.
5. Consider using rhymes, repetitions, and symbol patterns to make the plot more engaging.[13]

Events in the plot should flow naturally from one into another, and actions should be appropriately motivated. Rarely are capricious actions believable. Learners need to understand why a character acted in

---

[12]O'Connor, *Mystery and Manners*, p. 103.
[13]Maguire, *Creative Storytelling*, pp. 136–138.

a certain way or why events unfolded the way they did. The logic of motivation, then, contributes to learners' sense of the unity of the story.[14] For example, Amy Tan's *The Joy Luck Club* is the story of the relationships of a group of Chinese-American mothers and daughters. The story unfolds with both the intertwining of these women's lives in the contemporary world and with the individual stories of what happened to the mothers when they were in China before they came to the United States. As learners discover the mothers' stories, the larger story of the struggles and triumphs of two generations of Chinese-American women becomes more clear.

Generally, the plots of oral stories are fairly simple. For younger learners, chronologically sequenced plots are often best to allow learners to follow the story. Young learners also prefer action to exposition in a story. Learners of middle school-age and upward can enjoy more complex plots, including such literary devices as flashbacks, for example.[15] In creating original stories, religious educators should keep in mind the abilities of learners to process narrative and should construct stories appropriate to learners' abilities.

THEME

The theme is the major idea or the meaning of the story; it is what learners are to make of the human experiences rendered in the story.[16] The theme arises out of the confluence of characters and actions in the organic unity of the story. For example, one of the themes of May Sarton's *The Small Room* is vocation. This theme does not emerge out of discussions of vocation but out of the teaching experiences of the protagonist who, at the end of the academic year, chooses to return to the classroom because of her passion for teaching. Religious educators should be aware of the temptation to take an abstraction—like grace or redemption—and ask how they can concretely illustrate it in a story. Giving in to this temptation may result in some explication of the abstraction, but it probably will not result in an effective story.

In an effective story, the story itself is the meaning, and every word of the story is necessary for the meaning. Stories, then, cannot be

---

[14]Brooks and Warren, *Understanding Fiction*, p. 36.
[15]Russell, *Literature for Children*, p. 94.
[16]Brooks and Warren, *Understanding Fiction*, p. 177.

reduced to a proposition or thematic statement. In fact, stories move in just the opposite direction. Stories open rather than close; they offer options rather than answers, experiences rather than propositions. To explore the theme of a story is to explore its meaning, and the meaning of a story is always more than thematic statements about the story.

In creating an effective story, religious educators should begin by creating a world that exists independently in the imagination. In that world, characters act and are acted upon in such ways that one event leads to another, and each event contributes to the growing sense of the significance of the whole. As events take on significance in the larger work, meaning is created, and in effective stories this movement toward meaning reflects learners' own sense of moving toward meaning in their own life experiences.[17]

JONAH AND THE GREAT FISH

The biblical tale of the prophet Jonah offers an example of one well-constructed narrative that develops its character through his actions and conveys its theme through the action of the story. As James Michael Lee suggests, the Bible is essentially a religious instruction book. Its inspired writers wrote its stories, poems, sermons, and letters primarily for religious instruction purposes—to teach the people of God how to live as the people of God.[18] The story of Jonah is told to teach God's people the universality of God's love; God's love, the story teaches, extends to all people, and, by implication, the love of God's people should also extend to everyone, even to one's enemies.

The story of Jonah begins not with description or explanation, but with action. The Lord comes to Jonah and tells him to go to Nineveh to preach, but Jonah runs, attempting to escape from the presence of the Lord. Through this single action, the story tells us much about Jonah. He does not want to go to Nineveh—the capital of Assyria, the much-hated world power at that time. He is disobedient to the Lord, and he thinks he can run from the Lord. Jonah boards a ship to try to sail as far away as possible and then falls asleep. The Lord causes a great storm, and in the general panic the captain of the ship wakes

---

[17]Ibid., p. 178.

[18]James Michael Lee, "Religious Education and the Bible: A Religious Education-ist's View," in *Biblical Themes in Religious Education*, ed. Joseph S. Marino (Birmingham, Ala.: Religious Education Press, 1983), pp. 1–8.

Jonah to call on his God to save them. The passengers and crew cast lots to find out who has brought the storm upon them, and the lot falls on Jonah, who knows what the problem is. Jonah suggests the crew throw him overboard to quiet the sea, which they do with reluctance, and the sea becomes calm.

In this section of the story, learners see that Jonah knows he has done wrong by running from the Lord and apparently feels some guilt since he is so quick to recognize his responsibility for the storm. Learners also see here that Jonah is not willing for the entire ship to be lost on his account; he is willing to be thrown overboard for the sake of the others (Additionally, they see the sailors who are not Hebrews, behaving righteously—in contrast to Jonah who is not). All of the characteristics of the prophet are revealed simply through Jonah's actions; the narrative itself contains no description of the prophet. As an interesting side note to the story, learners are told that on the ship after the sea calms, the sailors offer a sacrifice and make vows to the Lord.

Jonah is swallowed by a great fish, and three days later Jonah prays to the Lord. Here the action conveys some of the book's humor as well as Jonah's character. Apparently, Jonah is stubborn enough that three days go by before he is willing to pray. The prayer contained in 2:2–9 probably represents the insertion of an independent psalm, but in the story it serves to add a note of the unexpected. It is a psalm of thanksgiving rather than a prayer of petition. Jonah fully expects the Lord's deliverance. Notice how subtly the biblical writer is creating a complex character through these actions—Jonah is disobedient but willing to give himself for others; he is stubborn but full of faith in the Lord. Jonah is no flat, one-dimensional character, and the second half of his story continues to develop his personality.

The call of the Lord comes to Jonah a second time. This time Jonah goes to Nineveh, but, when the people repent, Jonah gets mad. The truth of the matter is that Jonah hates the Assyrians and does not want to see them spared. So Jonah goes to a place outside the city to sit and watch what will happen. The sun beats down on Jonah, and the Lord creates a plant to provide shade for the prophet. The next day the Lord sends a worm to destroy the plant, and Jonah is furious about the injustice of it. The Lord gets the last word: Jonah is willing to feel pity for a plant but not for a city of more than 120,000 people. The action of the second half of the story ends much as the first—God shows mercy to people other than the Jews.

Hence the action of the story has created its religious instruction theme—the universality of God's love. This story is a reminder of the task of God's people to proclaim to all people the breadth of God's love and forgiveness. With no explanations or didactic interruptions, the action of the story builds this theme: the Lord calls Jonah, twice, to preach to Nineveh; the Lord spares the crew of the ship; and the Lord spares a penitent Nineveh. Then the Lord drives the point home to Jonah by creating a teaching situation in which Jonah can examine his own prejudices and attitudes. The story ends there, however. Learners do not know what Jonah does with this opportunity. Perhaps Jonah continues to sulk and goes home mad. Perhaps he sees the error of his prejudices. The story does not tell learners. Yet, here is learners' invitation to grapple with their own prejudices. What would they have done? The open-endedness of the story leaves room for struggle and decision on the part of learners. The Lord loves all people, but do they?

When I taught a Hebrew Bible survey course at a Christian college in Southern California, I wanted my students to get a sense of the relevance of biblical stories for our lives in contemporary America. So I developed a West Coast version of the story of Jonah. What, I asked myself, would happen if Jonah were set down in present-day Los Angeles? Here is the story that resulted:

Once upon a time, the word of the Lord came to Jonah, a true Southern California surfer-philosopher and coffee house guru who lived in a studio apartment just off Venice Beach.

"Jonah, get up. Go to San Francisco, the great bay city of Northern California, and preach against it, for their wickedness has come to my attention."

Now, Jonah didn't like this idea one bit, and so he packed his duffle bag, drove his VW van to the port of Los Angeles, and caught a ship going to Ensenada. This ship had no sooner gotten under way than a hurricane blew in from nowhere. Now, hurricanes are pretty rare on the West Coast, and the ship's crew was hardly prepared for the storm they found themselves in. Everyone thought for sure the ship was going to sink. The crew members began praying to their gods and throwing all their goods overboard to lighten the ship.

Jonah, meanwhile, had gone down into the ship's bunking quarters and had fallen fast asleep. The ship's captain found him there and woke him up.

"Hey, dude. Don't you know we're in the middle of this totally awesome hurricane, and we might sink any minute now? Get up and pray to your god. Maybe your god will save us. None of ours has."

Jonah wiped the sleep out of his eyes and went to join the others. By this time, they'd decided to throw dice and find out whose fault the hurricane was. So they threw the dice, and Jonah lost.

"Bummer, man," said one crew member. "So what gives? Who are you? Where are you from?"

Jonah answered, "I'm a Southern Californian from Venice Beach, and I'm running away from the Lord who wants me to go and preach to Northern Californians in San Francisco."

"Gnarly, man. So what are we supposed to do?"

"Throw me overboard."

The crew members dropped their jaws. "No way, man." And they tried and tried to get the ship back to Los Angeles. But their efforts were to no avail. So they prayed to the Lord. "Listen, Lord, we're really sorry about this, but this dude's got to go." So they picked Jonah up and pitched him overboard, and immediately the ocean calmed down.

"Awesome," the sailors said, and they agreed to go to church the very next Sunday.

In the meantime, Jonah had found himself in less than pleasant circumstances. The Lord had prepared this totally rad fish that gulped Jonah up as part of a seafood buffet. Now Jonah stayed in the belly of the fish for three days. At last, he decided to pray to the Lord.

"Lord, this is gross. There's some nasty stuff floating around in here. Now I know I really messed up back in L.A. But I'm grateful you're a loving and forgiving God, and I thank you already for getting me out of this mess. Amen."

No sooner had Jonah said amen than the Lord gave that fish such a case of indigestion that it vomited Jonah up right there on Laguna Beach.

"Dude," said one sun bather, "you don't look so hot."

Jonah hitched a ride with some Deadheads up to L.A. where he picked up his VW van and drove back home. He had just gotten a hot shower when the word of the Lord came to him a second time.

"Jonah, get up. Go to San Francisco and preach the message I'll give you."

"No prob, Lord. I'm on my way."

Jonah booked the next flight from LAX to SFO and by early evening he was in the Bay City. The fog was already rolling in. So Jonah decided to get a room for the night. The next morning, he started at 19th Avenue and worked his way through the financial district preaching the word of the Lord to the people of San Francisco.

"Hey dudes. You bunch of immoral, unethical Northern Californians. The poor wander your streets. Your youth kill one another for drug money. Your women and children are brutalized. The Lord is sick of you. In just a few days, the Lord is going to send the Big One. It's going to shake you from the TransAmerica building to the Golden Gate Bridge. And all the earthquake specifications in the world won't protect you from this one."

And the people of San Francisco believed God. So they proclaimed a day of prayer and fasting from Sausilito to South San Francisco. At last, word even reached the mayor's office, and she canceled the city council meeting to join in the prayer vigil. She even made an official proclamation to make that day a day of prayer to the Lord.

Now when the Lord saw what they did and how they began to plan for low-income housing, employment programs, rehabilitation centers, shelters, and other much-needed programs, the Lord decided not to destroy the Bay City.

Now this really peeved Jonah. So he said to God, "See, see! Didn't I tell you? And you wanted to know why I ran to Ensenada. I knew you were too nice to go through with it. I knew you'd wimp out of cleaning up that mass of immorality. Now I've been humiliated. I'd just as soon die."

And God replied, "So what's your problem?"

But Jonah just stormed out of the city and went over to Mill Valley. He found himself a spot at the top of the hill on Golden Gate Seminary's campus where he could watch and see if just maybe God would shake up San Francisco.

Now after a while, Jonah got hot sitting there in the sun. So the Lord caused a redwood tree to grow to give him shade. And so for a while Jonah just chilled out there under the redwood. But the next day, God sent the seminary's maintenance crew to cut down the tree because it interfered with the landscaping. That day, when the fog lifted, God sent record temperatures to Mill Valley. And Jonah was upset. "Just go ahead and kill me, God, just like you did that poor, innocent redwood tree. What did it ever do to you?"

And God replied, "Jonah, you feel sorry for that redwood tree that you didn't plant or water or make grow, and then you don't expect me to feel sorry for the people of San Francisco, who don't even know their left hand from their right?"

This story was always a success in class because learners readily identified with the places, language, and attitudes expressed in it. At other times, I asked students to retell other biblical stories in contemporary contexts. This process allowed them to understand the story better by placing it in a more familiar setting. Also, in order to be faithful to the original stories, learners had to examine them closely before adapting them. This process of translation encouraged deeper study and reflection while engaging learners in an enjoyable and creative task.

Because the basic plot and theme are already present, adapting a biblical story may be a good place for religious educators to begin creating their own stories. The important thing to remember is to let the story stand for itself. Let the action develop the characters and the theme. Avoid the temptation to explain, to moralize, or to sermonize. An effective story is itself the point. It will need no explanation. It will invite exploration by both those who hear it and those who tell it.

THE WORST CHRISTMAS PAGEANT EVER

Another story that I have told in a variety of settings grew out of a personal experience I had as a child. As the incident was shaped into a story, some elements were altered or exaggerated and others were invented as the story took on a life of its own beyond my simple reminiscence about what I remembered as The Worst Christmas Pageant Ever. The title was inspired by Barbara Robinson's children's book, *The Best Christmas Pageant Ever*. But the story is mine. I was there.

Every year my church produced a Christmas pageant at the civic auditorium in my hometown. Every year it was directed by Gaynelle Johnson, the pastor's wife. And every year it was the same Christmas pageant. The only thing that changed from year to year was the supporting cast. Six- seven- and eight-year-olds were silver bells. Nine-year-old girls were Christmas angels. So as you got older you got promoted just like in Sunday school.

It was Christmas 1969. I was finally nine years old. After nine long years of waiting I was going to get to be a Christmas angel. I could at last leave the ranks of those moronic silver bells. But alas, it was not to be.

That December Gaynelle Johnson got sick. Quick as a flash Judy Marshall stepped in to direct the Christmas pageant. Judy Marshall was Marty Marshall's mama. Marty Marshall was a year younger than I was. Eight years old. Eight, not nine, eight. Silver bell eight. Marty Marshall, however, did not want to be a silver bell. Actually, nobody did. Marty Marshall wanted to be a Christmas angel. I should have known. The handwriting was on the wall. Casting came around, and, sure enough, Marty Marshall was a Christmas angel, and, I, as the last of the nine year olds to have reached that highwater mark, was demoted to silver bell.

As some sort of consolation prize, I suppose, I was assigned to be the leader of the silver bells, a bunch of whiny six- seven- and eight-year-olds who were supposed to sing Christmas carols while costumed in cardboard bells covered in aluminum foil. I'm sure adults thought we were cute. I thought we looked like tiny captives in silver bell hell.

But, as they say, the show must go on, and on it did go. We were up first. Fifteen of us lined up on stage in our cardboard silver bells. In the wings Marty Marshall's mama was motioning for us to smile. Fourteen little kids grinned nervously. I simply stared straight ahead into the spotlight as if struck with stage fright. I tried to look like I might pass out. Out of the corner of my eye, I saw that ridiculous smile melt off Judy Marshall's face as she tried to decide what she would do with an unconscious nine-year-old on the stage.

Our first song was "Away in a Manger," which, of course, was pitched so high the first note could only be heard by small animals. Our next song was "Silent Night." When we got to the part about "'round yon virgin," I saw the older boys who were playing the shepherds start to giggle. Apparently they'd just found out what that line was all about. I myself had always been intrigued by the "round" part, assuming that it was an adjective describing Mary and thinking it had not been very polite of the songwriter to comment on her figure given her current state of affairs.

The last number for the silver bells was, of course, "Silver Bells." During this song, we were supposed to swing from side to side like ringing bells while we sang, "Silver bells, silver bells, it's Christmas time in the city. Ring-a-ling, hear them ring. Soon it will be Christmas day." Well, when we got to the ring-a-ling part Rusty Waters got so excited and rang so big that he knocked some six year old kid over, and he and his little cardboard bell rolled right off the stage. Dutifully I continued to sing as I heard Marty Marshall's mama order one of the big kids back stage to go and check on him. I smiled for the first time that evening.

When we finished singing, we left the stage. Then we could take off our bells and watch the rest of the performance from the back of the auditorium in seats that had been reserved for us. We got there just as the Christmas angels were about to leave the stage. As they turned to go, the wing of one of the bigger angels caught in Marty Marshall's hair. As the angel headed across the stage I heard Marty Marshall wail. The bigger angel, however, was determined not to stop until she had made her exit. Marty had no choice but to scurry off on the heels of the other angel. I smiled for the second time that evening.

Now, for most Christmas pageants, this would have been the end. The baby had come. The angels had sung. The shepherds had visited. But not this Christmas pageant. Oh no, it had only just begun. Our Christmas pageant went from the annunciation to the apocalypse. An audience, which had never seen this particular pageant, sat in hushed amazement as Jesus grew up, ministered, was crucified, rose from the dead, ascended, and returned. That's right. Returned. This particular pageant ended with the Great White Throne Judgment. The head deacon in a red devil costume pulled lost sinners shrieking and wailing off stage into the outer darkness and gnashing of teeth waiting in the wings.

This year Judy Marshall had taken it upon herself to play the trashy slut who gets thrown into the lake of fire. I thought it was appropriate. She had on a lot of makeup and a slinky red dress, which I figured she had gotten out of her own clothes closet anyway. After Jesus, who was wearing white and sitting on a throne, told her to depart from him, he never knew her, the devil started pulling her toward the wing, and she started screaming her head off. I thought the little kids' eyes were going to pop out. My guess is they've spent years in therapy since trying to rid themselves of that image.

I am not quite sure what happened next, but apparently the devil lost his grip on her, and she flew off in one direction and the devil in the other. When she hit the floor in that slinky dress, she just kept on sliding and slid right off into the wing that was supposed to be where The Saved were having The Marriage Supper of the Lamb. I heard the devil fall out in the lake of fire area, and, though I won't repeat what I heard him say, I thought it probably was the kind of thing the devil would say come judgment day.

At that point, the curtain came down, and before the audience had time to respond to the spectacle it had just seen, the pastor came out and had us close our eyes and bow our heads. After a few minutes of silence, we closed the pageant by singing "Joy to the World." As we sang that song, I thought about how no matter how bad things are, the Christmas pageant included, the joy of Christmas really is for the whole world, and isn't the miracle of Christmas, after all, that every year, no matter what, the Christ still comes!

When I went outside the theater, the stars were shining brightly above. As I went to heave my cardboard silver bell into the dumpster, I saw Marty's little angel wings stuffed into the garbage, and I saw Marty sitting on the back steps, ever so slightly whimpering. I disposed of my costume and went and sat down beside Marty.

"What's wrong?" I asked.

"It was a disaster. An absolute disaster," she cried.

I put my nine year old arm around her eight year old shoulders and said, "Now, it wasn't that bad."

"Really?" she brightened.

"Really. It was a Christmas pageant no one will ever forget."

She looked at me and smiled. Somewhere in the distance we heard a radio playing, "Silver bells, silver bells. It's Christmas time in the city. Ring-a-ling. Hear them ring. Soon it will be Christmas day." And I smiled for the third time that evening.

PART III
DEVELOPMENT AND STORYTELLING

14

Children and Storytelling

Miss Binney stood in front of her class and began to read aloud from Mike Mulligan and His Steam Shovel, a book that was a favorite of Ramona's . . . . As Ramona listened a question came into her mind, a question that had often puzzled her about the books that were read to her . . . . Now that Ramona was in school, and school was a place for learning, perhaps Miss Binney could answer the question. . . . "Miss Binney, I want to know—how did Mike Mulligan go to the bathroom while he was digging in the basement of the town hall?"[1]

—Beverly Cleary

As a child, I loved stories—Bible stories, biographies, mysteries, adventures. At church I heard stories of Abraham and Sarah, Moses and Miriam, Jesus and the little children. I also heard stories of missionaries like Lottie Moon, who shared God's love in China, and the many missionaries who still worked all over the world to show God's love. As soon as I could read, I had a book in my hands (or my nose in a book, as my mother usually put it). In my imagination I created stories in which I was the hero, scoring the winning basket or saving the world from a mad scientist. Stories formed the milieu in which I came to construct my identity, and many of these stories became integrated into my own personal myth, both as a child and now as an adult.

---

[1]Beverly Cleary, *Ramona the Pest* (New York: Dell, 1968), pp. 22–23.

By the time children reach kindergarten, they have developed a sense of story from their encounters with storytelling experiences, whether in formal storytelling sessions (for example, children's story hour at the library) or in informal adult conversations (for example, parents recounting to one another the day's experiences).[2] Young children begin to develop an understanding of story conventions such as syntax, word choice, text structure, character types, settings, and events.[3] Although very young children tell stories that utilize narrative structures, often the sequence of events in their stories is arbitrary, and the events are not tightly linked by any causality.[4] Jean Piaget found that very young children tend to tell stories with vague pronoun references and suggested that this phenomenon results from children's egocentric perspective which does not allow them to recognize the informational needs of the listener.[5]

By age five, children have developed a much more complex understanding of story. On average, five-year-olds tend to tell stories that are three times as long as those from two-year-olds and contain twice as many characters and incidents.[6] These stories take on more formal linguistic conventions, such as formal opening phrases, past tense, and formal closing. Dialogue becomes a common element in the stories of kindergartners, who also create more cohesive links from event to event than do two-year-olds. Nonetheless, five-year-olds frequently fail to bring their stories to a satisfying resolution.

In learning these story conventions, children are also learning how to organize their events and characters into a single, unified tale. Very young children simply "heap up" characters and events with few links from one item to the next. Yet even very early in life, children develop two organizational devices that they impose on this "heap" of information. One is centering or maintaining some central element throughout the story and tying other information to that element. The

---

[2]Arthur N. Applebee, "Children's Narratives: New Directions," *The Reading Teacher* 34 (November 1980): 137.

[3]Ibid.

[4]Susan Kemper and Linda L. Edwards, "Children's Expression of Causality and Their Construction of Narratives," *Topics in Language Disorders* 7 (December 1986): 14.

[5]Jean Piaget, *The Language and Thought of the Child*, 3d ed., trans. Marjorie and Ruth Gabain (London: Routledge and Kegan Paul, 1959), p. 99.

[6]Applebee, "Children's Narratives," p. 138.

other is chaining, in which each event implies, leads to, or motivates the next.[7] This sense of story is firmly rooted in children by the time they reach school age. This set of expectations about the nature of story subsequently guides them in their reactions to new stories and in their own storytelling experiences.[8]

This developing sense of story appears to be an interaction between the internal structure within the text of a story and a story schema held in the mind of the learner.[9] "Story grammar" describes the linguistic structural organization of the story, whereas "story schema" describes the internal cognitive structures that exist in the minds of learners. Piaget suggests that cognitive structures develop throughout childhood, and thus the development of story schemata is likely to follow developmental patterns of cognition. Empirical research suggests that children are sensitive to story structures and that certain structures are more memorable than others.[10] This apprehension of story structure seems to involve both story grammar itself and the developing story schema of the child.

This cognitive schema sets up expectations for what is coming next during encoding and operates in reconstruction of story information during recall. The story schema allows the child to determine what information is considered most important, and developmental changes in story schemata have been most apparent in children's determination of the relative importance of story information.[11]

For example, children tend to focus on actions—initiating events, resolutions, and what happened in between the beginnings and endings. This focus reflects an emphasis on physical causality. Adults, on the other hand, add more a complex emphasis on the major goals of the characters that provide a motivational connection between

---

[7]Ibid., p. 140.

[8]Ibid., p. 141.

[9]Gorden Bower, "Experiments on Story Understanding and Recall," *Quarterly Journal of Experimental Psychology* 28 (November 1976): 511–534; Gorden H. Bower, John B. Black, and Turner J. Turner, "Scripts in Memory for Text," *Cognitive Psychology* 11 (April 1979): 177–220; David E. Rummelhart, "Notes on Schema for Stories," *Representation and Understanding: Studies in Cognitive Science*, ed. Daniel Bobrow and Allen Collins (New York: Academic Press, 1975).

[10]Daniel D. Hade, "Children, Stories, and Narrative Transformation," *Research in the Teaching of English* 22 (October 1988): 311.

[11]Stephanie H. McConaughy, "Developmental Changes in Story Comprehension and Levels of Questioning," *Language Arts* 59 (September 1982): 82.

beginnings, endings, and actions. Adults also tend to make inferences about internal responses and dispositions of characters; children tend to make fewer inferences and, when they do, their inferences still tend to refer to actions rather than internal states.[12] Children's emphasis on physical causality indicates a less cognitively complex schema, whereas adults' emphasis on psychological causality suggests a more cognitively complex schema. Hence, differences in story schemata represent different levels of comprehension of the complexity of the same story information.[13] This understanding of the interaction of story schema and comprehension may be summarized in three assumptions:

1. Changes in cognitive schemata represent differences in the level of complexity for comprehension.
2. A higher level of complexity subsumes a lower level of complexity.
3. The higher the level of complexity in the schema required the greater the difficulty of a specific comprehension task.[14]

Children's sense of story, then, has numerous implications for religious educators of children. The stories that children hear shape their understanding of story. Thus, early experiences with stories are essential in children's developing a narrative framework from which to understand and to tell stories. Since life experiences occur in the form of narrative, a sense of story helps children begin to impose order on the chaos of experience and to derive meaning from their experiences.[15] Because the level of cognitive development is related to the functioning of the story schema, developmentally appropriate stories and techniques for teaching stories have more impact on children. Thus stories that focus on action and move logically through action-motivated sequences of events are more fully accessible to children than stories that rely on inferences of internal motivation. As children encounter developmentally appropriate stories, these stories can become means for facilitating further development in a number of ways—linguistically, cognitively, affectively, behaviorally, socially, and religiously.

---

[12]Ibid., p. 583.
[13]Ibid., p. 585.
[14]Ibid.
[15]See Jerome Bruner, *Actual Minds, Possible Worlds* (Cambridge: Harvard University Press, 1986).

STORIES AND LANGUAGE DEVELOPMENT

Children's facility in language develops quickly. Most children speak their first words at about one year of age and around eighteen months begin to put two words together.[16] All children seem to go through the same stages of language development, but the rate of development may vary greatly from child to child. On average, by the age of three, children have vocabularies of nine hundred words and have added adverbs, pronouns, and prepositions to the nouns, verbs, and adjectives they attained earlier. By age four, their vocabularies include about 1,500 words, and they are able to create grammatically correct sentences. By this time, children also have developed the ability to use past tense. During this period, children frequently use language to explore their world by asking why and how. Storytelling experiences can encourage language development in preschoolers by increasing their vocabularies, allowing them to identify and name objects and actions, and encouraging them to discover their world through language.[17]

Elementary age children continue to develop more complex language structures as they gain greater control over the various forms of language. They begin to use complex sentences, adding adjectival, conditional, and subordinate clauses as they progress in sophistication. During this period, stories can provide models for children's expanding language structure. Opportunities for children to tell their own stories will also provide occasions for them to use more complex sentence and narrative structures. In religious education, storytelling can assist children in learning the language of theology and religion.[18]

---

[16]Roger Brown and Collin Fraser, "The Acquisition of Syntax," in *Verbal Behavior and Learning: Problems and Processes*, ed. Charles N. Cofer and Barbara S. Musgrave (New York: McGraw-Hill, 1963), pp. 158–209.

[17]For example, Schickendanz found that when adults read stories to young children, children learn new information, new vocabulary, information about books, and the concept of "story." Judith A. Schickendanz, *More than ABCs: The Early Stages of Reading and Writing* (Washington, D.C.: National Association for the Education of Young Children, 1986).

[18]James Michael Lee distinguishes theological and religious language. Theological language, he contends, is primarily cognitive language used to talk about God; religious language is primarily affective and behavioral language used to talk with God or to relive one's encounters with God. *The Content of Religious Instruction* (Birmingham, Ala.: Religious Education Press, 1985), p. 280.

Since most of the vocabulary of theology has little to do with concrete objects, very young children may be able to use theological words, but they do so with a very superficial (if not mistaken) understanding of the words.[19] Young children learn the vocabulary of theology by connecting new words with words and conventions they already know.[20] For example, I once taught a group of preschoolers a song about the three Hebrew children in the fiery furnace. Later I heard one of the little girls singing the song—about Shadrach, Meshach, and a billy goat. Nonetheless, from their participation in a religious environment, children learn theological words and by age six have a limited understanding of some theological concepts.[21] Moving from simple words, such as kindness, gentleness, and love, to more complex words, such as justice and compassion, the stories of religious education can help children begin to develop a vocabulary with which to talk about theology. Furthermore, because of the central role of language in shaping identity, children's development of the language of theology can also facilitate their growing identity as children of God.

More significantly, stories can be used in religious instruction to help children develop religious language. Religious language is the language that learners use to talk to God or to express their experiences of encounter with God.[22] In other words, religious language "is a symbolic expression of religious experience."[23] For this reason, stories are an important and powerful way of teaching religious language. Religious language tends to be ambiguous and analogous because it is rooted in experience and in interpretation of experience. Stories reflect this particularity of individual experience and offer a verbal expression and interpretation of often profound religious events. The utility religious language has for religious instruction may also be said to be true of the value of stories (as a form of religious language) for religious instruction: religious language and stories (1) reflect and express the realities they symbolize; (2) provide deeper and more educational meaning to experience; (3) evoke cognitive, affective, and lifestyle

---

[19]George C. Brandeburg, "The Language of a Three-Year-Old Child," *Pedagogical Seminary* 22 (March 1915): 89–120.

[20]Eve. V. Clark, "Meanings and Concepts," in *Handbook of Child Psychology*, ed. P. H. Mussen (New York: Wiley, 1983), 3:816–817.

[21]F. A. Josephina, "A Study of Some Religious Terms for Six-Year Old Children," *Religious Education* 56 (January-February 1961): 24–25.

[22]Lee, *Content of Religious Instruction*, p. 281.

[23]Ibid., p. 285.

responses in the learner; (4) describe significant religious understanding, events, and experiences, in addition to performing religious acts in and through the very words themselves.[24]

Six-year-old Courtney Quattlebaum had heard the stories of Jesus all her life. One day her aunt Tisa, a seminary student in religious education, asked Courtney some questions about the Bible stories Courtney knew. "Who was Mary?" "Who was Joseph?" "Did Jesus have any brothers or sisters?" At that point, Courtney gave an interesting answer: "No. Jesus was an only child." Tisa replied, "I don't know, Courtney. I think maybe he had a few." Insistent, Courtney responded, "Well, that's not what we read in the Bible at Sunday school." It took a few moments for the answer to dawn on Tisa. What Courtney had read in the Bible at Sunday school was John 3:16: "For God so loved the world, He gave His only begotten son." Jesus was an only child!

STORIES AND COGNITIVE DEVELOPMENT

Cognition involves perception, memory, reasoning, reflection, and insight.[25] Perception is the detection, organization, and interpretation of data. Memory involves the storage and retrieval of the perceived data. Reasoning demands making inferences and drawing conclusions from the perceived data. Reflection involves evaluating ideas and solutions, and insight is the construction of new relationships between segments of knowledge.[26] Development in cognition comes as a series of qualitative changes in cognitive functioning rather than simply in quantitative increases in certain skills such as addition or subtraction. The impetus for these qualitative developments is a problem, challenge, or conflict. The previous stage poses the learner with a problem that is resolved through processes of assimilation or accommodation, and its resolution brings about a new developmental achievement. This growth process occurs through the constant reciprocal interactions of persons and their environments, particularly their social environments.

Jean Piaget identified four stages of cognitive development through which persons move: sensorimotor, preoperational, concrete

---

[24]Ibid., p. 287.

[25]Paul Henry Mussen, John Janeway Conger, and Jerome Kagan, *Child Development and Personality* (New York: Harper and Row, 1979), pp. 234–235.

[26]Ibid.

operational, and formal operational.[27] The sensorimotor stage covers birth to about twenty-four months and functions mainly through sensory inputs that result in motor outputs. I discuss formal operational thought, which begins in adolescence, in chapter 15, "Adolescents and Storytelling."

Preoperational thought is characterized by a number of particular cognitive operations. Preoperational children, ages two through five, think very concretely. They do not analyze or synthesize; rather, they judge events by their outer appearance, regardless of any internal logic. Thus their understanding of objects, events, and relationships depends on external attributes that the children can perceive. They begin to learn to organize their world on the basis of what they see— color, shape, size, use. This process reflects the centrism of preoperational thought. Young children tend to lock in on one particular dimension of an event or object and are unable to integrate two aspects into one judgment. Thus preschoolers learn to follow one type of classification through to completion (for example, color or shape). Their thinking also moves transductively and in one direction. Children's thought moves from particular to particular without implicit or explicit connection, though they are able to retell short stories if the material is presented in a meaningful sequence. They are not able, however, to reason the converse of a given statement. As mentioned previously, preschoolers are also egocentric and thus dependent on their own perceptions and unable to take the perspective of another.

Religious educators should be aware of young children's cognitive capacities and tell stories appropriate to children's developmental level. These stories may both affirm the abilities already developed by preoperational children and stimulate movement toward the next stage of cognitive development, concrete operations, which emerges during the early elementary years.

In concrete cognitive operations, children aged six through eleven begin to manipulate their environment mentally. They are able to deal with logical relationships, though their thinking still refers only to tangible objects which can be subjected to real activity. They develop abilities to conserve, classify, associate, and reverse. These cognitive

---

[27]See Jean Piaget, *Psychology of Intelligence* (New York: Harcourt, Brace, 1950); Jean Piaget, *The Origins of Intelligence in Children* (New York: International Universities Press, 1952); Jean Piaget, *The Construction of Reality in the Child* (New York: Basic, 1954).

abilities form the basis of concrete operational logic. During this period, children are also learning to read and write, and their attention span is increasing.

During childhood, storytelling can be used effectively as a means for developing children's abilities to handle basic operations of thinking: observing, comparing, classifying, hypothesizing, organizing, summarizing, applying, and criticizing.[28] Picture storybooks are especially useful in developing observational skills. Children can describe the actions and objects they see depicted in the illustrations. Comparative skills can be developed through comparisons of illustrations in picture books or through comparisons of settings, characters, or actions in stories themselves. Children can develop classification skills through concept books (which introduce color, shape, size, or use), through tales in which classifications emerge, or through classifications of stories themselves or characters within stories. Asking children to predict what a story is about based on its title or cover or asking them to predict the outcome of a story can facilitate development in skills of hypothesizing. Story plots help children develop organizational skills. Chronology is a difficult if not impossible concept for young children. Strong sequential plots allow children to discover the organizational movements of narrative. Having children retell a story reinforces its organizational structure. Especially useful with young children are cumulative tales because they repeat the sequence of events with each new element that is added. Young children should also be given opportunity to evaluate stories at their level, which encourages the development of critical skills. This occurs when children sense the appropriateness, reliability, value, and authenticity of the story.[29]

Of particular importance in facilitating cognitive development through storytelling are the level and type of questioning procedures used to explore stories. The following ordered set of questions is based on developmental changes in story schemata and story structure. The causal inference schema is most appropriate for exploring religious stories with very young children, whereas the social

---

[28]Dorothy Strickland, "Promoting Language and Concept Development,"in *Literature and Young Children*, ed. Bernice Cullinan and Carolyn Carmichael (Urbana, Ill.: National Council of Teachers of English), p. 55.

[29]Donna E. Norton, *Through the Eyes of a Child: An Introduction to Children's Literature* (Columbus, Ohio: Merrill, 1983), p. 14.

inference schema requires more complex thinking, which may emerge as early as middle school. Since, of course, the social inferences depend on the action of the story, reference to the physical causality of the story is appropriate at any level.

A. Causal Inference Schema (What happened)
   1. Most important elements
      When did the story begin? (setting: time)
      Where did the story begin? (setting: time)
      Who was the story about? (setting: characters)
      How did the story begin? (initiating event)
      What event started the story action? (initiating event)
      How did the story end? (resolution)
   2. Supporting details
      What did _____ try to do about _____? (attempts)
      What happened when _____ did _____? (outcomes)
      Then what happened? (sequence of attempts and outcomes)
B. Social Inference Schema (Why it happened)
   1. Most important elements
      What did _____ want? (goal)
      What did _____ want to accomplish in the story? (goal)
   2. Supporting details
      Why did _____ do _____? (internal response)
      What did _____ think/feel to cause _____? (internal response)
      What did _____ want to do then? (internal response)
      How did _____ feel in the end? (reaction)
   3. Character disposition
      What was _____ like? (character trait)
      What did _____ do or say to show what he/she was like?
      (character trait and behavioral consequences)
C. Going Beyond the Story Text
   What was the moral of the story? (implications of story text)
   What was the message the author was trying to tell the reader? (author purpose)
   Do you agree with the author's message? (reader's reaction)
   Do you think the story was true to life? (reader's reaction)
   How does this story relate to your own experiences? (reader's prior knowledge)[30]

---

[30]McConaughy, "Developmental Changes," p. 586.

These questions can be used to facilitate comprehension of any story. At the same time they can foster development in any of a number of emerging cognitive skills in young children. Storytelling and discussion can both affirm abilities of cognition that have already appeared and pose problems that demand resolution through a new development achievement of assimilation or accommodation. These cognitive processes are important factors in children's success in school and adults' success in life. Early experiences with stories provide one way for enhancing the development of these processes and facilitating growth from childhood through adulthood.

Cognitive development in children is an important part of children's ability to develop increasingly sophisticated religious ideas and beliefs. For very young children, religious concepts are practically impossible, limiting religious perception to external events related to personal immediate needs.[31] As children move from preoperational thought to concrete operations, their concrete literalism continues to make teaching conceptual beliefs impractical, if not impossible. Stories, however, do provide a significant way for religious educators to help children learn some of the key cognitive content of religion by connecting narrative information to children's experiences. Even so, in religious education, cognitive goals are appropriately secondary to affective ones in which children learn religious feelings, emotions, attitudes, values, and love.[32]

STORIES AND SOCIAL LEARNING

Learning occurs in a social context in which children develop behaviors, attitudes, beliefs, and values through interaction with their families and culture groups.[33] Children's experiences with primary caregivers, other family members, religious educators, and other significant people affect their sense of self as well as their ability to

---

[31]David J. Ludwig, Timothy Weber, and Douglas Iben, "Letters to God: A Study of Children's Religious Concepts," *Journal of Psychology and Theology* 2 (Winter 1974): 31–35.

[32]See Lucie Barber, *The Religious Education of Preschool Children* (Birmingham, Ala.: Religious Education Press, 1981).

[33]James Michael Lee, *The Flow of Religious Instruction* (Birmingham, Ala.: Religious Education Press, 1973), pp. 60–73.

express emotions, develop empathy, and act compassionately.[34] These early experiences play a powerful role in shaping the personalities of children. The stories children experience are also important elements in social learning in general and in religious learning in particular. Stories, as part of children's social and religious milieu, can help shape their sense of self and facilitate development in religion.

Psychosocial Development

Erik Erikson suggests that children move through four stages of psychosocial development: trust versus mistrust, autonomy versus shame and doubt, initiative versus guilt, and industry versus inferiority.[35] Each stage centers on a crisis that, when successfully completed, provides positive capacities for facing life. The first stage occurs in infancy, beginning with the dependability of the primary caregivers. Children's earliest experiences of provision or neglect will shape their basic capacity to trust. If basic needs are met, children develop a sense of the essential trustworthiness of others and a fundamental sense of their own trustworthiness. This basic sense of trust later in life becomes the basic capacity for religious faith. If children's needs are not met, they develop a sense of mistrust and may become suspicious, withdrawn, and lacking in self-confidence. As James Michael Lee points out, trust is one of the most important favorable attitudes toward God, and trust is essential for mature faith and religious life.[36]

The crisis of the second stage turns on children's ability to exert influence on their own behavior. As children begin to do things on their own, they seek independence. At the same time, the children's

---

[34]Research indicates that children who develop secure attachments with caregivers develop more positive behaviors, are more sociable, independent, and empathic, and show greater self-esteem. Leah Matas, Richard A. Arend, and L. Alan Stroufe, "Continuity of Adaptation in the Second Year: The Relationship between Quality of Attachment and Later Competence," *Child Development* 49 (September 1978): 547–556; Donald L. Pastor, "The Quality of Mother-Infant Attachment and Its Relationship to Toddler's Initial Sociability with Peers," *Developmental Psychology* 17 (May 1981): 323–335; L. Alan Stroufe, "Infant Caregiver Attachments and Patterns of Adaptation in Preschool: The Roots of Maladaptation and Competence," *Minnesota Symposium on Child Psychology*, ed. M. Perlmutter (Hillsdale, N. J..: Erlbaum, 1983), 16: 41–81.

[35]Erik Erikson, *Childhood and Society*, 2d ed. (New York: Norton, 1963).

[36]Lee, *Content of Religious Instruction*, pp. 57–59.

physical, social, and psychological dependence on primary caregivers creates a sense of doubt about the children's ability to exercise their own wills. This doubt is compounded by shame at children's instinctive revolt against their previous dependency. Successful resolution of this crisis leads to a sense of will—children know when and when not to assert themselves. Failure in this stage will lead children to turn against themselves or feel shame about attempts to assert themselves. Such a person may become manipulative, legalistic, and controlling. Thus, religious educators should take care to create a learning environment in which children are encouraged to be active and make decisions rather than sit passively and do only as they are told.

The third crisis of psychosocial development demands that children, who now know they are persons, discover what kind of persons they are. The important developments during this period are especially significant for religious education: language develops so that understanding occurs; increased motor skills result in increased locomotion, and imagination expands. As children begin to explore the world and push out their boundaries, parents' and religious educators' responses to children's newly acquired abilities have much to do with the degree of confidence the children develop. Successfully met, the crisis of initiative versus guilt facilitates development of a sense of purpose. Children are able to take on and succeed at new challenges. Unsuccessfully resolved, this crisis leads to a sense of guilt over goals and acts resulting from newly acquired locomotive skills. In order to assist children in resolving this crisis, religious educators should provide opportunities for children to take initiative using their imaginations, language, and bodies. Stories provide an excellent means for children to make up, tell, and act out experiences in ways that validate their initiative and help them develop a sense of purpose.

The fourth crisis of childhood is closely related to schooling and quite possibly to formal religious instructional settings. Children begin to move outside the bounds of the family and need to discover skills and tools to cope with their environment. During this time, children learn to do meaningful work, applying themselves to skills and tasks, learning the tools and tricks of the trade of the world, and adapting themselves to the work ethic of their world. Resolved successfully, this stage allows children to develop a sense of competence. If it is not resolved, this crisis can create a tendency to avoid developing new skills, satisfaction with minimum productivity, or compulsive working to demonstrate competence. Religious educators can address this crisis by affirming children's growing competencies and by providing opportunities for children to succeed at tasks such as writing letters to missionaries or helping deliver food to a hungry family.

Stories can provide ways by which religious educators can help children deal with these life crises. First, stories allow children to see that their experiences are common to other children and are also natural experiences of childhood. In identifying with characters in stories, children are able to understand their own experiences as a typical part of growing up. Second, stories present options for behavior in dealing with life experiences. Stories can provide a number of examples of ways to deal with problems and thus can promote discussions about appropriate behaviors and responses. Third, stories stimulate a sense of self and self-worth. This function of stories is especially significant for religious instruction and I give it greater attention in the following section.

One of my favorite children's books illustrates how stories can address many of children's psychosocial issues. Beverly Cleary's *Ramona the Pest* (as well as the several other books in her Ramona series) provides direct, concrete examples of the crises children face daily. In this book, Ramona begins school and there confronts issues of autonomy, industry, self-understanding, and relationships. Throughout the story, learners follow the perils and pitfalls of kindergarten and have an opportunity to experience many of their own triumphs and failures in Ramona's story.

Stories and Sense of Self

Empirical research indicates that personal narratives told by adults play a powerful role in childhood social learning.[37] Furthermore, children tend to learn to understand and express who they are through their routine participation in personal storytelling.[38] Three narrative practices seem especially relevant to children's social construction of self: (1) significant adults tell stories about a child in the child's presence; (2) significant adults intervene in a child's storytelling; and (3) children appropriate others' stories as their own.[39]

---

[37]Peggy J. Miller and Barbara B. Moore, "Narrative Conjunctions of Caregiver and Child: A Comparative Perspective on Socialization through Stories" *Ethos* 17 (Dec. 1989): 43–64.

[38]Peggy J. Miller et al., "Narrative Practices and the Social Construction of Self in Childhood," *American Ethnologist* 17 (May 1990): 295.

[39]Ibid., p. 296.

Significant adults often tell stories about a child to another person in the child's presence. These stories serve a number of functions for the child: they provide information about the child and the child's activities, and they convey messages about the significance and organization of the child's experiences. As significant adults selectively tell some stories and not others, they signify which experiences are tellable and, in the telling, reconstruct the experience, demonstrating what the components are, how they relate, and why they are significant.[40] Such narratives thus provide children with models for interpreting their own experiences. This narrative practice is further significant because in it significant adults treat the child as a subject, an actor whose experiences are worth telling. This practice also implies a significant level of intimacy between the child and the adult. Telling stories in the child's presence raises the issue of entitlement to tell stories. Generally, shared experiences are co-owned, giving both parties entitlement to tell the stories. These conditions for joint ownership are more likely to develop in intimate relationships than in nonintimate ones.[41]

Recognizing the importance of telling stories about a child in the child's presence can provide religious educators with an important tool for assisting parents and other adults in facilitating religious instruction for children. Because stories told about the child in the child's presence treat the child as an actor and imply intimacy, these stories can act as a means to build both identity and self-esteem. Through these stories, children can recognize themselves as valued by significant adults and accepted by the culture in which they live. Thus religious educators should encourage adults to tell stories about children in the children's presence and should assist adults in identifying appropriate stories and in developing good techniques for telling these stories. For example, if a child does a good deed, such as helping an elderly neighbor clear leaves from the yard, a parent may tell the story of the yard clearing in the presence of the other parent, a grandparent, or a friend at church, and in the telling of the story the parent may include reference to religious notions of care and concern for others.

The intervention of significant adults in a child's storytelling conveys messages about how to interpret and create accounts of one's

---

[40]Ibid., p. 297.
[41]Ibid., p. 298.

experiences.[42] While affirming the child as an actor with valuable experiences, this practice reinforces the child's status as a child, not yet fully competent to narrate his own experiences. The adult may either collaborate with the child in developing the narrative or offer another perspective on the experience being recounted. Either way, the adult suggests to the child ways to interpret her experience and ways to tell the narrative of the experiences to others. In religious instruction, this practice can also help construct experience within a religious context. For example, a parent may help a child tell a story by asking questions that further the narrative and provide a religious framework for its interpretation. Returning to the example of helping an elderly neighbor clear leaves from the yard, a parent may help the child tell the story by asking questions such as, Why was it important to help Mr. Smith? Or does helping others make God happy?

In a third practice, children appropriate others' stories as their own. Apparently entitlement to tell the story is established by the positing of parallel experiences.[43] In this experience, children enter the story of the other, vicariously reexperiencing the event narrated. The appropriation of another's story makes this reexperiencing explicit. The distinction between the child's experience and the other's is blurred. This process begins with the stories of those in the immediate environment of the child, but once children's access to the stories of others expands, experiences not otherwise available to them become available. "The power of stories to amuse or frighten, anger or excite, rests on a felt overlap with the narrator's recounted experience. When children inhabit environments rich in personal storytelling, they encounter again and again such moments of personal extension. It is not surprising that they come to make narrative-mediated identifications."[44] This practice suggests the importance of personal storytelling in religious instruction. As adults tell their stories of religious living, children can experience these stories and claim them as their own. From adults' stories, children can learn how to live religiously.

Through the stories they hear and tell in the context of personal relationships, children develop a sense of self. They come to understand what their significant experiences are and how to interpret and recount

---

[42]Ibid., p. 302.
[43]Ibid.
[44]Ibid., p. 306.

them. They also learn that they are actors in their own right and persons of value, though they still occupy child status. Through stories, children are also able to experience vicariously both experiences similar to their own and experiences otherwise unavailable to them. In religious instruction, these significant storytelling experiences can help children both understand and express their developing sense of self, particularly as a religious being, as they interact with significant adults in formal and informal religious instruction environments.

Stories and Moral Development

Although much of the research in stages of moral development has been shown to display gender biases,[45] some general characteristics of children's moral growth can be drawn from the work of Jean Piaget and Lawrence Kohlberg. Very early, preschool children begin to develop understandings of right and wrong from their immediate environment.[46] From their primary caregivers, they receive examples of acceptable behavior which they imitate. The physical consequences of actions determine their rightness or wrongness. Avoidance of punishment and deference to power are valued in their own right.

As children move into elementary school, changes occur in their moral development.[47] They begin to develop a sense of equality and fairness and to take into account situations and motives. Their sense of rules becomes more flexible than their original rigidity in regard to codified behaviors. Peers and significant adults outside the family become important factors in moral decision making during this period. Expectations of others are significant norms for determining right behavior. Whereas Kohlberg's research with boys indicates these norms center on issues of fairness and justice, Carol Gilligan's studies indicate that for girls norms of behavior center on relationships and caring.[48] These gender differences are likely related more to social construction than biological predisposition. Of most relevance is the

---

[45]For example, see Carol Gilligan, *In a Different Voice: Psychological Theory and Women's Development* (Cambridge: Harvard University Press, 1982).

[46]Jean Piaget, *The Moral Judgment of the Child*, trans. Marjorie Gabain (New York: Harcourt, Brace, 1932), p. 2.

[47]Lawrence Kohlberg, "Moral and Religious Development in the Public Schools: A Developmental View," in *Religion and Public Education*, ed. T. Sizer (Boston: Houghton Mifflin, 1967), p. 171.

[48]Gilligan, *In a Different Voice*, pp. 24–39.

observation that by early childhood, children have already developed a very strong sense of sex roles.

Stories can facilitate moral development in religious instruction in a number of ways. Stories can provide a means for children to become sensitive to their own and others' feelings. Stories can allow children to look at relationships with family, friends, and significant adults and to explore the feelings and problems associated with those relationships. Stories can also encourage the development of important social and religious skills such as sharing, taking turns, and playing cooperatively. Stories can introduce children to different experiences of the world, thus challenging their rigidly held rules of behavior. And finally, stories can help children develop nonstereotypical understandings of roles and behaviors.

Stories and Gender

Religious instruction provides a significant context for children's ongoing construction of their gender identity. Religious institutions have both explicitly and implicitly contributed to the construction of highly stereotypical notions of gender and have even insisted on the God-ordained enforcement of these roles. Instead of facilitating children's religious growth, such stereotypes have tended to limit available options for girls and boys in cognitive, affective, and lifestyle experiences and expressions.[49] However, religious instruction has the potential to act as a liberating rather than limiting force by challenging sex-role stereotypes and encouraging children to develop into the persons God has created them to be and to become the Christians God has called them to be.

Kohlberg has suggested that children construct sex-role stereotypes as they perceive rules in the world around them. As children begin to construct their gender identity, they increase their same-sex preferences in order to seek out information and behaviors congruent with their gender identity. Their moralization of sex-role stereotypes increases from ages five to eight. These behaviors are highly dependent on social expectations and reinforcements. In studies of the stories children compose and in studies of children's preferences in stories

---

[49]For an excellent resource on gender and gender relations in Christianity, see Mary Steward Van Leeuwen, ed., *After Eden: Facing the Challenge of Gender Reconciliation* (Grand Rapids, Mich.: Eerdmans, 1993).

told to them, researchers have found a high degree of sex-role stereotyping among both boys and girls.[50]

In stories told by children, empirical researchers have noted that the characters, attributes, and actions of the stories reflect sex-role stereotyping. Girls tend to tell more stories about girls, and boys tend to tell more stories about boys, although girls are more likely to tell stories with male characters than boys are likely to tell stories with female characters. Among their characters, girls tend to introduce more friendly characters who offer assistance, whereas boys introduce more aggressive behaviors and attempts to master situations.[51] Stories by both girls and boys tend to portray male characters as more violent in their approaches to conflict and more varied in their occupations, whereas female characters tend to be more traditional in their occupations and less violent in their approaches to conflict.[52] One study notes an interesting developmental change in the assignment of attributes among female story writers. Below grades 5–6, females tend to ascribe more personal and ability traits to male rather than female characters; yet by grades 5–6, the reverse occurs. Researchers Mary Trepanier and Jane Romatowski suggest that girls moving toward the identity development of adolescence have a stronger sense of self-awareness and awareness of characteristics of others like themselves and thus assign more personal and ability traits to female characters.[53]

Studies also indicate sex-role stereotyping in children's preferences and responses to stories. Girls tend to prefer stories with female characters and feminine activities and least prefer stories with male characters and masculine activities; the reverse is true for boys. The second preference for both boys and girls centers on the sex

---

[50]Marion H. Libby and Elizabeth Aries, "Gender Differences in Preschool Children's Narrative Fantasy," *Psychology of Women Quarterly* 13 (December 1989): 293–306; and Mary L. Trepanier and Jane A. Romatowski, "Attributes and Roles Assigned to Characters in Children's Writing: Sex Differences and Sex-Role Perceptions," *Sex Roles* 13 (September 1985): 263–272.

[51]Libby, "Gender Differences," p. 300

[52]Kate Pierce and Emily D. Edwards, "Children's Construction of Fantasy Stories: Gender Differences in Conflict Resolution Strategies," *Sex Roles* 18 (April 1988): 393–404.

[53]Trepanier and Romatowski, "Attributes and Roles," p. 271.

appropriateness of the activity rather than the sex of the character.[54] Another study found gender differences in the emotions children attribute to characters with whom they identify. Boys tend to attribute more anger to themselves more frequently than girls, whereas girls tend to attribute more sadness and fear to themselves more frequently than boys. Also, boys' first responses to the stories typically were more intensely angry and more intensely happy than were girls' first responses.[55]

Since sex-role stereotyping is constructed out of social interactions, stories in religious instruction can provide one means for reinforcing or challenging such stereotypes.[56] Stories that offer nonstereotyped sex roles can offer positive models for boys and girls and can act as powerful stimuli for helpful discussions about sex roles. What seems to be needed in religious instruction is stories that depict both boys and girls, as well as men and women, engaging in nonstereotypical activities. For example, a story being used to teach children to share may feature girls playing with matchbox cars or a story being used to teach children to help others may show a boy helping his father prepare dinner for the family. Another story may feature a woman minister or a male nursery worker. By utilizing stories that challenge stereotypical gender notions, religious educators can help children expand their experiences and options and can prepare them to be more well-rounded, capable adults.

Stories and Religious Thinking

Influenced primarily by the work of Jean Piaget in cognitive development, pioneering work in children's religious thinking[57] was done by

---

[54]Jerri Jaudon Kropp and Charles F. Halverson, "Preschool Children's Preferences and Recall for Stereotypes Versus Nonstereotyped Stories," *Sex Roles* 9 (February 1983): pp. 261–272.

[55]Leslie R. Brody, "Sex and Age Variations in the Quality and Intensity of Children's Emotional Attributions to Hypothetical Situations," *Sex Roles* 11 (July 1984): 51–59.

[56]For more on the construction of gender, see Ellyn Kaschak, *Engendered Lives: A New Psychology of Women's Experience* (New York: Basic, 1992). For an excellent resource on gender in education, see Ann Diller et al., *The Gender Question in Education: Theory, Pedagogy, and Politics* (Boulder, Colo.: Westview, 1996).

[57]The form of thinking described here could more correctly be labeled "theological thinking" because it focuses primarily on cognitive activity about God rather than

David Elkind in the United States and Ronald Goldman in England.[58] Using Piaget's categories, their research indicates that the development of children's religious thinking follows along the same lines of cognitive development described by Piaget, and that mental ability and age are more significant factors affecting the development of children's religious thinking than are specifically religious variables such as church attendance or Bible reading.[59] Their findings suggest that religious instruction in the cognitive domain can be effective only within the framework of developmentally appropriate substantive and structural contents. Because young children are unable to deal with abstractions necessary for theological and religious reflection, religious instruction must move its focus from abstract concepts to an emphasis on children's experience, and religious instruction must develop models for teaching children that are appropriate to the cognitive abilities of the child. Thus, for example, instead of attempting to teach children about abstractions such as sin, grace, or redemption, religious educators should attempt to teach children to share, to be kind, to help others. Sharing, being kind, and helping others are all religious ideals that can be embodied in children's concrete experiences and are therefore appropriate to children's cognitive abilities.

Recognizing that religious thinking is only one aspect of religiosity, other researchers have begun to explore the personal commitment and application of religious thinking in terms of faith. Of particular note is

---

with God. Since, however, the researchers referenced in this section used the term "religious thinking" to describe their work, I shall likewise use that term in this section.

[58]David Elkind, "The Child's Conception of His Religious Denomination: I, The Jewish Child," *Journal of Genetic Psychology* 99 (1961): 209–225; David Elkind, "The Child's Conception of His Religious Denomination: II, The Catholic Child," *Journal of Genetic Psychology* 101 (1962): 185–193; David Elkind, "The Child's Conception of His Religious Denomination: III, The Protestant Child," *Journal of Genetic Psychology* 103 (1963): 291–304; David Elkind, *The Child's Reality: Three Developmental Themes* (Hillsdale, N. J.: Erlbaum, 1978); Ronald Goldman, *Religious Thinking from Childhood to Adolescence* (New York: Seabury, 1968); Ronald Goldman, *Readiness for Religion: A Basis for Developmental Religious Education* (London: Routledge and Kegan Paul, 1965).

[59]Ibid. See also B. A. Kingan, *A Study of Some Factors Hindering the Religious Education of a Group of Primary School Children* (MEd thesis, University of Liverpool, 1969).

the work mentioned earlier of James Fowler.[60] Although limited and debatable at numerous points, particularly at Fowler's delineation of faith as a cognitive activity, Fowler's stages of faith offer some images of the cognitive issues of faith that people address at particular junctures in their lives.[61] These stages actually begin with a prestage of undifferentiated faith in which experiences of trust, hope, and love are fused. The fund of basic trust that emerges during this stage becomes the basis for the faith that develops later.

Intuitive-projective faith begins around age two with the convergence of thought and language. This convergence allows the use of verbal symbols in speech and ritual play to help children organize their sensory experience in meaningful ways. During this time, children combine fragments of stories and images given to them by their cultures into their own clusters of associations dealing with God and the sacred. The imagination has a significant role to play in intuitive-projective faith. Children are beginning to grasp and unify their experiences through images and stories that reflect their intuitive understanding and feelings toward the world, and they are responsive to stories that capture and stimulate their imaginations. Negatively, religious instruction can exploit children's imaginations by emphasizing images of sin, hell, and the devil. Positively, religious instruction can provide quality images and stories that stimulate and guide children's imaginations. At this point, religious educators do not need to worry about the orthodoxy of children's images and stories. Their faith is filled with fantasy, and their imaginative processes are not governed by logic. Rather, religious instruction needs to provide a place in which children's images can be expressed and valued as they are formed. These early images are often long lasting and influential in learners' later lives.

Transition to mythic-literal faith occurs with the emergence of concrete operational thought. Mythic-literal children begin to differentiate between what is real and what is make-believe. Of special significance is the emergence of their ability to create stories as ways of finding

---

[60]James Fowler, *Stages of Faith: The Psychology of Human Development and the Quest for Meaning* (San Francisco: Harper and Row, 1981).

[61]A particularly useful exploration and critique of Fowler's theory is Craig Dykstra and Sharon Parks, ed., *Faith Development and Fowler* (Birmingham, Ala.: Religious Education Press, 1988).

and giving coherence to their experiences, though they cannot yet generalize life meanings from their stories. These children also begin to appropriate the stories, beliefs, and observances that symbolize belonging to their particular communities. Beliefs and symbols are accepted literally, as are moral rules and attitudes. Transition to synthetic-conventional faith, which generally occurs around adolescence, results from contradictions in experiences and stories that lead to reflections on meanings. This transition is made possible by the advent of formal operational thought.

Fowler's descriptions of children's cognitive growth in faith make evident the significance of narrative in the development of the cognitive component of children's faith. The stories and images of the faith community provide stimulants for the religious imagination of children, as well as sources of identity for children to appropriate as members of the faith community. The ability to generate narratives allows children to begin to give coherence to their experience and to bind their experiences together in meaningful ways.[62]

The stories adults tell children that are most meaningful seem to be the ones that relate to the experiences of the child. Although Goldman suggests that young children need not be taught theological or religious concepts, research indicates that children, given something familiar to their experience, can discover some general meaning applicable to themselves in religious stories.[63] Other empirical researchers have suggested that biblical stories can be told to young children together with mythologies of other religious traditions to help them begin to experience the unity of the religious experience of humanity.[64] Another empirical researcher, on the other hand, has insisted on the importance of story as an art form that creates images rather than concepts and requires imagination rather than cognition to create meaning.[65]

---

[62]For a helpful resource on imagination and education, see Kieran Egan, *Imagination in Teaching and Learning: The Middle School Years* (Chicago: University of Chicago Press, 1992).

[63]Kenneth E. Hyde, *Religion in Childhood and Adolescence* (Birmingham, Ala.: Religious Education Press, 1990), p. 118.

[64]F. D. Doran, *Myth, Bible, and Religious Education* (Ph.D. Thesis, University of Exeter, 1978).

[65]Jack. G. Priestly, "Concepts with Blurred Edges: Story and the Religious Imagination," *Religious Education* 78 (Summer 1983): 377–389.

Stories capture and stimulate the imagination and provide experiences of enchantment and wonder. Children's developmental characteristics certainly affect their level of understanding of a story, but their inability to grasp its full implications from an adult perspective should not preclude religious stories that have layers of meaning beyond the intellectual grasp of children simply on that basis. Rather, stories should be told, including those from scripture and the religious tradition of the children's faith community, that reflect experiences relevant to the children.[66] Whenever children are able to identify with a character of an action of the story, they are able to learn something from the story. Bible stories should not be told, however, to children as if they are different from other stories. The literalism demanded by many religious educators who tell children these stories often becomes an obstacle for children as they move into formal operational thought and reject these stories as "mythological" or "not true." If children are allowed to experience Bible stories as an art form, then they are later able to appreciate the truths of the stories.

Children are able to respond to God in developmentally appropriate ways, and the stories they experience engage their imaginations in ways that open them to the mystery, enchantment, and wonder that they will later be able to name God. Although their cognitive structures are certainly involved in their developing faith, these structures are not the whole of faith, which demands response and commitment in addition to cognition. Stories can encourage children toward developmentally appropriate response and can create an openness and ongoing receptivity to the stories and experiences of faith that are relevant to their lives.

Stories and Affectivity

Religious instruction in the affective domain is essential in teaching religious living.[67] The affective content of religious instruction teaches feelings, emotions, values, attitudes, and love, which tend to be more powerful motivators of religious living than cognitive

---

[66]One study indicates that young children are able to remember more details from a story if the story is based on events familiar to them. Judith Hudson and Katherine Nelson, "Effects of Script Structure on Children's Story Recall," *Developmental Psychology* 19 (July 1983): 525–635.

[67]James Michael Lee, *The Content of Religious Instruction* (Birmingham, Ala.: Religious Education Press, 1985), pp. 196–257.

contents such as information, knowledge, or understanding.[68] Piaget himself claims that while cognition supplies essential developmental structures, affect provides the motivational energy.[69] Furthermore, he argues, needs and values motivate action.[70] Current researchers assert that emotion systems seem to guide thought and action.[71] Consequently, because of the primary affective nature of stories, narratives can play an important role in children's emotional development and growth in religious living.

Children's affective lives are evident already in infancy.[72] As infants grow into toddlers and preschoolers, they also grow affectively, developing toward more complex emotional relationships, more varied, complex, and flexible ways of expressing emotions, better control of emotions, more ability to reflect on their own emotions and the emotions of others, representation of emotions through language and play, and linking individual emotions to culturally valued skills and standards.[73]

In young children, pretend play is important in developing emotional competence.[74] One study found that toddlers are most expres-

---

[68]Ibid., p. 205.

[69]Jean Piaget, *Intelligence and Affectivity: Their Relationship during Child Development*, trans. T. A. Brown and C. E. Kaegi (Palo Alto, Cal.: Annual Reviews, 1981), p. 5. See also Dante Cicchetti and Petra Hesse, "Affect and Intellect: Piaget's Contributions to the Study of Infant Emotional Development," *Emotion: Theory, Research, and Experience: Vol. 2, Emotions in Early Development,* ed. Robert Plutchik and Henry Kellerman (New York: Academic Press, 1983), pp. 115–170.

[70]Jean Piaget, *Six Psychological Studies* (New York: Random, 1967), p. 6.

[71]See, for example, Gordan H. Bower, "Mood and Memory," *American Psychologist* 36 (February 1981): 129–148; J. J. Camps, et al., "Socioemotional Development," *Handbook of Child Psychology: Vol. 2, Infancy and Developmental Psychobiology,* ed. P. H. Mussen (New York: Wiley, 1983), pp. 783–915.

[72]Carol E. Izard and Carol Z. Malatesta, "Perspectives on Emotional Development I: Differential Emotions Theory of Early Emotional Development," in *Handbook of Infant Development*, 2d ed., ed. J. D. Osofsky (New York: Wiley, 1987), pp. 494–554; Carol Z. Malatesta, "The Role of Emotions in the Development and Organization of Personality," in *Socioemotional Development*, ed. R. A. Thompson (Lincoln: University of Nebraska Press, 1988), pp. 1–56.

[73]Marion C. Hyson, *The Emotional Development of Young Children: Building an Emotion- Centered Curriculum* (New York: Teachers College Press, 1994), p. 59.

[74]Carolyn Saarni defines emotional competence as "the demonstration of self-efficacy in emotion-eliciting social transactions," and she enumerates eight skills of emotional competence: (1). "awareness of one's emotional state, including the possibility

sive of emotions during pretend play.[75] Pretend play, as well as other creative outlets such as drawing, painting, and music, allow children to express feelings and to learn culturally appropriate ways of dealing with emotions.[76] Religious educators can use stories as a framework to help young children pretend, for example, to be characters in a story, such as the biblical story of David and Goliath, and to express the emotions those characters may feel. Children may also draw or paint a scene from a story, expressing the emotions they experience in the scene.

Emotions that are acquired in infancy and early childhood are refined in preschool and elementary years.[77] In this phase, children learn culturally appropriate ways to express their emotions, learning to laugh rather than jump up and down or connecting emotional

---

that one is experiencing multiple emotions, and at even more mature levels, awareness that one might also not be consciously aware of one's feelings due to unconscious dynamics of selective inattention" (2). "ability to discern others' emotions, based on situational and expressive cues that have some degree of cultural consensus as to their emotional meaning" (3). "ability to use the vocabulary of emotion and expression terms commonly available in one's (sub)culture and at more mature levels to acquire cultural scripts that link emotion with social roles" (4). "capacity for empathic and sympathetic involvement in others' emotional experiences" (5). "ability to realize that an inner emotional state need not correspond to outer expression, both in oneself and in others, and at more mature levels, the ability to understand that one's emotional-expressive behavior may impact on another and to take this into account in one's self-presentation strategies" (6). "capacity for adaptive coping with aversive or distressing emotions by using self-regulatory strategies that ameliorate the intensity or temporal duration of such emotional states (e.g., 'stress hardiness')" (7). "awareness that the structure or nature of relationships is in part defined by the quality of emotional communication within the relationship" (8). "capacity for emotional self-efficacy: The individual views her or himself as feeling, overall, the way he or she wants to feel." Carolyn Saarni, "Emotional Competence and Self-Regulation in Childhood," in *Emotional Development and Emotional Intelligence: Educational Implications*, ed. Peter Salovey and David J. Sluyter (New York: Basic, 1997) pp. 38–59.

[75]Judy Dunn and Jane Brown, "Relationships, Talk about Feelings, and the Development of Affect Regulation in Early Childhood," in *The Development of Emotion Regulation and Dysregulation*, ed. Judy Garber and Kenneth A. Dodge (New York: Cambridge University Press, 1991), pp. 89–108.

[76]Hyson, *Emotional Development of Young Children*, p. 154.

[77]Jeannette Haviland-Jones, Janet L. Gebelt, and Janice C. Stapley, "The Questions of Development in Emotion," in *Emotional Development and Emotional Intelligence*, pp. 235–240.

responses to new contexts and people. These refinements allow children to minimize expressions, exaggerate them, or cover them with other signals (as in smiling to cover disappointment). Such containment and enhancement strategies bring emotions into conformity with cultural expectations.[78]

Stories can offer important models of emotional competence, facilitating acquisition of emotions and refinement of emotional expression in children. Stories can teach children emotions by helping them experience and name a wide variety of emotions. Furthermore, stories can enable religious living by helping children express emotions in healthy ways that motivate and empower action. In particular, stories can allow children access to situations, emotions, and emotional experiences that are not common in their everyday experience.[79] Movies and television shows, in particular, provide narrative forms in which emotional content is easily decoded by children.[80]

Stories and Experiential Faith

Religious educator Bailey Gillespie argues that most of what religious educators think they are teaching young children in religious instruction is at best ineffective. Because very young children do not have the cognitive capability to synthesize and think logically they are not able to develop a conceptual knowledge of God. Yet many (if not most) religious instruction programs for children are primarily cognitive in nature. Gillespie argues that what can be most effective in the religious instruction of young children, then, is not cognitive content but faith experiences.[81]

Gillespie calls the faith of early childhood "borrowed," suggesting that the faith of young children is largely determined by the lives and actions of people who are significant to the child (Religious educator Bruce Powers names this phase "experienced faith").[82] Gillespie

---

[78]Ibid., p. 238.

[79]Aimee Dorr, "Contexts for Experience with Emotion, with Special Attention to Television," in *The Socialization of Emotions*," ed. Michael Lewis and Carolyn Saarni (New York: Plenum, 1985), pp. 60–61.

[80]Ibid., p. 68.

[81]Bailey Gillespie, *The Experience of Faith* (Birmingham, Ala.: Religious Education Press, 1988), p. 92.

[82] Bruce P. Powers, *Growing Faith* (Nashville: Broadman, 1982), p. 41.

suggests that even more important than telling the Christian story to young children is living the story with children.[83] In addition to adults' modeling of Christian living for children, significant adults, especially parents, can help children live the Christian story through the religious rituals that embody the story—worship, prayer, holiday celebrations. In these rituals, children participate directly in faith experiences that lay the groundwork for mature commitment later in life. Through storytelling in its many forms—oral telling, reading aloud, drama, film and video, visual art—young children can begin to learn their heritage in the community of faith and begin to sense their own importance in that heritage.[84] The concern for religious educators for young children is not that they form "right thinking" but rather that they find the faith community a place where they are welcomed, integrated, and valued—a place that provides a milieu for optimum growth in faith.[85]

Gillespie calls the faith of elementary aged children "reflected faith." Children's faith during this time is still somewhat borrowed, but developmental changes toward industry, individuation, differentiation, and personality lead toward children's owning of faith. In this phase, growth in faith comes as children accept challenges and learn to negotiate them successfully.[86] Powers describes this stage as "affiliative faith."[87] Children begin to internalize the faith and patterns of religious living they experience in the community around them and begin to reflect those back in their own attitudes, values, and behaviors.

Storytelling can be especially effective during this stage of childhood. Stories employ the imagination and the emotions and thus can teach the experiential and affective content of faith in the family and faith community, although the abstract cognitive content of faith may be beyond their grasp. The stories of Christian faith, in particular, teach children the attitudes, values, and behaviors of Christian living and help create a supportive and pervasive context in which children can experience themselves as part of God's community. For example, the biblical story of Jesus and the little boy who offers Jesus his fish

---

[83]Gillespie, *Experience of Faith*, p. 93.

[84]Ibid., p. 103.

[85]Daniel O. Aleshire, *Faithcare: Ministering to All God's People through the Ages of Life* (Philadelphia: Westminster, 1988), p.112.

[86]Gillespie, *Experience of Faith*, p. 111.

[87]Powers, *Growing Faith*, p. 42.

and loaves can help children learn that children have an important role to play in the faith community, and it can teach them the Christian value of sharing.

STORYTELLING WITH CHILDREN

Although I have already discussed a number of storytelling procedures, the developmental characteristics of children have specific implications for storytelling experiences with children. These characteristics also have implications for the ways religious educators use storytelling with children in religious instruction.

Because stories are significant in children's religious development, children need to experience stories. Stories help them internalize language patterns, develop intellectually, discover social roles, and grow in religious faith and morality. Religious educators can play an important role in providing children with access to stories through telling, reading, and dramatizing stories for children. Religious educators can also facilitate children's experiences with stories by talking about stories with children. In particular, religious educators can use their knowledge of story grammar to help children experience stories and remember the important elements in them.[88] Religious educators can use discussion to emphasize important aspects of the story; they can allow children opportunities to predict story information both before and during the story; they can ask questions that allow children to synthesize information and detect significant relationships in the story; they can encourage children to relate their personal experiences to the experiences of the characters; and they can create opportunities for children to retell stories.[89] By using such applications of story

---

[88]Maribeth Cassidy Schmitt and David G. O'Brien, "Story Grammars: Some Cautions about the Translation of Research into Practice," *Reading Research and Instruction* 26 (Fall 1986): p. 5.

[89]Research indicates that children learn language and syntax from the original version of a story and then follow that language and syntax in their retelling. The richer the original story, the richer the retelling. Hade, "Children, Stories, and Narrative Transformations," p. 320. In research related to children's retelling of written narratives, Rosen, then, argues that which stories are read to children do matter, and Rosenblatt contends that the text serves as a pattern for the child in retelling the story. Harold Rosen, "The Importance of Story," *Language Arts* 63 (March 1986): 226–237; Louise. M. Rosenblatt, *The Reader, the Text, the Poem: Transactional Theory of the Literary Work* (Carbondale, Ill.: Southern Illinois University Press, 1978).

grammar consistently and systematically with children, religious educators can help children internalize a strategy for dealing with the content of stories.[90]

Children also need opportunities in religious instruction to tell their own stories—stories of their life experiences, retold stories, stories they have made up, stories that have manifest or latent religious content. To lead children into storytelling, religious educators may first need to model storytelling and then help children develop their storytelling abilities by discussing good storytelling, having children act out a story, or having children draw scenes to tell a story. Personal stories are usually easiest for children to tell, since the basic elements of the story are readily available to them. In religious instruction, such stories may include telling of a time when they showed love to another person or a time when they helped their parents. Family stories also provide a good basis from which children can tell their own stories. Religious educators can stimulate children's family stories by suggesting that they recall an interaction with a family member or a special holiday.

Once children have learned to tell personal stories, they are ready to retell stories they have heard and liked. In this context stories work best that have a clearly defined main character, a relatively simple and straightforward plot, and a style which does not call for subtlety in interpretation.[91] Often folk stories or Bible stories, which originated in oral tradition, are good places for beginning storytellers to start. From retold tales, children may move on to original stories that express important facets of religious living for them. Sometimes creating an original story with a group in religious instruction offers a way for children to see how original stories are constructed. During this process, guidance from the religious educator is especially significant in helping children develop well-rounded stories with beginning, characters, atmosphere, action, conflict, resolution, and ending. Providing an appropriate religious instruction environment in which children can tell their stories is important as well. Group size, seating arrangement, and session length are all considerations in planning a storytelling event for children. Through these storytelling experiences, children can

---

[90]Schmitt, "Story Grammar," p. 6.

[91]Leland B. Jacobs, "Successful Storytelling," *Early Years* 15 (December 1984): 76.

develop their vocabulary and grammar of religious language and their facility in religious narrative, strengthen their sense of self, develop greater self-esteem, and give coherence and expression to their experiences of the world.

Thus experiences of hearing, telling, and dramatizing stories are incredibly significant for the religious instruction of children. Stories used in religious instruction should avoid abstract religious concepts and focus instead on life experiences relevant to children. Appropriate stories can provide models of behavior for children and help them cope with emotions and problems that arise in their lives. These life experiences can be brought into dialogue with the Christian story and the Christian experience in developmentally appropriate ways. Religious educator Marion Pardy suggests that the telling and teaching of the Christian story to children is analogous to teaching them their ancestral family: "Initially, children experience key members through visits, telephone calls, and/or letters, initiated by adults. Later through question of discussion they learn the meaning of names, 'Aunt Mary' (father's sister) or 'Grandpa' (mother's father). During this time they become conscious of stories about relatives living and dead (the emigration from another country, the pioneering, the tragedies, the jokes, and so forth) and eventually become conscious that these people and stories have molded the lives of their parents and are shaping their lives. Some stories are exaggerated (for example, an extraordinary tale that becomes embellished with each generation to illustrate the obstinancy of great-great-grandma); some are exciting; some are boring; all are a part of one's ancestral story. Some stories are not related to children until they are old enough to understand motive and circumstances; others are freely narrated before they fully comprehend the words. Later, children become aware that other families have their own stories. Ideally, they learn that their 'family tree' story is not better than another's but different, and because it is different, ritual activity and behavior may differ or be simply based on different stories. Children should encounter the Judaeo-Christian story through a similar mode."[92]

What is most significant in telling the Christian story to children is its context in the faith community. In the faith community, children

---

[92]Marion Pardy, *Teaching Children the Bible: New Models in Christian Education* (San Francisco: Harper and Row, 1988), p. 116.

experience the enactment of the Christian story long before they grasp its cognitive components. Children already participate in the story. The faith community allows children to see adults appropriating the Christian story and dealing with its complexities and ambiguities in the midst of their life experiences. This powerful modeling and appropriation of the Christian story invites children to participate in faith as a part of life and to participate in the Christian story as an integral part of their growing faith.

Religious educators should help the faith community be aware of how it uses the Christian story in its dealings with children. Bible stories should not be told to foster literal acceptance of historical data or moralistic behaviors based on traits wrenched from inappropriate use of a text. The Christian story should not be told to push children toward a conversion experience or to coerce them to adopt particular interpretations and theological propositions. Rather, Bible stories should be selected with children and their developmental needs and abilities in mind. The actions of the stories should be relevant to the experiences of children, and their experiences of the stories should be valued in their own right. Children's primary experiences of the stories of the Christian community will be affective—evoking feeling, emotions, and values—and behavioral, providing models for religious living. The focus of religious instruction for children should be here rather than on literal, moralistic interpretations that will not fit with the world children come to experience later in life.

Storytelling connected to children's developmental needs and abilities is a powerful religious instruction experience. When intentionally connected to the life of the faith community and the Christian story, storytelling experiences help children learn religious living. Through the stories they experience, children grow linguistically, cognitively, affectively, socially, morally, and religiously; through the narratives they experience and live, they experience God in their own developmentally appropriate ways. Early in the lives of children, religious educators can begin to enable Christian living by telling children stories and by inviting children to tell their own stories. The faith community context provides its own distinct hermeneutic, which reminds children that they are part of a living tradition of faith handed down through lives and stories. Although children will not fully comprehend the meaning of the stories they hear or the community which nurtures them, they will form long lasting images, feelings, and commitments growing out of the living narrative of which they are a part.

15

Adolescents and Storytelling

"Who are you?" asked the Caterpillar.
This was not an encouraging opening for a conversation.
Alice replied, rather shyly, "I—I hardly know, sir, just at pre-
sent—at least I know who I was when I got up this morning, but I
think I must have changed several times since then."[1]
—Lewis Carroll

I once spoke at a youth rally in Southern California. This is how I began: "When I was a teenager, I had to ride the big, old yellow bus to school each day. Occasionally, I'd run late and miss the bus, and my mother would have to take me to school in the car. Along the way, she always told me the same story. She'd say, 'When I was your age, I didn't have a mother who would drive me to school in a car. I had to walk six miles, rain or snow, uphill, with holes in my shoes to get to school.' It was during those rides that I learned a very important lesson: you can't believe everything adults tell you."

The religious education of adolescents may well be one of the most difficult tasks of the church. When dealing with the turmoil of adolescence, adults, even religious educators, may find themselves exasperated. Youth may not always listen to or believe parents or religious educators, and parents and religious educators may find themselves in desperation repeating the well-intentioned but useless cliches of their own adolescence: "If everybody else was going to jump off a building,

---

[1]Lewis Carroll, *Alice in Wonderland* (New York: Book Craft Guild, n.d.), p. 46.

would you jump too?" "Just wait until you have children of your own." "These are the best years of your life." "Nice girls don't telephone boys."

In addressing the teenagers at that youth rally, I talked to them about some of these fallacies of adolescence. They rolled their eyes with knowing recognition as I named each fallacy. In response to each fallacy, I told a Bible story—about people who did not look like everyone else, about families that did not get along, about people who faced peer pressure, and even about people who made big sexual mistakes. These stories held up a mirror before the adolescents at the youth rally in which they could see some part of themselves. Instead of finding yet another set of do's and don'ts, these teenagers were able to find themselves in the stories they heard that night.

Adolescents' search for identity offers religious educators an inestimable opportunity to help young people construct a Christian identity for themselves, and narratives can serve excellently as mirrors of identity for teenagers. I first fell in love with literature when I was in high school. Jim Moss, my tenthth grade English teacher, sent me home with a copy of *The Grapes of Wrath*, and from that story I learned what communion looks like in the world beyond the church walls. The stories I heard at youth camp, in Sunday school, in sermons, and in my own reading of Scripture became part of the identity I was shaping as a Christian and became embodied in the ways I began to choose to live in the world.

STORIES AND ADOLESCENT COGNITION

Especially significant to adolescents' understanding of story is the emergence of formal operation thought, which usually begins around eleven or twelve years of age and becomes firmly established by age fifteen.[2] Although not all adolescents achieve this stage, formal operations characterize the thought processes of most teenagers. A particularly significant aspect of formal operational thought is hypothetical-deductive reasoning. This form of cognition allows adolescents to move beyond the concrete to the abstract. Concrete operational thinkers think about objects, but formal operational thinkers are able to think about

---

[2]Gary L. Sapp, "Adolescent Thinking and Understanding," in *Handbook of Youth Ministry* (Birmingham, Ala.: Religious Education Press, 1991), p. 74.

ideas, concepts, abstractions. Thus they can think not only of what is but also of what might be. This ability allows them to develop hypotheses and explore them systematically. Furthermore, adolescents are able to make generalizations beyond their immediate experiences and environment. This awareness of what might be can even influence adolescents to reflect critically on their religious understandings.[3]

Formal operational thought also paves the way for further language development in adolescence. Adolescents become proficient in understanding and using abstract words. They also become capable of understanding metaphor, simile, irony, and sarcasm.[4] These developments allow adolescents to experience stories in new and rich ways as they bring their new critical skills to bear on story listening and storytelling.

Whereas concrete operational children summarize or retell stories they hear, formal operational adolescents are able to analyze stories and generalize about their meanings. Both of these processes demand the ability to go beyond the information given in the story. Analysis has to do with the structure of the story, in terms of its images and symbols. Children, on the one hand, will order a narrative into categories based on concrete attributes. Adolescents, however, will attempt to ascertain the reasons behind the characteristics. The focus shifts to how a story might have been structured in addition to how it actually is structured.[5] Consequently, adolescents develop aesthetic criteria for responding to a story, and they also turn their powers of analysis on their own personal responses to stories. An ability to consider cause and effect also develops as adolescents begin to explore connections between the structural characteristics of the story and the responses (interest or tedium) they had to it.[6]

Generalization has to do with the meaning rather than the structure of a story. It involves adolescents' understanding of the world through the story rather than simply their understanding of the story itself.[7]

---

[3]Ibid., p. 75.

[4]David Elkind and Irving B. Weiner, *Development of the Child* (New York: Wiley, 1978), p. 541; David Elkind, *Child Development and Education: A Piagetian Perspective* (New York: Oxford University Press, 1976), pp. 179–180.

[5]Arthur N. Applebee, *The Child's Concept of Story: Ages Two to Seventeen* (Chicago: University of Chicago Press, 1978), p. 109.

[6]Ibid., p. 112.

[7]Ibid., p. 110.

Generalization is the last process to emerge in formal operational thought regarding stories and usually appears around sixteen years of age. In this process, adolescents form abstract statements about the theme or meaning of the story. Although analysis may occur in isolation from generalization, generalization usually depends on analysis as its base for coming to a sense of the story's meaning. These two complementary processes allow older adolescents to construct implications from a story that transcend the specifics of the story itself. They understand that a story is a representation of one way life might be understood rather than a presentation of life as it is.[8]

Given their abilities to analyze and generalize, adolescents are ready to move into new relationships with stories. They are able to move beyond the concrete facts of the story to explore the structure of the story, the story's multiple meanings, and their own personal, subjective responses to the story. These abilities have important consequences for the ways religious educators use stories with adolescents. No longer, for example, can the Bible stories of childhood simply be retold. Critique of these stories must become a part of the religious instruction of adolescents. If youth are not allowed, encouraged, and aided in analyzing and generalizing in relation to Bible stories, they may find the stories simply untenable and dismiss them along with Santa Claus and the Easter Bunny. Religious educators should be aware of adolescents' developing analytical skills and facilitate the use of those skills in religious instruction. If encouraged to bring their new critical abilities to the biblical text, adolescents may be able to develop a greater understanding of the biblical stories.

Beyond Bible stories, adolescents' ability to analyze and to generalize also affects religious educators' choices about other stories to be utilized in religious instruction. Adolescents demand more depth to the stories they hear; they are more aesthetically critical of stories; and they will need more options for in-depth discussions of stories and explorations of their meanings.

Hearing and telling stories has often been confined to the religious instruction of children; yet storytelling has an important role to play for adolescents as well. Research has found a relationship between religious experience and creative arts. For example, one researcher

---

[8]Ibid., p. 125.

found that stories such as myths, legends, and sagas can provide ways for young people to recognize religious experiences and to cope with them.[9] Developing an understanding of the spiritual life is intimately connected to the development of the imaginative life, especially as the imagination is guided into creative forms of activity.[10] The link between creativity and spirituality provides an important reason for religious educators to use storytelling to facilitate development in adolescents.[11] For adolescents, storytelling can move away from simply the story itself toward the realities the story suggests, and response to story can move from simple engagement with characters and actions to changes within the self that result from learners' experiences with a story. For example, adolescents can understand Aslan the lion as a Christ figure in C. S. Lewis's *The Chronicles of Narnia*, and they can connect the character and actions of Aslan with their own experiences with Christ. Thus their encounter with Aslan in the story can facilitate both an affective response to Christ as well as deeper understandings of Christ. Whereas for children, *The Lion, the Witch, and the Wardrobe* (the first book of the *Chronicles*) is an exciting tale of Aslan's conflict with the White Witch, for adolescents the story functions also a reminder of the life, death, and resurrection of Christ and an invitation for them to respond to the risen Christ.

STORIES AND ADOLESCENT
PSYCHOSOCIAL DEVELOPMENT

Adolescents are developing in significant psychosocial ways that affect how religious educators use storytelling with youth. Young people are searching for identity and adopting the conventional morality and faith of their culture. They are developing more complex social roles and making more complicated and stressful decisions about their lives.[12] These issues offer religious educators numerous opportunities

---

[9]E. A. Robinson, "The Necessity for Dream: Religious Education and the Imagination," *Learning for Living* 14 (1975): 194–197.

[10]Kenneth E. Hyde, "Adolescents and Religion," in *Handbook of Youth Ministry*, ed. Donald Ratcliff and James E. Davies (Birmingham, Ala.: Religious Education Press, 1991), p. 126.

[11]Ibid.

[12]Sally L. Archer, "An Overview," in *Interventions for Adolescent Identity Development*, ed. Sally L. Archer (Thousand Oaks, Calif.: Sage, 1994), pp. 3–5.

to connect with the lives of adolescents through storytelling and to provide adolescents opportunities to deal with their issues through watching, enacting, hearing, telling, and discussing stories.

Stories and Adolescent Identity

Erik Erikson describes the psychosocial crisis of adolescence and identity versus role confusion.[13] Adolescence, according to Erikson, is a psychological stage between childhood and adulthood that is characterized by the mind of the moratorium, a space between childhood morality and adult ethics.[14] The primary concern of adolescents is developing self-identity. This task is accomplished in adolescence in two primary ways: youth compare the self they see in the eyes of others with the self they feel they are, and they experiment with personal choices related to identity. In response to drastic physiological changes and the uncertainty of their future adult roles, adolescents usually become overly concerned with establishing what appear to be terminal rather than transitory identity formations.

Feminist scholars point out that the identity development of adolescent girls is perhaps not best described by words typically used in describing psychological maturity—autonomy, separation, independence. Rather, these scholars suggest, young women develop a sense of self as a self-in-relation. In other words, the self is organized in relationships.[15] The growth of identity in late adolescence in particular is characterized by increased potential for mutually empathic relationships, the capacity to allow relationships to change, the ability to work through conflicts in relationships while continuing to value the emotional connection, and the capacity to feel empowered as a result of one's relationships.[16]

---

[13]Erik H. Erikson, *Childhood and Society*, 2d ed. (New York: Norton, 1963), p. 261.

[14]Ibid., pp. 262–263.

[15]Janet L. Surrey, "The Self-in-Relation: A Theory of Women's Development," in *Women's Growth in Connection*, ed. Judith V. Jordan et al. (New York: Guilford, 1991), p. 54. It is important to note that the gender differences observed by feminist developmental theorists do not imply that girls' or boys' differing identity development is a result of any essential biological characteristic of girls or boys. Rather, these gender differences likely arise from girls' and boys' differential sex role socialization.

[16]Alexandra G. Kaplan, Nancy Gleason, and Rona Klein, "Women's Self Development in Late Adolescence," in *Women's Growth in Connection*, p. 131.

With their quest for identity, adolescents develop a self-consciousness that David Elkind calls adolescent egocentrism.[17] Elkind means that adolescents are so self-absorbed that they assume they are the focus of attention for all others as well. In connection with the second egocentrism, adolescents also develop what Elkind calls a personal fable.[18] Not only do adolescents assume they are important to many others, but they also believe their personal feelings are original and unique to them. They become convinced that no one else has ever experienced things the way they do. Because of this sense of their own uniqueness, they often become convinced that they will never die (hence some of the foolish and dangerous behavior of many adolescents).

On the positive side, the personal fable may also have positive religious consequences. Psychologist Gary Sapp suggests that growing out of their desire for privacy and their belief in their personal uniqueness, adolescents may begin to confide in a personal God, turning to God as a trusted confidant. Consequently, adolescence can become a time when young people develop new forms of spirituality and open up new channels of communication with God. In addition, adolescents may internalize and generalize their sense of uniqueness in such a way that they come to a deeper experience and understanding of God's love for each individual human being.[19]

Significant to the psychosocial developments of adolescence is the role of society.[20] Connection with a peer group offers youth the opportunity to exhibit some uniformity of appearance and action. Adolescents have opportunities to follow the leadership of adults other than their parents, and they are often given opportunities to experiment with various tasks in the world of work through part-time, after-school jobs or summer jobs.

Successful resolution of the identity versus role diffusion crisis leads to a sense of identity, oneness with oneself, and affinity with one's community. Failure to achieve identity results in role confusion and low self-esteem, which manifest themselves in a number of ways:

---

[17]David Elkind, "Egocentrism in Adolescence," *Child Development* 38 (Winter 1967): 1025–1034.

[18]Elkind and Weiner, *Development of the Child*, p. 551.

[19]Sapp, "Adolescent Thinking and Understanding," p. 80.

[20]Erikson, *Childhood and Society*, pp. 261–263.

lack of self-confidence, poor academic achievement, impaired inter-personal relationships, hypercritical attitudes toward self, and excessive distress over personal faults.[21] Adolescents who do not know who they are are unable to make peace with themselves, their world, and their place in it.

Stories that depict Jesus as friend and emphasize his interest in and valuing of each person are particularly appropriate in the religious instruction of adolescents. Given adolescents' second egocentrism and their personal fable, stories of Jesus as friend can allow youth to feel an intimate, personal connection with Jesus. In addition, stories that allow adolescents to identify with protagonists struggling with identity issues can provide youth with models of others facing concerns similar to theirs and with possible options for behavior. Because story functions as a patterning of experience, stories can give expression to the fears and anxieties of adolescents and thus help begin to resolve them. In stories, adolescents can find a culturally constructed and appropriate framework for expressing, understanding, and overcoming their fears.[22] Encouraging adolescents to create and to tell their own stories may also powerfully address issues of identity, esteem, and anxiety, inviting youth to create a sense of self through the rendering of their experiences in story. For example, when the adolescents of my church returned from youth camp each summer, several teens were invited to share the story of their camp experience with the congregation during worship. The telling of these stories became a way of reinforcing the sense of self that was experienced during youth camp. Having youth tell these stories to the congregation during worship affirmed the importance and value of the youth to the congregation as well. This story-telling experience was especially significant for the young women who participated because it was the only time in the life of the church when they were allowed to speak from the pulpit during worship.

STORIES AND ADOLESCENT
MORALITY AND FAITH

As adolescents become capable of making more and more decisions for themselves, they begin to subject moral and religious ideas and

---

[21]Erik H. Erikson, *Identity: Youth and Crisis* (New York: Norton, 1968), pp. 165–196.

[22]Applebee, *Child's Concept of Story*, p. 133.

behaviors to critical examination. Childhood beliefs must be relinquished for new beliefs that grow out of the complex processes of formal operational thought. For some, belief develops into a committed faith; for others it fades and dies.[23] The church and the family have significant roles to play in the direction that adolescent faith takes. Adolescents need to find consistency between belief and behavior in both home and church, and in both they need to find a warm and caring environment that accepts them and allows them to struggle with their faith. For example, adolescents should be allowed and even encouraged to raise questions about their doubts and misgivings, and these questions should be treated with respect and openness. Their questions should not be stifled or given pat answers.

Lawrence Kohlberg has described moral development for adolescent males as oriented toward authority and the maintenance of the social order. Right is determined by fulfilling one's duty to society—obeying laws, contributing to society, one's group, or institutions.[24] On the other hand, Carol Gilligan explains that, for girls, moral decisions are made within a context of relationships and responsibilities in which awareness of the connections between people gives rise to a sense of responsibility for others and a need for response to others' needs.[25]

Interestingly, studies suggest that morality does not depend upon religion. Achievement of adolescent morality is not significantly related to religiousness, and no empirical evidence suggests that religious people are more moral than similar nonreligious people. Religiousness does tend to bring adherence to religious prohibitions, and a legalistic form of religious belief seems to be associated with conventional moral reasoning and may, in fact, have an adverse effect on the development of higher levels of moral judgment.[26]

Adolescent lifestyles are, however, closely connected with teens' religious commitment. This commitment can be a matter of adolescents' developing personal taste or it can give direction to all choices

[23]D. L. Williams, "Religion in Adolescence: Dying, Dormant, or Developing? *Source* 5 (1989): 1– 3.

[24]Lawrence Kohlberg, "Moral and Religious Education and the Public Schools: A Developmental View," in *Religion and Public Education*, ed. T. Sizer (Boston: Houghton-Mifflin, 1967), p. 171.

[25]Carol Gilligan, *In a Different Voice: Psychological Theory and Women's Development* (Cambridge: Harvard University Press, 1982), p. 30..

[26]Kenneth E. Hyde, *Religion in Childhood and Adolescence* (Birmingham, Ala.: Religious Education Press, 1990), pp. 285–286.

that adolescents make.[27] Religious behavior is an important indicator of one's religion, though it is not the sole indicator because it does not disclose motivation. Regular church attendance is a significant mark of religious commitment, particularly when it is accompanied by the practice of private personal prayer.[28] Church attendance has a significant relationship with positive attitudes toward religion, as does parents' religious behavior. Religious educator Kenneth Hyde concludes that church attendance and the maintenance of favorable religious attitudes are significant factors in the growth of religious understanding in adolescents.[29] Nonetheless, the relevant empirical research indicates a general decline in positive attitudes toward religion during adolescence. This trend indicates that religious educators must find ways to keep adolescents interested in religious growth. Hyde recounts the advice of an experienced teacher who found that older adolescents who discussed religious issues with proponents of Christianity adopted a critical stance toward Christian faith, but when confronted with critics of Christianity they adopted a stance of belief.[30]

Stories and Cognition in Adolescent Faith

James Fowler describes the cognitive aspect of adolescent faith as synthetic-conventional.[31] As formal operational thought brings adolescents the ability to reflect on their own thinking, they are able to see patterns arising out of their experiences and create myths of possible futures. Fowler claims the emergent strength of synthetic-conventional faith is the forming of a personal myth—that of becoming one's own person in identity and in faith.[32]

In their search for identity, adolescents must re-image God as having inexhaustible depths and knowing the depths of self and others. They need a God who knows, accepts, and affirms the self with its forming myths of personal identity and faith. Significant others

---

[27]D. E. Miller, "Life Style and Religious Commitment," *Religious Education* 76 (1981): 49–63.

[28]Hyde, "Adolescents and Religion," p. 120.

[29]Ibid., p. 123.

[30]Ibid., p. 124.

[31]James W. Fowler, *Stages of Faith: The Psychology of Human Development and the Quest for Meaning* (San Francisco: Harper and Row, 1981), p. 151.

[32]Ibid., p. 173.

become mirrors that contribute to the images of self that are forming identity and faith. When God is a significant other, commitment to God can exert a powerful influence on the ordering of adolescents' identity and values.

Adolescent faith is synthetic in that it is nonanalytical, and it is conventional in that adolescents see it as being the faith system of the entire community. Adolescent faith is not analytically examined faith. Values and commitment are deeply felt, but the value system itself has not yet been subject to critical examination.[33] The adolescent's cognitive faith system comes as a unified whole that provides a coherent orientation in the midst of other complex and diverse issues. The cognitive element of faith, then, provides a way of synthesizing values and information. Thus any attempt to demythologize elements of ritual or symbol feels like a fundamental threat to meaning because symbol and meaning are inextricably bound together.[34]

Synthetic-conventional faith is also conformist faith. The locus of authority for adolescents is external to the self. Generally, it is located in traditional authority roles or in the consensus of a valued group. Consequently, adolescents find themselves subject to the expectations of other. Although they feel that they make their own decisions, their decisions are actually greatly shaped and clarified by their understandings of the values of others.

Transition to individuative-reflective faith begins when adolescents perceive serious clashes or contradictions between valued authorities or marked changes by leaders or in policies or practices previously considered sacred and unbreachable.[35] These and other experiences challenge adolescents' perspectives and generally lead adolescents to reflect critically on how their beliefs and values were formed and how those beliefs and values are relative to the adolescents' own background. The stage is then set for the young adult quest to demythologize and criticize the tacit system of synthetic-conventional faith.

Religious educators as can use stories to challenge the tacitly held assumptions of youth and their excessive reliance on external authority. Stories that introduce adolescents to individuals, groups, and ideas different from their own may invite youth to begin to examine the beliefs and values they hold. Fowler warns that synthetic-conventional

---

[33]Ibid.
[34]Ibid., p. 163.
[35]Ibid., p. 173.

faith can become a long lasting or permanently equilibrated style of identity and faith if adults continue to conform to cultural norms and to rely on external authority for moral and religious decision making. Because challenges to the assumptions of synthetic-conventional faith feel threatening, people often avoid situations that might call on them to reflect critically on their faith and values. For example, when I taught Bible survey courses to first-year students at a conservative Christian college, many students avoided my sections of the course because of my reputation as a liberal professor who questioned the Bible. Other students who took my course were resistant to ideas that challenged their preconceptions about the Bible. During those years, however, I found that stories often allowed me to engage students in critical reflection when direct discourse faltered. When students heard Albert Schweitzer's and Rudolf Bultmann's ideas about the New Testament they would contend that these two biblical scholars could not possibly be Christians. I would then tell them stories of Schweitzer's calling to medical missions in Africa and of Bultmann's evangelical preaching and his opposition to Hitler. Usually, these stories gave students pause to begin to ask if Christian faith is determined only by a particular kind of biblical and theological orthodoxy.

Stories can provide a powerful tool to help adolescents begin to examine their faith. Through stories they can experience the world from other points of view and possibly begin to recognize the relativity of their own. Stories may also allow adolescents to begin to develop an appreciation for diverse experiences and values, and they may encourage youth to explore a wider range of options for their own beliefs and values.

Stories and Affectivity in Adolescent Faith

Emotions play a large role in adolescent experience. Jean Piaget suggests that with the advent of formal operational thought, adolescents develop emotional responses to ideas along with a concomitant desire to reform institutions and ideologies. He labels these responses "idealistic feelings" and claims that these feelings define the adolescent personality.[36] Other researchers concur, finding that for adolescents

---

[36]Jean Piaget, *Intelligence and Affectivity: Their Relationship during Child Development*, trans. T. A. Brown and C. E. Kaegi (Palo Alto, Calif.: Annual Reviews, 1981), p. 70.

emotions become the basis for identity and ideals. Thus when adolescents feel strongly about something, they care about it.[37] In keeping with psychosocial developmental changes, adolescents' emotional development also shifts away from a family focus and toward a peer focus. Consequently, emotions are becoming more attached to peer relationships, particularly romantic ones, and to situations in which friends are the primary participants.[38]

Religious educator Daniel Aleshire suggests that adolescence is a time when youth make some personal affirmation (or rejection) of the faith they have been taught by family and church. Although affirmation and commitment require some degree of cognition, their primary power to shape adolescent lives lies in affect.[39] By taking into account adolescent idealism and peer attachment, religious educators can create an effective learning environment in which youth are encouraged to affirm their faith and commit themselves to it. Both Aleshire and James Michael Lee agree that the affective dimension of adolescent faith is best shaped by teens' participation in the existential life of the faith community.[40]

Stories can be used as a significant part of adolescents' experience in the faith community. Stories of heroes of the faith community, such as Dorothy Day or Martin Luther King Jr., can provide appropriate models of faith and commitment in action and encourage the growth of adolescent idealism toward actual work for change within the world. Stories focusing on peer and romantic relationships can also provide models of healthy adolescent interactions. In particular, stories may help adolescents develop healthy attitudes toward their burgeoning sexuality. Research tends to indicate that attitudes are correlated with adolescent sexual behavior,[41] and religious educators may

---

[37]Jeannette Haviland-Jones, Janet L. Gebelt, and Janice C. Stapley, "The Questions of Development in Emotion," in *Emotional Development and Emotional Intelligence: Educational Implications*, eds. Peter Salovey and David J. Sluyter (New York: Basic, 1997), pp. 244–245.

[38]ibid, p. 246.

[39]Daniel O. Aleshire, *Faithcare: Ministering to All God's People through the Ages of Life* (Philadelphia Westminster, 1988), pp. 137–139.

[40]Ibid., p. 139; and James Michael Lee, "Procedures in the Religious Education of Adolescents," in *Handbook of Youth Ministry*, p. 248.

[41]Bonnidell Clouse, "Adolescent Moral Development and Sexuality," *Handbook of Youth Ministry*, p. 200.

use stories focusing on adolescent sexuality to help youth construct appropriate and healthy attitudes toward sexuality. Perhaps most significantly, stories can be used to help facilitate love for God and love for others. Adolescents need to feel that they are loved and accepted by others, including God. Stories of God's love for individuals, such as the story of Augustine, can be especially important in helping youth experience personally God's love for them. Stories can also demonstrate for youth how they can enact the love they feel for God and for others. Particularly helpful are stories of protagonists who embodied God's love in their actions, such as Mahatma Gandhi, Fannie Lou Hamer, or Martin Luther King Jr.

Stories and Adolescent Faith Experience

Bailey Gillespie labels the faith experience of early adolescence "personalized faith."[42] Personalized faith is characterized by its deeply personal nature, especially in relation to early adolescents' need to develop a strong ego center and their need to experience and express freedom. Consequently, Gillespie suggests religious educators should be concerned with helping early adolescents develop identity and learn to make decisions. These processes are interrelated as adolescents try on a variety of behaviors and begin to make choices about the people they want to be. James Cobble suggests there are two fundamental transitions in the early adolescents' faith experience: establishing a basis for their own faith apart from the beliefs of parents and other authority figures and clarifying what they believe to be the will of God for their lives.[43]

Both of these processes—developing one's own identity and learning to make one's own choices, particularly in terms of one's faith—can be enhanced by stories. Telling their own stories allows early adolescents to define themselves through the ways they create themselves as characters in their stories. Telling their own stories also helps them explore their own faith journeys and begin to construct those journeys as separate from, though related to, the journeys of their parents and other authority figures.

---

[42]Bailey Gillespie, *The Experience of Faith* (Birmingham, Ala.: Religious Education Press, 1988), p. 125.

[43]James Cobble, *Faith and Crisis in the Stages of Life* (Peabody, Mass.: Hendrikson, 1985), p. 47.

This is a true story, as, of course, all of mine are. I think I first took my own tentative steps toward claiming my faith as my own when I was about twelve or thirteen years old. My pastor always preached expository sermons, and we, the members of the congregation, were always encouraged to take copious notes in the margins of our Bibles. Being Baptists, we also were encouraged to read and study the Bible daily, an injunction I took quite seriously and zestfully, reading the entire Bible through each year from junior high through high school. In order to enhance my sermon and Bible study experiences, I had my parents purchase a hardcover Scofield Reference Bible for me. I underlined especially significant passages, took notes, and scribbled cross-references to other relevant passages. By the time I finished high school, that Bible was held together only by electrical tape and my refusal to give it up. Had anyone looked at my underlining and scribbling in that Scofield Bible, that person would have undoubtedly found me to be embracing the literalistic, fundamentalist faith of my church whole heartedly—unless that person found a slip of paper I kept tucked away in one of the lesser preached from books. For in my listening to sermons and attending Sunday school and reading the Bible daily, I had discovered things that troubled me—inconsistencies, contradictions, gaps. And on that slip of paper, for years, I had kept an ongoing list of these problematic passages. I never asked the pastor or a Sunday school teacher about them because I knew the response would deny the contradictions and assert that I did not understand the passages. But I knew it was more than that. I knew that answer would not be enough for me because I knew good and well what I had read. I knew then there were just some answers I was not going to find at church. Only when I went to seminary was I able to throw that list (and the Scofield Bible) away. But that is another stage of faith and another story.

As youth tell their own stories of faith and as they hear the stories of other youth, they can also begin to experience and appreciate both the uniqueness and diversity of individual lives, and the common features of human experience.[44] Furthermore, these personal stories of faith, as well as other forms of stories, can help early adolescents in their developing capacity for empathy. As adolescents participate in role taking (in this instance through the characters in stories), they

---

[44]Gillespie, *Experience of Faith*, p.147.

learn to take another's viewpoint and empathize with another's situation. Gillespie suggests that providing learners with opportunities to experience role taking optimizes faith development for early adolescents.[45]

Finally, stories can provide opportunities for early adolescents to explore decision making. At the core of stories is a dilemma, a conflict, with its concomitant moral and ethical options and their consequences. Experiences with stories in religious instruction can allow early adolescents to explore the options a character has, the decision making process a character uses, the choices the character makes, and the consequences of the character's decision. From their observations, learners can then be guided in making applications from the story world to their own lives and decision-making processes. For example, using the story of the Good Samaritan, religious educators can help young adolescents explore the options each character had, the decisions each character made, the motivations behind the decisions, and examples from their own lives in which they may find themselves in a similar situation.

Gillespie calls the faith experience of later youth "established faith."[46] The emphasis of established faith is on the creation of an ordered faith experience. Later adolescents seek to make meaning from their faith experiences, resulting in a coherent belief structure. This period is characterized by a sorting through and remythologizing of beliefs coupled with an intense focus on a personal relationship with God. Beliefs are generally redefined in relation to the personal stresses and crises of the individual adolescent's life. Consequently some previously held beliefs are rejected while others are maintained or modified. Later youth are especially concerned with the God's relevance to their lives in the here and now. If adolescents experience God as a way of making meaning, then their faith provides them with a way to evaluate previously held beliefs and organize their belief system.[47]

As later adolescents struggle to create their own identities, develop their own belief system, and make important lifestyle decisions, storytelling in religious instruction can assist with these developmental tasks. Stories can address many of the important contemporary issues

---

[45]Ibid., p. 139.
[46]Ibid., p. 152.
[47]Ibid., pp. 153–155.

facing later adolescents (for example, sexuality, career, drugs, friendships) and can help older youth form Christian values around these issues. Watching and discussing movies such as *The Breakfast Club* that deal with these topics in adolescents' lives is one way of facilitating dialogue about teens' values. Stories can also encourage older youth to develop a Christian lifestyle by providing models of religious behavior, as in stories of such people of faith as Sojourner Truth, George Fox, or Jimmy Carter. And stories can help older youth develop the abstract cognitive abilities that can assist them in constructing their belief system. Particularly helpful are stories that affirm God's presence and activity in the world.

Just before her fourteenth birthday, Therese of Lisieux experienced a profound conversion. The following spring she asked her father for permission to enter the Carmelite convent at Lisieux. He approved, but the local bishop felt that Therese was too young and denied her request. Shortly thereafter, Therese was in Rome and was granted an audience with Pope Leo XIII. Ignoring protocol, Therese asked the pope himself to allow her to enter the convent despite her young age. The pope told her to follow the orders of her superiors but assured her that if it were God's will for her to enter the convent a way would be made. After she returned home, she and her father persisted, and the local bishop at last granted approval. In April 1888, at the age of fifteen, Therese entered the convent. At twenty-three she contracted tuberculosis. During the months before she died she wrote her memoir and reflections on her spiritual journey. After she died, her writings were collected in a volume entitled *The Story of a Soul*, which was widely distributed and read. In most ways, Therese's life was not extraordinary. Her spirituality grew from her small, daily experiences and became known as the "Little Way." The "Little Way" is characterized by what Therese called spiritual childhood. For Therese, spirituality was found in childlike wonder at the presence of God in every little experience of life, and it involved love for and trust in God, simplicity, love for others, and search for truth.[48]

In effective religious instruction, adolescents can find a place to search for identity, struggle with beliefs, establish peer relationships,

---

[48]Joseph F. Schmidt, *Praying with Therese of Lisieux* (Winona, Minn.: Saint Mary's Press, 1992), pp. 14–28. See also *St. Therese of Lisieux: Her Last Conversations*, trans. John Clarke (Washington, D.C.: ICS, 1977); *Autobiography of St. Therese of Lisieux*, trans. Ronald Knox (New York: P.J. Kennedy, 1958).

develop attitudes and values, and make lifestyle decisions. Bible stories, stories of the faith community, personal stories, and many other kinds of stories should permeate the religious instruction of adolescents, offering them mirrors of identity, affirmation, and challenge. Stories can encourage adolescents' religious analytical ability, facilitate their creativity, nourish their spirituality, strengthen their values, deepen their understandings, and refine their decision making. When I was in high school, I read Shakespeare, William Faulkner, Flannery O'Connor, John Steinbeck, Eudora Welty. At church, I heard Bible stories, missionary stories, and stories of God at work in the everyday lives of ordinary Christians. Those stories became an integral part of my identity and my faith, so much so that to this day I cannot tell my story without those stories. Much more than the proscriptions and prohibitions of adolescence, the stories of my youth shaped who I was and who I am. The adolescent search for identity offers religious educators an invaluable opportunity to affirm young lives, and storytelling provides one important and effective tool for the religious instruction of adolescents.

16

Adults and Storytelling

I came here to create a world
As strong, renewable, fertile
As the world of nature all around me—
Learned to clear myself as I have cleared the pasture,
Learned to wait,
Learned that change is always in the making
(Inner and outer) if one can be patient,
Learned to trust myself.[1]

          —May Sarton

I think that because I work with college students, some part of me still believes that I am only eighteen years old. Or at least it did until the summer of 1998. My twenty-year high school reunion was held in June. I was unable to attend, but I have been receiving e-mail about it from a friend who was there. I found myself surprised when her first e-mail began with reports of all the health problems that people were facing. "When did they all get so old?" I found myself wondering. That same day, however, I was working on my computer, my right wrist in a brace from too much racquetball. The following Monday I began six weeks of physical therapy. I was in the process of buying my first house, and I was finishing my first book. That summer, I detected my first gray hair, and I no longer recognized my own body

---

[1]May Sarton, "Gestalt at Sixty," in *Selected Poems of May Sarton*, (New York: Norton, 1974), p. 84.

shape in the mirror. The summer of 1998 certainly destroyed any hope of continued illusion—I realized I was a middle adult.

Although Erik Erikson has defined three crises of adulthood—intimacy versus isolation, generativity versus stagnation, and ego integrity versus despair—he contends that generativity is the central issue of adult development.[2] Generativity is concern for establishing and guiding the next generation, creating something that will outlast oneself.[3] Drawing on Erikson's work, James Fowler enumerates six descriptors of the mature adult: (1) the mature adult has a repository of basic trust that expresses itself in a confidence that life does have meaning; (2) the mature adult has a sense of independence that allows her to hold fast to her principles; (3) the mature adult has a capacity for initiative and purpose; (4) the mature adult has the capacity for competent and effective contribution; (5) the mature adult has a well-defined sense of self; (6) the mature adult has a capacity for intimacy in close, personal relationships.[4] Carol Gilligan defines adult maturity as the convergence of an ethic of justice and an ethic of care. An ethic of justice, which proceeds from the premise of equality, presupposes that all people should be treated the same. An ethic of care, proceeding from the premise of nonviolence, assumes that no one should be hurt. In maturity, these perspectives converge in recognition of both the adverse effects of inequality and the destructiveness of violence, or a concern for both justice and care.[5]

Early theories of human development assumed that developmental tasks were completed by the end of adolescence, but work such as Erikson's has demonstrated that humans continue to develop throughout their lives. Hardly a period of stagnation, adulthood can be a time of significant growth psychologically, morally, and religiously. Unfortunately, the religious education of adults is often neglected, and a fertile opportunity to help adults grow in their religious lives is missed. Religious educators may readily understand storytelling as an appropriate procedure for teaching children and youth; they may not realize the effectiveness of storytelling with adults. The complexity and

---

[2] Erik Erikson, *Childhood and Society*, 2d ed. (New York: Norton, 1963), p. 266.
[3] Ibid., p. 267.
[4] James W. Fowler, *Becoming Adult, Becoming Christian* (San Francisco: Harper and Row, 1984), pp. 26–28.
[5] Carol Gilligan, *In a Different Voice: Psychological Theory and Women's Development* (Cambridge: Harvard University Press, 1982), p. 174.

richness of adults' lives, however, creates an excellent opportunity for religious educators to use storytelling to help adults live as faithful people in the world.

Adult educator Malcolm Knowles has posited four assumptions of adult learning.[6] First, as persons mature, their self-concept moves from dependence to self-direction. Religious educators should facilitate this movement, encouraging self-directedness in the religious instruction process. Second, adults accumulate a growing reservoir of experience that constitutes a rich resource for learning. Experiential learning generates greater learning than passive reception of information. Consequently, experiential techniques such as storytelling are excellent tools for adult religious instruction. Third, readiness to learn is closely related to the developmental tasks of learners' social roles. People are more ready to learn when they experience a need to learn in order to cope with life more effectively. Thus adult religious instruction should be organized around life needs of learners and sequenced according to their readiness to learn. Finally, a change in time-perspective occurs in adulthood that demands immediate rather than future application of knowledge, making adult learning more problem centered than subject centered. Consequently, adult religious instruction should organize learning experiences around applicable knowledge and skills related to the immediate life needs and concerns of adults.

Narrative experiences in religious instruction can prove especially fruitful in addressing adults' needs. Storytelling allows adult learners to direct their learning in ways significant to them. Because stories are not primarily propositional, they demand interpretation, and interpretation is greatly influenced by the experiences learners bring with them to the story. Thus narrative experiences allow adults to explore the story ideas and images most closely related to their own religious and personal experiences and interests. Storytelling also invites adults to draw from their reservoir of experiences to enhance the learning process for themselves and for others. Furthermore, storytelling allows adults to define important issues and to name and interpret their own experiences. Religious educators can make especially good use of personal storytelling to provide adults with opportunities to direct

---

[6]See Malcolm Knowles, *The Modern Practice of Adult Education* (Chicago: Follett, 1980).

their own learning, share the wisdom of their experiences, identify their needs, and construct solutions to pressing problems in their lives.

STORIES AND ADULT DEVELOPMENT

Stories that deal with themes related to the developmental tasks and characteristics of adults will be more effective in engaging adult learners in the stories. Research indicates that individuals at different life stages are likely to identify with different implicit thematic content.[7] This finding suggests that in religious instruction stories reflecting themes appropriate to learners' developmental stages will likely be more effective in facilitating the goals of religious instruction. One researcher developed an instrument that allows adult respondents to offer narrative descriptions of the impact of fiction on their experience. From these responses emerged such developmental themes as family of origin, marital and love relationships, friendship, maleness/femaleness, autonomy, and creativity/achievement. According to the researcher, the reports of the participants on fiction reading are replete with references to the central developmental tasks and themes of adulthood.[8] Her findings also suggest that adult readers partly assimilate the experience of transition via the aesthetic transaction with fiction.[9] The response of one participant illuminates this conclusion:

> I seem to read more when I am engaged in a spurt of emotional growth, when the assumptions and attitudes about life which I use to order my perceptions are undergoing revision. Part of my process of synthesizing a new world view and a definition of my personal role is to become aware of the perceptions of others. I read to see how other people deal with the problem of existence . . . in order to better redefine my own role.[10]

---

[7]Cynthia Adams et al., "Adult Age Group Differences in Story Recall Style," *Journal of Gerontology* 45 (July 1990): 25.

[8]Betty Mandl, "The Relationship of Fiction-Reading to Adult Development," ERIC Document Reproduction Service no. ED 203 282 (Boston: Boston University, 1981), p. 25.

[9]Ibid., p. 24.

[10]Ibid.

Understanding the stages and issues of adult development, then, is key in religious educators' ability to select and use stories in adult religious instruction.

Stories and Adult Cognition

Research indicates that cognitive development affects learners' responses to stories. A number of studies suggest that cognitive development plays an important response by prescribing the ways in which learners respond to a story.[11] Other researchers have found that response to literature involves understanding, the possession of information, the ability to grasp verbal and human complexities, psychological readiness to enter the world of the work, the use of evaluative criteria, and the ability to articulate critical statements.[12] Other researchers suggest that learners must approach a story text with a "spectator stance," that is, the reader must be able to approach the story as a valid depiction of possible experience.[13] Likewise, another researcher has found that the reader must be able to determine conventions that constitute the world of the text and must be able to infer conventions operating in the text by noting consequences of certain acts.[14] Studies have also found that learners' concept of story affects their response to a story.[15] What readers of a story know about literature—its creation, its purposes, and its effect—influences their response to the story, as does learners' prior knowledge.[16] Factors such as whether or not the reading is assigned, whether the reading context is a classroom or not, and why the reading is undertaken at all are

---

[11]Lee Galda, "Research in Response to Literature," *Journal of Research and Development in Education* 16 (Spring 1983): 2.

[12]Alan C. Purves and Richard Beach, "Literature and the Reader: Research in Response to Literature, Reading Interests, and the Teaching of Literature," (Urbana, Ill.: National Council of Teachers of English, 1972), p. 42.

[13]James N. Britton, *Language and Learning* (London: Penguin, 1970), pp. 97–125.

[14]Richard Beach, "Attitudes, Social Conventions, and Response to Literature," *Journal of Research and Development in Education* 16 (Spring 1983): 51.

[15]Galda, "Research in Response to Literature," p. 2; Bernice E. Cullinan, Kathy T. Harwood, and Lee Galda, "The Reader and the Story: Comprehension and Response," *Journal of Research and Development in Education* 16 (Spring 1983): 29–38.

[16]Beach, "Attitudes, Social Conventions, and Response to Literature," p. 50.

significant.[17] In summary, the cognitive abilities needed to allow learners to respond most fully to narratives are linked to the achievement of formal operational thought.[18]

Adulthood, then, is a life stage particularly suited to dealing with complex stories, especially literary tales. Adults have the greatest likelihood of having reached fully mature formal operational thought, although not all adults reach this stage or function primarily in it. Receptivity to complex stories is further enhanced in adulthood by the link between cognition, experience, and stories. Researchers suggest that many developmental trends that influence a reader's comprehension of a literary text are determined by life experiences and literary experiences.[19] Furthermore, other researchers have found that the reader's experiences influence their ways of responding to literature by providing keener insights into and closer identification with the experiences narrated in stories.[20] Simply because adults have had more experience than children or adolescents, they have greater potential to connect with the experiences of stories.

Differences in narrative ability and response also occur across adult life stages. Empirical research studies have found, for example, age-group differences in story recall style among adults. Young adults appear to focus on the propositional content and structure of stories in order to acquire and store information and knowledge. Thus for young adults, storing and recalling narratives is a highly literal and text-based mode of processing.[21] In contrast, older adults may focus more on experientially based transformations of a story's propositional content, shifting emphasis from the propositional content to the story's

---

[17]Galda, "Research in Response to Literature," p. 3; Purves and Beach, "Literature and the Reader," pp. 187–188.

[18]Galda, "Research in Response to Literature," p. 2.

[19]Cullinan, Harwood, and Galda, "Reader and the Story," p. 37.

[20]Purves and Beach, "Literature and the Reader," pp. 137–138.

[21]Louise M. Rosenblatt, "The Transactional Theory of the Literary Work: Implications for Research," in *Researching Response to Literature and the Teaching of Literature: Points of Departure*, ed. C. R. Cooper (Norwood, N.J.: Ablex, 1985), pp. 33–53.; J. M. Rybash et al., *Adult Cognition and Aging: Developmental Changes in Processing, Knowing, and Thinking* (New York: Pergamon, 1986); K. W. Schaie, "Toward a Theory of Adult Cognitive Development," *Journal of Aging and Human Development* 8 (1977–1978): 129–138.

underlying psychological and/or metaphorical significance.[22] In one study, middle-aged adults demonstrated a blend of both styles.[23] These studies indicate that as adults age they develop an integrative style of story recall in order to connect information in the story with personal knowledge and experience. This is an important fact for adult religious education storytellers to keep in mind.

Other studies suggest that the process of encoding propositions into highly integrated forms such as metaphor, morals, and sociocultural rules provides older adults with an efficient means for storing information and for transmitting cultural information to members of younger generations.[24] Research also documents that older adults tend to be effective storytellers.[25] Perhaps older adults have become increasingly skilled in telling stories with age, or perhaps they tell stories that they have practiced with retelling across time. Whatever the reasons, older adults seem to produce good stories from their repertoires of personal experiences.[26] Generally, people who listen to oral narratives prefer older adults as storytellers over younger adults. This could be the result of more highly developed skills across the life span, or it could result from the older generations' familiarity with oral

---

[22]James E. Birren, "Age and Decision Strategies," in *Interdisciplinary Topics in Gerontology*, ed. A. T. Welford and J. E. Birren (Basel, Switzerland: Karger, 1969); G. Labouvie-Vief, "Modes of Knowledge and the Organization of Development," in *Beyond Formal Operations 2: The Development of Adolescent and Adult Thinking and Perception*, ed. M. L. Commons et al. (New York: Praeger, 1989).

[23]Cynthia Adams, "Qualitative Changes in Text memory from Adolescence to Mature Adulthood" (Ph.D. diss, Wayne State University, 1986).

[24]David Olson, "The Language of Instruction: The Literate Bias of Schooling," in *Schooling and the Acquisition of Knowledge*, eds. R. J. Spiro and W. E. Montague (Hillsdale, N.J.: Erlbaum, 1977), pp. 65–89; Nancy Mergler and Michael D. Goldstein, "Why are There Old People: Senescence as Biological and Cultural Preparedness for the Transmission of Information," *Human Development* 26 (March-April 1983): 72–90.

[25]Nancy L. Mergler, Marion Faust, and Michael D. Goldstein, "Storytelling as an Age-Dependent Skill: Oral Recall of Orally Presented Stories," *International Journal of Aging and Development* 29 (1984–1985): pp. 205–228; Michael W. Pratt and Susan L. Robins, "That's the Way It Was: Age Differences in the Structure and Quality of Adults' Personal Narratives," *Discourse Processes* 14 (January-March 1991): pp. 73–85.

[26]Pratt and Robins, "That's the Way It Was," p. 83.

tradition.[27] Nonetheless, the implications for religious instruction are significant. Older adults could be made an integral part of religious instruction by calling on their storytelling abilities in a variety of religious instruction settings from the home to the classroom. Utilizing older adults as storytellers may both provide an effective storytelling experience for learners and offer an opportunity for older adults to feel themselves useful, contributing members of the faith community.

Stories and Adult Psychosocial Development

Erikson's three crises of adulthood correspond to the three major eras of adult life—young adulthood, middle adulthood, and older adulthood. Unfortunately, Erikson's model is based on an assumption of male development as normative, and so his description of adult development more accurately depicts adult male development. Erikson contends that identity formation precedes the development of intimacy. His first stage, trust versus mistrust, anchors development in relationship, but his subsequent stages point to a process of individuation. For males, identity does generally precede intimacy, but for females identity forms out of experiences of intimacy. In other words, identity is constructed as women come to know themselves as they are known in relationship with others.[28] Development, then, should not be equated only with separation. Rather, development should be defined to be inclusive of women's experience of the self in relationship.[29]

Young adulthood. Erikson calls the crisis of young adulthood intimacy versus isolation. This stage is characterized by the development of commitments to affiliations and partnerships and by the ethical strength to maintain these commitments. Successful resolution of this crisis leads to the capacity to love, and the individual is able to begin to take seriously the tasks of participation in community through career, citizenship, and love relationships. The potential negative of this crisis is distantiation—the individual may avoid intimacy from fear of loss of identity or may develop a readiness to isolate self from others.

Using the concept of life structures or underlying patterns, Daniel Levinson found that young adults face a number of developmental

---

[27]Ibid., p. 84.

[28]Gilligan, *In a Different Voice*, p. 12.

[29]See Judith V. Jordan et al., eds., *Women's Growth in Connection* (New York: Guilford, 1991).

tasks focused on building, evaluating, and restructuring an initial life structure, including making key choices about relationships/family, occupation, separation from family of origin, and lifestyle.[30] He contends that the sequence of structure building/maintaining and transitional periods holds true for both men and women, but gender significantly affects how men and women experience these periods.[31] Levinson's central concept in attending to gender differences in development is gender splitting. By gender splitting, Levinson refers to the creation of a rigid division between male and female, masculine and feminine. He identifies four basic forms of gender splitting: (1) the domestic and public spheres as social spaces for women and men respectively; (2) the traditional marriage enterprise, which defines women as homemakers and men as providers; (3) "women's work" and "men's work"; (4) the masculine and feminine split within the individual psyche.[32] In his empirical research, Levinson found significant differences between the experiences of homemakers and career women. During young adulthood, these women formed different inner scenarios for adult life centering on, to varying degrees, their internal traditional homemaker figure and their internal antitraditional figure. In each woman, one figure tended to dominate. Especially for the career women, the sense of conflict between the two figures was great. Levinson found that for homemakers the traditional pattern was hard to sustain and those who tried to maintain that pattern developed relatively unsatisfactory life structures. Career women attempted to reduce gender splitting and often found themselves in innovating positions without much support from the values of contemporary institutions.[33] Levinson's empirical research concludes that the self-development of both women and men is limited by gender splitting, and he suggests that a broadening of the meanings of gender can allow both women and men a greater range of options for building and maintaining life structures and making transitions from one season of life to the next.[34]

---

[30]Daniel J. Levinson, *The Seasons of a Man's Life* (New York: Ballantine, 1978), pp. 71–135.

[31]Daniel J. Levinson, *The Seasons of a Woman's Life* (New York: Knopf, 1996), p. 36.

[32]Ibid., pp. 38–39.

[33]Ibid., pp. 414–415.

[34]Ibid., p. 419.

Drawing on the empirical, social scientific research done on the self-in-relation, psychologist Ellyn Kaschak images identity as the self-in-context.[35] Kaschak points out that most theoretical discussion of identity seems to presuppose a fixed self, a personality that exists independently of context. She argues, however, that the self is a construct, an abstract concept by which meaning and consistency are attributed to a person in context. In other words, the self is an organizing metaphor. Consequently, she suggests, psychologists would be more accurate to speak of a sense of self, which includes the physical, cognitive, and affective experiences associated with the metaphor of self. She offers the example of a woman interacting with different people—her husband, children, clients, students, professors, and clergy. This woman, she explains, may draw on very different qualities depending on the person with whom she is interacting. Different circumstances call up different behaviors and experiences within a range of consistency. One's sense of self, then, is a function of one's experiences, one's social location (including one's race, ethnicity, class, and sexual identity), and the meanings one makes of those experiences.[36]

The work of Gilligan, Levinson, and Kashack suggests that women and men experience the psychosocial crisis of young adulthood differently and that young adults who build experiences and notions of intimacy and identity on rigid gender distinctions may find their initial life structures unsatisfactory. Consequently, religious instruction with young adults has the potential to address successfully issues of intimacy, identity, and gender in ways that expand learners' options and enhance the possibility of learners' building satisfactory initial life structures.

Stories have great power to challenge outmoded stereotypical notions of gender and suggest a wider range of options for behavior for women and men. Unfortunately, the church has often played a major role in codifying, institutionalizing, and enforcing gender roles, even using Bible stories such as the Fall narrative to justify un-Christian gender distinctions and the subordination of one group of human beings to another. The potential, however, of religious instruction to assist young adults in developing close, mutual, empathic relationships

---

[35]Ellyn Kashack, *Engendered Lives: A New Psychology of Women's Experience* (New York: Basic, 1992), p. 154.
[36]Ibid., pp. 154–155.

that are not based on gender stereotypes is great. Many Bible stories depict women and men acting in ways that stretched the limits placed on their behavior by gender roles—Deborah judged the people of Israel; David and Jonathan loved each other as brothers; Mary, the sister of Martha and Lazarus, sat at the feet of Jesus as a disciple; Jesus talked with a Samaritan woman in public. Biographies of women and men of faith also offer examples of people acting in accordance with the sense of self-in-context they are constructing—George Fox, Julian of Norwich, Sojourner Truth. Literary tales also offer a wealth of resources for stories to address issues of young adulthood. Gail Godwin's *Father Melancholy's Daughter* is an especially good example. In this story, the daughter of an Episcopalian priest struggles with her relationship to her father, her deceased mother, her mother's best friend, and her boyfriend, as she attempts to come to terms with her faith and her own calling to ministry. One empirical research study of fiction and adult development found that the theme of maleness/femaleness was referred to more than any other theme. Whereas 30 percent of the males in the study mentioned this theme, 85 percent of the females mentioned it. The researcher suggests that fiction may in a sense fulfill a mentoring role which has, on the whole, been lacking for women. She notes that two-thirds of the women in the study named a female author as important to them. She quotes the response of one woman:

> I am almost embarrassed to admit it, but I am drawn to works either by or about women in the same way I listen more keenly to female singers on the radio. Unconsciously I must be yearning for role models, for advice, for proof of what other women have done, for glimpses into their problems. There is always this hazy hope they will either reveal some path or secrets for me (i.e. teach me about life), or else they will express things I have subconsciously felt but never before seen in print. . . . Maybe they will clarify something I didn't even realize I was feeling.[37]

Since intimacy is a key issue of young adulthood, sharing personal stories within an ongoing, committed, safe group can be an effective means of developing relationships and building community. Sharing

---

[37]Mandl, "Relationship of Fiction-Reading to Adult Development," p. 27.

stories can help young adults learn to build mutually empathic relationships by enhancing their listening and self-disclosure skills. Furthermore, personal stories can also present a challenge to implicitly held notions of gender, race, and sexual identity. When I taught at a conservative Christian college, many of my students believed that gay and lesbian people were headed directly for hell. Once on a field trip to San Francisco, some of these students had an opportunity to meet some of the members of the Metropolitan Community Church of San Francisco, a congregation comprised most of gay men and lesbians. After listening to the stories of these gay Christians, most of the students in the group, although they still struggled with their beliefs about homosexuality, found a new openness to the possibility that these people were indeed their brothers and sisters in Christ. I have had similar results with fish bowl experiences in which I have placed women, people of color, or women of color in the fish bowl and asked them to talk about their experiences while the men or white students have listened. Inevitably, those on the outside, when we debrief the experience, exclaim that they did not know what the life of the others was like.

American cultural scripts about gender tend to limit the range of choices available to young adults who are seeking to establish relationships, occupations, and lifestyles. The stories of religious instruction can help young adults write their own scripts, redefining the nature of relationships, careers, and life choices. As young adults experience stories that challenge stereotypical notions of gender and posit alternatives for religious living, they can be empowered to construct their own ways of living as selves-in-context.

Middle adulthood. The crisis of middle adulthood, which Erikson terms generativity versus stagnation, brings to the foreground the central psychosocial issues of adulthood. The concern of this stage is establishing and guiding the next generation and securing for them the things necessary to ensure their successful development. Generativity also encompasses a sense of creativity and a desire to be productive a make a contribution to society. The potential negative of this crisis is that an individual may completely withdraw from society and become self-indulgent or may regress to a pseudo-intimacy.

Levinson suggests that for men, midlife begins with an assessment of the past and a subsequent restructuring of life choices. Central in middle-aged men's development is the resolution of four polarities: young/old; destruction/creation; masculine/feminine; and attachment/

separateness.[38] For men, Levinson contends, integrating these polarities is an essential part of individuation at midlife. In this process, men come to terms with being both young and old, destructive and creative, masculine and feminine, attached and separate. The integration of these polarities allows men to create a basis upon which a new life structure is formed.[39]

For women, Levinson also discovered significant developmental changes at midlife. In his study, homemakers tended to transform the traditional marriage enterprise during midlife. Many were divorced and/or remarried. For these women, motherhood was becoming a less central aspect of the life structure, and the terms of marriage and the marriage relationships were being modified.[40] Most had found traditional marriage to be a failure and wanted a different kind of marriage, family, and life structure in the next season of life.[41] The career women who had pursued the nontraditional dream of career and family also reappraised their life choices. They tended to be more realistic about the impact of sexism in work organizations and their own need for passionate engagement and equality in work and in love. These women hoped for more satisfactory and creative work in the future based on play, love, and contribution to society rather than proof of one's ability to compete in the workplace. Having juggled career and family in institutions that mostly gave lip service to the advancement of women's careers, these women wanted to create life structures in which occupation had a different place in the next season.[42]

The religious instruction of middle adults should concern itself with issues of generativity. Religious educators can facilitate religious growth in middle adults by helping them find fulfilling ways to be productive, creative, and contributing as religious persons. Storytelling can assist in this task in a number of ways. First, encouraging middle adults to create and express their own stories can offer them a sense of creativity and productivity. Second, storytelling may allow adults to review their lives and assess their contributions to society through their relationships and work. Finally, exposing middle adults

---

[38]Levinson, *Seasons of a Man's Life*, p. 197.
[39]Ibid., p. 209.
[40]Levinson, *Seasons of a Woman's Life*, p. 198.
[41]Ibid., p. 408.
[42]Ibid., p. 409.

to appropriate stories can provide them with opportunities to identify with the struggles of middle adulthood expressed in the stories. Psychologist Allan Chinen has linked a particular type of fairy tale with psychological development in middle adulthood. In a small number of tales across cultures middle adults are protagonists. Chinen enumerates five themes that emerge in these "middle tales": the loss of magic (namely, youthful inspiration), gender role and other train reversals, struggle with the shadow, healing power learned through encounter with death or demons, and humor embodied in the sacred clown.[43] He suggests that these middle tales reveal the psychology of midlife, particularly the transpersonal dimensions of development.[44] In planning religious instruction experiences for middle adults, religious educators should look for stories in which themes of generativity predominate. The stories should allow middle adult learners to identify closely with the characters and their experiences.

Older adulthood. Erikson labels the psychosocial stage of older adulthood ego integrity versus despair. This crisis centers on one's ability to accept the human life cycle as meaningful. This stage is characterized by reflection and evaluation of one's life and its meaning. Resolution of this crisis results in a sense of wisdom about life and a philosophy that extends beyond one's own life cycle. The individual finds a sense that life is meaningful and is able to accept her own death. In "Gestalt at Sixty," May Sarton pictures the achievement of ego integrity:

> I am not ready to die,
> But I am learning to trust death
> As I have trusted life.
> I am moving
> Toward a new freedom
> Born of detachment,
> And a sweeter grace—
> Learning to let go.[45]

---

[43] Allan B. Chinen, "Fairy Tales and Transpersonal Development at Mid-Life," *Journal of Transpersonal Psychology* 19 (1987): 99–132.

[44] Ibid., p. 99.

[45] May Sarton, "Gestalt at Sixty," p. 85.

The potential negative of this stage is despair, an experience that encompasses a sense that life is unjust or unfair, a fear of death, and bitterness about life. Such an individual is unable to accept aging or to find meaning in the life cycle. Instead of sensing satisfaction with life, this individual feels cheated by life and regrets the decisions he has made.

Storytelling in religious instruction may provide a way to assist older adults in achieving ego integrity. Through the stories they tell of their own lives, older adults may be able to construct patterns of meaning in their life experiences and develop a sense of meaningfulness about their existence. Intergenerational storytelling activities can create opportunities for older adults to share from their wealth of information, knowledge, and wisdom. This process can underline the continuing value of older adults to the life of the faith community and signify the contributions they can make to everyone in the congregation.

Allan Chinen has also identified a type of fairy tale that deals with the developmental issues of aging. In these elder tales, Chinen has identified six themes of older adulthood: poverty, self-reformation, transcendence, worldly wisdom, emancipated innocence, and mediation with the supernatural.[46] In youth tales the prince and princess marry and live happily ever after, but elder tales depict what ideally happens in the ever after. Elder tales, then, describe what might be in the third era of adult life. Chinen claims these tales exemplify the union of innocence with wisdom and magic with insight in later life.[47] In religious instruction, elder tales can provide models of older adults leading active and productive lives and can encourage older adults to continue to be active in the world.

Stories and Adult Moral Development

Although the higher levels of moral development are specifically adult realities, they are by no means certainties. In actuality, many adults remain in the lower stages of moral reasoning. Lawrence Kohlberg's stages of moral development point to some of the themes of moral decision making which are relevant in adult development,

---

[46]Allan B. Chinen, "Fairy Tales and Psychological Development in Late Life: A Cross-Cultural Hermeneutic Study," *The Gerontologist* 27 (June 1987): 340–345.

[47]Ibid., p. 345.

although, as acknowledged previously, his work is limited in its applicability because of its inherent gender bias.

Kohlberg describes two postconventional stages of moral reasoning. Stage 5 of his hierarchy of moral development is characterized by a contractual legalistic orientation. It recognizes the relativity of most values, rules, and norms established by the majority, although some values, such as justice, are not considered to be relative and are to be maintained in any society.

Stage 6 is characterized by self-chosen ethical principles and moral autonomy. The orientation of moral reasoning is not toward socially ordained rules but toward principles of choice involving appeal to logical universality and consistency. Social agreements are laws that are followed only as they cohere with these principles.

Carol Gilligan points out that women's perception of moral dilemmas, however, depends on an ethic of care, which is characterized by an emphasis on relationships and responsibilities rather than an abstract notion of justice. The dichotomy of care versus justice or responsibilities versus rights results from an emphasis on separation rather than connection or individuality rather than relationship. Gilligan recognizes that for women the context of moral discernment is a web of relationships. She suggests that both men and women need to move toward a maturity that balances separation and attachments, rights and responsibilities, justice and care.[48]

Storytelling can play a significant role in moral development in religious instruction. Stories can provide a challenge to conventional moral thinking and implicitly held moral assumptions. The ambiguities and complexities of stories have the potential to disrupt conventional attitudes and mores by presenting conflicting interpretations of life experiences and undermining external sources of authority. Stories also remind learners that more than one mode of moral reasoning is appropriate. Stories require both separate and connected knowing, a sense of justice and a sense of care.

The story of Jesus and the woman taken in adultery provides an excellent example of the importance of both justice and care. In this story, a group of men bring a woman who has committed adultery before Jesus, expecting him to condemn her, as the law demands. Jesus,

---

[48]See Carol Gilligan, *In a Different Voice: Psychological Theory and Women's Development* (Cambridge: Harvard University Press, 1982).

instead, simply says to them, "Let the one who is without sin cast the first stone." Judged by their own sins, her accusers go, leaving her alone with Jesus, who offers her forgiveness and encouragement.

Stories and Adult Faith Development

In 1996, I became a member of a multiracial, multicultural, open and affirming local congregation of the United Church of Christ. Members of my church are not overly concerned with theological orthodoxy. They do not worry about the authorship of the Pentateuch or the historicity of Genesis 1–11. But members of my church participated actively in the Civil Rights movement. They have stood in Christian solidarity with the farm workers in Oregon. They have ministered to people living with AIDS. They have provided financial assistance for young people to attend college. They have raised children who have learned to value diversity. In many of their daily acts, both large and small, these people have lived their biblical faith, even when that faith has meant facing hardship and struggle. They have built lives of personal devotion to God lived out in their relationships with others. From the stories I hear about the members of Ainsworth United Church of Christ, each Sunday I learn what it means to be the people of God.

The mature faith of adulthood is a faith that is personally owned and expressed in one's living. It is a lifestyle characterized by a love for one's neighbor and empowered by one's personal relationship with God.[49] Adult faith grows as learners are better able to love God and to exemplify that love in their commitments to work lovingly in the world. Religious educators can utilize storytelling in its many forms to facilitate adult faith development by helping learners own their own beliefs and convictions, love God more deeply, and embody that love in their actions.

Faith and cognition. Although many adults remain in the synthetic-conventional stage 3 of James Fowler's stages of faith, those who begin to move out of this nonanalytic, conformist stage undertake a long and often painful journey to own their own faith. The emergence of stage 4, individuative-reflective faith, depends on the disruption of learners' reliance on external authority and the parallel relocation of

---

[49]Walter Conn, *Christian Conversion: A Developmental Interpretation of Autonomy and Surrender* (New York: Paulist, 1986), p. 212.

authority within the self. Some learners may complete only one of these two tasks and become caught in the transition between stages 3 and 4. On the one hand, they may become aware of relativity through life experiences, but they may continue to rely on external authority as a means of coping with this relativity. On the other hand, they may relocate authority internally but never distance themselves from their assumptive value system.

Individuative-reflective faith is involved in the process of demythologizing. This process involves separating meaning from the symbol that expresses it. Learners translate meanings into propositions, definitions, and conceptual foundations. For many adults, this translation process can bring about a sense of loss, dislocation, grief, and even guilt. The emergent strength of this stage is the capacity for critical reflection on identity and outlook. The danger is an excessive confidence in the conscious mind and critical thought. Transition to stage 5 begins when learners begin to hear anarchic and disturbing inner voices and to sense a flatness of meanings. Stories, symbols, and paradoxes may break in on the neatness of recently established demythologized systems. Disillusionment with one's own compromises and recognition of life's complexity beyond the logic and abstract concepts of this stage prepares learners to move toward a more dialectical and multileveled understanding of truth.

Stage 5, conjunctive faith, then moves beyond either/or to both/and. This stage is able to see many sides of an issue simultaneously. Knowing becomes dialogical. The known is invited to speak its own word, and the knower accommodates knowing to the structure of the known before imposing her own categories own it. The reliance on the conscious of stage 4 gives way to an awareness of the unconscious in stage 5 and its attempt to integrate and reconcile the conscious and unconscious. This stage recognizes that truth is more than any single system or theory can grasp, and it recognizes that stories, symbols, and doctrines are inevitably partial, limited to a particular people's experience of God. Nonetheless, what is significant is not their relativity but the relatedness to the reality they mediate. Therefore, stage 5 is ready for significant encounters with traditions other than its own, understanding that truth resides in those traditions in ways that may complement or challenge its own. Consequently, in this stage, stories and symbols are no longer demythologized but are remythologized and self-authenticating. This second naivete submits itself to the initiative of the symbolic, reuniting symbol and meaning, reclaiming and reworking the past, and opening itself to the deeper voices of the self. The emergent strength of this stage is ironic imagination—the ability to see and be in one's own most powerful meanings while at the same time recognizing their relativity and partiality. The danger of this stage is paralysis—inaction that gives rise to complacency or cynical withdrawal due to a paradoxical understanding of truth. This stage, however, leaves learners caught between an untransformed world and a transforming vision of what the world might be. Few answer the call to actualization of the vision because of its radical demand for complete commitment, inclusivity, and action.

Adults who do answer this call live out in radical ways the implications of stage 6, universalizing faith, which Fowler admits is easier to describe by example than to define. Stage 6 is a disciplined activist incarnation, embodying the imperatives of absolute love and justice partially apprehended by stage 5. Stage 6 spends and is spent for the transformation of present reality. Its commitment to inclusivity, justice, and love is exemplified in the lives of such people as Mother Teresa of Calcutta, Martin Luther King Jr., and Jimmy Carter. These people call into question the blatant injustice in the world as well compromises that are sanctioned by conventional justice. Their stories remind Christians of their vocation to work and live in anticipation of the in-breaking community of God; they call Christians to spend their lives as part of God's reconciling, redeeming, and restoring work in the world.

Using stories in religious instruction can be an effective way of facilitating the cognitive aspect of faith development that Fowler outlines. Stories provide ways for adults to acquire, explore, expand, and express meaning, including (and especially) religious meaning. Stories are perhaps the most significant means the faith community has for passing on its heritage. A faith community's stories embody its identity in deeper ways than its doctrines or statements of faith. Its stories are its record of lived Christian faith. Stories also allow learners to explore and expand meanings. They allow learners to connect their life experiences to the normative stories of the community and to understand their life stories in light of the community's stories and vice versa. Stories can also challenge learners to critique and question their own religious tradition by inviting them to hear voices other than their own. Stories invite learners to express meaning by action in the world, and they themselves become vehicles through which learners express meaning.

Stories can also encourage the processes of demythologizing and remythologizing that are central to stages 4 and 5 of Fowler's schema. New stories can challenge codified stories and encourage demythologizing. For example, examination of the flood epics of other ancient civilizations can challenge flat, literal interpretations of the flood story found in Genesis. On the other hand, stories can also be used to stimulate movement to stage 5, conjunctive faith. Stories demand responses beyond demythologized propositions and extracted statements of meaning. Stories offer experiences that are beyond propositional expression. Myths and folktales, for example, may be especially appropriate in adult religious instruction as they bring to awareness the images of the unconscious that become significant in stage 5. Additionally, reclaiming the stories of one's own religious tradition is an important task of conjunctive faith. For example, stage 4, individuative-reflective faith, may demythologize Communion. The story that is embodied in that ritual may be lost to an awareness that the elements are nothing more than bread and grape juice (at least, in many Protestant traditions). Stage 5 allows the restoration of meaning to the ritual as a sacred part of one's spiritual tradition.

Finally, stories, particularly biographies and autobiographies of those who embody universalizing faith, can challenge adult learners to live out the radical call to be God's people. These stories stand as witnesses to the radical incarnation of Christian love to which the people of God are called. These stories, then, can become both critics and models for learners as they seek to live out God's reconciling love in the world. Good resources for religious instruction include the stories of Mother Teresa of Calcutta, Jimmy Carter, Dorothy Day, Thomas Merton, Mahatma Gandhi, Martin Luther King Jr., Albert Schweitzer, and Rigoberta Menchu.

Religious experience. Bailey Gillespie identifies three phases of faith experience corresponding to the three stages of adult life. Reordered faith, the faith experience of young adulthood, is characterized by restructuring, relearning, retesting, and sorting out both religious ideas and religious feelings.[50] During young adulthood, faith is put to the test as it encounters real life situations in career and relationships. Gillespie contends that faith is tested on two fronts:

---

[50]Bailey Gillespie, *The Experience of Faith* (Birmingham, Ala.: Religious Education Press, 1988), p. 178.

relevance and transference. The quest for relevance leads young adults to explore new experiences to see if they make sense. Often this quest results in feelings of doubt, reorganization, and disequilibrium. The process of transference explores how well religion has actually been learned. Transference shifts focus from theological concepts such as grace and forgiveness to their real-life incarnation in moral and ethical decision making. Gillespie suggests that the religious instruction of young adults provides opportunities for values clarification and application of religious contents to actual life experiences.[51] Sara Little adds that the religious instruction of young adults should also include procedures which involve metaphorical thinking, increase self- understanding, and allow self-direction.[52]

Storytelling in religious instruction with young adults can provide opportunities for values clarification, application, self-understanding, and self-directedness. For example, in Chaim Potok's *My Name is Asher Lev*, a young Hasidic artist finds himself only able to express his artistic vision only by painting crucifixes. Only this form expresses passionately enough the anguish of the world. At the cost of his family and his faith community, Asher Lev paints as an expression of his faith.

Gillespie identifies the faith experience of middle adulthood as reflective faith. Reflective faith is characterized by three directions— looking back, looking inside, and looking beyond.[53] In looking back, middle adults reflect on what has happened in life. In particular, they attempt to understand and come to terms with feelings in order to achieve peace. This looking back results in new ideas and feelings about God. Looking inside helps middle adults understand themselves in relation to God. This latter process is often characterized by a desire for spiritual power and insight. Looking beyond involves a growing sense of urgency that the work that needs to be done needs to be done now, and it provides the motivation for middle adults to make changes and project themselves beyond their immediate problems and situations.[54]

Stories offer an excellent way for religious educators to meet the religious needs of middle adult learners. Sharing life stories allows

---

[51]Ibid., p. 182.

[52]Sara Little, *To Set One's Heart* (Atlanta: Knox, 1983), p. 69.

[53]Gillespie, *Experience of Faith*, p. 198.

[54]Ibid., pp. 194–200.

learners to look back, inside, and beyond. Religious educator Anne Brennan suggests that religious instruction for middle adults is a dialogue involving the Christian myth, the larger biblical and historical story of the Christian community, and learners' personal stories. It provides one way to help learners discover their own inner experiences of the sacred. She suggests that learners explore their own personal stories and look for instances of the in-breaking of the sacred.[55] Both Gillespie and Daniel Aleshire suggest that middle adulthood is an especially appropriate time for religious educators to utilize Thomas Groome's Shared Praxis method in religious instruction.[56] Although it is a highly cognitive method, shared praxis allows learners to explore the biblical story in the context of their own personal stories.[57] Another useful method, which is inclusive of affective, behavioral, and cognitive components, is David Kolb's experiential learning cycle.[58] The experiential learning cycle can allow middle adults to bring their own stories, particularly the affective and lifestyle contents of those stories, into dialogue with the Christian story through a variety of levels of cognitive, affective, and behavioral experience.

Anne Tyler's *Earthly Possessions* is the story of a woman who decides to leave her husband. Her marriage is not working out. Her dreams have not been realized, and she has decided to move on. But, when she goes to the bank to withdraw enough cash to leave, she is taken hostage by a bank robber and forced into a stolen car bound for Florida. The experience sends her on a journey of reflection and self-discovery. By the time she walks away from her kidnapper she has recreated herself. She is able to return to her marriage and build a fulfilling relationship with her husband.

---

[55]Anne Brennan, "Myth in Personal Spirituality," *Religious Education* 75 (July-August 1980): 448.

[56]Gillespie, *Experience of Faith*, pp. 201–203. Daniel O. Aleshire, *Faithcare: Ministering to All God's People through the Ages of Life* (Philadelphia: Westminster, 1988), p. 168.

[57]Thomas Groome, *Christian Religious Education* (San Francisco: Harper and Row, 1980); Thomas Groome, *Sharing Faith: A Comprehensive Approach to Religious Education and Pastoral Ministry: The Way of Shared Praxis* (San Francisco: Harpercollins, 1991).

[58]David A. Kolb, *Experiential Learning: Experience as the Source of Learning and Development* (Englewood Cliffs, N.J.: Prentice-Hall, 1984).

Sometimes, when Saul can't sleep, he turns his head on the pillow and asks if I'm awake. We may have had a hard time that day: disagreed, misunderstood, come to one more invisible parting or tiny, jarring re-arrangement of ourselves. He lies on his back in the old sleigh bed and starts to wonder: will everything work out? Is he all right, am I all right, are we happy, at least in some limited way? Maybe we ought to take a trip, he says. Didn't I use to want to?

But I tell him, no. I don't see the need, I say. We have been traveling for years, traveled all our lives, we are traveling still. We couldn't stay in one place if we tried. Go to sleep, I say.

And he does.[59]

The faith of older adulthood is resolute faith, according to Gille-spie. Resolute faith involves making sense and making hope.[60] Mak-ing sense is the process of developing a clarity about what has hap-pened in life. Making hope allows older adults to face the future with a sense of purpose. In this sense, religious faith can stabilize life and fill it for older learners. Resolute faith is a caring faith. Out of their life experiences, older adults build a reservoir of compassion and val-ues. The religious instruction of older adults should provide ways to help older learners come to terms with the ending of life and provide them with ways to be of continued use in the faith community.

As suggested earlier, one way that older adults can play an active role in the faith community is through storytelling. A number of excel-lent stories are available that address the needs of older adults. An es-pecially good resource is May Sarton's *A Reckoning*. This novel is the story of a woman who learns that she has inoperable cancer. For her the illness becomes a journey during which to assess her life and come to terms with it. Through the story, she discovers the real connections of her life and at the end of the novel is able to let go of life with a sense of peace.

CONCLUSION

Stories take learners "elsewhere." When learners are engaged in a story, they are transported to another world. They have traveled to

---

[59] Anne Tyler, *Earthly Possessions* (New York: Berkley, 1977), p. 222.
[60] Gillespie, *Experience of Faith*, p. 212.

another place. When a shaman wakes up from an ecstatic trance, he tells the story of his visit to the spirit world. The soul journey and the stories told about it express a belief that the principal realities of life are to be found in the journeys of the spirit. The mystery and sacredness of life is to be found only by those who travel likewise. In this connection, Paul Zweig writes:

> A resemblance exists between the adventurer exploring the countries of the marvelous and the "absent" one: each finds his way to the "other" world and returns to tell the story. For each, the story is what he brings back; it is all he brings back, suggesting an essential connection between adventure and storytelling: a connection which becomes all the more complex, if we recognize the "transport" of the listener, the self-abandonment which it is the story's business to create, as a form of soul-journey. By entering the story, the listener not only allows himself to be transported into a particular narrative, he crosses the elusive barrier which divides the worlds. He makes a controlled excursion into the "elsewhere" of life itself.[61]

Storytelling in the religious instruction of adults provides an opportunity for adult learners to become adventurers, travelers on a journey of self-creation. In stories, adults can deal with pressing developmental issues and find ways to resolve developmental crises successfully and achieve maturity appropriate to their developmental stage. Most importantly, in stories adults can learn to live religiously in the world. From their excursions into the deep, sacred realities of "elsewhere," they can return challenged and renewed to live as the people of God. Life, as Frederick Buechner points out, is a sacred journey.[62] On their pilgrimage to Canterbury, Geoffery Chaucer's pilgrims decide to tell stories to pass the time and make the journey easier. The idea is still a good one. Stories in religious instruction can provide strength, challenge, and encouragement for the sacred journey each learner undertakes and can help learners as they strive to live faithful lives as God's people in the world.

---

[61]Paul Zweig, *The Adventurer* (Princeton, N.J.: Princeton University Press, 1974), p. 89.
    [62]Frederick Buechner, *The Sacred Journey* (San Francisco: Harper and Row, 1982).

Epilogue

A great Jewish scholar once asked a preacher what makes a parable so influential. He complained, "If I recite Torah, no one comes, but if I tell a parable, the synagogue is full."

The preacher replied, "I'll explain it to you with a parable." And he told this story.

> Once upon a time Truth went about the streets as naked as the day he was born. As a result, no one would let him into their homes. Whenever people caught sight of him, they turned away or fled. One day when Truth was sadly wandering about, he came upon Parable. Now, Parable was dressed in splendid clothes of beautiful colors. And Parable, seeing Truth, said, "Tell me, neighbor, what makes you look so sad?" Truth replied bitterly, "Ah, brother, things are bad. Very bad. I'm old, very old, and no one wants to acknowledge me. No one wants anything to do with me."
>
> Hearing that, Parable said, "People don't run away from you because you're old. I too am old. Very old. But the older I get, the better people like me. I'll tell you a secret: Everyone likes things to be disguised and prettied up a bit. Let me lend you some splendid clothes like mine, and you'll see that the very people who pushed you aside will invite you into their homes and be glad of your company."
>
> Truth took Parable's advice and put on the borrowed clothes. And from that time on, Truth and Parable have gone hand in hand and everyone loves them. They make a happy pair.[1]

Storytelling in religious instruction provides one effective way for religious educators to help learners think about, feel, and live the

---

[1]Beatrice Silverman Weinreich, *Yiddish Folktales*, trans. Leonard Wolf (New York: Schocken, 1988), p. 7.

truths of human experience, particularly human experience with the Divine. Parables, myths, folktales, literary tales, biographies, and children's stories can play an important role in addressing the educational needs of children, youth, and adults in religious instruction. Through stories, learners can gather new information, grasp new ideas, develop new values and attitudes, and learn new behaviors. Narrative's versatility makes it an excellent tool to help religious educators facilitate the desired goals of religious instruction.

The possibilities for narrative in religious instruction are practically limitless. This volume only begins to suggest the myriad ways religious educators may use stories to achieve cognitive, affective, and lifestyle goals in religious instruction. Because storytelling (like religious instruction) is both an art and a science, this volume can only serve as a guide to help religious educators develop their storytelling skills. Like all arts, storytelling requires commitment, practice, and creativity from religious educators. And, like all substantive and structural contents of religious instruction, the types of stories and the ways storytelling are used in religious instruction should grow out of the specific needs of the learners and the specific goals of the religious instruction event as identified through social scientific research.

To begin to use stories in religious instruction may seem a daunting task, especially as religious educators strive to become effective storytellers themselves. But stories are powerful, and we, as the people of God, participate in one of the most wonderful stories of all. Bible scholars use the phrase *Heilsgeschichte*, salvation history,[2] to describe this story that begins in the biblical stories of Abraham, Moses, and Jesus and continues in the lives of God's faithful people today.

People know that story only as it is passed on from one person to another in their words and, more importantly, in their lives. As I was growing up, I learned an old gospel hymn from those same people who first told me the story of God's love:

> I love to tell the story of unseen things above.
> Of Jesus and his glory, of Jesus and his love.
> I love to tell the story because I know 'tis true.
> It satisfies my longings as nothing else can do.

---

[2]See, for example, Johannes Munck, *The Acts of the Apostles* (Garden City, N.Y.: Doubleday, 1967).

I love to tell the story. 'Tis pleasant to repeat
What seems each time I tell it more wonderfully sweet.
I love to tell the story for some have never heard
The message of salvation from God's own holy word.

I love to tell the story for those who know it best
Seem hungering and thirsting to hear it like the rest.
And when in scenes of glory I sing the new, new song
'Twill be the old, old story that I have loved so long.

I love to tell the story. 'Twill be my theme in glory
To tell the old, old story of Jesus and his love.[3]

The old, old story can make a difference in learners' lives. The connection of learners' stories to the gospel and to other stories can create a profound learning experience that helps learners think, feel, and live differently. With his stories, Jesus taught his followers how to live as members of the community of God. His stories taught them to love their enemies, to include the excluded, to give extravagantly, and to forgive without limit. His disciples seized upon those stories and began to live them. And they told those stories (and more) to generations who did not see Jesus but met him in the stories told and lived by his followers through the years.

One of the tasks of religious instruction is to continue to introduce learners to the good news of the gospel by telling the stories of Jesus and by helping learners live the gospel in their own lives. In addition, religious educators can enable learners to live faithful lives by using other stories from the vast wealth of human narrative to teach religious living. Entertaining, engaging, awe-inspiring, and sometimes even life-changing, these stories, however, are not ends in themselves but are a means toward achieving the goals of religious instruction. Because storytelling is an effective educational tool, religious educators should include storytelling in their repertoire of instructional procedures.

Tisa Lewis is an excellent teacher and a delightful storyteller. She once told me that after ten years of teaching she decided that if a point cannot be illustrated with a story, she generally does not bother with

---

[3]Katherine Hankey, "I Love to Tell the Story," *Baptist Hymnal* (Nashville: Convention Press, 1975), 461.

the point. For her, the stories make the content come alive in her classes.

Religious instruction should create an environment rich with stories. Having spent many years in seminary and in my early teaching career grappling with the complexities of theology, I find myself having now come back to stories. What invigorates my religious living are the stories of the church, the stories of my own experiences, the stories of the great writers, the stories of the people I love. A religious instruction environment permeated by stories can provide a space in which learners struggle with meaning-making, feeling, and living in process enriched by an abundant narrative tradition.

An old pastor visiting a country jail came upon a despondent young man. "Leave me alone, pastor. I'm no good," the young man moaned. "Everything I have touched has been bruised. I have influenced others to turn to a life of crime. I have deeply wounded the only ones who care for me—my mother, my wife, and our young daughter. There is no hope for me."

The old man was silent for a moment before he spoke. "The hurt that you have inflicted on others may never be healed. What you have done is most serious. What you need now is to find a new compass, a new way to walk." He paused before he continued. "We must begin by teaching you some new stories."

"Stories!" the young man thundered. "I speak to you out of despair and you talk to me of idle tales? I live without hope and you speak to me of happy endings? If my life is to be spent behind bars, I may need new facts, but I certainly do not need fiction."

When the outburst had subsided, the pastor placed a caring hand on the young man's arm. "Humor an old man. Listen to one tale."

Once a very bad man died and went before the judgment throne. Before him stood Abraham, David, Peter, and Luke. A chilly silence hung heavy in the room as an unseen voice began to read the details of the man's life. There was nothing good that was recorded. When the voice concluded, Abraham spoke: "Men like you cannot enter the heavenly kingdom. You must leave."

"Father Abraham," the man cried, "I do not defend myself. I have no choice but to ask for mercy. Certainly you understand. Though you lied to save your own life, saying your wife was your sister, by the mercy of God you became a blessing to all nations."

David interrupted, "Abraham has spoken correctly. You have committed evil and heinous crimes. You do not belong in the kingdom of light." The man faced the great king and cried, "Son of Jesse, it is true. I am a wicked man. Yet I dare ask you for forgiveness. You slept with Uriah's wife and later, to cover your sin, arranged his death. I ask only forgiveness as you have known it."

Peter was next to speak. "Unlike David, you have shown no love to God. By your acid tongue and your vile temper you have wounded the Son of God." "I should be silent," the man muttered. "The only way I have used the blessed name of Jesus is in anger. Still, Simon, son of John, I plead for grace. Though you walked by his side and listened to words from his own lips, you slept when he needed you in the garden, and you denied him three times in his night of greatest need."

Then Luke the evangelist spoke. "You must leave. You have not been found worthy of the kingdom of God."

The man's head bowed sadly for a moment before a spark lit in his face. "My life has been recorded correctly," the man began slowly. "I am guilty as charged. Yet I know there is a place for me in the blessed kingdom. Abraham, David, and Peter will plead my cause because they know of the weakness of man and the mercy of God. You, blessed physician, will open the gates to me because you have written of God's great love for the likes of me. Don't you recognize me? I am the lost sheep that the Good Shepherd carried home. I am your younger, prodigal brother."

And the gates opened and Luke embraced the sinner.

"You see," the old pastor concluded, "I want you to learn stories, not as an exercise in fiction, but in order to walk in mercy. Stories will help you find your way."[4]

---

[4]William R. White, *Speaking in Stories* (Minneapolis: Augsburg, 1982), p. 119, related in William J. Bausch, *Storytelling: Imagination and Faith* (Mystic, Conn.: Twenty-Third, 1984), pp. 36-38.

Appendix: Selected Resources for Storytelling in Religious Instruction

MYTHS

Bailey, J. R., et al. *Gods and Men: Myths and Legends from the World's Religions*. New York: Oxford University Press, 1994.

Birch, Cyric. *Chinese Myths and Legends*. New York: Oxford University Press, 1994.

Erdoes, Richard, and Alfonos Ortiz, eds. *American Indian Myths and Legends*. Pantheon, 1984.

Guerber, H. A. *The Myths of Greece and Rome*. Mineola, N.Y.: Dover, 1993.

Pelton, Mary Helen, and Jackie DiGennaro. *Images of a People: Tlingit Myths and Legends*. Englewood, Colo.: Libraries Unlimited, 1992.

FOLKTALES

Andersdatter, Karla, and C. E. Brookes. *The Woman Who Was Wild and Other Tales*. Wilmette, Ill.: Chiron, 1994.

Buber, Martin. *Tales of the Hasidim: The Early Masters*. London: Thames & Hudson, 1956.

————. *Tales of the Hasidim: The Later Masters*. London: Thames & Hudson, 1956.

Creeden, Sharon. *Fair Is Fair: World Folktales of Justice*. Little Rock, Ark.: August House, 1995.

Davis, Donald. *Jack Always Seeks His Fortune: Authentic Appalachian Jack Tales*. Little Rock, Ark.: August House, 1992.

DeSpain, Pleasant. *Thirty-three Multicultural Tales to Tell*. Little Rock, Ark.: August House, 1993.

Hamilton, Virginia. *The People Could Fly: American Black Folktales*. Westminster, Md.: Knopf, 1993.

Hejduk, John. *Aesop's Fables*. Libertyville, Ill.: Daedalus, 1992.

MacDonald, Margaret Read. *Tom Thumb*. Phoenix: Oryx, 1993.
McClintock, Barbara. *Animal Fables from Aesop*. Boston: Godine, 1992.
Pijoan, Teresa. *La Cuentista: Traditional Tales in Spanish and English*. Santa Fe, N.M.: Red Crane, 1994.
Reneaux, J. J. *Cajun Folktales*. Little Rock, Ark.: August House, 1992.
Sherman, Josepha. *Rachel the Clever and Other Jewish Folktales*. Little Rock, Ark.: August House, 1993.
Sherman, Josepha. *A Sampler of Jewish-American Folklore*. Little Rock, Ark.: August House, 1992.
Vigil, Angel. *The Corn Woman: Stories and Legends of the Hispanic Southwest*. Englewood, Colo.: Libraries Unlimited, 1995.
Young, Richard, and Judy Dockery. *African-American Folktales*. Little Rock, Ark.: August House, 1993.

BIOGRAPHY/AUTOBIOGRAPHY

Augustine, Saint. *Confessions*. Trans. William Watts. Cambridge: Harvard University Press, 1960-1961.
Cleaver, Eldridge. *Soul on Fire*. Waco, Tex.: Word Books, 1978.
Day, Dorothy. *The Long Loneliness*. New York: Harper, 1952.
Goodrich, Francis. *The Diary of Anne Frank*. New York: Random House, 1956.
Haven, Kendall. *Amazing American Women: 40 Fascinating 5-minute Reads*. Englewood, Colo.: Libraries Unlimited, 1995.
Kerr, Hugh T., and John M. Mulder. *Conversions*. Grand Rapids, Mich.: Eerdmans, 1983.
Lewis, C. S. *Surprised by Joy: The Shape of my Early Life*. New York: Harcourt, Brace, and World, 1955.
Merton, Thomas. *The Seven-Storey Mountain*. New York: Harcourt, Brace, and Jovanovich, 1978.
Schweitzer, Albert. *Out of My Life and Thought: An Autobiography*. Trans. A. B. Lemke. New York: H. Holt, 1990.
Gilbert, Olive. *Narrative of Sojourner Truth*. Mineola, N.Y.: Dover, 1997.

CHILDREN'S LITERATURE

Cleary, Beverly. *Ramona the Pest*. New York: Scholastic Book Services, 1968.

Danzinger, Paula. *The Cat Ate My Gymsuit*. New York: Delcorte, 1974.
Hoffman, Mary. *Amazing Grace*. New York: Dial Books for Young Readers, 1991.
L'Engle, Madeline. *A Wrinkle in Time*. New York: Farrar, Straus, and Giroux, 1962.
Lewis, C. S. *The Chronicles of Narnia*. New York: Collier, 1970.
_____. *Perelandra*. New York: Macmillan, 1968.
Scieszka, John. *The Frog Prince Continued*. New York: Viking, 1991.
_____. *The True Story of the Three Little Pigs by A. Wolf*. New York: Viking, 1989.

LITERATURE

Atwood, Margaret. *Alias Grace*. New York: Talese, 1996
_____. *The Handmaid's Tale*. Toronto: McClelland and Stewart, 1985.
Dubus, Andre. *The Times Are Never So Bad*. Boston: Godine, 1983.
Hawthorne, Nathaniel. *The Scarlet Letter*. New York: Viking, 1983.
Hesse, Herman. *Journey to the East*. New York: Farrar, Straus, and Giroux, 1956.
Lewis, Sinclair. *Elmer Gantry*. New York: Dell, 1958.
Lewis, Sinclair. *It Can't Happen Here*. New York: New American Library, 1970.
_____. *Main Street*. New York: Library of America, 1992.
O'Connor, Flannery. *Everything that Rises Must Converge*. New York: Farrar, Straus, and Giroux, 1965.
_____. *A Good Man is Hard to Find*. New Brunswick, N.J.: Rutgers University Press, 1993.
_____. *Wise Blood*. New York: Farrar, Straus, and Giroux, 1952.
Percy, Walker. *The Moviegoer*. New York: Knopf, 1962.
Price, Reynolds. *The Tongues of Angels*. New York: Atheneum, 1990.
Salinger, J. D. *Franny and Zooey*. New York: Little, Brown, 1961.
Sams, Ferrol. *Run with the Horsemen*. New York: Penguin, 1982
_____. *The Whisper of the River*. Atlanta: Peachtree, 1984.
Silko, Leslie Marmon. *Almanac of the Dead*. New York: Penguin, 1991.
Walker, Alice. *The Color Purple*. New York: Washington Square, 1982.

———. *Possessing the Secret of Joy.* New York: Hancourt, Brace, and Javanovich, 1992.

BIBLE STORIES

Bible Stories and Activities for Children. Nashville: Abingdon, 1992.
Bicknell, Treld. *A Child's Bible.* Mahwah, N.J.: Paulist, 1986.
Boomeshine, Thomas E. *Story Journey: An Invitation to the Gospel as Storytelling.* Nashville: Abingdon, 1988.
Jordan, Clarence. *The Cotton Patch Version of Matthew and John.* New York: Association Press, 1970.
———. *The Cotton Patch Version of Luke and Acts: Jesus' Doings and Happenings.* New York: Association Press, 1969.
Williams, Michael E., ed. *The Storyteller's Companion to the Bible.* Nashville: Abingdon, 1995.

Index of Names

Index of Subjects